Once There Was and Was Not

# Once There Was and Was Not

ARMENIAN TALES RETOLD

by Virginia A. Tashjian

Based on Stories by H. Toumanian

Illustrated by Nonny Hogrogian

Little, Brown and Company · *Boston* · *Toronto*

LIBRARY OF CONGRESS CATALOG CARD NO. 66-11000

FIRST EDITION

*Published simultaneously in Canada*
*by Little, Brown & Company (Canada) Limited*

PRINTED IN THE UNITED STATES OF AMERICA

IN MEMORY OF MY SISTER ARMANE A. MANUELIAN

—AND FOR HER THREE S's—

SHANT, SHAHAN AND SEVAN

# Contents

# Author's Note

THE ARMENIANS, *an ancient people who have lived since prehistoric times in the northeastern part of Asia Minor on a lofty plateau south of the Caucasus Mountains, have long possessed a body of folklore and legend, hero tales and tales of gods and giants almost unknown to the English-speaking world.*

*Some of these tales are stories of the common folk who have the universal faults and foibles of ordinary people and who are sometimes the victims of trickery and of enchantment, while others deal with the realm of spirits and monsters.*

*Armenian writers and historians throughout the centuries have recorded the "other world" beings, and there have been, in the past, several writers of Armenian fables (including Mkhitar Gosh, Vartan Aiketzi, Moses Kashankatvatzi) whose stories are even today household favorites.*

*The seven folk tales in this collection tell of the common folk—their own quiet humor and their peculiar resolutions of problems. They are a modern retelling of stories told by folklorist Hovhannes Toumanian, who lived from 1869 to 1923.*

*Some of them will be reminders of folk tales from other parts of the world. A talking fish is, indeed, a well-known device used throughout folklore, while "The Miller-King" is certainly a variant of "Mighty Mikko" in Finnish folklore and of "The Good Man and the Kind Mouse" from the folklore of Chile.*

# Once There Was and Was Not

# The Foolish Man

ONCE THERE WAS AND WAS NOT IN ANCIENT ARMENIA a poor man who worked and toiled hard from morn till night, but nevertheless remained poor.

Finally one day he became so discouraged that he decided to go in search of God in order to ask Him how long he must endure such poverty—and to beg of Him a favor.

On his way, the man met a wolf.

"Good day, brother man," asked the wolf. "Where are you bound in such a hurry?"

"I go in search of God," replied the man. "I have a complaint to lodge with him."

"Well," said the wolf, "would you do me a kindness? When you find God, will you complain to Him for me, too? Tell Him you met a half-starved wolf who searches the woods and fields for food from morning till night—and though he works hard and long, still finds nothing to eat. Ask God why He does not provide for wolves since He created them?"

"I will tell Him of your complaint," agreed the poor man, and continued on his way.

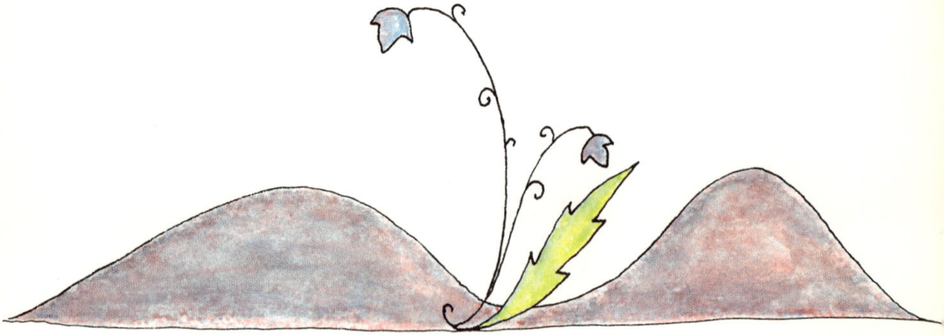

As he hurried over the hills and through the valleys, he chanced to meet a beautiful maid.

"Where do you go in such a hurry, my brother?" asked the maid.

"I go in search of God," replied the man.

"Oh, kind friend, when you find God, would you ask Him something for me? Tell him you met a maid on your way. Tell Him she is young and fair and very rich—but very unhappy. Ask God why she cannot know happiness. What will become of her? Ask God why He will not help her to be happy."

"I will tell Him of your trouble," promised the poor man, and continued on his way.

Soon he met a tree which seemed all dried up and dying even though it grew by the side of a river.

"Where do you go in such a hurry, O traveler?" called the dry tree.

"I go in search of God," answered the man. "I have a complaint to lodge with Him."

"Wait a moment, O traveler," begged the tree, "I, too, have a question for God.

"Please ask Him why I am dry both in summer and winter. Though I live by this wet river, my leaves do not turn green. Ask God how long I must suffer. Ask Him that for me, good friend," said the tree.

The man listened to the tree's complaint, promised to tell God, and continued once again upon his way.

Finally, the poor man reached the end of his journey. He found God seated beneath the ledge of a cliff.

"Good day," said the man as he approached God.

"Welcome, traveler," God returned his greeting. "Why have you journeyed so far? What is your trouble?"

"Well, I want to know why there is injustice in the world. Is it fair that I toil and labor from morn till night—and yet never seem to earn enough for a full stomach, while many who do not work half as hard as I live and eat as rich men do?"

"Go then," replied God. "I present you the Gift of Luck. Go find it and enjoy it to the end of your days."

"I have yet another complaint, my Lord," continued the man—and he proceeded to list the complaints and requests of the starved wolf, the beautiful maid, and the parched tree.

God gave appropriate answers to each of the three complaints, whereupon the poor man thanked Him and started on his way homeward.

Soon he came upon the dry, parched tree.

"What message did God have for me?" asked the tree.

"He said that beneath your trunk there lies a pot of gold which prevents the water from seeping up your trunk to your leaves. God said your branches will never turn green until the pot of gold is removed."

"Well, what are you waiting for, foolish man!" exclaimed the tree. "Dig up that pot of gold. It will make you rich—and permit me to turn green and live again!"

"Oh, no," protested the man. "I have no time to dig up a pot of gold. God has given me the Gift of Luck. I must hurry and search for it." And he hurried on his way.

Presently, he met the beautiful maid who was waiting for him. "Oh, kind friend, what message did God have for me?"

"God said that you will soon meet a kind man who will prove to be a good life's companion to you. No longer will you be lonely. Happiness and contentment will come to you," reported the poor man.

"In that case, what are you waiting for, foolish man?" exclaimed the maid. "Why don't you stay here and be my life's companion."

"Oh, no! I have no time to stay with you. God has given me the Gift of Luck. I must hurry and search for it." And the man hurried on his way.

Some distance away, the starving wolf impatiently awaited the man's coming, and hailed him with a shout.

"Well, what did God say? What message did He send to me?"

"Brother wolf, so many things have happened since I saw you last," said the man. "I hardly know where to begin. On my way to seek God, I met a beautiful maid who begged me to ask God the reason for her unhappiness. And I met a parched tree who wanted God to explain the dryness of its branches even though it stood by a wet river.

"I told God about these matters. He bade me tell the maid to seek a life's companion in order to find happiness. He bade me warn the tree about a pot of gold buried near its trunk which must be removed before the branches can receive nourishment from the earth.

"On my return, I brought God's answers to the maid and to the tree. The maid asked me to stay and be her life's companion, while the tree asked me to dig up the pot of gold.

"Of course, I had to refuse both since God gave me the Gift of Luck—and I must hurry along to search for it!"

"Ah-h-h, brother man, and what was God's reply to me?" asked the starving wolf.

"As for you," replied the man, "God said that you would remain hungry until you met a silly and foolish man whom you could eat up. Only then, said God, would your hunger be satisfied."

"Hmmmmmm," mused the wolf, "where in the world will I find a man more silly and stupid than you?"

And he ate up the foolish man.

# The Miller-King

ONCE THERE WAS AND WAS NOT IN ANCIENT ARMENIA a poor miller who was barely able to make ends meet. One morning he went out to start up the waterwheel of his mill and, when he returned, the piece of cheese he had left on the table for his noonday meal had disappeared.

At the end of the day, he went out to shut off the waterwheel, and when he returned this time, the piece of crusty bread he had saved for his supper had disappeared.

"How could this be?" wondered the miller. "Who is stealing my bit of food?" And that night, he set a trap.

The night passed. When morning came, the miller found a fox caught fast in the trap.

"Ho! You miserable thief you! I'll show you what it is to steal my food!" shouted the miller and went after the fox with a broom.

The fox begged for mercy. "Don't kill me," he pleaded. "What is a piece of cheese or a crust of bread that you wish to kill me for that? Set me free . . . I promise to reward you for your kindness."

The miller listened and, being a kindly man at heart, set the fox free. At once, the fox hurried to the royal stable belonging to the king of that land. Searching carefully, he found a gold piece on the stable floor. Quickly he presented himself at the palace and was ushered in to the king.

"Long live Your Majesty," said the fox, bowing low. "I have come to ask a favor. My master, the miller-king who lives not far from here, is engaged in counting his gold, but alas, he has no proper means of measure. Would you kindly lend us your measuring basket? I promise you we will return it promptly."

"I have never heard of this miller-king," frowned the king. "Who is he?"

"To be sure, you do not know him yet, Your Majesty," replied the fox. "He is a very rich king, and I am his vizier.

Please lend us this measuring basket to measure his gold and then you shall meet him."

The king agreed. Taking the basket out of sight of the palace, the fox carefully placed the gold piece which he had found in the stable in the bottom of the basket. Later that evening he returned the basket to the king.

"Oh-h-h," he said, pretending to be weary, "how my master thanks you. We're both so tired, but thanks to your basket, we finally finished measuring the gold."

The king rubbed his chin. "Can it really be that this miller-king is so rich he measures his gold by the basket?" he wondered. Taking the basket, he shook it. A gold piece fell out.

The next day, the fox appeared once again before the king.

"LONG LIVE YOUR MAJESTY," he said, bowing low. "My master, the miller-king, has some precious jewels he needs to count. May we impose on Your Majesty's kindness and borrow the measuring basket once more? I promise to return it by nightfall."

Once again, the fox took the basket out of sight of the palace. He had found a pearl somewhere behind the king's stable, and he placed it in the bottom of the basket.

When evening came, he returned the basket to the king.

"Oh-h-h," he groaned, "how tired I am! We had such a time measuring all the jewels. My master deeply thanks Your Majesty for the use of the basket."

The king reached for the basket. As he did so, the pearl fell out. The amazed king wondered how anyone could be rich enough to measure precious jewels by the basket.

Several days passed. Then the fox reappeared at the palace, and this time asked the king for the hand of his daughter, the princess, as wife to the miller-king.

Remembering the riches of his neighbor, the king happily agreed to the match and ordered the palace staff to prepare at once for a wedding. All was confusion in the palace as the hasty plans got under way.

Meanwhile, the fox hurried to the flour mill and congratulated the poor miller. "I have received the king's own permission for you to have his daughter as your wife," he said. "Come! Hurry and make ready! We are going to your wedding."

"What!" exclaimed the bewildered miller. "Have you gone out of your mind? What have you done? Who am I to marry a king's daughter? I have no decent means of livelihood, no house, and not even any clothes other than the wretched things I now wear!"

"Don't worry. Leave everything to me." The fox assured the miller, and he hurried back to the king.

"Your Majesty, the most terrible tragedy has taken place," he announced. "The miller-king and his retinue were on their way here for the wedding when suddenly enemy soldiers attacked and robbed him of everything.

"Fortunately, my master escaped. He was able to take refuge in a broken-down mill not far from here. But you must give me clothes and horses so that he may come to his wedding in proper style. Then he plans to hurry on to take revenge on the enemy who attacked him."

The king immediately gave the fox some clothes fit for royalty and dispatched enough horses and guards to escort his future son-in-law properly to his bride's home.

The fox hurried back to the mill with the clothes. Long before the guards and horses arrived he had dressed the poor miller in the princely garments. Then he helped him mount one of the royal horses.

Escorted by the palace guards, the miller arrived at the palace in a solemn, dignified procession. The poor miller, who had never seen a palace before in his life, was tongue-tied. He looked about him in amazement. He stared first at his own clothes, then at the finery about him, and was unable to utter a word.

"Why does your master stare about so, brother fox?" asked the king. "You would almost think he had never seen such clothes or even such a palace."

"Oh, no, Your Majesty, it isn't that at all! He is simply comparing your palace with his own. Of course, he finds quite a difference," answered the fox.

Next came the dinner to celebrate the coming wedding. So many courses of rich foods were served that the bewildered miller did not know which ones to take, nor indeed how to eat them.

"Why does your master not eat, brother fox?" asked the king. "Isn't he hungry?"

"How can he eat, Your Majesty? He is thinking of the thieves who robbed him on the road. You cannot imagine how much they took, nor what a blow the attack was to my master's dignity. How can he eat?" replied the fox.

"Ah-h-h, try not to worry, my dear son-in-law," consoled the king. "Such things happen. Let us hope future tragedies will be as small as this one. In the meantime, there is the wedding . . . Let us be merry and gay and forget sad things."

And so the wedding took place. For seven days and seven nights there was feasting and dancing and merriment.

The fox acted as the best man. The king presented his daughter a fine dowry, and after the seventh day he bade her farewell as she prepared to leave with her husband. According to the custom, the wedding guests formed a procession in order to escort the bride and groom to their own home.

"Do not hurry," said the fox to the guests. "Let me go on ahead and prepare the house a little to receive the bride." And he hurried on before them.

Soon he came upon a hillside of vast fields where herds of cattle were grazing.

"Who owns these herds of cattle?" the fox questioned the nearby farmers.

"Why, the shah, of course," they replied.

"Bah! Never speak of the shah again—or it will go ill with you. The king who follows right behind me with his guards is very angry with the shah and orders anyone beheaded who mentions his name. If he should ask you who owns these herds, answer, 'The miller-king,' or your heads will suffer!"

With this warning, the fox hurried on. Soon he came upon grazing flocks of sheep.

"Who owns these flocks of sheep?" asked the fox.

"Why, the shah, of course," replied the shepherds.

Repeating the same warning as before, the fox hurried on. He came to vast acres of farmland being tilled by hard-working farmers.

"Who owns these farmlands?" he asked.

"Why, the shah, of course," was the answer.

The fox repeated his warning.

He came upon hayfields where men were gathering hay.

"Who owns these hayfields?" the fox asked, and received the same answer: "Why, the shah, of course."

Once again, the fox repeated his warning. Finally, he reached a beautiful palace which was the residence of the shah himself.

"O shah, most honorable shah," said the fox, "do you see the cloud of dust in the road yonder? It is the king who comes with his soldiers. How can you sit so calmly? The king is angry with you and comes to kill you and take over all your possessions. Flee now—while there is yet time! Once I enjoyed your hospitality here, and since I never forget a kindness, I have come to warn you."

"What shall I do? Where shall I go?" cried the frightened shah, who could already see the king and his company far off in the distance.

"Go anywhere—as far from here as possible. Flee for your life," urged the fox, and he helped the shah escape from the back door of the palace.

In the meantime, the wedding procession continued down the road. It was led by the miller and his bride dressed in their royal garments and followed by the wedding guests and the horse guards walking to the music of the royal musicians.

The procession reached the herds of cattle.

"Who owns these herds?" asked the wedding guests.

"Why, the miller-king, of course," replied the farmers.

The procession reached the hillside where the flocks of sheep grazed peacefully.

"Who owns these sheep?" came the question.

"Why, the miller-king, of course," was the answer.

The procession continued on its way and came to the fields where the workers toiled.

"Who owns these fields?"

"Why, the miller-king, of course."

The procession reached the hayfields.

"Who owns these fields?" "Why, the miller-king, of course," replied the farmers.

Amazed were all the wedding guests and soldier guards, but most amazed of all was the poor miller-bridegroom!

In this way, the procession finally reached the front gate of the shah's palace where the fox, the best man, welcomed the bride and groom and their guests. Once again the feasting and merrymaking started, and continued for seven days and seven nights until the guests and soldier guards finally bid the bridal couple farewell and left for home.

The miller-king and his bride lived happily in their palace, and with them lived happily ever after the fox. As for the shah—no one has ever heard of him since that time. Probably he is running away from the angry miller-king to this very day.

## The Master and the Servant

ONCE THERE WAS AND WAS NOT IN ANCIENT ARMENIA a pair of brothers so poor they could not keep a roof over their heads. They finally decided that while the younger brother remained at home to tend house, the elder would go out to look for work that would support them both.

After some searching, the elder brother at last found employment as the servant of a very rich man.

"If you agree to work for me, however," said the rich man, "you must promise to stay until the call of the cuckoo in the spring."

The elder brother agreed.

"There is still another condition," the rich man went on. "You must agree to a bargain. You must promise not to lose your temper while you are working for me. If you should lose it, you must pay me one thousand silver pieces as forfeit. On the other hand, if I lose my temper, I'll pay you one thousand silver pieces. What do you say? Do you agree to the bargain?"

"But I don't own one thousand silver pieces," protested the elder brother.

"In that case, instead of paying the money, you must work for me for ten years," said the rich man.

At first, the elder brother was afraid to agree to such a bargain. "But I really have no choice," he thought to himself. "My brother and I need the money and I will just make up my mind not to lose my temper no matter what my master does."

"It's a bargain!" he said aloud.

Both master and servant signed an agreement, and the elder brother started to work.

Early the next morning, the rich master sent the servant out to the fields to harvest the grain.

"Go quickly," he ordered, "and continue working while it's light. Come back only when darkness falls."

The servant hurried to the fields. He worked hard all that day and when twilight came he returned home, tired and weary.

"Why have you come back so soon?" asked the rich man.

"The sun has set—and so I came home."

"That's not what I told you to do!" shouted the master angrily. "I told you to work while there was light. It is true that the sun has set, but the moon has come out. That gives light!"

"What kind of reasoning is that?" exclaimed the amazed elder brother.

"What! Are you losing your temper?" asked the master.

"No! I'm not losing my temper," stammered the elder brother. "What I meant to say was that I'm a little tired and I ought to rest."

Wearily, the elder brother returned to the fields. He worked hard and long by moonlight. Then as soon as the moon disappeared, the sun rose from the east. He continued to work by sunlight until, exhausted, he fell to the ground.

"To the devil with your farm and your money and with you, too!" murmured the youth wearily.

"What! Have you lost your temper?" asked the master, suddenly appearing in the fields. "Remember our bargain!

If you have lost your temper, you must either give me one thousand silver pieces or ten years of your service."

The poor youth did not know what to do. He neither had one thousand pieces of silver—nor could he bear to work for such a taskmaster for ten long years. In despair, he gave the master a signed note, promising to pay him one thousand silver pieces in the future. Then, empty-handed, he returned home to his brother.

"Did you make a fortune?" the younger brother greeted the elder. And the elder brother told him everything that had happened.

"Stay home and rest yourself. Don't worry," said the younger brother consolingly. "It's my turn to find work while you tend house." And he went immediately to the home of the same rich man to ask for work as a servant.

"If you want to work for me," said the rich man, "you must promise to stay until the call of the cuckoo in the spring."

The younger brother agreed. The rich master offered the same bargain to the younger brother: If the boy should lose his temper, he must forfeit one thousand silver pieces or ten years of service as a servant. If the master should lose his temper first, however, he must forfeit one thousand silver pieces.

"Is it a bargain?" asked the rich man.

"Oh, no! That's hardly worth bargaining for," scoffed the younger brother. "If you lose your temper, you must pay me two thousand pieces of silver. If I lose my temper, I will either forfeit two thousand silver pieces or work for you for twenty years."

"It's a bargain!" The greedy master quickly agreed to the new terms. They signed the agreement, and the younger brother started to work.

Night passed and morning came, but the young servant did not get out of bed. The master angrily paced the floor; the servant still slept. Finally, the master rushed into the boy's bedroom. "Get up! Get up! Do you realize it's nearly noon?" he shouted.

"What! Are you by chance losing your temper?" asked the servant, lifting his head from the pillow.

"Of course I'm not losing my temper!" answered the frightened master, lowering his voice. "I'm only reminding you that we must go to harvest the grain."

"Oh, well, then . . . if you're not angry, we'll go right along," said the boy. Slowly he got out of bed and slowly began to put on his clothes.

The rich man impatiently paced back and forth—and still the boy continued to dress.

"Hurry, boy! You're taking too long to get dressed!" exclaimed the master.

"What! Are you losing your temper?" asked the servant.

"Who is losing his temper? Certainly not I! I just mean to remind you that we are late!"

"Oh, well, then . . . I will be ready soon," replied the younger brother.

By the time the servant finished dressing, by the time they arrived at the fields, it was already noon.

"It would look silly to start work now when all the others are eating their noon meal," said the servant. "Let's eat first; then we can go to work."

They sat down together and ate. "It is customary for working people to take a short nap after a noonday meal," said the younger brother and stretched himself out on the ground. He fell asleep at once and did not wake up till nightfall.

"Wake up! Wake up! It's dark already and only our grain is not yet harvested. Cursed be the one who sent you to me! I'm ruined!" shouted the rich man in despair.

"What! Can it be you are losing your temper?" asked the servant, waking up.

"Who's losing his temper? I'm not!" the master exclaimed. "I only mean to remind you that night has fallen. It's time to go home."

"Oh, well, then . . . that's different. I thought you might have forgotten our bargain."

They returned to the house to find that unexpected guests had arrived. The master ordered the servant to go out and kill a sheep for supper.

"Which one?" asked the boy.

"Whichever one comes along," answered the master impatiently. "But hurry!"

A few moments later, some of the other servants came running in to their master.

"Master! Master! Hurry! Your new servant has killed all the sheep in your flock!"

The rich man rushed out and found that all his sheep had, indeed, been slaughtered. Out of his mind with anger, he shouted to the boy, "What have you done, you fool? May your house be ruined as you have ruined mine! Why have you killed all my sheep?"

"But master, you told me to kill whichever sheep came along. They all came along—and I killed them all according to your orders. And I do think you've lost your temper this time, haven't you?"

"No! I have NOT lost my temper," screamed the master. "Alas! I am only heartbroken to have lost all my sheep."

"Oh, well, then . . . as long as you haven't lost your temper, I'll continue to work for you," replied the servant.

From that moment on, however, the rich man thought only of how he could get rid of his servant. By their agreement, the boy was to work until the call of the cuckoo in the spring. It was still winter, however, and the spring cuckoo was months away.

Finally, the master thought of a plan. He took his wife into the woods, put her up in a tree, and told her to call, *Cuckoo, cuckoo* when he returned later with the servant.

Back at the house, he ordered the servant to accompany him on a hunting trip into the woods. As soon as the two entered the woods, the man's wife in the tree called out, *Cuckoo, cuckoo!*

"Aha!" said the master. "Listen! There is the call of the cuckoo, I do believe. According to our agreement, your months of work for me are over."

The younger brother thought for a moment. He suspected a plot.

"No! No! Who ever heard of a cuckoo singing in the middle of winter? It must be a very strange cuckoo, indeed. I will kill it immediately." Saying this, he aimed his bow at the tree.

The rich man fell upon the younger brother. "Don't shoot! Don't shoot! Ah-h-h-h—black was the day you came to me!" he shouted. "What trouble I'm in because of you!"

"What! Is it possible you are losing your temper?" asked the servant.

"Yes! Yes! Yes! I'm losing my temper! This is enough! I'll pay any price to get rid of you! I made the bargain—and I'll suffer the losses! Just get out of my sight!" screamed the rich man at the top of his voice.

So it was that the rich man eagerly paid two thousand silver pieces to the servant. The younger brother, in turn, paid off his elder brother's debt of one thousand silver pieces. Then he put the remaining one thousand silver pieces into his pocket and headed happily for home.

## The Talking Fish

ONCE THERE WAS AND WAS NOT IN ANCIENT ARMENIA a man who was very poor—and though he tried to better himself, still he remained poor. At last he was able to find work as a fisherman's helper. Thus he could bring home a fish or two each day, which enabled him and his wife to live.

One day the fisherman caught an unusually beautiful fish, which he handed to his helper to put into the fish sack. It was still early so the fisherman then went off to fish some more.

The fisherman's helper gazed long and thoughtfully at the fish in his hands. "Oh, Lord," he thought, "this is a breathing living creature, like us. Tell me, does this fish not have parents as we do? And friends? Doesn't he, too, understand something of this world? Doesn't he feel happiness and pleasure and pain as we do?"

As the man silently thought these things, the fish began to speak in a human voice.

"Listen to me, brother man," he said. "I was playing in the river rapids. In my pleasure, I forgot to be careful and fell into the fisherman's net. And now—now, I know that my parents are searching for me, and weeping at my absence. My friends are saddened, and I, as you can see for yourself, am panting for breath and fighting for my very life.

"I want to return to my family, to play in the clear water once again. Ah, fisherman's helper, take pity on me. Throw me back into the river. Give me my freedom. Open the net and let me go."

Thus pleaded the fish in a faint voice while his mouth opened and closed in weaker and weaker gasps.

The fisherman's helper took pity on the fish. He lifted him up and threw him back into the river.

"Go, sweet fish," he said, "your parents must not weep, nor should your friends be saddened. Go to live and play among them."

When the fisherman returned to find that his helper had released the fish, he was furious and scolded the man sharply. "You fool!" he shouted. "I work hard catching fish, and you take the result of my labor to throw it back into the river! Go and die from starvation for all I care!" Seizing the empty sack from his helper's hands, he pushed him on his way.

"Ah-h-h, now where shall I go? What shall I do? How shall we live?" despaired the poor man as he made his way homeward to his wife.

It happened that along the way he met a demon leading a cow behind him. Although the demon was in the disguise of a human being, the man recognized him nevertheless.

"Good day, brother-to-be," called out the demon. "Why do you look so grieved? What painful thoughts make you look so sad?"

The poor man recounted all that had happened to him and how he was now out of work with no hope of employment and no means of livelihood for himself and his wife.

"Listen to me, friend," said the demon. "I will make a bargain with you. I will lend you this milk cow. You may keep her for exactly three years and each day she will give enough milk for you and your wife to live more than comfortably.

"At the end of that time, however, I shall come and ask you a question. If you answer correctly, my cow is yours.

Otherwise, you and your wife belong to me and must do my bidding forever. Is it a bargain? What do you say?"

The poor man thought quickly. "One thing is certain," he said to himself. "Without the cow, we shall starve. With the cow, at least we shall live comfortably for three years. And who knows what will happen then? God is good—and a door to good luck may open somehow. We might even be able to think of the right answer to the demon's question. Who knows?"

"It is a bargain," agreed the poor man and, leading the cow, he made for home.

For three years, the man and his wife milked the cow, and the sale of leftover milk, cream, butter and cheese brought them the extras of life. Indeed, they were so happy that they did not heed the swift passing of time until the three years were up and the day of the demon's visit was at hand.

The man and his wife did their daily chores with heavy hearts, and at dusk sat sadly in front of the house wondering how they were to answer the fateful question to be put to them. Who could tell what the demon would ask? What human being could read the mind of a demon? Alas! Anything might happen when a man did business with a demon, or accepted favors from one!

Too late, the man regretted the bargain he had made three years ago, although at that time, he told himself, he had had no other choice.

As dusk deepened into night, and the couple anxiously awaited the demon's coming, a handsome young stranger approached them.

"Good evening," he said. "I have traveled a long way. It is very late and I am tired. Would you accept a guest this night?"

"Why not, brother traveler? A guest belongs to God and man. But we must warn you that is it dangerous to be near us tonight. Three years ago we borrowed a cow belonging to a demon on condition that he be permitted to ask us a question at the end of that time. If we answer correctly, the cow is ours. Otherwise, we become his slaves. Now the time is up; the demon is to come this very night and we don't know how to answer him. Whatever happens, we are to blame, but what if harm comes to you, young stranger?"

"Don't worry about me," smiled the strange youth. "Whatever happens, I shall share your fate."

In the middle of the night after all three had wearily retired there came a loud knock at the door.

"Who is it?" called the man.

"The demon. I have come; I want my answer."

"What answer?" The couple were so frightened they could hardly speak.

"Don't be frightened," said the strange youth. "I shall answer him in your place. Do not say another word."

"I've come," repeated the demon.

"I have come, also," replied the stranger from behind the door.

"Where have you come from?" the demon demanded.

"From the far shores of the sea."

"How did you get here?"

"I saddled the lame water buffalo and mounted it to come," replied the stranger.

"Was the sea so narrow, then, that you could cross it thus?"

"Narrow! Why, the sea is so vast that an eagle cannot fly from one shore to another."

"Is an eagle so tiny, then?"

"Tiny! Why, the shadow of an eagle's wings can cover a whole city!"

"Well then, is a city so small?"

"Small! Even a swift hare cannot run from one end to the other without weariness."

"Well then, is a hare so little?"

"Little! Why, its fur will stretch to make a grown man's coat—and his hat and boots besides!"

"Well then, is a man such a dwarf?"

"A dwarf! Why, a rooster crowing from a man's knee can hardly be heard by the man's ear."

"Well then, is a man deaf?"

"Deaf! Why, a man can hear the sound of an insect eating grain in the field."

The demon was thoroughly confused by now; he realized that behind the door stood a wise and unbeatable spirit. Knowing that he was beaten, the evil one disappeared silently into the darkness.

The old couple, saved from an unknown fate, rejoiced at their good fortune, and finally all three returned to bed. In the morning, the young traveler thanked the couple for their hospitality and prepared to depart.

"We cannot let you go. You have saved our lives," exclaimed the old man and his wife. "How can we ever repay your kindness? You must stay longer with us."

The stranger insisted that he must leave and said he expected no payment.

"At least, tell us your name," begged the old couple. "If we can't repay you, at least we will know whom to bless in our prayers."

"A kindness is never lost—even if it is thrown into the water," said the stranger. "I am the talking fish whose life you saved three years ago. And I came here to repay my debt."

With that, the young stranger disappeared before the eyes of the old man and his wife.

## Shrovetide

(*Carnival days of merrymaking just before Lent*)

ONCE THERE WAS AND WAS NOT IN ANCIENT ARMENIA a couple who could not get along with one another. The man called his wife a fool; the wife called her husband the same—and they argued from morn till night.

One day the man went to the village and brought home one hundred measures of rice and fifty measures of butter. When the wife saw so much rice and butter, she lost her temper.

"When I call you a fool, you get angry," she shouted, "but fool you are! Why did you buy so much rice and butter? Are you going to celebrate your son's wedding or your father's name day?"

"What wedding! What name day! Stop shouting!" answered the husband. "I bought this for Shrovetide."

The wife quieted down and put away the rice and butter.

Several weeks passed. The wife waited and waited patiently but Shrovetide did not come. One day while she sat alone outside her front door, she saw a stranger walking down the street with quick determined steps.

"Oh brother, brother," she called to him. "Stop a moment."

The man stopped.

"Brother, tell me. Are you, by chance, Shrovetide?"

The stranger realized that the woman was not quite right in her head and, in order to humor her, he replied, "Yes, sister, I am, indeed, Shrovetide. What do you want of me?"

"Well, I want to say that I think it's about time you appeared! We are not your servants, you know! We have kept your rice and butter long enough! Come and take them away at once!"

"Don't be angry, my sister," answered the man, smiling.

"I was just coming to get my rice and butter, but I couldn't seem to find the right house!"

"Well, now that you have found it, take away your property." The stranger walked into the house, took the one hundred measures of rice and the fifty measures of butter and left.

Soon afterwards, the woman's husband returned home.

"Well," said the wife, "Shrovetide finally came and I gave him his things!"

"What Shrovetide? What things?"

"Why, the rice and butter, of course. I saw him walking towards our house searching for us. I hailed him, scolded him properly and gave him his things."

"Oh, you fool! I always said you were a fool! Which way did he go?" shouted the angry husband.

"That way."

Jumping on his horse, the husband went in search of Shrovetide. Further along the road the stranger heard someone following him. He turned around, and guessed that the rider must be the husband of the foolish woman. Quickly he hid the rice and butter behind some bushes.

"Good day, brother," the husband greeted the stranger.

"Good day to you."

"Have you seen anyone else traveling along this road?"

"Why yes, I have."

"Did he, by chance, carry a large bundle on his back?"

"Yes, he had some rice and butter."

"Ah, that's the man I seek," said the husband. "How long ago did he pass?"

"Oh, quite some time ago."

"Will I catch up to him if my horse hurries?"

"I don't think so," answered the stranger. "Your horse would have to hurry along on his four feet, while the man could hurry along on his two feet much faster, since he has less feet to worry about."

"Then what shall I do?" asked the foolish husband.

"Well, why don't you leave your horse with me? With only your own two feet to worry about, you could probably overtake him," answered the crafty stranger.

"You speak the truth; if you would be kind enough to mind my horse, I'll do as you say." And the foolish husband dismounted. Leaving his horse with the stranger, he hurried along on foot.

As soon as he disappeared down the road, Shrovetide loaded the rice and butter on the back of the horse and rode off in the opposite direction.

Meanwhile, the husband walked and walked and overtook no one. In disgust, he returned to the place where he had left his horse and found neither horse nor stranger. Wearily, he went home and told his wife all that had happened.

Once again they began to argue. He called her a fool and shouted about the rice and butter. She called him a bigger fool and screamed about the horse. They argued from morn till night, and no doubt are arguing till this very day.

As for Shrovetide: he probably hears them and smiles.

## The White Snake

ONCE THERE WAS AND WAS NOT IN ANCIENT ARMENIA a very wise king who seemed to have knowledge of all things. It was as though the wind whispered the most secret of secrets into his ear.

Every day, the king practiced a most peculiar custom. Before each meal, a certain servant was ordered to bring a small covered dish to the royal bedroom, place it on the table, and then depart—leaving the king alone with the dish.

This peculiar custom continued for some years, until one day the servant could no longer contain his curiosity. Before bringing the dish to the king, he first carried it secretly into his own room—and slowly uncovered it . . . A cooked white snake lay coiled within the dish.

Unable to stop himself, the servant cut off a piece of the snake meat and ate it. As soon as his tongue touched the meat, the youth was aware of a peculiar chirping and warbling of birds on the branches of the trees just outside the open window of his room.

He listened, and to his astonishment, realized that he was able to understand the language of the birds! And as he heard the many tales told to each other by the birds and insects on the trees, the servant knew that the snake meat which he had swallowed had given him the power to understand the speech of all animals.

It so happened that on that very day, the queen lost her most prized ring. Since this faithful servant was the only one who had access to all rooms in the palace, suspicion fell upon him—and the courtiers declared that he must, indeed be the thief!

The king summoned the youth and threatened him: "If the ring is not returned by sunrise tomorrow, OFF WITH YOUR HEAD!"

The servant swore his innocence, but the king would not listen. "You will produce either the ring or the identity of the thief by sunrise tomorrow if you wish to keep your head," he repeated.

Trembling with fear and anger, the faithful servant went out to the courtyard to think of a way out of his predicament. As he paced back and forth, his eyes absently gazed upon some ducks in the nearby pond. They were huddled together, resting and cleaning their feathers with their flat bills. They were probably telling each other of the tasty catch of fish which each had had for breakfast that morning.

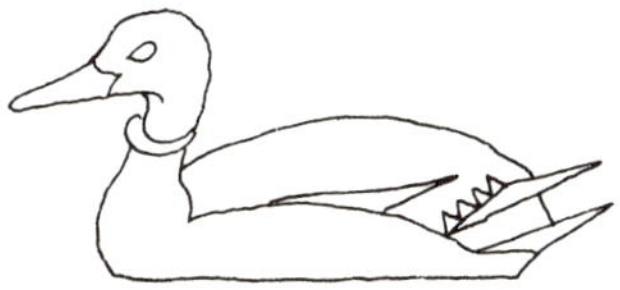

One of them stretched up and boasted, "As for me, I admit I was too greedy! I swallowed the queen's ring that had fallen beneath her window. But I'm paying for it, now! My stomach feels so heavy and tight!"

The servant leaped forward and grabbed the duck by his neck. He ran to the kitchen with the squawking bird and shouted to the cook, "Kill and pluck this duck! He has grown too fat for his own good!"

"You are right," agreed the cook. "He is a fat one, indeed—just right for roasting." And with that, he chopped off the duck's head. As he cleaned the bird's stomach, out came the queen's ring.

Thus, the servant was cleared of blame. The king, ashamed of his doubt of the boy, offered to grant him any request he wished to make, as well as a permanent place in the palace.

The servant refused all favors. He begged only for the gift of a horse, enough money for a few meals, and his freedom to go out and see the world. And with the king's blessing, he set off.

He traveled far; he traveled wide. One day he came upon three fish lying by the side of a brook. They had accidentally leaped out of the water, and now, unable to get back in, they lay helpless, dying of thirst.

The servant listened to the fish telling one another of their sad fate. He felt sorry for them and, dismounting from his horse, threw them back into the brook. At first, the half-dead fish swam in circles under the surface of the water, trying to revive themselves. Then they raised their heads out of the brook and called out, "We will never forget your kindness to us, good lad. Some day, perhaps, we shall be able to reward you."

The servant continued on his way. Soon he became aware of a faint moaning sound beneath his feet. He looked down and saw a swarm of crawling ants. He bent an ear down to the ground and heard the ants complaining. "Alas! If only big men and giant beasts would leave us alone—and walk elsewhere! See how this stupid horse with his enormous feet tramples our homes and families."

The servant felt sorry for the ants and turned his horse off to a side path, whereupon the king of the ants hailed the youth. "Thanks, kind soul. With God's help, we will not be long beholden to you."

The youth traveled up the narrow path into the forest. As he passed under a tree, he heard two crows fluttering about on the edge of their nest and soundly scolding their young.

"Children, we can't find food for you forever! You're

old enough now to go seek your own food. Get up and fly!"

The frightened, hungry young crows tried to test their wings, but fell to the ground, cawing wildly.

*We're baby crows—unwanted and poor.*
*We have no nest, nor wings that are sure.*
*Where shall we find food and a home, too?*
*Where shall we go—what shall we do?*

The servant's heart was filled with pity. Without thinking of the long or the short of it, he gave the baby crows the few crumbs of bread he had left from his last meal.

"Thank you, lad," called the crows. "Be sure we will repay your kindness some day."

The youth continued on his way and traveled far until he reached a large city where the streets were filled with excited people. Soon a royal messenger on horseback came down the street, calling out to all who would listen:

"THE KING'S DAUGHTER SEEKS A HUSBAND. WHOSOEVER WISHES THE POSITION MUST PERFORM A HEROIC DEED. IF SUCCESSFUL, HE GAINS THE PRINCESS AS WIFE; IF HE FAILS, HE SHALL FORFEIT HIS HEAD."

In the next few days, many brave young men came to try for the position—and lost their heads for their trouble.

One day, however, the servant saw the king's daughter at the palace window. Immediately he fell deeply in love with her. Though he knew the dangers and pitfalls connected with the venture, he presented himself at the palace and asked for the hand of the princess.

He was accepted as a candidate and escorted immediately to the shore of the sea. There the king himself took a gold ring from his finger, threw it into the sea and said, "This shall be your heroic deed. You must retrieve my ring from the sea. If you succeed, my daughter is yours. If you fail, you shall yourself be thrown into the sea to drown."

The courtiers who accompanied the king, and the common people besides, felt sorry for the brave youth who was about to drown. But while he pondered his fate for a moment, three fish came swimming toward the servant—the same fish he had rescued in the past. The middle one carried a seashell in his mouth, which he dropped in front of the waiting youth. When the lad picked it up, he found the gold ring resting inside.

The rejoicing of the servant and the courtiers was quickly cut short when the proud princess scorned the humble servant for her husband. She demanded further proof of his worth and imposed a second test.

The princess went into the fields behind the palace and

with her own hands gathered ten bags of grain. She then scattered the grain upon the ground. "You must gather every bit of this grain into the ten bags before sunrise," she said. "If you miss even one kernel, you will lose your head."

Left alone in the field, the poor servant once again pondered his miserable fate and, being weary, fell asleep. When he awakened in the morning, he could hardly believe his eyes. There, resting before him, were ten bags of grain neatly packed—and nary a kernel on the ground! The ants whom he had befriended in the past had returned his favor and collected the grain.

Although the king's daughter received the grain with amazement, she was still not ready to accept the humble youth as husband.

"You have successfully performed two tasks," she said, "but in order to become my husband, you must bring me the sacred apple from the Tree of Life."

The youth had never heard of such an apple, nor did he know where it might be found. Nevertheless, he started on his way, traveling from mountain to valley in search of the sacred apple.

One day, tired and discouraged, he sat beneath a tree in a forest to rest. Suddenly he heard a rustling of leaves above him—and a golden apple dropped into his lap. Then three crows flew down from the top of the tree and alighted on the servant's knee.

"We are the three crows whom you once saved from starvation. When we grew up and heard of your search for the sacred apple from the Tree of Life, we traveled over hill and ocean to bring you the apple you seek."

The servant thanked the crows, and with the sacred apple in his hand, started on his way back to the princess.

The princess gazed upon the fruit. "I have no further objection to you as my husband," she said to the youth, whereupon they halved the apple and ate it together. Immediately, the princess's heart was filled with love for the servant.

They were married—and lived happily ever after.

# Nazar the Brave

ONCE THERE WAS AND WAS NOT IN ANCIENT ARMENIA a peasant named Nazar who was both lazy and stupid. Worse than that, Nazar was a terrible coward. He was afraid of everything: of the light and of the dark, of the day and of the night. He did not dare to take a step by himself. Hanging on to his wife's apron strings from morning till night, he followed the poor woman wherever she went.

Thus people called him Nazar the Fearful.

One night his wife stepped out to the back of the house for a moment. As usual Nazar followed right behind her. It was a brilliant, moonlit night and the stars shone brightly over the mountains.

"Ah, wife," sighed Nazar, "what a wonderful night for a robbery! My heart tells me to go and rob the caravan of the rich shah who visits our land from India."

"Oh, be still!" said his wife angrily. "Who are you to talk of robbing a caravan!"

"Why won't you let me rob the shah's caravan?" scolded Nazar. "That's just the way you are! Never letting me do anything! Am I not a man? Do I not wear the hat of a man? Why do you stop me?"

Sick of her husband's empty boasts, Nazar's wife ran into the house and slammed the door in his face.

"All right," she called out. "Go ahead and rob the shah's caravan. And don't come back here till you do!"

Poor Nazar was frightened out of his wits at this turn of events. In vain did he beg and plead with his wife to rescue him.

The hours passed. Weariness finally overcame him and he fell asleep.

The night was a hot and sticky one, and morning came slowly. Thousands of flies swarmed over Nazar's face, sticking to his nose and his lips. Without opening his eyes, and still half asleep, he angrily raised his hand and slapped at the flies. Dead flies fell all about him. Nazar opened his eyes and saw the dead flies on the ground beside him.

"What is this?" he said in amazement. And he began 

to count the number of flies he had killed at one blow. There were so many that he lost count.

"Ah! What a brave man I am! And I never knew it until today! To think that I who can kill a thousand living things at one blow have been waiting hand and foot on such an ungrateful wife as mine!"

Quickly he got up and went off to see the village priest.

"Bless me, Father," he said.

"God's blessings on you, my son," replied the priest.

"Father, you don't know . . . let me tell you . . ." And Nazar recounted the tale of his bravery. He begged the priest to record his courageous deed so that all might know of it.

Laughing, the good-natured priest took a piece of cloth and, in jest, printed in large letters the words:

NAZAR THE BRAVE, OUR MIGHTY HERO,
FELLS A THOUSAND AT A SINGLE BLOW.

Nazar attached the cloth to the end of a long pole as a banner, tucked a rusty sword he had found into his belt, mounted his neighbor's donkey and rode off. He traveled and traveled on a road which led out of the village and through a forest.

As he left his home farther and farther behind, Nazar became more and more frightened. To keep up his spirits, he began to talk to himself and to scold the poor donkey in loud tones. The farther he traveled, the more frightened he became, and the more frightened he was, the louder he shouted. The poor bewildered donkey brayed louder in reply.

All this commotion disturbed the peace of the birds, who started to screech. The timid rabbits scurried into their burrows, and the frogs jumped into the water from their lily pads.

A well-to-do peasant, who was leading his horse back from market through the forest, heard all the noise and shouting.

"Oh my!" said the peasant. "It must be thieves!" Leaving his horse in the forest, he took to his heels and fled for his life.

When Nazar approached the spot, he saw a horse with an expensive saddle standing unattended. Getting off his donkey, he mounted the horse and continued on his way.

He traveled and traveled . . . how far he did not know, until he reached a village from which came sounds of the zoorna.* A wedding feast was in progress in the center of the village.

"Good day," said Nazar as he rode toward the gathered wedding guests and dismounted.

"Good day to you, stranger, and a thousand welcomes. Come and join us. Any guest is both God's and ours."

*Bugle.

The villagers took Nazar with his banner, to the head of the table and offered him food and drink. They were curious to know who this stranger might be and what his banner said, but since they were simple peasants who could not read, the printed words remained a mystery. Each guest in turn nudged his neighbor and whispered, "Who is he?" until, finally, the question reached the village priest sitting at the head of the table.

The priest leaned over and spelled out the words on the banner:

NAZAR THE BRAVE, OUR MIGHTY HERO,

FELLS A THOUSAND AT A SINGLE BLOW.

He read them to himself, repeated them to the one sitting next to him, who, in turn, repeated it to his neighbor—all the way down to the foot of the table until all the wedding guests knew the identity of the guest.

NAZAR THE BRAVE, OUR MIGHTY HERO,

FELLS A THOUSAND AT A SINGLE BLOW.

"Ah-h-h," said one who loved to boast. "So it's Nazar the Brave! Oh, I remember him well, but I didn't recognize him. He has changed greatly since I saw him last."

Several others pretended to remember him and began to whisper to one another what they remembered of Nazar's past bravery.

"But if he is so famous and important, how is it that he has no servant to attend him?" asked one of the guests.

"That is his desire," replied another. "He is too humble to keep a servant. Once I, too, asked him that very question and he answered that the whole world was his servant. What need did he have for one?"

"But how is it that such a man carries no real sword—only a small rusty one in his belt?" another guest wondered aloud.

"What need would Nazar have for a large shiny blade? Anyone can be brave with a sharp weapon. Only Nazar can perform bravely with a small rusty one!" came the reply.

The astonished villagers were very impressed with the famous guest. They drank many toasts in his honor. The village orator arose and with great dignity delivered a long speech of welcome to the hero, while the village troubadour sang a song praising his deeds of valor.

When darkness finally ended the wedding celebration, the villagers presented Nazar with gifts and bade him farewell.

Nazar rode away from the village, trembling with fear at the darkness and the strange unfamiliar roads. Finally he reached a wide, open green field. Frightened and weary, he dismounted to let his horse graze. He thrust his banner into the ground, huddled fearfully beneath it and fell asleep.

The field belonged to seven giants, who lived in a castle on top of the mountain overlooking the open space. In the morning the giants looked out and saw that someone had dared trespass on their land. Angrily, they shouldered their clubs and tramped down to the field to find Nazar fast asleep under a banner which read:

NAZAR THE BRAVE, OUR MIGHTY HERO,

FELLS A THOUSAND AT A SINGLE BLOW.

"It's Nazar the Brave!" exclaimed the giants. "The hero we have heard so much about from all the villagers." And they gazed fearfully at the man who could kill a thousand at a single blow.

Suddenly Nazar awoke. When he opened his eyes and saw seven giants armed with clubs towering over him, his stomach turned over! Trembling like a fall leaf he tried to crawl under his banner.

When the giants saw him turn pale and tremble, they were frightened.

"Nazar the Brave is angry," they said. "And now he will kill us at one blow." They fell upon their knees before Nazar and pleaded with him.

"Oh, Nazar the Brave, we have heard of your fame and have long wished to meet you. We are honored to have you as our guest. Come to our home on top of yonder hill and meet our beautiful sister. Accept us as your servants and brothers and do us the honor of breaking bread with us."

Nazar collected his wits and permitted himself to be led to the giants' castle, where he was treated as an honored guest. Indeed, so well did the giants tell the tales of Nazar's bravery to their beautiful sister, Yar, that she promptly fell in love with him.

About this time, a man-eating tiger suddenly appeared in the countryside, terrifying the people. All agreed that the tiger must be killed—but who was brave enough to try? "Nazar the Brave, of course! Who else?" exclaimed the villagers, and they came to Nazar for help.

As soon as Nazar heard the word tiger, he began to shake with fright and ran out of the castle to go back to his own village and his wife.

The people, however, thought that he was running to kill the tiger.

The beautiful Yar called after him, "Nazar, my brave hero, where do you go without weapons? At least take this knife with you." And she hurriedly brought him a knife to help him perform his deed of bravery.

Grabbing the knife, Nazar ran into the forest as fast as he could go and scrambled to the top of the tallest tree he could find. Scared out of his wits, he held on for dear life, hoping never to see the tiger.

As luck would have it, the tiger chose that very moment to walk through the forest, and decided to lie down and rest under that same tree!

When Nazar looked down and saw the tiger, his liver turned to water. He trembled and shook so that he lost his hold on the tree. Down he fell, right on the back of the tiger!

The startled beast jumped up, furiously trying to shake off the strange burden on his back. Roaring wildly, the tiger ran out of the forest, while Nazar, quaking with fear, hung on for dear life.

What a sight it was for the people who waited on the outskirts of the village!

"Look!" they said. "Look! Nazar has tamed the tiger and is riding him like a horse!"

Gaining courage from Nazar's bravery, the villagers surrounded the tiger and killed him.

Slowly, Nazar regained his senses. Taking a deep breath, he opened his eyes and said, "Alas! Why did you kill the beast? I was going to keep him for a horse!"

News of this new deed of bravery spread throughout the countryside. All the people turned out to welcome Nazar and do him honor. The beautiful Yar decided to marry the hero, who had by now forgotten all about his first wife. A wedding was celebrated for seven days and seven nights and there were many toasts to praise the courage of the groom and the beauty of the bride.

Some weeks later, the giants received word that their neighbor king from the south was marching against them in battle. This same king had long been in love with Yar and reports of her marriage to Nazar had angered him into an open declaration of war.

The giants came to Nazar for help. Proclaiming him general in charge of their armies, they gave him full command.

At mention of the word war, Nazar quaked with fear, and started to run out of the castle back to his own village.

The people thought that Nazar was rushing to fight the enemy with his bare hands.

"Come back, brave Nazar," they begged. "How can you go into battle unarmed and on foot?" The beautiful Yar pleaded with her brothers to restrain her brave husband.

News of Nazar's great courage spread throughout the army and made the soldiers eager to follow such a commander. Indeed, Nazar's fame spread even to the enemy.

The soldiers helped Nazar mount a horse saddled especially for battle. Hundreds of men on horseback waited for his commands. Nazar's horse moved, and off went the army to battle.

Nazar's horse, sensing that his rider had no control, bolted straight ahead toward the enemy camp. Nazar's soldiers, thinking that their commander was leading a charge, galloped after him.

When the frightened Nazar realized that his horse was leading him right into the midst of the enemy, he decided to save himself by jumping off the horse into a tree along the way. He grabbed for a branch, but the tree was a dead one, and a great part of it broke off in his hand!

When the enemy saw the famed hero, Nazar, galloping toward them with a tree in his hand, they cried, "Run for your lives! Nazar the Brave is coming to kill us, and he's tearing up the trees by the roots as he comes!"

Many were killed in that terrible battle. Those who survived surrendered to Nazar and swore him full allegiance.

What pomp and ceremony ushered Nazar back to the giants' castle! He was proclaimed king of the land by the grateful people and given all manner of gifts and honors. The seven giants became his seven viziers and helped him to rule wisely and well forever after.

But whenever the talk turned to his bravery and his courage, Nazar always smiled mysteriously and said, "What bravery! What courage! My friends, it is LUCK that rules the world."

THE MIDDLE EAST
Irrigated land and oases
Grass land (dry farming or grazing)
Desert
Elevations over 2,000 meters
CASPIAN SEA
U
Tabriz
Resht
Meshed
Mosul
Hamadan
Teheran
Tigris
Kermanshah
P E R S I A
Baghdad
Isfahan
A
Q
Euphrates
Basra
Shiraz
Abadan
KUWAIT
Bushire
PERSIAN GULF
Bandar Abbas
BAHREIN
Muscat
Riyadh
J D I
A R A B I A
O M A N
ADEN PROTECTORATE
Sana
YEMEN
Aden
ibouti
Berbera

# FOOD AND INFLATION IN THE MIDDLE EAST 1940-45

*Publications of the Institute*

CURRENT SERIES

STUDIES ON FOOD, AGRICULTURE, AND WORLD WAR II
STUDIES IN COMMODITY ECONOMICS AND AGRICULTURAL POLICY
STUDIES IN TROPICAL DEVELOPMENT
MISCELLANEOUS PUBLICATIONS

DISCONTINUED SERIES

COMMODITY POLICY STUDIES
FATS AND OILS STUDIES
WAR-PEACE PAMPHLETS
WHEAT STUDIES

A complete list of publications
of the Food Research Institute
will be furnished on request.

*A Publication of the*
FOOD RESEARCH INSTITUTE
STANFORD UNIVERSITY

*One of a group of studies on*
FOOD, AGRICULTURE, AND WORLD WAR II

# FOOD AND INFLATION IN THE MIDDLE EAST
# 1940-45

By

E. M. H. LLOYD, C.B., C.M.G.



Stanford University Press
STANFORD, CALIFORNIA

# FOOD RESEARCH INSTITUTE

Established at Stanford University, Stanford, California, in 1921, jointly by Carnegie Corporation of New York and the Trustees of the Leland Stanford Junior University, for research in the production, distribution, and consumption of food.




STANFORD UNIVERSITY PRESS, STANFORD, CALIFORNIA

PUBLISHED IN GREAT BRITAIN BY GEOFFREY CUMBERLEGE,
OXFORD UNIVERSITY PRESS, LONDON





PRINTED AND BOUND IN THE UNITED STATES OF AMERICA BY STANFORD UNIVERSITY PRESS

*Library of Congress Catalog Card Number: 55-6686*

# DIRECTOR'S PREFACE

This book is the ninth to appear in the Food Research Institute's projected series of some twenty volumes designed to illuminate the complex aspects of food, agriculture, and World War II. These studies fall broadly into groups focusing upon commodities, upon wartime management of food and agriculture in important regions of the world, and upon international organizations created to cope with wartime food problems of common concern to member governments.

This volume, however, treats both of regional management in the Middle East and of the functioning of an Anglo-American organization, the Middle East Supply Center. The setting is a region composed of several political entities not accustomed to concerted action or to provision of statistical records, and of populations little urbanized and not highly literate or self-disciplined. Central problems for Anglo-American solution were the relatively elementary and tractable one (as compared, for example, with equitable consumer rationing) of avoiding bread riots in the cities through collection and supply of the basic food, grain; and the complicated and recalcitrant one of restraining general price inflation in the face of inescapably heavy military expenditure in a crucial theater of war. Readers will find here a probing discussion of the connection between inflation and urban food provisioning and, for the first time, the story of the effort to check inflation by sales of gold.

The author, Mr. E. M. H. Lloyd, served in 1943 and 1944 as Economic Adviser to the British Minister of State in the Middle East. His long and wide experience in food and agriculture and associated wartime problems, and in international affairs, is reflected in activities ranging from Assistant Secretary, Ministry of Food, in World War I, author in 1924 of a well-known book on *Experiments in State Control at the War Office and the Ministry of Food*, through service in the British Food Mission to the United States in 1941 and 1942, with the United Nations Relief and Rehabilitation Administration in Southeast Europe in 1944–46, with the Food and Agriculture Organization of the United Nations in 1946 and 1947, to Under

Secretary of the British Ministry of Food until his recent retirement. I take occasion here to thank him on behalf of the Food Research Institute for his contribution of this book to our series in the face of many and varied obligations elsewhere.

Grateful acknowledgment is made to the Rockefeller Foundation for a grant of funds that made possible the preparation and publication of this work. The Foundation is in no way responsible for the treatment of the subject. The final responsibility, in general, rests with the author himself.

M. K. Bennett
*Director*

Stanford, California
April 1956

# FOREWORD AND ACKNOWLEDGMENTS

The story I have to tell is about the impact of the war on Middle East food and agriculture and the part played by the Middle East Supply Center (MESC), in co-operation with the governments of a score or more countries, in maintaining the food supply of the towns and averting the threat of famine. My firsthand acquaintance with the Middle East and its problems was limited to the two critical war years 1943 and 1944, during which I served as Economic Adviser to the British Minister of State in the Middle East. My first acknowledgment therefore is to the authors of the many books and official reports which I have consulted in sketching the background to wartime developments.

I have received permission from the British Government to make use of official records, particularly the monthly letters, agricultural reports, and special reviews written by officers of MESC during the war. I am specially indebted to Sir Keith Hancock for allowing me to make use of historical notes by Mrs. Warner on the origin and early struggles of MESC; and to Professor Sayers and Miss Behrens for showing me draft chapters in their forthcoming volumes in the official History of the Second World War (U.K. Civil Series) entitled *Financial Policy 1939–45* and *Merchant Shipping and the Demands of War*. Among those who have been kind enough to supply information or to read various chapters I would specially thank the following: Max Nicholson, R. G. A. Jackson, Sir Keith Murray, and George Woodbridge on the work of MESC; Charles Empson on Egyptian cereals; Sir Edward Spears on the OCP in Syria; Sir Reader Bullard and G. F. Squire on cereals collection in Persia; and W. A. B. Iliff and Arnold France on problems of inflation and the sale of gold. Needless to say, the author alone is responsible for errors of fact and interpretation.

I am particularly grateful for the friendly guidance and encouragement I have received from Merrill K. Bennett, Director of the Institute; and I am under special obligation to Miss Rosamond Peirce for wrestling with the uncertainties of Middle East statistics and preparing the statistical tables in the Appendix. Last but not least, I should like to express warm thanks to Mrs. Young for her patient care in seeing the book through the press.

E.M.H.L.

BROADMOOR NEAR DORKING
SURREY, ENGLAND
September 1955

# CONTENTS

## PART I: FOOD AND AGRICULTURE BEFORE THE WAR



## PART II. THE WORK OF THE MIDDLE EAST SUPPLY CENTER

## PART III. CEREAL IMPORTS AND COLLECTION SCHEMES



## PART IV. THE MENACE OF INFLATION

## APPENDIX AND INDEX

# Part I

# FOOD AND AGRICULTURE BEFORE THE WAR

## CHAPTER 1

# GENERAL SURVEY

### THE REGION DEFINED

During World War II the term Middle East, rather than Near East, was adopted by the military authorities to designate a region that for strategic and economic purposes had certain elements in common and could conveniently be treated as a unit. Before the war the Middle East sometimes meant Arabia, Mesopotamia, Persia, and Afghanistan; while the Near East comprised Greece, Bulgaria, Turkey, the Levant States, Palestine, and Egypt. Some writers went so far as to extend the Near East to include the whole area from Afghanistan to Greece, but excluded Egypt. Since the war the two terms have become virtually synonymous and there is no accepted convention as to their precise meaning. In the present survey, which deals with the food supply of the Middle East during the war years, particularly as it was affected by the work of the Middle East Supply Center (MESC), it will be convenient to follow the practice of that body, which was based on administrative and political considerations rather than on any geographical convention.

The countries that came within the jurisdiction of MESC varied from time to time as the fortunes of war and administrative decisions dictated. Egypt was the center of what Fisher (*1*, p. 1) calls "a military province stretching from Iran to Tripolitania," which came into being during the war and was named "Middle East." Here was the General Headquarters of the Middle East Command; the offices of the British Minister of State in the Middle East (hereafter called Minister of State), of the American Economic Mission, and of the Anglo-American MESC; and the vast naval and military supply bases of Alexandria and Suez. Surrounding Egypt were the British-administered territories of Anglo-Egyptian Sudan (often called simply Sudan), Palestine, and Cyprus. To the east were the liberated territories of Ethiopia, Eritrea, and British, French, and ex-Italian Somaliland; and on the west Cyrenaica and Tripolitania, now united in the state of Libya.

In the early days of MESC the needs of Greece were prominent; but after the German occupation of Yugoslavia, Bulgaria, Greece, and Crete, the Balkans were cut off from the rest of the Middle East and dropped out of MESC's sphere of responsibility, until plans for supplying them with food imports after liberation led to the creation of a Balkan stockpile of cereals in 1944. The beleaguered island of Malta was represented at the first conference of Middle East territories and drew most of its supplies of cereals and other essential imports from Middle East stocks at Alexandria. The needs of Turkey for cereal imports were a source of anxiety to MESC in 1941 and 1942; but in later years her import requirements were looked after by a separate Anglo-American Co-ordinating Committee and passed out of MESC's jurisdiction. After the British and Free French forces liberated Syria and Lebanon in 1941 the feeding of these territories became of major concern; and shortly afterward the needs of Iraq, Persia, and the Sheikdoms of the Persian Gulf became an additional responsibility. Saudi Arabia, Aden Colony and Protectorate, and Yemen completed the outer ring.

In its official publications MESC listed 27 territories with whose import requirements and food supplies it had to deal. They may be grouped as follows:

Western: Cyrenaica, Malta, Tripolitania

Central: Cyprus, Egypt, Lebanon, Palestine, Syria, Transjordan

Eastern: Aden Colony, Aden Protectorate, Iraq, Persia, Persian Gulf Sheikdoms (Bahrein, Kuwait, Muscat, Oman, Qatar, Trucial Oman), Saudi Arabia, Yemen

Southern: British Somaliland, Eritrea, Ethiopia, ex-Italian Somaliland, French Somaliland, Sudan

It will not be possible to deal in detail with wartime developments in each of these territories. Many will be referred to only in so far as their food supply became of special concern to MESC. Main emphasis will be given to those territories in the central and eastern groups where military operations, or the presence of Allied forces involving large military expenditure, created inflationary conditions and a threat of food shortage. Egypt, Palestine, Syria, Lebanon, Persia, and Iraq were the countries with which for political, strategic, and economic reasons MESC was chiefly concerned.

These six countries were more advanced politically and economically than the remaining territories. They are now all independent sovereign states, but during the war Palestine was under a British mandate, and Syria and Lebanon were still under a French mandate. Trade and industry were relatively more important in them than in the rest of the area and they had as a consequence a larger urban population to be fed—a point of special importance in dealing with wartime food supplies.

## LAND AND CLIMATE

Geologically the Middle East falls into three broad divisions. First, a stable basement of archaic rocks in the south, including Arabia, Sinai, and most of Egypt and Cyrenaica; second, a folded irregular mountain zone in the north running from Turkey through northern Iraq to Persia; and third, an intermediate zone of sedimentary limestone underlying the Fertile Crescent, which stretches from Palestine through Syria and the valley of the Tigris and Euphrates to the Persian Gulf. These sedimentary rocks are said to have been laid down some fifty million years ago when the Mediterranean and the Indian Ocean were joined by the ancient Sea of Tethys.

The greater part of the Middle East consists of desert or semidesert steppes, and less than 3 percent of the total area is cultivated land. The whole of Egypt outside the valley of the Nile, most of Arabia except for Yemen and Aden Protectorate, the greater part of Sudan, and most of the central plateau of Persia consist of rainless or almost rainless deserts.

The climate of the Middle East is influenced both by its land structure and by the air currents coming from neighboring regions. From the continent of Asia comes a cold and dry polar air over the mountains of Anatolia and Persia; from the interior of India and Pakistan comes the hot, dry monsoon air, that has lost most of its original moisture on arrival in southern Persia; and from the Mediterranean and the Atlantic Ocean, between October and May, come the maritime air currents which provide most of the region's scanty rainfall. The Middle East serves as a connecting link between two of the hottest parts of the world, the Sahara and northwest India, and yet forms part of the continent of Asia, where in winter extremes of cold are found. None of these three adjoining regions provides rain. Cold spells of Siberian origin bring frost; and hot air from the south brings scorching heat and dust storms. Only from the west, and mainly in late winter and early spring, comes a series of moisture-laden depressions and cyclonic disturbances similar to those experienced in more temperate latitudes.

Middle East countries thus fall into three categories: (1) in the northwestern belt of countries—Cyprus, Syria, Lebanon, and northern Palestine—the climate is much influenced by the Mediterranean. The chief rainfall is from November to March; the summer period from May to October is practically rainless. (2) Egypt, Sinai, southern Palestine, northern Sudan, and most of Arabia have an extremely low rainfall, averaging less than 100 millimeters (4 inches) a year. Wide areas of Egypt and Arabia may be without rain for years on end. (3) In the southern belt, comprising southern Sudan, Ethiopia, Eritrea, Somaliland, Aden, and Yemen, the chief rainfall is in the summer months. Moisture-laden air currents are brought by the southwest monsoon between July and September across central Africa from the South Atlantic. The main source of the flood waters of the Nile is the rain falling on the mountains of Ethiopia, which comes mostly from the Atlantic and not from the Indian Ocean (*2*, p. 28). Aden Protectorate gets a certain amount of rain in March, April, and May from the Indian Ocean.

Insufficient rainfall is the chief feature which limits food production. The region lies in a desert belt with a rainfall for the most part less than 200 millimeters, which is the lower limit for wheat, and for about half the area less than 100 millimeters, which is the lower limit for barley. Only in southwest Arabia, in southern Sudan, and on the shores of the Caspian Sea does the annual rainfall exceed 600 millimeters (*3*, p. 7).

The hot and dry climate reduces the volume of water in the rivers through evaporation; and in the mountainous regions much of the rain is carried out to sea by torrential floods. The soil erosion caused thereby is aggravated by deforestation and uncontrolled grazing. Rainfall varies from year to year, and from earliest times irrigation by means of pumps, dams, and canals has been used to regulate the supply of water, so as to mitigate droughts and floods and extend the range of cultivation. Except in the Tigris and Euphrates valleys the relatively small volume of river water limits the area that can be irrigated. Even in Egypt, where irrigation has been developed on the largest scale, the volume of unused water is small in relation to the need. The problems of water supply and irrigation are discussed in chapter 32.

Land structure, climate, and rivers have influenced the way of life of the Middle East for thousands of years. The desert area in the south is the home of pastoral nomads, living much as their remote ancestors must have lived five or ten thousand years ago before the invention of agriculture. In the north are a mountain people split up into tribal groups and struggling against a harsh environment.

The middle zone and the Nile Valley, since the dawn of history, have been the home of settled agriculture and the arts of civilization; and, since it has always been open to invasion by conquerors, it has been for thousands of years the melting pot of races.

### DISTRIBUTION OF POPULATION

The supply of water has largely determined the distribution of population, the development of agriculture, and the growth of cities. About 75 percent of the population of the area is settled rural, 15 percent nomadic, and 10 percent urban. The bulk of the population is concentrated in towns and villages situated in river valleys, or on hillsides and coastal plains watered by mountain ranges near the sea. There are 25 cities in the area with a population exceeding 100,000, the three largest being Cairo with more than 2 million in 1947, Alexandria with about 900,000, and Teheran with 600,000. The nomads are for the most part pastoral, living on the fringe of the deserts or in the mountain ranges of Kurdistan and southern Persia. In the Arabian peninsula, including Jordan, nomads are estimated to be about 30 percent of the population, in the Sudan 25 percent, and in Persia, Iraq, and Syria between 10 and 15 percent.

During the war, when imports of food and consumer goods had to be reduced to the minimum to save shipping, control of distribution presented a baffling problem. The settled population in the villages and farms had enough food, but were short of consumer goods—clothing, kerosene, soap, hardware, and tools. The chief difficulty that faced governments and MESC was to induce them to sell their surplus cereals to feed the towns. Rationing by household cards was introduced in the towns but not in the villages; and special steps had to be taken to ensure that nomad tribes obtained their share of bare necessities by allocating supplies to tribal sheiks.

### POVERTY AND ILLITERACY

The population of the area before the war was about 75 million, and had probably been increasing for several decades at a rate somewhat greater than the world average of 1 percent per annum. This was notably the case in Egypt and Palestine, where fairly reliable data are available. Illiteracy was high, for the region as a whole probably reaching 80 percent. The percentage of children attending elementary schools had been rising since World War I; but only in Palestine and Lebanon did it approach 75 percent. In Egypt it was about 50 percent and in Persia and Iraq only about 20 percent. In

Arabia, Ethiopia, and Sudan the percentage was still lower (*3*, p.10).

Lack of educational facilities was paralleled by the backward state of medical and public-health services. Endemic diseases, including malaria, bilharziasis, and ancylostomiasis, had been intensified by the extension of irrigation. Typhoid, dysentery, and trachoma were largely due to overcrowding and to polluted water supplies. The low level of education and public health and the high density of population in relation to natural resources were reflected in a low level of income. The average annual per capita income in Middle East countries is roughly indicated by the following approximate estimates for 1949 published by the United Nations (*3*, p. 12); conjectural estimates for 1939 at prewar prices have been added. The figures are in dollars:

| Country | 1939 | 1949 |
|---|---|---|
| Palestine | 100 | ... |
| Lebanon | 70 | 140 |
| Syria | 63 | 100 |
| Egypt | 58 | 100 |
| Persia | 50 | 85 |
| Iraq | 48 | 85 |
| Saudi Arabia | 30 | 45 |
| Yemen | 30 | 40 |

Low national incomes were accompanied by marked inequality of distribution. The mass of the population consisted of peasants, sharecroppers, pastoralists, and laborers, living on the margin of subsistence with incomes barely sufficient to provide the necessities of life. At the other extreme was a relatively small class of landowners and merchants living in comparative luxury and disinclined to devote their resources to industrial development. Between the wealthy and the very poor there was a small but growing middle class, which was slowly making its influence felt in economic and political developments holding out promise for the future.

### LAND TENURE

Among the social factors impeding progress was, and still is, the traditional system of land tenure. In many countries titles to land are matters of dispute. Egypt is the only country with a complete cadastral survey and registration of landholdings. Registration of land, but not of water rights, was carried out in Transjordan before the war; but only a beginning had been made elsewhere (*4*, p. 15).

The prevailing system based on the Ottoman code recognizes

five main types of landholding. *Mulk* is land held in freehold ownership. *Miri* denotes land originally held by the state and transferred in return for services formerly rendered to the sultan. *Waqf* is land held under a religious or charitable trust, the revenues of which are applied for the maintenance of persons or institutions. *Matrukhi* means land used for public benefit, such as village threshing floors or grazing grounds used in common. *Masha*, which is found mainly in eastern Syria and Transjordan, is a form of communal ownership under which the land is reallotted at intervals of three years or so at the end of each crop rotation. This custom, which originated when the tribe first settled, has resulted in course of time in one individual's holdings being scattered in small strips in different parts of the village area. Even when periodical reallocation ceased, excessive fragmentation of holdings tended to persist (*1*, pp. 180–81).

The effect of the traditional systems of land tenure is to discourage agricultural improvement. With few exceptions large holders of *mulk* or *miri* land tend to be absentee landlords living in the towns and receiving rent in cash or in kind collected by agents. Under the other types of holding cultivators have little security of tenure and are tempted to exhaust the soil with no thought of the future. Fragmentation of holdings leads to serious loss of efficiency. The former director of the Land Survey Office in Syria and Lebanon estimated this loss of efficiency at about 30 percent—10 percent due to loss of time in walking from one strip to another in different parts of the village area, 10 percent due to loss of land through the multiplication of boundaries, and 10 percent due to waste from excessive seeding (*4*, p. 20). Jacques Weulersse in his *Paysans de Syrie et du Proche-Orient* quotes a case of a village in Lebanon where 2,140 hectares were divided into 32,643 separate plots (*1*, p. 182). One of the obstacles to the introduction of contour plowing is the prevalence of narrow strips running up and down and not along the hillsides (*5*, p. 56).

During the last few decades, growth of population and land hunger have strengthened the position of large landlords. In Egypt in 1933 about 40 percent of the land was held in estates of over 50 acres by less than 1 percent of the total landholders, while two-thirds of the landholders held on an average only two-fifths of an acre each. The commonest form of tenancy is sharecropping or *metayage*. Under this the landlord provides seeds and other requisites and receives 50 percent or more of the yield after payment of taxes. Cash rents are the exception, being found mainly in the neighborhood of cities, where profits are relatively high, and on the edge of the desert, where the landlord seeks to avoid the loss that might result from a Bedouin raid. Before the war many tenants and sharecroppers lived in a state of chronic indebtedness to landlords and usurers. During the depression of the thirties, when prices of cereals and other crops touched very low levels, large numbers of cultivators were forced by the burden of debt to sell their holdings to merchants and landlords in the towns. This tendency was especially pronounced in Syria and Iraq. Under such conditions landowners might acquire whole villages without any change in the existing methods of strip cultivation.

## CITATIONS

*1* W. B. Fisher, *The Middle East. A Physical, Social and Regional Geography* (London, 1950).

*2* E. B. Worthington, *Middle East Science . . .* (London, 1946).

*3* United Nations, *Review of Economic Conditions in the Middle East, Supplement to World Economic Report 1949–50* (New York, March 1951).

*4* Doreen Warriner, *Land and Poverty in the Middle East* (Royal Inst. Internatl. Affairs, London, 1948).

*5* B. A. Keen, *The Agricultural Development of the Middle East . . .* (London, 1946).

## CHAPTER 2

# FOOD PRODUCTION AND CONSUMPTION

### THE AGRICULTURAL PATTERN

Except in Egypt, and parts of Palestine and Lebanon, extensive rather than intensive cultivation is practiced, with methods and implements that go back to Biblical times. Wooden plows drawn by oxen, hand sickles for reaping, threshing floors where animals tread the corn, and use of manure as fuel are common features throughout the area in spite of the gradual introduction on large farms of tractors and modern agricultural machinery. The peasants live in compact villages rather than in scattered homesteads, and leave home only under strong pressure. Conservatism and lack of enterprise have their roots embedded in Arab culture and the Moslem way of life. Among the scientifically educated minority there is growing awareness of the need for modern improvements; but among the mass of the peasantry and the village elders, to whom the peasants look for guidance, reverence for tradition carries with it distrust of any novelty. Sometimes this is carried to an extreme degree. In a village visited by young social workers from the American University at Beirut, the elders were only persuaded with great difficulty to accept piped water. They feared, at first, that water carried in a pipe would have a bad taste, and they preferred to get their water from the village pond. However, after an explanation of the connection between impure water and high infant mortality (which the elders attributed to the will of Allah), they were eventually persuaded by one of the party, who was able to quote from the Koran that Allah helps those who help themselves.

The traditional methods of cultivation are simple but effective. In areas of low rainfall of between 100 and 200 millimeters, like the Negeb in southern Palestine and parts of Syria, Iraq, and Transjordan adjoining the desert, barley is the only crop grown and appears to have been cultivated by the same method for countless generations. A description was given by Lowe at the Conference on Middle East Agricultural Development (*1*, p. 31):

When the rains appear due, in late September or October, the day's task is broadcast with seed-barley among the remains of stubble and dry weeds and the simple nail-plough is brought into action to loosen the surface and bury the grain. The nail-plough is a simple triangle of metal, which loosens the surface and gives partial covering to the seed; it is drawn by a camel, a mule, or a team consisting of an ox with an ass; it does not turn the soil, but runs a few inches below the surface which is thus loosened and thus enabled to receive the seed. If good rains fall, germination follows, and if fair rains continue, so does growth until the harvest is ready. If continuation of rain does not follow, the seedlings die and the so-called "afir"-sowing has failed, which is just too bad, but not unexpected. It is locally estimated that crops run on a seven-year cycle which contains about three good crops—according to the local modest standard—three partial successes, when one reaps little more than the seed sown, and one total failure when the seed would have been more usefully consumed as food.

The sowing of barley may continue until about mid-December by which time it is normally completed. No further attention is given until harvest which takes place between the end of April and the end of May. The crop is harvested by uprooting the plants or more rarely with a sickle and transported to a threshing-floor of hardened earth, where the grain is trampled out by animals and cleaned by hand. The remaining mixture of chaff and broken straw is used for fodder.

In many respects Middle East agriculture resembles that of medieval and feudal Europe. Most of the food is produced for consumption by the growers or for barter and sale in villages and neighboring towns. Specialization and the growing of crops for a distant market or for export is the exception. Cotton in Egypt and Sudan, citrus fruits in Palestine, and dates in Iraq are the chief crops grown for export.

Of the cereals produced, wheat and barley are winter crops. The summer crops are sorghum and millet where rainfall or irrigation permit; maize which is grown mainly in Egypt; and rice which is grown in alluvial soil in the Nile Delta and southern Iraq, and on the Caspian shore in Persia. Wheat and barley are native to the Middle East and may have originated there. Barley grows wild, and cultivated wheat may have arisen as a hybrid from emmer and einkorn, both of which grow wild in parts of Syria (*2*, p. 188). Barley is eaten as a bread grain less than wheat and is largely fed to livestock, particularly draft animals. Maize, introduced from North America, has become the most important bread grain consumed in Egypt and has largely taken the place of sorghum and millet. In the southern belt of countries, the predominant bread grain is either sorghum or white millet (*Pennisetum*), particularly in Sudan, Ethiopia, Eritrea, and parts of southern Arabia.

The principal fruits are olives, figs, dates, apricots, and grapes;

bananas and citrus fruits are comparatively recent introductions from other parts of the world. Apples are grown in a few places, mostly in Syria and Lebanon. Olives are of special importance and are either eaten as cured fruit or crushed to make oil, the stones being fed to livestock. Traditionally the oil was used both as an illuminant and for soapmaking, but kerosene is now taking its place for lighting and imported oils are used for soap. Figs are well adapted for countries with a Mediterranean climate of winter rains and dry summers, and flourish best in the Euphrates Valley near Antioch and in gardens around Damascus and Beirut. Vines grow well on well-watered hills in Cyprus, Syria, Lebanon, and Palestine, and mainly supply grapes for eating rather than for wine making. The date palm, an exceptional crop, needs a hot dry summer, yet a good supply of underground water, and provides one of the principal items of diet in Iraq, southern Persia, Arabia, parts of Egypt, and Libya. It is found in desert oases as well as in river valleys. Because of their high sugar content and keeping qualities dates are an ideal food for nomads.

The growing of vegetables flourishes near towns, the most important vegetable crops being onions, beans, tomatoes, cucumbers, and to a less extent potatoes. Edible herbs are common everywhere. Nomad tribes collect and eat the seeds and leaves of many wild desert plants. For a few weeks in the spring "the steppe presents an amazing picture of luxuriant, almost lush, vegetation." In the desert a shrub of the pea family called camel thorn "exudes a brown, sweetish sap, which when hardened on contact with the atmosphere forms the Biblical manna" (*2*, pp. 72, 73).

The culture of mulberries and silkworms was introduced into Syria and Lebanon from China in Byzantine times. During World War II there was some expansion of silk production in Lebanon for sale to the British Ministry of Supply for use in making parachutes.

## LIVESTOCK AND PASTORALISM

The Middle East is the home of pastoralism but has next to no livestock industry in a Western sense. Before the war, mixed farming and intensive animal husbandry were mainly confined to the Jewish settlements in Palestine and to a few modern farms in Egypt. Specialized dairy production had developed in the neighborhood of cities, and in Cairo, Damascus, and Beirut stall-fed cows were kept. Cattle and buffaloes were kept primarily as draft animals, along with donkeys and mules. Beef production was low and of poor quality and, except in Egypt, fodder crops were rarely grown to fatten animals. One of the main reasons for the low level of livestock production has been pressure of population on the resources of land and water. The best land must be reserved for growing crops for human consumption and animals must make do with stubble and straw, eked out by a small ration of barley.

In steppe and mountain regions sheep and goats predominate, under the guidance of nomad herdsmen moving from summer to winter pastures on the fringe of the deserts. They yield milk and cheese, wool and hair, and a little meat. The typical fat-tailed sheep of the Middle East yields as much as 10 pounds of fat from its tail. The nomad tribes of the Arabian desert live largely on the milk of camels, sheep, and goats, supplemented by dates and wild plants and a relatively small amount of grain. Mutton is reserved for feasts and occasions of hospitality.

Hogs are reared by Christians of Palestine and Lebanon but not by Moslems and Jews. In the climate of the Middle East hogs are prone to disease; the Mosaic ban on pork may have had some justification on health grounds. Water buffaloes are found in great numbers in the Nile Delta, in lower Iraq, and on the shores of the Caspian. They are tough and docile workers in the paddy fields and yield excellent milk and meat.

Donkeys, rather than horses, are used for transport of men and goods. Cyprus specializes in the breeding of mules. Camels are found everywhere and, until the advent of automobiles, were the only means of transport in the desert.

## FOOD SUPPLY AND PATTERN OF CONSUMPTION

Before the war the Middle East was broadly self-sufficient in staple foods, but the dietary pattern was poor by Western standards. There was a relatively small net export of grains balanced by net imports of sugar and oilseeds; and the important export trade in citrus fruits from Palestine and in dates from Iraq offset the area's imports of tea, coffee, and small quantities of canned and processed foods.

It was extremely difficult during the war to obtain any reliable figures of prewar food consumption per head, and the best that can be given now are only what the Food and Agriculture Organization of the United Nations (FAO) calls (*3*, p. 91) "approximations" which "indicate merely the order of magnitude of consumption levels." For the Middle East as a whole (excluding Turkey) with a prewar population approaching 75 million, total grain production was probably about 15 million tons, or 200 kilos per head per year. In the eight countries for which official estimates are shown in Appendix Table IV, production was just under 10 million tons for a population of 48 million, or 208 kilos per head. After allowing for seed, waste, and animal feed, human consumption of flour or meal probably averaged about 165 kilos per head, ranging from 182 kilos in Egypt to 150 kilos or less in Ethiopia and Arabia. This compares with prewar figures of 90 kilos in the United States and 94 kilos in the United Kingdom (*4*).

Estimates of consumption of other foods are even more conjectural and only orders of magnitude can be indicated. On the basis of FAO's food balance sheet for Egypt (*4*) and approximations given by FAO for other countries (*3*, p. 91), the following table has been constructed giving the broad pattern of Middle East prewar per capita food-consumption levels as compared with Italy and the United States:

| Item | Middle East | Italy | United States |
|---|---|---|---|
| Kilos per year: | | | |
| Grains, as flour | 165 | 177 | 90 |
| Roots, pulses, and nuts | 15–25 | 59 | 71 |
| Sugar and syrup | 11 | 7 | 49 |
| Fats and oils | 5 | 12 | 22 |
| Meat, eggs, and fish | 15 | 33 | 85 |
| Fruit and vegetables | 100–200 | 84 | 184 |
| Milk and cheese | 50–100 | 42 | 177 |
| Calories per day | 2,200 | 2,689 | 3,164 |
| Protein (*gm. per day*): | | | |
| Total | 70 | 86 | 90 |
| Animal | 10–12 | 20 | 52 |

The chief feature of the Middle East pattern of consumption, shared by most countries with low income per head, is the high proportion of total calories taken in the form of bread grains, ranging from 63 percent in prewar Palestine to 71 percent in Egypt. By contrast, in the Middle East the percentage of calories from sugar and fats is only about a third of what it is in the United States and a fourth in absolute amount; and consumption of meat, fish, and eggs is only about a sixth. But in spite of this the consumption of meat, sugar, and fats is not so low as in India and many other countries with low incomes per head. Total protein intake in the Middle East ranges around 70 grams per day, of which animal protein supplies

10–12 grams; whereas in the United States, out of a total of 90 grams, animal protein supplies 52 grams. In India and China the prewar figures given by FAO are total protein, 56 and 71 grams respectively; and animal protein, 8 and 6 grams. In spite of the predominance of cereals in the diet, the Middle East is not quite so vegetarian as India and China.

The consumption of protective foods—milk and cheese, fruit and vegetables—though it varies widely between different countries and social groups, compares not unfavorably with that of some other countries of higher income rating. Milk is obtained from sheep, goats, camels, and buffaloes as well as from cows, and has for thousands of years been the traditional food of nomad pastoralists. Among fruits, dates are a Middle East specialty and olives, figs, and grapes go back to Biblical times and earlier. The fairly high level of these protective foods and the low consumption of refined sugar are favorable factors in the average diet.

But the important question for the student and the administrator is not the average for each nation, or for an area as a whole like the Middle East, but the variations in time and place among different sections of the population. As to this, little is known and a few remarks must suffice.

### DIETARY SURVEYS

Nutritional surveys in Palestine before and during the war clearly brought out the contrasts in the diets of Jews and Arabs, urban and rural. A survey published in 1931 under the auspices of the Jewish Agency (*5*) showed that Ashkenazic or European Jews consumed more meat, milk, and butter than Oriental Jews and had a higher calorie intake. Rural Jewish families ate more than urban groups; and children had an excess of fat in the diet. Among rural Arabs the average calorie intake of adults (3,700) was higher even than that of rural Jews (3,500) but protein intake was low. Semi-agricultural Bedouins consumed more milk than the fellahin, preferred butter oil, when available, to olive oil, and ate more meat and vegetables than the villagers. In all groups the diets fell off in the winter; the rural Arabs' calorie intake was 20 percent greater in spring and summer when milk and eggs were plentiful. The main conclusions drawn were that in Palestine, where 70–80 percent of income was spent on food, economic status was the chief determining factor in nutrition; that the high fat intake typical of average diets in Europe is not needed and may be harmful in subtropical regions; that the diet of adults was nearer to the optimum than that of the children; and that there was much scope for increased consumption of milk and vegetables.

The most marked differences are between the diets of nomadic tribes and agricultural communities, the former eating more milk and milk products and the latter more cereals and pulses. It may be conjectured that among the nomad tribes of Arabia little more than a third of total calories is derived from cereals and pulses, about a third from milk, ghee, and curds, and the remaining third from dates, wild plants, meat, mutton fat, camel fat, wild animals, and even locusts. According to Musil (*6*), who lived among the Rwala Bedouins, locusts are much sought after; they taste, he says, "like the tails of crayfish." In Somaliland the staple foods are rice, dates, milk, and ghee, with some mutton and camel flesh. According to the *Annual Medical and Sanitary Report for 1935* (*7*), during good seasons there was an abundance of milk available in the interior of the country and the Somalis were beginning to appreciate the value of green vegetables. Among the nomadic tribes of the Sahara, Galan (*8*) reports that the diet consists mainly of milk, butter, and curds; small amounts of millet, wheat, and barley are included when the tribe settles long enough to obtain a crop; leaves of wild plants are eaten; and dates and meat are much prized by those who can get them. He adds that in seasons of drought, when pastures are poor and food is scarce, the children, from weaning age to 15 years, are most affected. Adults withstand the poor diets better, but their physique is stunted and they have a low resistance to tuberculosis, malaria, and trachoma. On the other hand dental caries is almost unknown.

In 1935 MacLennan (*9*) studied the diet of 1,030 individuals from four semi-nomadic Bedouin tribes in Transjordan after a series of years with poor rains. Their diet consisted of unleavened bread, olives in season, small quantities of grapes, figs, dates, melons, and tomatoes for the richer families, and milk products for those who possessed goats or camels. Of the 1,030 persons examined, only 16 percent were well nourished and 33 percent were definitely undernourished or emaciated. Tuberculosis was frequent and there were some signs of scurvy; but dental caries was infrequent and pellagra, beriberi, and other deficiency diseases were not observed. A later study by Avery Jones (*10*, p. 161) concluded that even in the good years 1937–39 only a minority of the Bedouins had an adequate diet.

They have no reserves to fall back on except their livestock—a form of capital that quickly depreciates; but the tribal tradition of generosity is strong and leads to sharing of food and giving relief to the needy in bad times.

In contrast to nomadic tribes, those engaged in settled agriculture live mainly on cereals. Wheat, rice, or maize, ground at home or in local mills, may supply up to 80 percent of the calories, mainly supplemented by pulses, olive oil, and fresh or sour milk. During the war, the writer was informed that in Palestine an Arab heavy worker would eat as much as 1,000 grams of unleavened bread in a day with the addition of a few olives. Milk, meat, fish, and fruit are highly prized, but the amount obtained varies locally and depends on the season and the resources of the peasant family. In a study of the diets in the Gezira area of Sudan, Culwick (*11*) found that among the poorest households up to 75 percent of the total calories and 97 percent of the protein was obtained from home-produced sorghum eaten either as a thin pancake (*kisra*) or a thick gruel (*lugma*). In places studied outside the Gezira area the primary need was for more food, particularly milk. Children showed seasonal fluctuations of growth and babies gained weight erratically, falling off in condition after six months. What was needed was not only improvement in the milk supply, but redistribution within the family to give priority to expectant and nursing mothers, infants, and young children. But, the author concludes, this would involve modifications of social traditions.

Farther south, among the Azande in southwestern Sudan, according to a study by the same author (*12*), the calorie intake was mainly derived from cassava supplemented by sesame and peanuts. Vitamins A and C were adequately supplied by leafy vegetables, mangoes, and sweet potatoes. The vitamin A intake during the rainy season appeared high enough to carry most people over the dry season, when the intake was low. The two months, April and May, were noted as the "stress period," when work in the fields is hardest and the women, especially, get exhausted and lose weight.

## NUTRITIONAL DEFICIENCIES

The facts brought out in these and other nutritional surveys, of which there have been all too few in the Middle East, point to wide variations—seasonal, local, and group—which are concealed in national averages derived from estimates of crops and population. The latter give no answer to the questions how the total quantity of food is distributed, who goes short, for how long, and for what reason. Though there is evidently a close correlation between poor diets and low incomes, the traditional diet of the poorest natives in southern Sudan may be superior to that of a wage earner in Cairo or Teheran—especially if the latter gets his calories largely from white flour and refined sugar. In a study of dental caries in relation to diet in central Africa, Sudan, and Egypt, Price (*13*) found that a high degree of immunity to caries was observed in tribes living on the best native foods, and that the incidence became greater as he traveled down the Nile to Khartoum and Cairo. The tribes with almost complete immunity had a diet of high vitamin and mineral content, and were much superior physically to those lacking protective foods.

The chief dietary deficiencies of the urban workers, and of the majority of peasants, appear to be due to insufficient milk, fruit, and vegetables rather than to persistent lack of calories. There is generally enough food to stave off hunger and prevent loss of body weight, but not enough of the right kind of food to provide adequate nutrition, and above all not enough to enable mothers to rear healthy children and avoid heavy child mortality. In groups where calories are too low, chronic undernourishment results in spare physique and low vitality. Bennett (*14*, p. 200) has pointed out that "low physical activity and accompanying low calorie ingestion . . . is probably a common phenomenon. But it is not properly to be interpreted as signifying presence of hunger . . . People can clearly ingest relatively little and still not be hungry or losing body weight." This probably applies to large sections of the population in the Middle East, where low output per capita and lack of vigor are associated with poor diet and poor health—including helminthic infections. Seasonal or "preharvest" hunger for a month or two before the harvest is well known, and is apt to occur, not every year, but once or twice in a decade whenever there is a crop failure and peasants are unable to borrow or draw on reserves. But widespread famines, such as occurred in Europe in 1315 and in India and China in recent times, have not been frequent in the Middle East. Famine involving excess mortality took place during World War I, particularly in Syria (see chapter 4, following); but between the wars there were few, if any, recorded instances of famine over wide areas, partly because improvements in transport and administration enabled supplies to be sent promptly to deficit areas. In Egypt there has been no year when deaths exceeded births since 1919, the year of the influenza epidemic; the high death rate then may have been partly due to the effects of wartime food scarcity. Elsewhere there are insufficient data to show when deaths due to famine or food shortage have exceeded births. An instance occurred in 1943 and 1944 in the Hadhramaut in southern Arabia, where a succession of years with poor rainfall culminated in conditions of real famine; and the severe malaria epidemic on the sugar estates of Upper Egypt in 1944 was partly due to lack of sufficient food.

### CALORIE REQUIREMENTS AND POPULATION GROWTH

The striking fact about Middle East food and agriculture before the war was that, in spite of low productivity, crop failures, periodic shortages, and occasional famine conditions, the population did not decrease but continued to increase—not of course at the maximum possible rate but at a rate somewhat higher than the world average of 1 percent. This suggests that the food supply in terms of calories was not grossly inadequate. In Egypt the increase of population that has taken place during the last 70 years carries with it the presumption that total calorie supplies have not been below requirements, except possibly toward the end of World War I, when deaths exceeded births for the first time on record. For the period 1934–38 this is confirmed by FAO's estimates (*15*), which show that the average supply of calories per head per day was 2,450, compared with requirements estimated at 2,390—the latter figure including an allowance of 15 percent for wastage between retail purchase and actual consumption.

If we ask why the population of Egypt did not increase faster and why it increased for so many decades at the steady rate of 12 per 1,000, it is not easy to find a satisfactory answer. Disease and lack of medical attention obviously played an important part. But if the food supply available was just about sufficient to meet the calorie requirements of the population, *with its existing age and sex distribution and current fertility and mortality rates*, this may provide an important clue. The fact that high specific death rates are found among infants, children under 10, and persons over 55, while death rates between the ages of 10 and 55 are not excessively high, suggests that the effects of food shortage are felt most among the old and the very young. When food is limited, it is the workers who need and receive priority and thus have a greater chance of survival than the non-workers. In the majority of households the food available is sufficient to feed those who survive but would often be insufficient to rear to maturity all those who are born. Undernourishment of mothers, infants, and children may in fact be one of the main reasons why, in spite of the high birth rate, the population increased by little more than 1 percent per annum instead of by 2 or 3 percent, as in some tropical islands.

To sum up, the pattern of Middle East food consumption before the war was superior to that of some countries in Asia and South America, but was markedly below that of Western countries. Food supplies were insufficient in quality rather than in quantity and any improvement tended to increase the numbers to be fed rather than raise the nutritional level. Periodic and local shortages, and in particular undernourishment of mothers and children, prevented the population from increasing faster than it did. Total food supplies just about kept pace with the calorie requirements of the growing population, but were never sufficient for rearing to maturity more than a fraction of those born each year.

## CITATIONS

*1* B. A. Lowe, "Dry Farming in the Beersheba District of Palestine," in *The Proceedings of the Conference on Middle East Agricultural Development, Cairo, February 7th–10th, 1944* (Middle East Supply Centre, Agr. Rpt. No. 6, Cairo, 1944).

*2* W. B. Fisher, *The Middle East. A Physical, Social and Regional Geography* (London, 1950).

*3* FAO, *Report of the Second Near East Meeting on Food and Agricultural Programs and Outlook, Bloudane, Syria, 28 August—6 September, 1951.*

*4* FAO, *Food Balance Sheets* (Washington, D.C., April 1949).

*5* I. J. Kligler, A. Geiger, S. Bromberg, and D. Gurevitch, "An Inquiry into the Diets of Various Sections of the Urban and Rural Population of Palestine," *Bulletin* . . . (Palestine Econ. Soc., Jaffa), 1931.

*6* Alois Musil, *The Manners and Customs of the Rwala Bedouins* (New York, 1928), ch. v.

*7* Somaliland Protectorate, *Annual Medical and Sanitary Report for 1935.*

*8* P. Galan, *Study of the Nutritional Problem in the Hoggar* (Institut Pasteur d'Algérie, Algiers, 1951).

*9* N. M. MacLennan, "General Health Conditions of Certain Bedouin Tribes in Transjordan," *Transactions. Royal Society of Tropical Medicine and Hygiene* (London), 1935.

*10* E. B. Worthington, *Middle East Science . . .* (London, 1946).

*11* G. M. Culwick, "Diet in the Gezira Irrigated Area, Sudan" (Sudan Surv. Dept., No. 304, 1951).

*12* G. M. Culwick, *A Dietary Survey Among the Zande of the South-Western Sudan* (Sudan Govt., 1950).

*13* W. A. Price, "Field Studies Among Some African Tribes on the Relation of Their Nutrition to the Incidence of Dental Caries and Dental Arch Deformities," *Journal of the American Dental Association*, May 1936.

*14* M. K. Bennett, *The World's Food* (New York, 1954).

*15* FAO, *Calorie Requirements. Report of the Committee on Calorie Requirements . . .* (Washington, June 1950), and *Second World Food Survey* (Rome, November 1952).

CHAPTER 3

# EGYPT AND SUDAN

## EGYPT (*1*)

Egypt, with an area of about a million square kilometers, or 250 million acres, is about the size of Spain, or of Arizona, New Mexico, and Colorado put together. But only a little more than 2 percent of the area—24,000 square kilometers—is cultivated land. The rest is bare desert. The agricultural area consists of the valley and delta of the Nile, which flows through Egypt for 950 miles of its total length of 4,000 miles.

On this small and densely crowded area there lives a population now estimated at over 20 million, compared with 9.7 million in 1897. According to the census of 1937, when the population was 15.9 million, 25 percent were classified as urban. For planning food distribution during the war, it was reckoned that in 1943 about 3.7 million out of 17 million lived in towns of more than 20,000 inhabitants.

The rapid increase of population during the last fifty years was made possible not by extension of the agricultural area—the land under cultivation only increased by about 5 percent between 1905 and 1945—but by a phenomenal rise in production per hectare. This was brought about partly by growing two and sometimes three crops during the year on the same land, partly by higher yields—the yield of wheat rose 25 percent and that of maize 15 percent between 1917 and 1937—and partly by the development of high-quality cotton. These improvements were made possible by extension of irrigation and by heavy application of fertilizers.

The rich black loam of Egypt, accumulated over thousands of years by alluvial deposits, results from soil erosion in the mountains of Ethiopia. The White Nile, which rises in central Africa and joins the Blue Nile near Khartoum, loses much of its water in the vast papyrus swamps of the Sudd in southern Sudan. The flood waters in the summer come mainly from the muddy torrents of the Blue Nile and the Atbara, which have their source in Ethiopia. Before the building of the Delta and Asyut barrages and the great dam at Aswan, the area that could be sown with crops depended each year on the size of the Nile flood. But since 1902, when the Aswan Dam was completed, continuous or "perennial" irrigation has become possible and the flow of water can be systematically regulated to meet the needs of cultivators. At the Aswan Dam the Nile is at its lowest at the end of May, rises slowly until mid-July, and reaches its maximum at the beginning of September. It then falls slowly through October and November. At Cairo the maximum rise of about 4 meters is reached at the beginning of October.

There are now two systems of irrigation. The older "basin" system, under which the land is divided into banked areas varying from 2,000 to 20,000 hectares, is said to have been invented by King Mena about 4000 B.C. Water is admitted during the flood period to an average depth of three feet and is left on the land for about 40 days. After the water has been run off, the seed is broadcast on the silt that is left behind. The newer system of perennial irrigation, which is made possible by dams and barrages and involves digging a network of canals and regulating the flow of water through sluices, has been rapidly extended until now it covers more than four-fifths of the cultivated area. Only about 360,000 hectares in Upper Egypt are left under basin irrigation (*2*, p. 70).

Under perennial irrigation crops may be obtained twice and even three times during the year from the same land. The agricultural year is divided into three seasons: *nili*, when the Nile is in flood from September to November; *shetwi*, or winter season, from December to March; and *sefi*, or summer season, from April to August. Maize, rice, and millet are both *nili* and *sefi* crops. Wheat, barley, clover, and beans are among the *shetwi* crops. Cotton, sugar cane, groundnuts (peanuts), and sesame are *sefi* crops grown in the summer. The acreage under crops harvested or used for pasture each year is about 60 percent greater than the total area of cultivated land.

Cereals and pulses can be grown under basin irrigation; cotton, cereals, sugar, vegetables, onions, rice, and fruit are grown under the perennial system. The most important cash crop is high-quality cotton, which before the war contributed about 75 percent in value to Egypt's exports. During 1934–38 the area under cotton averaged 746,000 hectares, under wheat 588,000 hectares, and under maize 649,000 hectares (*3*). Cotton, maize, wheat, and berseem (Egyptian clover) accounted for 75 percent of the area under crops, with barley, rice, sugar, beans, millet, onions, and vegetables covering most of the remaining 25 percent. Rice, the second largest export crop, is mainly grown in the northern Delta, being sown in the spring and harvested in September.

Before the war Egypt produced almost enough food to meet her internal demand. Her main exports, apart from cotton, were rice, onions, sugar, and cottonseed oil and cake. She imported small amounts of meat, dairy products, potatoes, nuts, and oils, and her total requirements of coffee and tea. An essential import, on which her agriculture depended, was fertilizer—averaging about 500,000 tons, mostly Chilean nitrates. Average consumption was 60 kilos per hectare, compared with 38 in the Netherlands and 15 in Denmark (*4*, p. 29). During the war, shortage of shipping necessitated drastic reduction in fertilizer imports, which led to a fall in yields and the need to import cereals.

For bread grains, Egypt supplied her requirements of wheat with an average production of about 1.2 million tons and net imports of only 7,000 tons, consisting mainly of hard wheat used in macaroni and other pastes for European consumption. Egyptian wheat is a cross between hard and soft wheat and is cultivated mainly in Upper Egypt under both basin and perennial irrigation; but it has been extended into the Delta to some extent in recent years. High yields are normally obtained, the prewar average being 20 quintals per hectare, compared with about 15 in France and 10 for the world outside the USSR. During the war, when yields fell owing to shortage of fertilizers, the lowest point touched was 13.6 quintals per hectare in 1944.

But wheat was not the only bread grain and in fact contributed only about 30 percent of the total food grains (including rice) used for human consumption. The most important food grain for the mass of the peasantry was not wheat but maize, which accounted for 47 percent of the human consumption of flour and meal. Sorghum or giant millet came next (13 percent), followed by rice (9 percent).

Wheat straw or *tibn*, which contains a fair amount of grain mixed with it owing to primitive methods of threshing and winnowing, is much in demand for animal feed. In 1937–39 the amount of wheat *tibn* was estimated by Anis (*5*) at nearly 2 million tons. Wheat offals at 86 percent extraction provided a further 140,000 tons of animal feed. About three-fourths of the barley crop (170,000 tons) and 5 percent of the maize crop (80,000 tons) are estimated to have been used for livestock feed; but these figures are highly conjectural. The main source of feed is the berseem crop, which before the war was sufficient to feed about 2 million cattle and buffaloes.

About 750,000 milch cows received supplementary rations of cottonseed cake (263,000 tons) and beans (68,000 tons). Sheep, goats, and poultry lived mostly on waste, weeds, and stubble.

The following estimates of prewar human consumption of grains, pulses, and potatoes are taken from Egypt's food balance sheet for the years 1934–38, published by the Food and Agriculture Organization of the United Nations (FAO) (*6*, p. 283):

| Item | Gross (*1,000 metric tons*) | Extraction rate (*percent*) | Net (*1,000 metric tons*) | Net per capita | |
|---|---|---|---|---|---|
| | | | | Kilos per year | Calories per day |
| Wheat | 1,002 | 86 | 862 | 54.9 | |
| Wheat, imported | 16 | 75 | 12 | | |
| Maize | 1,436 | 95 | 1,364 | 85.6 | |
| Millet and sorghum | 410 | 92 | 377 | 23.7 | |
| Rice | 412 | 65 | 268 | 16.8 | |
| Barley | 30 | 60 | 18 | 1.1 | |
| Total grains | 3,306 | — | 2,901 | 182.1 | 1,752 |
| Potatoes | 49 | — | 49 | 3.1 | |
| Sweet potatoes | 24 | — | 24 | 1.5 | |
| Total potatoes | 73 | — | 73 | 4.6 | 11 |
| Pulses | 300 | — | 300 | 18.8 | 200 |
| Grand total | — | — | — | — | 1,963 |

Pulses, consisting mainly of broad beans and lentils, were an important food of the fellah and have traditionally been regarded as more suitable for the climate of Egypt than potatoes. But one of the minor effects of the war has been an increase in potato production from about 50,000 tons before the war to 200,000 tons in 1947/48. Production and consumption of pulses have declined by about 10 percent.

Large white maize is eaten as the staple food grain by a large proportion of the population, particularly in Upper Egypt. The proportion of wheat to maize in the national diet before the war was about two to three; but in the poorest peasant families, according to a family-budget enquiry published by Cleland (*7*), wheat was only an eighth to a tenth of the maize consumed. As a rough approximation, it would seem that before the war a quarter of the population, mainly those living in cities and townships, consumed about 75 percent of the wheat with an annual consumption of 160 kilos per head; while the remaining three-quarters, consisting of the mass of the peasantry, consumed only 18 kilos of wheat per head, or about 10 percent of their total consumption of cereals. Of the other grains, all but a small proportion would be eaten by the poorest 75 percent of the population, with maize and millet predominating. Rice is of minor importance and is eaten mainly in the northern Delta, where it is grown; before the war there was an average export surplus of 145,000 tons of paddy. Prewar consumption of refined sugar was about 10 kilos per head per annum, with an additional 4 kilos consumed in the form of syrup and molasses, mostly obtained from home-produced cane averaging over 2 million tons.

During the war the area under cotton was more than halved in order to grow more cereals, and special efforts were made to expand the production of rice and sugar for export. Egypt was thus able to make an important contribution toward saving shipping and making the Middle East more self-supporting in food.

## SUDAN

Sudan has an area of 2.5 million square kilometers, two and a half times that of Egypt, with only about two-fifths of the population. It is bounded by Egypt on the north; by the Red Sea, Eritrea, and Ethiopia on the east; by Kenya, Uganda, and the Belgian Congo on the south; and by French Equatorial Africa on the west. Its greatest length north and south is 1,650 miles and its greatest width 900 miles.

The population was estimated to be about 7 million during the war and 8.2 million in 1949. It is supposed to have been 9 million in 1884 and to have decreased to 2 million owing to war, famine, and pestilence during the Mahdi troubles; but these estimates are highly conjectural. Between 4 and 5 million Arabic-speaking Moslems live in the north and central belts, and the remainder consists of primitive African tribesmen living in the tropical south (*8*). The only complete census that has been undertaken for any part of Sudan was in the town of Omdurman in November 1944 in connection with wartime rationing.

The incidence of rainfall divides the country into three parts. The most important is the central belt which has large fertile areas, including the rain-fed pastures of Kassala and Tokar, the Gezira plain, and the gum forests of Kordofan. Here the annual rainfall varies between 100 and 500 millimeters and is concentrated in the late summer months, July to October. The northern desert belt, through which passes the narrow valley of the Nile, extends for 400 miles to the Egyptian frontier and has an irregular rainfall of less than 100 millimeters. In the south there is an equatorial belt of savanna forest and marsh—including the vast area of the Sudd, 150 miles from the source of the Nile. Here the rainfall is sufficient for cultivation, but development is hampered by lack of communications and a sparse and primitive population.

Soils and climate provide for a wide variation of crops, including cereals and cotton in the central zone and coffee, oil palms, and other tropical products in the south. The staple food crop is sorghum or millet of various kinds, estimated before the war at about 700,000 tons. Cassava is found in the tropical south. Wheat, pulses, and vegetables are grown in the northern province, and during the war wheat was grown in the Gezira and White Nile areas to take the place of 25,000 tons normally imported. South and southeast of the Gezira plain, sorghum is grown by the so-called *harig* system of cultivation. The grass is burned before the early summer rains and the grain is then sown and left untended until the return of the nomad tribes for the harvest in January and February. In southern Sudan even more primitive methods of shifting cultivation are practiced (*9*, p. 8).

In recent years there has been a great development of modern irrigation along the valley of the Nile, particularly in the Gezira area of 2 million hectares lying between the Blue and White Niles, where nearly 400,000 hectares are now irrigated from the Sennar Dam.

The Gezira Cotton Scheme presents features of special interest. Long-staple cotton is grown as a winter crop, with millet included in the rotation as a food crop. The Scheme is operated on a partnership basis between the government, the cultivators, and a managing body originally provided by the Sudan Plantations Syndicate and the Kassala Cotton Company. When the companies' concessions came to an end in 1950, management was vested in a public-utility board. The shares of the three partners in the Scheme are 40 percent for the government, 40 percent for the peasant cultivators, and 20 percent for the managing body. The government assumed control of the land, compensating the owners by paying them a rent equivalent to the highest market rate before the Scheme started and giving them a prior right to continue as cultivators under the Scheme.

The tenant provides no capital, pays no rent for land or water, and gets his crops free of tax. Instruction, supervision, and tools are provided for him as a charge on the three partners. Apart from his cash returns for cotton, the tenant harvests an average crop of 3.5 tons of sorghum, sufficient to provide food for his family and the labor employed; he can also grow a leguminous crop for livestock and a vegetable crop for his own use. Since the Scheme started, a substantial reserve fund has been accumulated in addition to the cash payments distributed each year. In 1947 cash payments to 20,600 tenants amounted to over 1 million Egyptian pounds. Each tenant's share in the profits is based on the yield of cotton from his own holding; his grain and other crops belong to him (*8*, pp. 32–34).

In 1941 a start was made in setting up village councils. There are now 240 of these councils, employing agricultural supervisors selected by the tenants themselves and covering more than 80 percent of the total irrigated area. Keen (*9*, p. 91) in his survey of Middle East agriculture refers to the Gezira project as "an illustration of how agricultural progress and rural development can best be made . . ."

The chief exports of Sudan are cotton, oilseeds, hides and skins, and gum arabic, of which Sudan is the world's principal source of supply. Cattle, sheep, and goats are kept by pastoral and nomadic tribes, and there are possibilities of building up an export trade in meat products.

The following approximate estimates of prewar and postwar production and livestock numbers are based on figures prepared for FAO's Near East regional meeting in 1951 (*10*):

| Crop | Area (*1,000 hectares*) | | Production (*1,000 metric tons*) | |
|---|---|---|---|---|
| | Prewar | 1946–49 | Prewar | 1946–49 |
| Millet and sorghum | 1,100 | 1,280 | 700 | 720 |
| Wheat and barley | 11 | 13 | 9 | 13 |
| Maize | 11 | 17 | 12 | 16 |
| Pulses and potatoes | 6 | 7 | 5 | 6 |
| Cotton | 173 | 155 | 53 | 51 |
| Cottonseed as oil | — | — | 16 | 16 |
| Sesame and peanuts, as oil | — | — | 36 | 63 |

| Livestock | Prewar (*million head*) | 1947–49 (*million head*) |
|---|---|---|
| Cattle | 2.7 | 3.5 |
| Sheep | 2.5 | 5.5 |
| Goats | 2 | 4.3 |
| Camels | 1 | 1.5 |

These estimates of food production, which are themselves conjectural and do not include cassava and other tropical products produced and consumed in southern Sudan, should be related to the food requirements of the Arabic-speaking population in the north of between 4 million and 5 million, and not to those of the total population. In the southern region the Sudan government reports (*8*, p. 37) that "the production of cash crops has been subordinated to the over-riding need to increase the bulk and variety of native diet and the success already attained is manifest by the present infrequency of food shortages in an area in which famine was formerly perennial." In the towns of Khartoum and Omdurman the infant-mortality rate in 1945 was 78 per 1,000 in both and the general death rate was 14 in the former and 12.5 in the latter. These figures compare favorably with corresponding rates of 199 and 29.5 in 1940 for urban districts in Egypt (*8*, p. 85). Indeed they suggest that the level of food consumption of the urban population may have been higher in Sudan than in Egypt.

During the war, by growing more wheat and exporting less millet, Sudan was able to produce enough cereals to feed itself without imports and made few calls on the Middle East Supply Center except for sugar and some rice. On the other hand, in 1943 and 1944, it was able to supply large quantities of cottonseed to offset the acute shortage of oils and fats in Egypt that resulted from reducing cotton acreage in order to expand wheat acreage.

## CITATIONS

*1* Charles Issawi, *Egypt: An Economic and Social Analysis* (Royal Inst. Internatl. Affairs, London, 1947).

*2* A. N. Cumberbatch, *Egypt . . .* (Gt. Brit., Bd. Trade, Comm. Rels. and Exports Dept., Overseas Econ. Survs., 1952).

*3* Internatl. Inst. Agr., *International Yearbook of Agricultural Statistics, 1941–42 to 1945–46* (Rome, 1947).

*4* Doreen Warriner, *Land and Poverty in the Middle East* (Royal Inst. Internatl. Affairs, London, 1948).

*5* M. A. Anis, in *L'Egypte contemporaine* (Société khédiviale d'économie politique, de statistique et de législation, Cairo), March 1945.

*6* FAO, *Food Balance Sheets* (Washington, D.C., April 1949).

*7* W. Cleland, *The Population Problem of Egypt* (Lancaster, Pa., 1936).

*8* Sudan Govt., *The Sudan, A Record of Progress, 1898–1947* (1948).

*9* B. A. Keen, *The Agricultural Development of the Middle East . . .* (London, 1946).

*10* FAO, *Report of the Second Near East Meeting on Food and Agricultural Programs and Outlook, Bloudane, Syria, 28 August—6 September, 1951.*

## CHAPTER 4

# CYPRUS, PALESTINE, SYRIA, AND LEBANON

### CYPRUS

The island of Cyprus lies 60 miles west of Lebanon and 40 miles south of Turkey; it has an area of 9,250 square kilometers, with a population of 371,000 in 1937 and 450,000 in 1946. It has been administered by Britain since 1878 and became a crown colony in 1914. Four-fifths of the inhabitants are Greek Christians and most of the rest are Moslems of Turkish descent (*1*, p. 120).

The island is divided by a central plain, the Mesaoria, bounded by mountain ranges rising to 900 meters in the north and 1,800 meters in the south, with a narrow coastal plain at the foot of each range. The climate is Mediterranean with winter rainfall varying from 250 millimeters on the plains to over 600 millimeters on the southern mountains (*2*, p. 2). The winter is mild and the summer long and hot. Less than a quarter of the total area is cultivated (including fallow), 18 percent is forest, and 45 percent is pasture and rough grazing.

The chief agricultural products are wheat, barley, vetches, potatoes, oats, carobs—obtained from a leguminous tree similar to the American mesquite—olives, oranges, and grapes. Small amounts of flax, tobacco, and silk are produced. The principal exports, apart from copper and other minerals, are carobs, potatoes, wines, oranges, and live animals, particularly asses and mules. Sheep and goats numbered 485,000 before the war and cattle 40,000. Prewar figures of area, production, and net trade for the principal crops are given below (*3*). Production and trade figures for the war years are contained in Appendix Tables IV and V.

| Crop | Area (*1,000 hectares*) | Production (*1,000 metric tons*) | Net exports (*1,000 metric tons*) |
|---|---|---|---|
| Wheat | 74 | 59 | 23[a] |
| Barley | 46 | 44 | 5 |
| Oats | 5 | 4 | — |
| Potatoes | 3 | 24 | 13 |
| Pulses | 6 | 4 | .. |
| Citrus fruit | — | 14 | 11 |

[a] Net imports.

Figures for food consumption per head in 1934–38 and in 1946–49, as estimated by the Food and Agriculture Organization of the United Nations (FAO), show some improvement (*4*, pp. 60–61):

| Item | 1934–38 | 1946–49 |
|---|---|---|
| Kilos per year: | | |
| Cereals | 169.3 | 174.1 |
| Roots and pulses | 31.4 | 42.6 |
| Sugar | 9.1 | 8.3 |
| Fats | 6.9 | 7.8 |
| Meat, eggs, and fish | 16.9 | 23.8 |
| Fruits and vegetables | 78.3 | 88.9 |
| Milk and cheese | 96.1 | 95.0 |
| Calories per day | 2,345 | 2,483 |
| Protein (*gm. per day*): | | |
| Total | 65.1 | 70.7 |
| Animal | 10.9 | 13.9 |

The most noteworthy advances were in meat, fish, and eggs, and in fruit and vegetables; but increased production of milk and cheese fell short of the increase in population. Consumption of animal protein is higher than in other Middle East countries, except in prewar Palestine and postwar Israel.

In contrast with most Middle East countries, farms for the most part are owned by the cultivators or held under a tenancy which gives security of tenure. Partly as a result of this, co-operative credit and marketing societies have taken root and developed rapidly since 1934. The co-operative movement was strengthened during the war by being used as a government agency both for collection of produce and for distribution of farm requisites (*1*, p. 128). Subdivision of the land into strips, plowing up and down slopes instead of on contours, and uncontrolled grazing of flocks of sheep and goats have contributed, as elsewhere in the Middle East, to low yields and soil deterioration. Insufficient rainfall and hot dry summers, when the temperature reaches 110° F., check the growth of natural pastures suitable for cattle and dairy cows.

Progress in mixed farming and dairying depends on pasture improvement and better irrigation. The chief problem in Cyprus is to conserve the winter rainfall, to make full use of springs and wells, and to control flood water. Ingenious systems have been developed for controlling the flow of underground waters and increasing the storage capacity of natural underground reservoirs. Almost every village has a minor irrigation scheme, and local committees contribute to the cost of maintaining and improving irrigation tanks and adits. Rural areas are well served with roads, but defective road drainage has been responsible for serious soil erosion. In recent years active steps have been taken to check the growing impoverishment of the soil, and substantial grants have been made from the Colonial Development and Welfare fund for improvement of agriculture and animal husbandry in order to meet the increased food requirements of a rapidly growing population (*1*, p. 131).

In 1946, when the population had increased to 450,000, the birth rate was 32.4 per 1,000, the infant-mortality rate 70.9, and the crude death rate only 8.5 compared with 10 in the United States and 12 in the United Kingdom. The exceptionally low death rate—one of the world's lowest—combined with the high birth rate has meant that the population has increased by nearly 30 percent in the 15 years between the two last censuses (*1*, p. 121). This is a remarkable testimony to the rapid advances in economic development, education, and health services which have taken place during the last 20 years; and they were not interrupted but were even intensified by the impact of war. Unless there is a fall in the birth rate, there is danger in the future that increase in numbers may handicap the plans embodied in the government's ten-year development program for raising the national income per head.

## PALESTINE

Prewar Palestine was about the size of Vermont but had more than twice as many inhabitants. Its area was 27,000 square kilometers, of which 700 consisted of the inland waters of Lake Huleh, Lake Tiberias (Sea of Galilee), and half of the Dead Sea. Of the land area, nearly half was the semidesert area of southern Palestine known as the Negeb. The population, including nomads, was reckoned at 757,000 in 1922 and had more than doubled in 1942 to over 1.6 million (*5*, p. 4).

The central hill range is divided into two parts. The northern part, which is mainly basaltic, extends from Nazareth to the Anti-Lebanon Mountains of Syria; and the southern part, which starts at Mount Carmel, south of Haifa, and proceeds eastward to Nablus and then south along the Judean hills to Beersheba, consists of porous limestone. The northern and southern hills are separated by the plain of Esdraelon, which has a heavy but fertile soil. The coastal plain has a sandy soil and extends for about 190 kilometers in length and 20–30 kilometers in width between the Mediterranean and the foothills of the central range. East of the central range is the narrow valley of the Jordan, which reaches its lowest point in the Dead Sea, 390 meters below sea level—the deepest depression on earth.

The climate is predominantly Mediterranean but wide variations occur over short distances. Within two to three hours one could motor from temperate sunshine on the coast near Tel-Aviv up to the cold and damp hilltops of Jerusalem and then down to the tropical zone of the Dead Sea. Winter rainfall decreases rapidly from north to south. On the coastal plain it ranges from about 500 to about 250 millimeters, in the hills from 800 to 600 millimeters, and in the Jordan Valley from 500 millimeters in the north to virtually none at the Dead Sea. Of greater importance is the wide annual variation of rainfall, which ranges from about half to nearly double the annual average. Over a period of fifteen years, the total rainfall in the wettest years has been three times the amount in the driest years. The dry seasons are the worst for agriculture, but excessive rainfall coming at the wrong season may also have disastrous results. The rainy season is divided into "early rains" from October to January and "late rains" from February to April. The length of season during which rain falls varies greatly and may be decisive in determining crop yields. In the Negeb, with an average rainfall of 220 millimeters and a range from 336 millimeters in 1933–34 to 130 in 1935–36, successful cultivation of barley was entirely dependent on the rainfall. In three years out of seven there were good crops, in three years partial failures, and in one year a total loss (*6*, p. 29).

Soil erosion has been accentuated by deforestation and uncontrolled grazing of goats. In the hill country after heavy rains the water pours down in torrents, cutting deep gullies and shifting the beds of local wadis. Most of the silt is deposited on the plains and not carried out to sea; but the effect is to leave the hillsides denuded of topsoil and too rocky for cultivation.

In the cultivated area widely different systems of agriculture were practiced before the war. The most primitive type was found in the area of low rainfall south of Beersheba, where barley alternates with fallow. Elsewhere the commonest system practiced by the Arabs was a two-year rotation. A winter crop of wheat or barley was rotated with a winter crop of pulses or with a summer crop of millet or sesame. A three-year rotation combining all three could also be used. The chief defect of these systems was that they did not provide enough animal fodder for the whole year. Livestock were either treated as nomadic flocks or pastured on stubble and unplowed lands.

The methods adopted by Jewish settlers represented a radical departure from the traditional Arab system. Mixed farming was introduced on unirrigated land; and then further developments of mixed farming took place on land irrigated in various ways. In the 10-year period of most rapid development between 1926–30 and 1936–40, agricultural crop production (excluding citrus fruit) increased by about 75 percent, or more than 5 percent per annum. This was due mainly to the phenomenal growth of Jewish agriculture, stimulated by import of capital, growth of industry, and increase of population (*7*).

The contrast between Jewish and Arab methods of production is brought out by the following estimates, in Palestinian pounds (£P), of income from agriculture, published by the Palestine government in 1946 (*8*, pp. 25–27):

| Item | Arab | Jewish | Total |
|---|---|---|---|
| Income from agriculture (including fisheries and forests) (*million £P*) | 20.4 | 9.1 | 29.5 |
| Persons fully engaged (*thousands*)[a] | 152 | 24 | 176 |
| Income per person (*£P*) | 134 | 379 | 168 |

[a] The number of persons actually engaged in agriculture, etc., is understated owing to the exclusion of part-time family labor on Arab farms and calculation from man-days worked in Jewish agriculture.

One of the main reasons for the difference between the incomes of the two communities was that Arab farming was predominantly cereal growing, while the Jews obtained higher incomes from mixed farming, dairying, and fruit and vegetable growing.

The most highly specialized branch of production was the growing of citrus fruit for export, which contributed four-fifths of Palestine's total exports. About 30,000 hectares had been planted before the war, of which about two-thirds were of full bearing age; roughly half the area was owned by Jews and half by Arabs. In 1939 citrus exports reached 13 million cases valued at £P 3.7 million. Olives were to be found all over the central and northern areas and the value of their output during the war, when citrus exports ceased, exceeded that of the citrus groves.

Of Palestine's total land area of 2.63 million hectares, the cultivated land rarely exceeded one-quarter. The maximum area cultivated during any of the years 1936–42 was 780,000 hectares. In 1943 the cultivated area was 624,000 hectares or about 24 percent of the total area. Of this, 175,000 were under wheat and 148,000 under barley, with recorded crops of only 66,000 tons of wheat and 62,000 tons of barley. This was the year of lowest yields during the war.

The vagaries of the climate and the uncertain rainfall are reflected in wide variations in cereal production, shown in Appendix Table IV. Taking the average prewar production of wheat, barley, and millet in the years 1934–38 as 100, production of these cereals in 1940 was 146 and in 1943 only 78.

Before the war Palestine was largely dependent on imports of cereals, sugar, rice, oilseeds, and livestock products to feed her growing urban population, which increased from 387,000 in 1931 to 742,000 in 1942. Average production and net imports of food and feed during 1934–38 were as follows, in thousand metric tons (see *3* and Appendix Tables IV and V):

| Product | Production | Net imports | Total supply |
|---|---|---|---|
| Wheat (and flour as wheat) | 87 | 70 | 157 |
| Barley | 67 | 14 | 81 |
| Millet (durra) | 49 | .. | 49 |
| Maize | 7 | 5 | 12 |
| Rice, milled | — | 16 | 16 |
| Sugar | — | 25 | 25 |
| Oilseeds, as oil | 10 | 9 | 19 |
| Potatoes | 8 | 16 | 24 |
| Pulses | 6 | 2 | 8 |
| Meat | 8 | 8 | 16 |
| Poultry and fish | 2 | 8 | 10 |
| Eggs | 6 | 9 | 15 |
| Dairy products, as milk | 100 | 90 | 190 |

Assuming that about two-thirds of the barley, half the millet, and one-fifth of the maize were normally fed to livestock, imports supplied about 40 percent of the grains (including rice) for human consumption. All the sugar was imported and about half the meat and livestock products. Out of a total population averaging 1.25 million in 1934–38 the urban population constituted between 40 and 45 percent. It thus appears that, while the rural population was broadly self-sufficient, except in sugar, most of the imported food was needed to feed the towns. In practice, of course, there was an exchange of products between town and country. The Jewish population of the towns with their higher dietary pattern obtained supplies of meat, milk, eggs, fruit, and vegetables from home production, while consumer goods and part of the imported rice and sugar went to the villages.

During the war years, when imports were cut and rationing had to be strictly enforced in the towns, the urban population suffered much greater deterioration in their diet than the villages with their traditional diet of cereals, olives, and figs. The government's efforts to cope with this situation by controlling distribution and introducing an ambitious points-rationing scheme are described in chapter 24.

## SYRIA AND LEBANON

Syria and Lebanon were formerly provinces of the Ottoman Empire. By the Treaty of Sèvres in 1920, they were established as two states administered under French mandate, which formally came to an end in 1945 when the two states became members of the United Nations. Under the mandate they maintained a currency and customs union and had a joint budget for matters of common interest. Syria, including Latakia and Jebel Druze, which were separate governments under the French administration, comprises an area of 181,000 square kilometers. The population was estimated at 3 million in 1944 and 3.5 million in 1949. Lebanon, with 10,000 square kilometers, had a population of 1.06 million in 1944, according to a special census taken for purposes of bread rationing, and 1.2 million in 1949.

Lebanon consists of a narrow coastal strip and the western slopes of the Lebanon Range, which rises steeply from the Mediterranean to a height of 3,000 meters. Between the mountains of Lebanon and Anti-Lebanon lies the Bekaa Valley, a continuation of the great north-to-south rift running through the Dead Sea to the Gulf of Aqaba. The dividing watershed is found near Baalbek, site of the ruins of the Roman temple of Jupiter. From here the Orontes flows northward until it reaches the sea near Antioch, and the Litani southward—starting toward the Jordan Valley, turning abruptly westward, and finally reaching the sea just north of the Palestine frontier. Numerous smaller streams also flow westward into the Mediterranean.

Lebanon is much better supplied with water than Syria, owing to the mountains which precipitate rain from the Mediterranean. Rainfall is confined mainly to the winter season, from mid-November to the end of March. At Beirut the average annual rainfall is 900 millimeters; 1,200 meters above Beirut it is 1,500 millimeters; and at Damascus, 60 miles inland, it falls to 250 millimeters. The coast of Lebanon has more than twice as much rain as Southern California, but much is lost in torrential downpours which either soak through the calcareous limestone or eat away the surface soil and wash it out to sea. In early spring, the Adonis River and the sea at its mouth are stained blood red from the soil washed down from the mountains. According to Greek legend, probably dating from Phoenician times, the river is tinged each year with the blood of Adonis, slain by a wild boar on Mount Lebanon (*9*, p. 336).

In the dry season, especially in the autumn just before the rains, a hot wind (or sirocco) from the south, corresponding to the khamsin in Egypt, may bring humidity down to less than 10 percent. The temperature at Beirut ranges from over 38° C. to a minimum, only rarely reached, of −1° C. in winter with an annual average of 20° C.

Only cereals requiring little rain can be grown without irrigation because of the dry summer. Olives, vines, and mulberry trees abound on the mountainsides, and during the war tiny plots of wheat and corn could be seen growing among the fruit trees on the hillside terraces. Lebanon drew about half of its grain supply from Syria, mainly to feed the city of Beirut and its neighborhood. The pattern of landownership is similar to that of Western Europe, with a large class of small-scale peasant owners and a high density of rural population.

Most of Syria consists of an undulating plateau which descends in the northeast to the valley of the Euphrates and the great plain of Jezira. By contrast with the intensive cultivation in Lebanon, where almost the whole cultivated area is under crops each year, the dry plains of Syria are only cropped one year in two, and before the war about one-third of the cultivated land was under fallow. The principal crops grown are wheat, barley, and millet. A prevalent rotation is wheat or barley followed by fallow followed by lentils or vetch. Cereal production is carried on for the most part on large fields divided into long strips. The greater part of the land belongs to large absentee landowners and is cultivated by small sharecroppers. The sharecropper has little incentive to change his methods of cultivation and many of the landowners have little interest in undertaking long-term improvements in their land.

In the northeast corner, the large area of Jezira between the Tigris and Euphrates is potentially fertile and has sufficient winter rain for wheat growing. In Roman times it was one of the Empire's chief grain-growing areas. Before World War II, largely because of malaria and lack of population, the greater part was uncultivated. It was here that special efforts were made during the war to increase the wheat supply of the Middle East by mechanized farming with Lend-Lease tractors, but these efforts were hampered by the shortage of trained personnel to maintain the tractors.

The waters of the Orontes and the Euphrates have not yet been brought under control with large irrigation works. Around Damascus there is a large area depending on the waters of the Awaj and the Barada (the Abana and Pharpar of the Old Testament) where land utilization shows a regular sequence determined by the amount of irrigation available: first, dairy farms and market gardens, then fruit plantations intercropped with vegetables and cereals, then olives and vines, and lastly cereals bordering on arid pastures next to the desert.

Before the war Syria and Lebanon had a fairly large livestock population, including nearly half a million cattle and about 3.5 million sheep and goats. In spite of a drop during the war years their numbers are greater today than they have ever been. Nomadic sheep and goats provide meat, milk, and wool. In the neighborhood of Beirut and Damascus there is a well-defined breed of dairy cattle.

In 1944, out of a total population of 4 million in the two states, about one-third lived in towns, distributed as follows: Aleppo, 339,000; Damascus, 303,000; Beirut, 247,000; Homs, 106,000; Tripoli, 78,000; Hama, 75,000; Deirez-Zor, 65,000; and Latakia, 39,000. Nomads and semi-nomads were estimated at about half a million. The rural population of about 2.7 million, from a cropped area of about two-thirds of a hectare per head, was normally just able to feed itself and provide a surplus for the urban population of 1.25 million. In the five years 1934–38 production of wheat and barley averaged 813,000 tons and in 1938, 1940, and 1943 approximated 1 million tons. But the poor harvests of 1937, 1941, and 1942 averaged less than 750,000 tons, which meant that the towns could not be fed without imports.

The fear of wartime shortage was ever present. In World War I the failure of the 1916 harvest, largely due to a plague of locusts, created an acute shortage. According to a despatch dated July 15, 1916, from the American Consul General (cited in *10*, p. 203), the streets were filled with starving women and children. In his history of this period, George Antonius (*10*, p. 203) writes that "the shortage was made more serious by maladministration, defective transport services, the depreciation of currency, and above all by profiteering and a dastardly collusion between Turkish officials and certain Syrian merchants. The poorer people were starving." In the two years that followed, before British and French forces occupied Beirut, it was reported that "not less than 300,000 people died of hunger or of disease due to malnutrition" (*10*, pp. 240–41).

In 1941 and 1942 the specter of famine again loomed large in the towns of Syria and Lebanon. Drastic intervention by the Allied authorities was needed to prevent a repetition of the unrest and starvation of 1916/17.

## CITATIONS

*1* Royal Inst. Internatl. Affairs, *The Middle East . . .* (London, 1950).

*2* B. A. Keen, *The Agricultural Development of the Middle East . . .* (London, 1946).

*3* FAO, *Yearbook of Food and Agricultural Statistics, 1952* (Rome, 1953).

*4* FAO, *Current Development of and Prospects for Agriculture in the Near East. Second Near East Meeting on Food and Agricultural Programs and Outlook, Bloudane, Syria—28 August 1951* (July 12, 1951).

*5* Jewish Agency for Palestine, Econ. Res. Inst., *Statistical Handbook of Middle Eastern Countries . . .* (Jerusalem, 1945).

*6* B. A. Lowe, "Dry Farming in the Beersheba District of Palestine," in *The Proceedings of the Conference on Middle East Agricultural Development, Cairo, February 7th–10th, 1944* (Middle East Supply Centre, Agr. Rpt. No. 6, Cairo, 1944).

*7* R. R. Nathan, D. Gass, and D. Creamer, *Palestine, Problem and Promise* (New York, 1947).

*8* P. J. Loftus, *National Income of Palestine* (Palestine Govt., 1946).

*9* Sir James Frazer, *The Golden Bough* (New York, 1927).

*10* George Antonius, *The Arab Awakening* (London, 1938).

CHAPTER 5

# IRAQ AND PERSIA

## IRAQ

The Kingdom of Iraq, established under a British Mandate in 1920, became an independent state and a member of the League of Nations in 1932. Its area is about 435,000 square kilometers, divided into two distinct regions—a northern rain-fed zone of which only 15 percent is cultivated and a south-central irrigated zone of which about two-thirds is under crops. The desert area in the northwest provides extensive grazing after the winter rains and resembles the adjoining area in Syria. The southern region, which depends on irrigation from the Tigris and Euphrates, has climate and potentialities similar in some respects to the valley of the Nile in Egypt. The annual rainfall in the south is insufficient for arable farming and around Baghdad is only about 100–125 millimeters.

Compared with Egypt, the water resources of Iraq are little used and there is large scope for development of irrigation under properly controlled conditions. There seems little doubt that irrigation was practiced successfully in quite early times and reached an advanced stage in the reign of Harun-al-Rashid. But the Mongol invasions in the thirteenth century caused widespread destruction from which the country has never fully recovered. There is nothing in Iraq corresponding to the intricate system of reservoirs and barrages under centralized government control which exists in the Nile Valley. Establishment of such a system would need the prior agreement of Turkey and Syria, which control the headwaters of the Euphrates.

In the absence of planned development, much of the cultivable area has gradually gone out of cultivation owing to insufficient drainage and accumulation of salts in the soil. It is estimated that serious deterioration has taken place in about 60 percent of the area covered by flow irrigation and that more than a million acres could be reclaimed by development of soil drainage.

Though the area of Iraq is nearly twice that of Great Britain, its population is only about one-tenth. In 1937 the population was estimated at 3.67 million, in 1943 at 4.0 million, and in 1947 it was 4.8 million, according to a census taken in October of that year. The population of the principal towns (to the nearest thousand) in 1947 was: Baghdad, 400,000; Mosul, 203,000; Basra (1937), 180,000; Karbala, 123,000; and Najaf, 107,000—giving a total of 1.01 million or 21 percent of the total population. Iraq with one-fourth Egypt's population has a cultivable area two to four times as great. Given a maximum development of irrigation under a strong central government, the population—or agricultural exports—might be much larger. But with present methods of cultivation the existing population would be insufficient for any large extension of the area under cultivation. Rapid extension of the area under irrigation would involve either considerable immigration or the introduction of large-scale mechanization. The present policy of the Iraq government favors mechanization.

The cropped area (including fallow) is estimated at about 2.3 million hectares, out of a cultivable area variously estimated at 6.6–14.4 million hectares. Of the cropped land, 600,000 hectares are in the rainfall zone and 1.7 million in the irrigation zone, divided into 1.2 million hectares of *shetwi* (winter) crops, 400,000 under *sefi* (summer) crops, and the remainder under dates and orchard crops (*1*).

The principal cereal crops are barley, wheat, rice, and millet. Barley is Iraq's most important crop, and is mainly produced as a winter crop in the northern plains and in the central irrigated zone in the provinces of Kut and Muntafiq. Average production in the five years before the war was 575,000 tons, yielding an exportable surplus of over 200,000 tons. Wheat production averaged 478,000 tons in 1934–38, with an average export of 53,000 tons. The best wheat is grown in the rain-fed northern plains, though it is also grown in the irrigated zone. It is especially liable to attack by the sunn pest and by the Moroccan locust. In 1944, the worst year of the war, wheat production fell to 330,000 tons, and after the war the 1947 harvest was only 235,000 tons.

Rice is grown as a summer crop in the marshes of the lower Euphrates and Tigris, and to a small extent under irrigation in the valleys of Kurdistan, and is harvested between September and November. Before the war, average production for the five years 1934–38 amounted to 205,000 tons, with a small export of 1,400 tons. Rice was a remunerative crop, but under a law passed in 1932 its cultivation was restricted to certain areas because of the large amount of water it required.

Maize, millet, and sorghum are grown as summer crops in the south. Official figures of prewar production are lacking, but prewar estimates supplied by the Food and Agriculture Organization of the United Nations (FAO) at their second regional meeting in Syria in 1951 include 120,000 tons for millet and sorghum and 15,000 tons for maize. Exports of millet and sorghum in 1934–38 averaged 27,600 tons.

Iraq dates are sold to more than 40 countries and provide about 80 percent of the world's supply. Before the war the value of date exports exceeded that of cereals, but during and after the war cereals have been in greater demand and many countries have placed restrictions on imports of dates. Production in the three years 1936–38 averaged 260,000 tons. In 1947 production was 300,000 tons, and 226,000 tons valued at 4.7 million dinars were exported, chiefly to India, the United Kingdom, Egypt, and the United States, which between them took about two-thirds of the total exports. The main producing area is near Basra where the Tigris and Euphrates join to form the Shatt-el-Arab. There are said to be about 350 varieties of dates grown in Iraq, although only four are normally exported (*2*, p. 19). Inferior dates are used locally for the manufacture of alcohol and of date syrup, which is consumed as a substitute for imported sugar. There is no recorded production of sugar beets or sugar cane in Iraq.

Cotton cultivation was increasing before the war, production of ginned cotton averaging 16,000 tons in 1934–38. During and after the war it declined to a low point of 7,000 tons in 1948. Production is now increasing and a new spinning and weaving mill is using Iraq cotton of good quality. Cotton is mainly grown in the neighborhood of Baghdad.

Prewar production of vegetable oils, including olive oil, has been roughly estimated at about 10,000 tons. Large quantities of oilseeds, however, were not processed into oil but went for direct consumption. There is therefore special difficulty in estimating consumption of fats and oils in Iraq, a problem discussed later in chapter 28.

Little information is available about vegetables and fruits, other than dates. They are grown mainly in the Diyala area, although there is some production for local consumption throughout Iraq. There is no official estimate of citrus-fruit production, but excellent oranges are grown near the Diyala River. Beans and pulses are not eaten as much as in Egypt; prewar production is thought to have been not more than about 5,000 tons, which is the official estimate for 1948. The climate of Iraq is not well suited to potatoes; prewar production probably did not exceed 5,000 tons on an area of about 2,000 hectares.

Sheep are kept mainly by nomadic tribes, though the numbers have never been accurately known. In December 1939 the number registered for taxation was 5.5 million. A more reliable census in 1946 gave the number as 8 million. Iraq wool finds a ready market for carpet manufacture. Production before the war was about 7,000 tons and was estimated at 11,000 tons in 1947. Goats numbering between 2 and 3 million are found in all parts of Iraq. Nomad tribes use goat hair for making tents, and in the settled areas where grazing is insufficient for sheep or cattle they keep goats for milk. In 1938 cattle and buffalo were estimated at 350,000 and in 1948 at 950,000. Oxen are mainly used for plowing in the northern zone. About 300,000 camels are kept, mainly by Bedouin tribes.

The system of land tenure is one of the chief handicaps to expansion of production. There are few peasant proprietors, the land being for the most part owned by absentee city landlords or by tribal sheiks. The actual cultivator is usually a sharecropper and often receives only 30–40 percent of the crop. Tenants have no legal security and their labors are usually directed by subsheiks or *sirkals* acting as head of the local clan. This system has come about from the gradual disintegration of the old tribal system of landownership which prevailed when the tribe itself was a political unit performing many of the functions now taken over by the state. Under the tribal system there was no clear definition of individual ownership, but with the economic development that has taken place during the last 30 years tribal chiefs have had a strong inducement to acquire legal ownership of the land. This tendency has been strengthened both by the profitability of grain exports and by the extension of pump irrigation and mechanization. In the southern zone of flood irrigation the sheik and the *sirkal* between them may take up to 80 percent of the crop, leaving the cultivator between 20 and 30 percent.

In the northeastern rainfall zone around Mosul and Kirkuk as much as 75 percent of the land is held in small and medium-size farms averaging up to 50 hectares. Where the land is held by a large proprietor his share of the profit is much less than in the south and usually amounts to only 10–20 percent. Before the war sharecroppers and small peasant proprietors were overburdened with debt, but the high prices of grain obtained during the war helped to reduce their burden.

The establishment of large farms owner-operated with modern machinery is handicapped by the scarcity of farm laborers; labor tends to be especially short at harvest time. In the irrigated zone ownership of water rights is almost more important than ownership of land. Improvement of irrigation results in a shift of sharecroppers from the less-watered land. In general, agricultural development is handicapped partly by the ignorance of the fellahin and partly by lack of incentive under the present system of land tenure.

## PERSIA

Persia (or Iran) is the second largest country in the Middle East, covering 1.6 million square kilometers. The population was estimated at about 16 million at the outbreak of the war, and the urban population in 25 towns of over 50,000 was somewhere between 2 and 2.5 million. Persia lies along the fold of the earth's crust that stretches from the Alps to the Himalayas and forms the connecting link between the Taurus Mountains of Turkey and the mountain ranges of Afghanistan and Baluchistan. It is bounded on the north by the USSR and the Caspian Sea, on the east by Afghanistan and India, on the west by Iraq and Turkey, and on the south by the Persian Gulf.

The country is divided into three main zones. In the north are the Elburz Mountains, reaching a height of 5,600 meters, which descend to a narrow coastal plain on the fringe of the Caspian Sea. In the center is a high plateau ranging from 1,200 to 2,400 meters, which is traversed by minor mountains and valleys running northwest and southeast. The capital, Teheran, lies on this plateau in a saucer-like plain south of the Elburz Range. In the southwest the Zagros mountain belt, which runs parallel to the Persian Gulf and the Tigris River, consists of a series of strongly folded and overthrust structures which look from the air like gigantic waves of rock breaking on the plains below. Adjoining Iraq at the head of the Persian Gulf lies another plain cut by the river Karun only a few hundred feet above sea level.

Persia is subject to extremes of heat in summer, brought by hot dry winds from India, and to unusual cold in winter, brought by cold dry air from Siberia. Except on the shores of the Caspian nearly all the rain comes from the Mediterranean or the Black Sea and is largely intercepted by the western highlands (*3*, p. 269). The climate of the central plateau is continental and semiarid. Rainfall in the northwest is about 250 millimeters and falls off progressively toward the desert areas of the southeast. The southeastern desert is 2,000 kilometers long and varies from 250 to 500 kilometers in width. Along the shore of the Caspian Sea and the foothills of the Elburz Mountains there is abundant rainfall most of the year and a fairly mild climate; average annual rainfall is about 1,250–1,500 millimeters in the west and 500 millimeters in the east. At the head of the Persian Gulf the winter rainfall is scanty, from 100 to 300 millimeters. Summers are hot and oppressive, with the temperature rising to 46° C., and winters are mild. The Karun Valley is fertile, but much of the land is alkaline and suffers from lack of drainage. In Khuzistan the temperature rises to 49° C. in July and the average rainfall is 300–400 millimeters. In the central plateau water is scarce and frequently brackish. Salt marshes and lakes are fed by small rivers with no outlet to the sea; and much of the soil is too salty for cultivation (*4*, p. 6).

Only about 10–15 percent of the land area is cultivated, 15 percent is rough pasture, and another 15 percent is under forest. A further 20 percent could be cultivated if suitable irrigation were possible, but at least 30 percent of the total area is desert and infertile (*5*). Wheat, barley, millet, and rice are the principal crops, the latter being grown mostly on the shores of the Caspian Sea. The main wheat-producing areas are the provinces of Khurasan in the northeast, Azerbaijan in the northwest, Kermanshah and Khuzistan in the west, and Fars in the south.

The normal system of peasant cultivation is to leave a third to a half of the land in fallow. Irrigation water is obtained either by gravitation from rivers which maintain a flow from spring to autumn, or more frequently from *qanats* or underground watercourses; these *qanats* start from the foothills and collect water for long distances, sometimes 10 or 12 miles, before they rise above the surface and reach the lands to be irrigated. Cereal and other crops may be watered at intervals from March to June and summer crops from May to September. The return on irrigated land for wheat and barley is rarely more than tenfold and usually less. Where dry farming is practiced, as in some parts of the central plateau between 1,800 and 2,400 meters, the timing and results of cultivation depend on the rainfall. Wheat and barley are sown as soon as the ground is softened by the first rain, which may begin early in November or may be as late as the first week of January. Wheat is harvested toward the end of April and the beginning of May in the south, but two and a half months later in the northwest and at altitudes above 1,800 meters. In the Persian Gulf area the crop depends on good rainfall from the middle of February to the end of March. If this occurs, a yield of twentyfold may be obtained, whereas if there is no rain in February or March, even after good rains from November to January, the harvest is a failure. In this area records show that during cycles of 11 years one will be a good year, two or three medium, four poor, and two to three a failure (*5*).

Other cereals grown as summer crops are millet, sown in the spring, and maize, sown at the end of May and harvested in September. Lentils, beans, and peas are grown as winter crops. Cotton is grown in many places and production in the five years before the war averaged 34,000 tons. Production of vegetable oils is limited and before the war was mainly derived from cottonseed. Total production according to official estimates averaged about 9,000 tons, of which 7,000 tons were cottonseed oil. Tea and sugar were mostly imported, but 12 percent of the tea and 20 percent of the sugar were home-produced.

Fruits and vegetables are grown in abundance. Experts believe that the parents of many of the cultivated fruits of Europe are derived from the province of Azerbaijan and the southern Caucasus. There were substantial exports of fresh and dried fruit and nuts before the war, including raisins, apricots, almonds, and dates. Other exports included rice, opium, and medicinal herbs.

The numbers of livestock are quite uncertain. In 1937 the number of sheep was estimated at 14 million and of goats about 7 million. The number of cattle before the war was reckoned at 2.9 million, asses at 1.18 million, camels at 600,000, and horses and mules at 350,000. There was an important export both of raw wool and of carpets and rugs, and more than half a million lambskins were exported, mainly to the USSR (*6*).

Lack of reliable statistics makes it difficult to assess Persia's prewar consumption of staple foods. Even if population and crop statistics could be trusted, the wide variations in diet—between rich and poor, urban and rural, villagers and nomadic tribesmen—tend to make the national average misleading.

There is doubt about the population because there has never been a complete census. The International Institute of Agriculture (IIA) gave a figure of 15 million for 1937. The United Nations (*7*) gives 16.2 million for 1937 and over 19 million for 1951. The IIA put wheat production at 2.02 million tons in 1934–37, whereas the FAO uses a prewar average for three years of 1.87 million tons. Combining these different prewar estimates gives a range of 115–35 kilos for wheat production per head or 92–108 kilos for flour consumption. Even 135 kilos seems a low figure for a country that consumed wheat as its staple bread grain and had an average export of

22,500 tons. If all the barley and other grains are included, the total grain production becomes 216 kilos per head, which exceeds the average for other Middle East countries. Human consumption of grain as flour may be between 160 and 170 kilos per head. Approximate figures for consumption per head of cereals and other foods are given by FAO as follows (*8*; *9*, pp. 90, 91):

| Item | Kilos per year | | Percent of total calories |
|---|---|---|---|
| Cereals, as flour | 162 | | 67 |
| Roots and pulses | 11 | | 4 |
| Sugar and fats | 6 | | 4 |
| Fruit and vegetables | 118 | | 11 |
| Meat, eggs, and fish | 19 | | 4 |
| Milk | 93 | | 10 |
| Total | ... | | 100 |
| Total calories per day | | 2,010 | |
| Protein (*gm. per day*): | | | |
| Total | | 65 | |
| Animal | | 10 | |

Nomadic tribes comprising 15 percent of the population must have consumed more milk and less cereals and sugar per head than the national average, and the urban population more sugar and fats and less milk. The most important uncertainty is the total consumption of milk and its distribution between different groups, since the amount of milk available for consumption by mothers and children appreciably influences the rate of increase of the population. In this respect Persia with her large numbers of livestock—if the numbers are not overestimated—compares favorably with Egypt. In other respects, particularly in the consumption of roots and pulses, Persia is given a lower consumption than Egypt, but this must be largely conjectural owing to incomplete records of production.

As in other Middle East countries, improvement of agricultural techniques is handicapped by the traditional system of land tenure. Most of the land is owned by large absentee landlords and only about 30 percent belongs to peasants or small proprietors. The usual term of lease is three to five years and takes the form of a crop-sharing agreement. The share going to the landlord and the cultivator depends on their respective contributions of land, water, seed, draft animals, and labor. The share taken by the landlord varies in different districts from one-third to three-quarters, depending on whether he provides seed and draft animals as well as land and water. In addition, the peasant in many areas is liable for customary dues and servitudes, including labor service. The mass of the peasants live in mud-brick hovels on the margin of subsistence, and are frequently burdened with debt. Public-health and education services are almost completely lacking, and clothing and fuel are scanty and hard to come by. Outside the rice-growing area in the north and the date groves in the south, the main diet of the peasant is bread made of wheat or millet supplemented by soup made of peas and other pulses and a little meat. In the summer he gets fruit and vegetables; and if he owns a flock or can afford to buy them, he also eats cheese and curds. His chief luxuries, when he can afford them, are tea and sugar (*10*, p. 389).

In the uplands of central Persia it is said that one harvest in every five years will be good, three indifferent, and one a complete failure; but not infrequently two good years or two bad years will come successively. Widespread famine no longer occurs, but local famines from total crop failure are not uncommon; and nearly everywhere, when crops are indifferent, some peasants go short for a month or so before the next harvest. Insecurity and poverty are the dominant features in the lives of the peasants (*10*, pp. 219–22).

## CITATIONS

*1* United Nations, Conciliation Commis. for Palestine, *Final Report of the United Nations Economic Survey Mission for the Middle East. Part II. The Technical Supplement* (Lake Success, N.Y., Dec. 28, 1949); and Doreen Warriner, *Land and Poverty in the Middle East* (Royal Inst. Internatl. Affairs, London, 1948).

*2* F. H. Gamble, *Iraq* . . . (Gt. Brit., Bd. Trade, Comm. Rels. and Exports Dept., Overseas Econ. Survs., 1949).

*3* W. B. Fisher, *The Middle East. A Physical, Social and Regional Geography* (London, 1950).

*4* B. A. Keen, *The Agricultural Development of the Middle East* . . . (London, 1946).

*5* A. I. Tannous, "Agricultural Production and Food Consumption in Iran," *Foreign Agriculture* (U.S. Dept. Agr., Off. For. Agr. Rels.), February 1944.

*6* N. S. Roberts, *Iran* . . . (Gt. Brit., Bd. Trade, Export Promotion Dept., Overseas Econ. Survs., 1948).

*7* United Nations, *Demographic Yearbook, 1953* (New York, 1953).

*8* FAO, *Second World Food Survey* (Rome, November 1952).

*9* FAO, *Report of the Second Near East Meeting on Food and Agricultural Programs and Outlook, Bloudane, Syria, 28 August—6 September, 1951.*

*10* A. K. S. Lambton, *Landlord and Peasant in Persia* (London, 1951).

## CHAPTER 6

# ETHIOPIA, ERITREA, AND THE SOMALILANDS

### ETHIOPIA

Ethiopia is about the same size as Egypt, with an area of just over 1 million square kilometers. Before the war it had no coastline and was surrounded by Kenya, Sudan, Eritrea, and French, British, and Italian Somaliland. In the absence of a census its population was unknown. The International Institute of Agriculture (IIA) gave a figure for 1936 of 5.3 million (*1*), and the United Nations (*2*) gives 15 million. During the war Worthington (*3*, p. 182) took 8 million as the mean of estimates ranging from 5 to 16 million.

The country is exceptionally broken and mountainous, with fertile soils of basaltic origin in the valleys and on the plains, and a plentiful rainfall exceeding 1,000 millimeters at high altitudes. Most of the rain comes in the summer months, with "little rains" in March and April also. Good rains and variations of soil and altitude provide excellent conditions both for agriculture and for livestock production. But, as Keen observes (*4*, p. 9), the high plateaus, where pastures are good and the land is suitable for mixed farming, are given over mainly to arable farming, while in the low plains of Danakil and Somali, which are less suitable for livestock, nomadic herdsmen keep cattle of poor quality and resist attempts at agricultural settlement.

The following estimates of land distribution in 1951 have been given by the Food and Agriculture Organization of the United Nations (FAO), in million hectares (*5*):

| | |
|---|---|
| Cultivated land | 11 |
| Meadows and pastures | 50 |
| Forests | 3 |
| Unused, potentially productive | 8 |
| Waste | 34 |
| Total | 106 |

The capital, Addis Ababa, lies on the central plateau at a height of 2,400 meters and has a population variously estimated between

200,000 and 400,000. It is linked by the only railway in Ethiopia with the Red Sea port of Djibouti in French Somaliland. The provinces of Harar, Cherchar, and Hadama in the south normally produced a surplus of wheat, maize, and sorghum, and the central province of Dessie also produced a surplus, mainly of wheat. The north was deficient in grains and drew its supplies from the south.

The main cereal harvest follows the summer rainy season and extends from September to December according to climate and altitude; but subsidiary harvests also take place at other times of the year in special regions. The cereals most commonly eaten are durra or giant millet and teff or *taff* (*Poa abyssinica*) which is related to the South African fodder crop known as *taff* grass. This is a small grain producing a fine gray flour and is preferred as a bread grain to durra. Wheat is mainly grown as a cash crop and is thought to be about 70 percent hard wheat.

Durra or giant millet (sorghum) is grown in the hot lowlands. *Dagusa* is a dwarf millet sometimes grown with cotton and coffee; and teff is grown on flat lowlands where it is too hot for wheat. All these are used in breadmaking. Wheat is grown in the highlands above 1,800 meters, but best yields occur above 2,400 meters (*6*; *7*, p. 244).

The following conjectural estimates of crop production, in thousand metric tons, before the war and in 1948, are taken from FAO's report in 1951 (*8*, pp. 75–79):

| Crop | Prewar | 1948 |
|---|---|---|
| Millet | 1,350 | 1,730 |
| Barley | 127 | 800 |
| Wheat | 100 | 200 |
| Maize | 91 | 170 |
| Pulses | 200 | 250 |

In addition, about 5,000 tons of oats and 3,000 tons of potatoes were produced in 1948. The production of teff, for which no figure is available, may have exceeded that of wheat and maize combined.

Prewar numbers of livestock are put as high as 18 million cattle, 6 million sheep, 8 million goats, and 2 million camels. In 1948 they were about the same except that the number of sheep was thought to have risen to 17 million.

Lack of communications and tribal traditions are among the chief handicaps to economic development of agriculture. With the exception of coffee and hides and skins, which are Ethiopia's staple exports, there is little production for market. The country is self-supporting in food, with a marked difference in pattern of consumption between the nomadic herdsmen in the north, whose staple food is milk, and the settled farmers of the highlands, who live mainly on cereals and pulses.

Buxton (*9*, p. 166) refers to the diet of the Danakil tribe of nomad herdsmen, who use camels for transporting their women and children and have little to do beyond feeding and milking their cattle. "It is only at rare intervals or on special occasions that they eat grain or kill animals for meat. Nor do they mix blood with their milk as is done by the Somalis and various other tribes in East Africa and the Sudan. . . . As milk is their staple diet I was not surprised at the Danakil's ability to take a gallon or so at a draught." Gifts of food given on special occasions may include chickens, eggs, honey, and corncobs.

In view of the contrasting diets of herdsmen and arable farmers, figures of national consumption per head would have little meaning in Ethiopia, even if there were reliable figures both for food and for population. But so far as the figures for crops and livestock can be trusted, there seems some ground for supposing that Ethiopia was fairly well fed by Middle East standards. During the war the reports were of surpluses that could not be transported rather than of shortages.

When the Middle East Supply Center (MESC) was looking to Ethiopia to export cereals for neighboring deficit countries, particularly Aden and Somalia, the surpluses that might be obtained from 1942 crops compared with actual exports in 1943 were estimated as follows, in thousand metric tons:

| Item | Surplus | Exports |
|---|---|---|
| Wheat and flour | 22 | 16.0 |
| Millet | 28 | 3.6 |
| Maize | 12 | .9 |
| Barley | 3 | — |
| Total | 65 | 20.5 |

## ERITREA

Eritrea, now reunited to Ethiopia, was established as an Italian colony in 1890. It runs for 670 miles along the African coast of the Red Sea between Sudan and French Somaliland, and has an area of

124,000 square kilometers. In June 1942 its population was 803,-300, including 58,200 Europeans and Italian refugees from Ethiopia. The indigenous population of 745,100 was divided about equally between Coptic Christians in the central plateau round Asmara and Moslems in the western province and eastern lowlands.

The country is divided by a mountainous plateau which rises gradually from north to south and reaches 2,400 meters on the border of Ethiopia. Between this central spur and the frontier with Sudan lies an arid plain which has potentially rich soil but a summer rainfall of only about 300 millimeters. Much of it is given over to nomadic tribes, but settled agriculture has begun to be developed, partly by Sudanese and West African immigrants. The northern part of the central plateau is occupied by nomad pastoralists. Part of the southern plateau is settled but much of the land is of poor fertility. Summer rainfall here is about 500 millimeters. The coastal plain and the foothills have a winter rainfall and in the fertile areas are fairly densely settled. But food production is insufficient for the needs of the area owing to primitive methods and the hostility of nomad pastoralists to settled agriculture (*4*, pp. 8–9).

Before the war Eritrea was not self-supporting in staple foods. Prewar production of wheat had averaged only 4,000 tons and net imports of wheat and flour were about 8,000 tons, mainly for the Italian population of 50,000. The native population consumed other grains—barley, millet, maize, and teff, in that order. According to figures published by FAO, the total cultivated area in 1948 was 222,000 hectares, or 2 percent of the total area. FAO's estimates of prewar production (*5*) and wartime estimates by the British Military Administration are given below (*10*, p. 135):

| Crop | Area (*1,000 hectares*) | | | | Production (*1,000 metric tons*) | | | |
|---|---|---|---|---|---|---|---|---|
| | Prewar | 1941 | 1942 | 1943 | Prewar | 1941 | 1942 | 1943 |
| Wheat | 6.0 | 5.9 | 11.8 | 3.4 | 4.0 | 1.6 | 6.0 | 2.5 |
| Barley | 18.0 | 11.8 | 19.5 | 25.0 | 10.0 | 7.2 | 10.0 | 20.0 |
| Sorghum | 32.0 | 17.5 | 48.6 | 36.0 | 18.0 | 10.0 | 26.8 | 17.4 |
| Maize | 7.0 | 8.1 | 17.9 | 10.1 | 4.0 | 4.7 | 14.6 | 7.6 |
| Millet | ... | 5.9 | 4.0 | 10.2 | ... | 3.7 | 4.0 | 4.0 |
| *Dagusa* | ... | 3.0 | 6.3 | 6.7 | ... | 1.2 | 3.2 | 5.6 |
| Beans | 13.0 | 4.9 | 5.2 | 3.9 | 6.0 | 2.5 | 3.6 | 2.0 |
| Potatoes | — | .3 | .7 | .4 | — | .6 | 1.5 | 2.0 |
| Teff | ... | — | — | 7.7 | ... | — | — | 8.0 |

The population of Eritrea in June 1942 was estimated by the British Military Administration to be distributed as below. Rough estimates of grain supplies needed to feed the different groups are added in a second column:

| Population | Number | Grain requirements (*1,000 tons*) |
|---|---|---|
| Europeans | 58,200 | 10–12 |
| Natives in towns | 140,000 | 20–28 |
| Natives in villages | 471,500 | 75–95 |
| Natives, nomadic | 133,600 | 10–15 |
| Total | 803,300 | 115–150 |

Assuming that the wheat was mainly eaten by the Europeans, domestic production of 4,000 tons and imports of 8,000 tons would be about sufficient for their needs. The grain consumption of the nomadic tribes, consisting of barley, sorghum, and teff, is unlikely to be included in the official figures, and the same can be said of part at least of the local production and consumption of grain on settled holdings. The official estimates of production would be sufficient to cover the requirements of the towns and may correspond fairly closely with farm production for sale. If total production of grain was no more than, say, 80,000–100,000 tons, which seems possible, the balance of supplies consumed may have come from unrecorded imports from Ethiopia across the land frontier. Livestock numbers are put by FAO at 1.2 million cattle, 1.5 million sheep and goats, and 68,000 camels.

About three-quarters of the recorded crop production in Eritrea was obtained from the densely populated and well-watered highlands of the Alto Piano lying between 1,500 and 2,400 meters above sea level. The rainfall ranges from 500 to 600 millimeters and mainly occurs in June, July, and August. Some rain may fall in the spring and is sometimes sufficient for maize and the larger types of durra; but more usually barley and wheat, which require a shorter growing season, are grown in the drier areas. Teff is an important crop, much grown in Eritrea as in Ethiopia, and is widely preferred to harder grains owing to the ease with which a soft flour can be produced by the simple process of rubbing it with the hands. With native methods of cultivation, the tillable area of the highlands is cultivated as intensively as the limited rainfall permits. The native plow serves to loosen the soil without causing soil erosion and a rough system of contour plowing is not uncommon, giving rise to low terraces which serve to retain water and check erosion. Deep plowing with tractors would have deleterious effects on the soil. Little or no fertilizers or manure are applied to the soil and the poorer land is left fallow every third or fourth year. Higher yields could be obtained from a careful application of fertilizers; but heavy use of nitrates, particularly in areas of uncertain rainfall, would be disastrous. The better course would be to seed the land now left fallow with leguminous crops such as clover or vetch. Beans are a popular crop in Eritrea; they not only improve the soil but serve as a useful source of protein.

As elsewhere in the Middle East, the system of land tenure tends to discourage productivity. Some areas are occupied by permanent tenants, but most of the land is held under a system of tribal or communal custom, under which redistribution of holdings takes place every three to seven years. Continual change of tenants and competition for land from pressure of population discourage improved methods of cultivation and tend to promote soil exhaustion.

The density of population in the more climatically favored highlands is in striking contrast with the relative underpopulation of the lower and hotter areas of the south. In the irrigated zone of Ali Gebir cotton was being developed by the Italians before the war; but elsewhere the prevalence of malaria and insecurity resulting from the movement of nomadic tribes have discouraged intensive settlement.

After the surrender of Asmara to British troops in April 1941 the feeding of Eritrea gave cause for temporary anxiety, which was intensified when the port of Massawa became an important American and British naval and air base with a large influx of Italian and local labor. The needs of Eritrea were included in MESC's food-import programs for the Mediterranean and Red Sea area; but in 1942 the shortage of shipping led to increased emphasis on the need for expanding local production of cereals. By 1943 the country was almost self-supporting except for imported sugar, tea, and canned milk, and some grain from Ethiopia.

### FRENCH SOMALILAND

French Somaliland lies at the southern end of the Red Sea between Eritrea and British Somaliland. Its area is 22,000 square kilometers and its population in 1937 was 46,000. The capital is the important port of Djibouti (population 15,000) which is connected by rail with Addis Ababa and provided before the war the sole outlet for Ethiopia's foreign trade.

In the hinterland, the native population of herdsmen subsist mainly on a diet of milk and meat, with millet as their chief bread grain. Indigenous grain production may have been about 5,000 tons, since the recorded imports of 4,000 tons—mostly rice and wheat flour shipped from India via Aden—were mainly required to feed the urban population. In 1943, when rice imports ceased, wheat flour and millet had to be obtained from Ethiopia.

French Somaliland was impoverished by the war through the loss of much of its entrepôt trade, especially during the year and a half before the colony joined the Free French at the end of 1942. Published figures show a sharp decline in livestock numbers between 1936 and 1945, as follows, in thousand head (*11*):

| Animal | 1936 | 1945 |
|---|---|---|
| Cattle | 7 | 3 |
| Camels | 30 | 8 |
| Sheep | 363 | 35 |
| Goats | 220 | 120 |
| Asses | 3 | 6 |

The number of goats fell by nearly a half, cattle by 60 percent, camels by 70 percent, and sheep by more than 90 percent. Asses, on the other hand, doubled in number.

The catastrophic fall in sheep numbers must have taken place mainly on account of food shortage during the six-month blockade of Djibouti from June to December 1941 (*12*, p. 252).

### BRITISH SOMALILAND

British Somaliland, with an area of 176,000 square kilometers, lies between French Somaliland and Somalia. In 1937 it had a population of about 350,000 and in 1949, 500,000. It was a grain-importing country before the war and to a less extent during the war. Prewar imports of wheat and flour averaged 12,700 tons and of rice 10,730 tons. The population is almost entirely pastoral and nomadic, and indigenous production of grain, chiefly millet, was probably less than 10,000 tons.

In 1943, when India could no longer supply rice, the United Kingdom Commercial Corporation undertook to send supplies of wheat and millet from Ethiopia and to keep a reserve stock at Diredawa sufficient to implement a guaranteed supply of 700 tons per month. But owing to the efforts made to increase local production, combined with the activities of Arab traders, the guaranteed amount was not taken up and total grain imports in 1943 were less than 2,000 tons.

As in neighboring countries the staple food of the Somali tribes comes from their flocks and herds in the form of milk and meat. According to Buxton (*9*, p. 166), the Somalis are accustomed to drink blood with their milk. The numbers of livestock in 1937 and 1946 were estimated as follows, in thousand head (*13*):

| Animal | 1939 | 1946 |
|---|---|---|
| Cattle | ... | 250 |
| Camels | 1,000 | 1,240 |
| Sheep | 3,000 | 3,000 |
| Goats | 2,000 | 2,000 |

## SOMALIA

Somalia, or ex-Italian Somaliland, which was occupied by the British in February 1941 and is now a United Nations trust territory administered by Italy, is bounded on the west by British Somaliland, Ethiopia, and Kenya, and has a coastline of about 4,000 kilometers facing the Indian Ocean. It covers an area of 514,000 square kilometers with a population of about a million before the war. The bulk of the population consists of pastoral nomadic tribesmen living on a diet of meat, milk, and eggs with relatively small amounts of grain, mainly millet.

The Italians had established agricultural settlements in an irrigated zone north of the capital of Mogadishu, mainly for the production of cotton, sugar, oilseeds, and bananas for export to Italy. Partly to insure a supply of native labor for Italian-operated farms, the Italians had done little to develop the native agriculture itself. Production and area in 1934–36 as given by FAO was as follows (*11*):

| Crop | Area (*1,000 hectares*) | Production (*1,000 metric tons*) |
|---|---|---|
| Sugar cane | .. | 36.0 |
| Maize | 14 | 13.9 |
| Cottonseed | 5 | 1.4 |
| Sesame | 3 | .7 |
| Cotton | 5 | .5 |

Prewar imports of grain amounted to about 11,000 tons—mostly rice, oats, and barley. During the 12 months July 1942 to June 1943, MESC records show that imports were less than 300 tons of wheat and flour from Ethiopia and 50 tons of maize from Kenya.

As a result of the growing shortage of tonnage and supplies, steps were taken by the British Military Administration to encourage native cultivation and to switch production on the irrigated area from cotton to rice and maize. In August 1943 estimated crop production was as follows, in thousand metric tons (*14*):

| Type | Millet | Maize | Rice | Total |
|---|---|---|---|---|
| Native cultivation: | | | | |
| Summer ........ | 40 | 9 | — | 49 |
| Winter ......... | 21 | 4.5 | — | 25.5 |
| Total ......... | 61 | 13.5 | — | 74.5 |
| Irrigated area: | | | | |
| Summer ........ | — | 3.1 | .4 | 3.5 |
| Winter ......... | — | 3.1 | 1.2 | 4.3 |
| Total ......... | — | 6.2 | 1.6 | 7.8 |

Early in 1944, when there was a severe drought and famine conditions were reported in the sparsely populated province of the extreme northeast, arrangements were made to ship 1,500 tons of millet from Ethiopia.

Numbers of livestock before the war were estimated at just over a million cattle, 2.5 million goats, 2 million sheep, 800,000 camels, over 11,000 asses, and about 3 million chickens (*13*).

Since the war, cotton cultivation has again expanded under the stimulus of high prices. In 1951/52, 1,800 tons were produced from 20,000 hectares. Owing to the prosperity of cotton cultivators and the increased demand for labor there has been a change in the dietary pattern of Somalis. Less millet is eaten than before the war and the younger generation are acquiring a taste for wheat bread and pastes in place of millet. Rice has remained the preferred food of the older generation, when they can afford it.

## CITATIONS

*1* IIA, *International Yearbook of Agricultural Statistics, 1938–39* (Rome, 1939).

*2* United Nations, *Demographic Yearbook, 1952* (New York, 1952).

*3* E. B. Worthington, *Middle East Science . . .* (London, 1946).

*4* B. A. Keen, *The Agricultural Development of the Middle East . . .* (London, 1946).

*5* FAO, *Yearbook of Food and Agricultural Statistics, 1952* (Rome, 1953).

*6* Italo Papini, *La Produzione dell'Etiopia* (Rome, 1938).

*7* Major R. E. Cheesman, *Lake Tana and the Blue Nile* (London, 1936).

*8* FAO, *Current Development of and Prospects for Agriculture in the*

*Near East. Second Near East Meeting on Food and Agricultural Programs and Outlook, Bloudane, Syria—28 August 1951* (July 12, 1951).

*9* D. Buxton, *Travels in Ethiopia* (London, 1949).

*10* Lord Rennell of Rodd, *British Military Administration of Occupied Territories in Africa, 1941–47* (London, 1948).

*11* FAO, *Yearbook of Food and Agricultural Statistics—1947* (Washington, 1947).

*12* G. Kirk, *The Middle East in the War* (London, 1952).

*13* FAO, *Yearbook of Food and Agricultural Statistics, 1949* (Washington, D.C., 1950).

*14* Captain R. F. Birch, Unpublished report on cereals supply in the Middle East, 1945.

# CHAPTER 7

# LIBYA, TRANSJORDAN, AND ARABIA

## LIBYA

Tripolitania and Cyrenaica are now united in the state of Libya, which covers an area of the North African desert exceeding 1.5 million square kilometers—more than half as large again as Egypt. Before the war the population was about 850,000, including some 30,000 Italian colonists.

Along the coastal belt there is a scanty rainfall of 100–300 millimeters during the winter months, and some irrigation water is obtained from wells and artesian bores. A hot dry wind from the south called the *Ghibli* comes in the spring and summer and often causes great damage to vegetation and crops. Along the coast of Tripolitania there are large areas of date palms intercropped on a two-year rotation with cereals or vegetables. In Cyrenaica the chief cultivated area is a segment of rich soil with fair rainfall stretching for about 500 kilometers between Bengazi and Derna (*1*, p. 11). It was here on the plain of Barca that the British Military Administration in 1942/43 made great efforts to obtain a crop of wheat. It was originally planned to cultivate 8,000 hectares, but owing to dry weather in the first year only about 1,000 tons of wheat were harvested from 2,000 hectares.

The main cereal grown by the Arabs both for human and for animal consumption is barley. On the foothills of the Jebel Akhdar Range an exceptionally good barley is grown. Before the war this found a ready market in Europe for brewing beer; but a good crop depends on the right quantity of rain and the absence of parching winds during the ripening period. Barley is also grown in depressions and wadi beds wherever runoff water accumulates.

Before the war, figures published by the International Institute of Agriculture (IIA) gave a production of 16,000 tons of wheat with net imports of 60,000 tons, and 38,000 tons of barley with net imports of 8,000 tons—10,000 tons of imports less 2,000 of exports (*2*). In the light of wartime experience it seems probable that this prewar estimate for barley production left out of account some of the barley grown in the interior. In 1943 during the first year of the

British Military Administration barley production was estimated at about 75,000 tons and in 1946 at 92,000 tons. In 1944 there was a surplus for export just before the harvest and it was found possible to ship 2,600 tons of barley to Cyprus and 2,000 tons to Malta. In 1946 barley exports reached 24,000 tons.

Numbers of livestock were officially published for December 1938, and it is of interest to compare these with estimates of the Middle East Supply Center (MESC) for 1944 after the fighting in North Africa was over (in thousand head):

| Animal | 1938 | 1944 |
|---|---|---|
| Cattle | 70 | 40 |
| Camels | 86 | 70 |
| Sheep | 877 | 625 |
| Goats | 705 | 700 |
| Asses | 40 | 35 |

Goats, camels, and asses, belonging in the main to nomad herdsmen, suffered less or recovered more quickly from the effects of war than cattle or sheep. Before the war there was an extensive trade with Egypt in cattle, sheep, and camels, the animals being taken on the hoof during the period when grass was growing along the southern pasture belt. Farther south in the Oases of Cufra near the frontier of Egypt there were extensive groves of date palms, said to number over a million trees.

In Greek and Roman times Libya may have had a larger agricultural population or a climate more propitious for agriculture than today. In the *Odyssey* (*3*), Menelaus says he roamed there "gathering much livelihood," and praises it as a land "where lambs are horned from birth. The ewes yean thrice a year; and neither lord nor shepherd lack cheese or meat or fresh milk."

## TRANSJORDAN

Before the war Transjordan was an Arab state east of Palestine with an area of about 90,000 square kilometers and a population estimated in 1937 at 300,000, of whom 260,000 were Moslems and 30,000 were Arab Christians. In addition there were about 10,000 Circassians who had come from the Caucasus in czarist times, and lived in colonies established by the Turkish government after the Russo-Turkish wars of 1870. After World War I the country was for a time under British mandate but became an independent state bound by treaty to Britain. After the partition of Palestine it was enlarged to include Arab Palestine and became the present Hashemite Kingdom of Jordan.

The western frontier of Transjordan passed down the center of the Jordan Valley to the Gulf of Aqaba. From the Jordan Valley the land rises abruptly to the mountains called in the Bible Gilead, Moab, and Edom, which reach 1,350 meters above sea level. From these highlands the land slopes away to the north and east, merging into the Syrian and Arabian deserts. The most fertile area lies to the west of the Hejaz railway, which runs parallel to the Jordan at a distance of about thirty miles. Here there is a winter rainfall which diminishes from north to south as in Palestine. Eastward the rainfall becomes negligible (*4*, p. 4).

Wheat, barley, millet, sorghum, and pulses are the principal crops grown, and vines and olives flourish on the hillsides. In the lower-rainfall areas toward the east dry farming is practiced with uncertain yields of barley or sorghum. Of the total area of 9 million hectares the cultivated land, including fallow and vineyards, was only about 5 percent, and only half of this on the average was cropped. Of the cropped area of 225,000 hectares, wheat accounted for 160,000 hectares, barley and millet 35,000, and pulses and legumes 30,000. In 1934–38 wheat production averaged 81,000 tons with an export surplus of 22,000 tons, leaving about 200 kilos per head for home consumption (*2*). Owing to uncertain yields exports varied greatly from year to year, and there is evidence to show that seminomad tribes living in the low-rainfall areas bordering on the desert suffered from periodic food shortage (*5*).

In 1941 there were thought to be about 500,000 goats and 325,000 sheep; estimates by the Food and Agriculture Organization of the United Nations for prewar are 439,000 and 224,000. Only about 60,000 cattle were kept and plow oxen were mostly imported from Syria. Of special interest for its bearing on similar problems in other Middle East countries was the reorganization of land settlement and the reform of land tenure which was carried through in Transjordan between 1933 and 1942 (*6*, pp. 77–79).

## ARABIA

The Arabian peninsula, with a population in the region of 10 million, is about the same size as Sudan and three-quarters that of India. Like Sudan and Egypt it is mostly desert or semidesert steppe, and apart from the oases in the interior the areas where intensive agriculture is possible are limited to the rain-fed highlands and valleys round the coast. The most fertile areas are Asir and parts of the Hejaz in western Saudi Arabia, and Yemen and parts of Aden Protectorate in the south. The peninsula was to a large extent self-supporting in food, but imports of cereals and rice into Saudi Arabia, Aden, and the Persian Gulf Sheikdoms were important before and during the war.

### SAUDI ARABIA

In the interior of Saudi Arabia nomadic tribes move with a seasonal rhythm in search of vegetation for their flocks of sheep and goats, growing an occasional catch crop of barley or millet and obtaining fresh water and dates in numerous scattered oases.

In the eastern provinces of Hasa and Nejd there are a number of small irrigated areas where settled agriculture is being developed, the chief crops being wheat and millet, with some maize and alfalfa (*1*, p. 91). In southern Asir on the west coast good farmland is found at an elevation of about 2,100 meters above sea level. Part of this is in narrow valleys irrigated from wells; but the greater part consists of ancient rock-faced terraces which have been in continuous use for centuries. These lands are dependent on rainfall estimated at 300 millimeters annually and full use is made of runoff water from the adjacent slopes. The principal crops grown on the irrigated land are grain sorghum, barley, spring wheat, and alfalfa. In addition, peaches, figs, apricots, pomegranates, grapes, and almonds are grown, and many vegetables including onions, potatoes, tomatoes, cabbages, melons, peppers, and radishes. The type of farming in Asir, as in Yemen, is often of a high standard. An agricultural mission of American experts, who visited the area from May to December 1942, were impressed with the excellent condition of the terraces and the way in which full advantage was taken of any rain and floodwater from the adjacent slopes. "The Western world," they reported (*7*, p. 140), "especially the farmers of the United States of America, can learn much about soil and moisture conservation from the mountain farmers of Saudi Arabia."

No figures of agricultural production or complete records of food imports are available. Prewar grain imports were estimated at about 60,000 tons, of which half was rice, 40 percent wheat and flour, and 10 percent maize and barley. India was the chief source of supply for rice and wheat. When grain exports from India ceased in 1942, MESC had to send supplies for eastern Saudi Arabia from stocks in the Persian Gulf, and for the towns of Mecca and Medina from the

Middle East pool at Suez. Recorded imports in 1943, mostly of wheat and flour, were 44,000 tons, of which two-thirds went to Jedda. In addition there were unrecorded imports by land and sea of barley and millet from Iraq and Yemen (*8*).

### YEMEN

Yemen, with a population of 3–4 million and an area of 195,000 square kilometers, lies at the extreme southwest of Arabia. Though it is now a member of the United Nations and of the Arab League, its agriculture remains almost a closed book. It used to have an important export trade in the famous Mocha coffee, but coffee is not now cultivated on a large scale.

Climatic conditions are similar to those in adjoining Asir, and the land structure resembles Lebanon with its coastal plain and inland mountain range. The chief rains fall in July to September and minor rains in March; the annual rainfall on the highlands ranges from 500 millimeters to 1,000 millimeters (*9*, p. 433).

The coastal plain, up to 50 miles wide, has a scanty vegetation and supports a semipastoral population of African origin. Above 900 meters carobs, figs, and walnuts appear. The most productive land is above 1,350 meters. Millets, wheat, barley, and alfalfa grow well on the highlands together with a wide variety of fruits and vegetables. *Pennisetum,* or bulrush millet (dukhn), grows best up to 600 meters, and sorghum (durra) above 600 meters and up to 2,700 meters. Cultivation is intensive and the traditional system of terracing is remarkable. Irrigation from ancient cisterns and by underground channels, with shafts at intervals like *qanats* (underground watercourses) in Persia, is well established (*10*, p. 234).

Before and during the war Yemen was self-supporting in cereals and other foods, and made no claims on MESC for shipping or supplies. If the land feeds a population of 3–4 million—the United Nations (*11*) gives a figure of 4.5 million for 1949—the production of cereals, mostly millets but also wheat, barley, and some maize, cannot fall far short of 800,000 tons. This is a pure guess. But in reaching a total for Middle East food supplies to compare with the Middle East's estimated population it has to be remembered that there are some millions of people for whom no food is included in official statistics.

### ADEN COLONY AND PROTECTORATE

The area of this British territory is 316,000 square kilometers with a population estimated at 600,000 in 1937, and 650,000 in

1949. Aden Colony, which covers 200 square kilometers including the island of Perim, had a population of 48,000 in 1931 and 81,000 in 1946 (*11*; *1*, p. 104). The island of Sokotra, attached to Aden, has an area of 3,600 square kilometers, and a population of 12,000, mostly engaged in fishing and animal husbandry.

The protectorate is in a summer-rainfall zone depending on the northeast monsoon from March to May and on the southwest monsoon from July to September. Some rain is also brought to the coast by winter storms from the Indian Ocean. The amount of rainfall is irregular and insufficient, except in the western part adjoining Yemen, and has to be supplemented by conserving erratic floodwater by dams and terracing.

Apart from a narrow coastal plain the country is mountainous, rising to over 2,100 meters. The cultivation of the soil is simple but effective. Soil and water are conserved by field terraces and by controlling the runoff water from the bare hillsides. This system is of ancient origin and has contributed to building up soil of high fertility over a fairly wide area.

The main crop grown in the west is millet, both sorghum and *Pennisetum*, the latter being grown in areas below 1,800 meters. Wheat and barley are summer crops. Sesame, cowpeas, and gram are grown, and potatoes were introduced into the highlands in 1939 (*4*, p. 10).

In the Hadhramaut, where rainfall is lower and agriculture competes with the pastoral industry, there is great pressure of population and the soil is less fertile. Cultivation is concentrated round wells and in flood-irrigated wadis. Sorghum is planted in the spring and again in August or September. Wheat, which is less frequently grown, is sown in December by drilling and deep sowing. Subsidiary crops include alfalfa, tobacco, and various vegetables; and there is a traditional export of honey to Java to supply the needs of emigrants from the Hadhramaut. One of the chief handicaps, apart from erratic rainfall, is a tendency for the soil to become saline; this leads to the abandonment of wells and formerly productive areas. There is also an ever-present risk of famine from drought or locusts.

The needs of Aden Colony and Protectorate for imported supplies received high priority from MESC, particularly when India had to stop her traditional exports. During the war years there was a succession of poor harvests in the Hadhramaut, leading to famine conditions in 1943, when special steps had to be taken to send wheat and millet from Ethiopia.

### MUSCAT AND OMAN

Muscat and Oman, with an area of 212,000 square kilometers and a population of about half a million, lies at the extreme southeast of Arabia between Aden Protectorate and the Persian Gulf. Cereals are grown in the west, where there is sufficient rainfall in the mountains, and in the coastal plain of Batina in the east. Dates, pomegranates, limes, and dried fish are the principal exports, and rice is the chief imported food. Camels are bred in the interior. Agriculture could be developed with better control of floodwater from the mountains, but in general rainfall, soil, and climate are unfavorable for cultivation (*1*, p. 110).

### SHEIKDOMS OF THE PERSIAN GULF (*1*, pp. 112–18)

Trucial Oman, with a population of 80,000, and Qatar, with 25,000, have little agriculture and apart from some date cultivation the main occupations are pearl fishing, for export to India, and boatbuilding. Until 1820 the coast had been for centuries the haunt of pirates who preyed on shipping in the Gulf. The staple food is rice, which was normally supplied from India, but this trade was interrupted by the war.

Kuwait, near the head of the Persian Gulf, covers an area of 21,000 square kilometers, with a population of 170,000 (or including a neutral zone in the south, half a million on 50,000 square kilometers). It has one of the largest oil fields in the world, which produced 16 million barrels in 1947, and an excellent harbor. The town of Kuwait, with a population of 70,000, is mainly engaged in dhow-building and trade. Dates, cereals, fruits, and vegetables are grown for local consumption, but the main food is rice imported from Iraq or from India.

The total area of the Bahrein Islands is 600 square kilometers, with a population of 110,000, of whom 40,000 live in the port of Manama. Bahrein is the shipping and trading center of the Persian Gulf and the headquarters of the pearling industry. Production of oil reached 8 million barrels in 1937/38 and has remained at about that figure. There is little agriculture and the main food import is rice.

In February 1943, when supplies of rice from India ceased, the annual requirements of Kuwait, Bahrein, Muscat, the Trucial Coast, and eastern Saudi Arabia were reported to MESC to be about 60,000 tons of rice. MESC could only offer wheat flour and barley as substitutes and the records show that in 1943 the Persian Gulf Sheikdoms reluctantly accepted 21,000 tons of flour and 3,000 tons of barley, while eastern Saudi Arabia took 15,000 tons of flour and 1,000 tons of barley.

This sudden and enforced change in diet from rice to wheat flour caused discontent and threatened to have political repercussions. Indeed it was feared that, if the pearl fishers did not get their normal diet of rice, dates, and fish, the pearl-fishing fleet, which normally starts operations in May and continues for four or five months, might stay at home and create trouble. In March 1944 it was found possible to send some 1,500 tons of rice from Iraq—the first consignment that the Persian Gulf Sheikdoms had had for nearly a year; and for a time their demands appear to have been met to some extent by smuggling rice out of India and Iraq in dhows. Finally in June 1944 MESC prevailed on the Iraq government to allow export to the Persian Gulf Sheikdoms through normal trade channels; and when the Sultan of Muscat visited Cairo that summer he was able to tell MESC's director of food and agriculture that he was satisfied with the existing arrangements.

## CITATIONS

*1* Royal Inst. Internatl. Affairs, *The Middle East . . .* (London, 1950).

*2* IIA, *International Yearbook of Agricultural Statistics, 1941–42 to 1945–46* (Rome, 1947).

*3* *Odyssey*, Book IV, line 85.

*4* B. A. Keen, *The Agricultural Development of the Middle East . . .* (London, 1946).

*5* N. M. MacLennan, "General Health Conditions of Certain Bedouin Tribes in Transjordan," *Transactions. Royal Society of Tropical Medicine and Hygiene* (London), 1935.

*6* Doreen Warriner, *Land and Poverty in the Middle East* (Royal Inst. Internatl. Affairs, London, 1948).

*7* U.S. Agr. Mission to Saudi Arabia, *Report . . .* (Washington, 1943).

*8* Captain R. F. Birch, Unpublished report on cereals supply in the Middle East, 1945.

*9* W. B. Fisher, *The Middle East. A Physical, Social and Regional Geography* (London, 1950).

*10* Hugh Scott, *The High Yemen* (London, 1942).

*11* United Nations, *Demographic Yearbook, 1952* (New York, 1952).

Part II

# THE WORK OF THE MIDDLE EAST SUPPLY CENTER

CHAPTER 8

# HOW WAR CAME TO THE MIDDLE EAST

For more than five thousand years the Middle East has been fought over by rival empires. Assyrian, Babylonian, Egyptian, Persian, Greek, and Roman conquerers came and went. Then in the seventh century A.D. came the Mohammedan conquest, which in less than a hundred years spread to India and central Asia in the east and to Spain and France in the west. The height of Arab power was reached under the Omayyad dynasty at Damascus; this was overthrown by the Abbassids, who established themselves at Baghdad in Iraq, and under Harun-al-Rashid achieved a high level of civilization at a time when western Europe under Charlemagne was emerging from the Dark Ages.

In 1055 the Abbassid caliphs came under the control of Seljuk Turks, who fought the Crusaders and the Frankish Kingdom of Jerusalem. In the thirteenth century four disastrous invasions of the Mongols, which did lasting damage to the irrigation works of the Euphrates Valley, brought to an end the Seljuk sultanate in Asia Minor. From that time the Ottoman dynasty arose; and in 1453 the capture of Constantinople brought to a close the Eastern Roman Empire.

The Arab conquests established the Arabic language and the religion of Islam, which have lasted with little change for more than a thousand years; but it was the Turks who established a unified political system and rule of law. During its decline the Ottoman Empire became corrupt and inefficient, and the Janissaries, who were responsible for military and civilian administration, became increasingly arbitrary and rebellious. Throughout the eighteenth and nineteenth centuries the Ottoman Empire lost territory in Europe and, after Napoleon's invasion in 1800, Egypt became virtually independent. In 1881 the French annexed Tunisia and in the following year the British occupied Egypt. The Italians took Libya in 1911. In 1918 the Young Turks' revolution and the abdication of Sultan Abdul-Hamid did little to stop the breakup of the Empire, and after World War I (when Turkey was on the side of Germany) the dissolution was completed by the Arab revolt. France received a mandate for

Syria and Lebanon, and Great Britain for Iraq, Palestine, and Transjordan. In 1924 Hejaz was annexed by King ibn-Saud of Arabia and Yemen became an independent state.

From 1920, Britain and France had established themselves as the predominant powers in the Arab world and at the same time had encouraged the growth of Arab nationalism. The Arab independence movement was led by a group of political leaders of whom Nuri Pasha as-Said of Iraq was one of the most active. But the separate development of each territory tended to accentuate disunity and personal rivalries. Arabia under King ibn-Saud was an independent monarchy; Egypt, a constitutional monarchy; Iraq, semi-independent under British guidance; Syria and Lebanon, under indirect French rule; and Palestine and Transjordan, under British mandate with the Jewish National Home, enjoying some degree of autonomy under the Jewish Agency for Palestine.

In the 1930's a new threat to the stability of the Middle East came from Italy. Mussolini's ambition was to dominate the Mediterranean and re-establish something like the old Roman Empire. The conquest of Tripoli from Turkey had been followed by the seizure of Cyrenaica and the suppression of the Senusi. This brought an Italian army to the frontier of Egypt. In 1936 Mussolini conquered Ethiopia in defiance of the League of Nations; and Italian East Africa (as Ethiopia, Eritrea, and Italian Somaliland were now called) completed the encirclement of Egypt and Sudan on the east.

When General Wavell was appointed General Officer Commanding-in-Chief, Middle East, in July 1939, the area over which his command extended was about three million square miles and included Palestine and Transjordan, Cyprus, Egypt, and Sudan. In addition, he was responsible for the land forces in British Somaliland, Aden, and Iraq, and on the shores of the Persian Gulf, which brought him into contact with the Commander-in-Chief, India. He had to cooperate with two naval Commanders-in-Chief and with the Air Officer Commanding-in-Chief, Middle East, and was responsible for co-ordinating British defense plans with the French military authorities in North Africa, Syria, and French Somaliland, and so far as possible with the Turkish and Greek General Staffs (*1*, p. 193).

When war broke out in September 1939, the military position in the Middle East was extremely vulnerable. The chief dangers were the presence of large Italian armies in Cyrenaica and Ethiopia, and the potential threat of Germany to Turkey and Greece. The first object of British strategy, as in World War I, was to safeguard communications with India and the Far East, and to keep open the Red Sea, the Suez Canal, and the Mediterranean for ocean shipping. The second main object was to build up resistance to attack on Turkey, Greece, and the Balkans as the first line of defense against invasion by land of Egypt, Syria, Palestine, Iraq, Persia, and eventually India. The Italian forces in North Africa totaled about 215,000 men. Some nine divisions were in Tripoli facing the French in Tunisia and Algeria, and another five in Cyrenaica. In addition there were about 225,000 Italian troops in Ethiopia and Eritrea. To set against these large forces General Wavell had little more than 50,000 men—barely sufficient to defend the Suez Canal, Alexandria, and the Nile Delta. When he took over his command he had only one incomplete armored division (the 7th, which later became famous as the "Desert Rats"), one brigade of the 4th Indian Division, several British battalions, and four regiments of artillery. A second infantry brigade arrived from India in the middle of August. This meant that the Italians in the west had a superiority on paper of about four to one. On the eastern frontier of Egypt it was much greater—at least seven to one (*1*, pp. 196, 197).

Until war broke out, General Wavell was only authorized to have "a small planning and co-ordinating staff" consisting of his Chief of Staff, Major General Arthur Smith, four second-grade staff officers, and an aide-de-camp. The administrative services for the troops in his vast area remained the responsibility of the War Office in London. Two years later, when Wavell left the Middle East to become Viceroy of India, his headquarters staff consisted of 350 officers. This rapid growth was sometimes criticized by those unfamiliar with the vast range of operational and administrative problems involved. It was a case of starting from scratch and improvising to meet each crisis as it came. As Major General Collins points out in his life of Lord Wavell, "Throughout Wavell's time in the Middle East, it was the administrative services that were to be his Achilles' heel and to provide him with the problems that were most difficult to solve" (*1*, p. 195).

Soon after war broke out, Wavell appointed Brigadier (later General) B. O. Hutchison to take charge of administrative planning. This proved to be a most successful choice. Eighteen months later General Hutchison became one of the chief originators and first chairman of the Middle East Supply Center (*1*, pp. 212, 431).

In November 1939 an inter-Allied meeting in Paris was attended by Wavell and Hutchison. One of the items discussed was a project drawn up by General Weygand, the French Commander-in-Chief, Syria, for an Allied landing in Salonika. Neither the French nor the British had troops to spare for such a purpose, but the discussions led to two important decisions in London. First, Wavell's proposal to take over executive control of administrative services was approved; and second, it was decided to proceed at once with building a base in Egypt for 6 divisions. This was later expanded to 12 and in July 1941 to 18, by which time the "ration strength" of the army in the Middle East, including its labor force, had reached nearly a million men (*1*, p. 218).

The task that thus fell on General Hutchison and his "Q" staff was of baffling complexity. Apart from the dearth of munitions and military stores, shortages of coal, timber, and mechanical transport were chronic. None of these could be obtained in the Middle East and their supply from the United Kingdom was limited by shortage of shipping. Fortunately, relations between General Hutchison and the "Q" staff in the War Office were excellent. Good progress was made in building up the vast military base at Suez during the first six months of 1940.

With the intervention of Italy in June 1940 the Mediterranean was closed to sea transport and supplies for the Middle East had to be shipped round the Cape of Good Hope — a distance of 12,000 miles instead of 2,000 miles from home ports. This added ten weeks to the time taken to obtain supplies, and at the outset involved an awkward gap during which no ships arrived. These were the critical months when preparations were being made to ward off the threatened Italian attacks from North Africa, Ethiopia, and Eritrea. During this period the Italians, moving from Ethiopia, successfully invaded and occupied British Somaliland, but it was not until the middle of September 1940 that Marshal Graziani started to cross the frontier into Egypt from the west. On reaching Sidi Barrani the Italians came to a halt and Wavell began to plan the counterattack which resulted in a sweeping victory. At the start, the administrative plan provided for maintaining the offensive for less than a week; actually the campaign lasted two months. In two months British forces had advanced 200 miles to Bengazi and had captured 130,000 prisoners, 1,290 guns, and 400 tanks. Capture of Italian gasoline and transport helped to make this possible.

The closing of the Mediterranean brought about radical changes in the internal arrangements for supply and transport in Egypt. Instead of supplies arriving in Alexandria and being distributed by rail to the front, ships coming around the Cape had to discharge at the south end of the Suez Canal in the Red Sea where port and rail facilities were extremely limited. An immense program of port and railroad development had to be undertaken. Coal imports had to be cut down to save shipping and locomotives had to be converted from coal to oil. The shipping shortage was further aggravated by lack of unloading and transport facilities, which involved serious delays in the turn-round of ships in port.

From closure of the Mediterranean in 1940 until final victory over Rommel in 1943 there was constant conflict between rival claims for tonnage — first, between munitions and other military stores and equipment, and, second, between military and civilian imports. The first problem, difficult though it was, formed an essential part of staff planning; in the Middle East, as in other campaigns, there was continual uncertainty as to whether "teeth" or "tail" should have priority of tonnage. But when there was superimposed on this the need for deciding what priority to give to the whole range of civilian imports, the problem became almost insoluble. The Middle East depended for its essential imports on shipping and on sources of supply controlled almost entirely by Britain or the United States; but, if the claims of the military authorities were to be paramount and essential civilian imports were to be excluded or subjected to arbitrary interference, the strategic consequences might have been disastrous. Famine and civil unrest had at all costs to be avoided; and a reasonable degree of political stability and popular acquiescence in the war effort had to be preserved (*1*, p. 272).

These problems became acute after the Italian invasion of Greece on October 28, 1940. The Greek government appealed for military aid from Britain in accordance with the guarantee given by Mr. Chamberlain in April 1939, and Mr. Churchill responded in the words: "We will give you all the help in our power. We will fight a common foe and we will share a united victory" (*2*, p. 533). This undertaking, as he points out, was ultimately made good, but only after a disastrous interval of nearly four years of enemy occupation.

## CITATIONS

*1* Major General R. J. Collins, *Lord Wavell* (London, 1948).

*2* W. S. Churchill, *The Second World War: Their Finest Hour* (Houghton Mifflin Co., Boston, 1949).

CHAPTER 9

# ORIGIN OF THE MIDDLE EAST SUPPLY CENTER

The immediate effect of British support for the Greeks was an increased demand on shipping for supplies of all kinds. Greece was cut off from her customary sources of supply of coal, steel, chemicals, raw materials, machinery, and oil, and was also in urgent need of wheat and barley. These would have to come from supplies transported by the long route via the Cape. They could be met only in part by drawing on stocks in Egypt or by diverting shipments destined for Palestine or Turkey. The difficulties of co-ordinating the requirements of Greece with those of Middle East countries led to the setting up in London of a committee under the chairmanship of Lord Hankey. Its first task was to settle policy issues arising out of the new demands of Greece; but in addition it had to co-ordinate procurement and shipping programs for the whole eastern Mediterranean and the Middle East. Co-ordination of plans and their execution were secured by meetings at the Ministry of Shipping of officials drawn from the service departments, and from the Ministries of Supply, Food, and Economic Warfare.

Meanwhile the Egyptian government was making representations to the British Embassy in Cairo, expressing growing concern. In a memorandum dated November 6, 1940, they pointed out that reduction of imports and local purchases by the British army were creating an acute shortage of civilian supplies, particularly of coal, iron and steel, and paper. They asked that sufficient shipping should be allocated to bring supplies to Egypt and that the British should assist in procurement and shipment from neutral countries, particularly the United States. These representations prompted Sir Miles Lampson (later Lord Killearn) to propose a regional organization to deal with supply problems of Egypt and neighboring countries. Many of these latter depended on exports and re-exports from Egypt, which were now subject to the Egyptian government's system of export licensing. The Embassy was being called upon to intervene to prevent control of exports throttling the economies of neighboring countries, particularly Palestine, Greece, and Malta. Only a regional body could adjudicate between the rival claimants and co-ordinate their reasonable requirements with those of the armed forces. The Embassy pointed out that the question of shipping priorities was being dealt with in London without sufficient information about the needs of Middle East countries. A central organization was needed to collect such information and to advise on the allocation of shipping space from the United Kingdom and other sources to all countries in the Middle East.

This proposal was strongly supported by General Headquarters (GHQ), Middle East, which advocated close liaison between a Middle East organization and the Eastern Group Supply Conference which had been set up in Delhi to deal with supply problems arising in India and Southeast Asia. A Middle East Provision Office was in fact set up in Cairo early in 1941 as an offshoot of the central Provision Office in Delhi.

In January 1941 an interim reply was sent from London, suggesting that the best way to give immediate help to Egypt would be to extend the activities of the United Kingdom Commercial Corporation (UKCC) to the Middle East. This body had been created by the Treasury to undertake purchases and sales on government account in the Balkans and Turkey. It had an office in Egypt under a Middle East Board of Directors (MEBOD) which handled shipping and storage problems, and it was thought that this office might purchase and ship supplies for the Egyptian government. This suggestion was welcomed by the Embassy and GHQ as a partial solution, but they pointed out that UKCC, as a commercial concern, could not co-ordinate requirements and determine priorities between the different territories. What was needed was a regional body, representing governments, which would be responsible for:

*a*) investigation of the import requirements of each territory;

*b*) stimulation of local production to meet deficiencies;

*c*) channeling of demands for essentials to the UKCC;

*d*) determination of priorities of supply and transport to the several territories; and

*e*) recommendation of shipping priorities in concert with GHQ.

As regards its constitutional position the Embassy proposed that governments of the territories should be invited to grant it powers of control over their supplies.

Further consideration of the Cairo proposals was undertaken by a committee under the chairmanship of Sir Arthur Salter (now Lord

Salter), who was at the time Parliamentary Secretary of the Ministry of Shipping, a post to which he had been appointed by the Prime Minister because of his unique experience as the architect of inter-Allied shipping control in World War I. The Ministry was also fortunate in having among its wartime recruits E. Max Nicholson, who, as the initiator and secretary of Political and Economic Planning (always known as PEP), had made his name as an economic analyst during the prewar depression. Salter and Nicholson welcomed the idea of a regional body to co-ordinate Middle East shipping programs. They saw it not as an executive board with plenary powers but as a planning and consultative body, analogous in some ways to the Program Committees of the Allied Maritime Council in World War I, to which the shipping authorities could look for help and guidance in settling civilian import priorities and loading programs. Experience of shipping control in World War I had shown that, even if it had been politically possible, it was unnecessary from the shipping standpoint to go as far as the Embassy suggested and try to persuade governments in the Middle East formally to surrender their power to control imports to a supranational executive. In so far as they were dependent on Allied shipping, their total imports were in fact under control. What was needed was that they should use the powers they had to regulate and select the imports required; no outside body could do this for them or against their will.

Nicholson drew up a proposal for what he called a Middle East Supply *Centre*. (This was the spelling of the official title in London and Cairo, but the American spelling was used in Washington.) He suggested that a three-tiered organization was needed: first, a British mission in each territory capable of estimating civil requirements; second, a regional center to arrange for these requirements to be met as far as possible from local resources; and, third, a clearing center in London to arrange for supplies and shipping from outside the area. In most of the territories a suitable local body already existed. In Greece there was an Anglo-Greek Co-ordinating Committee, and in Turkey and Egypt there were branches of the UKCC. In British colonies and protectorates requirements were presented by the administrations to the Colonial Office. The London Committee would act as the top tier for determining questions of policy. The regional center now proposed would supervise and co-ordinate the territorial bodies and execute the policies laid down in London.

This proposal was well received by other departments. Neither the Foreign Office nor the Colonial Office liked the political and constitutional aspects of the plan for a supply board, and the supply and service departments were prepared to accept a co-ordinating body to screen requirements and draw up programs. The chief criticism of the plan came from UKCC, which urged that there was no advantage in introducing a regional body between the territories and London, and that it would hinder rather than help the procurement of supplies and allocation of imports.

Discussion of these and other issues, such as the position of the chairman and the relations of the Center to the Embassy and to GHQ, continued in February and early March of 1941. It was finally decided that a Middle East Supply Center (MESC) should be established in Egypt under the chairmanship of General Hutchison, Deputy Quartermaster General, Middle East, with Sir Alexander Keown-Boyd, who had had experience of both commerce and civil administration in Egypt, as civilian vice-chairman and executive officer. Though its function would be to deal with civilian authorities in the area, it was decided to launch it as an offshoot of GHQ responsible to the Commander-in-Chief, Middle East, whose jurisdiction extended over all the territories concerned. As the Center had been initiated by the Ministry of Shipping and was primarily intended to save shipping, it was agreed that that department should be responsible for setting it up, engaging the staff, and providing it with funds to operate. MESC owed much to Nicholson. It was largely through his initiative and his help in selecting key personnel for the job, that MESC came to play so important a role in stimulating local production and in providing technical aid on problems which ranged from breeding fish to census techniques and the destruction of locusts.

The first meeting of MESC was convened by the Embassy and took place in Cairo on April 24, 1941. It was attended by General Hutchison Keown-Boyd, Mr. C. Empson, Commercial Counsellor in the Embassy at Cairo, Colonel V. B. Gray, chairman of MEBOD, and representatives of the governments of Palestine, Malta, Cyprus, and Sudan. There were also present representatives of the British Ministry of Shipping in Egypt; the Commander-in-Chief, Mediterranean; the Administration of Occupied Enemy Territories; the East African War Supplies Board; and the Local Provision Office of GHQ, Cairo.

### SCOPE AND TERMS OF REFERENCE

The meeting first discussed a draft of MESC's terms of reference based on the agreement reached with London. In addition to Egypt, Sudan, Palestine, Malta, and Cyprus, the area of the Center's responsibility originally included Turkey, Greece, Yugoslavia, and ex-Italian East Africa. The possibility of including British East Africa was debated, but a decision was reached that it should be excluded, except as a supply area, on the ground that imports into British East African territories were already co-ordinated by the East African Governors' Conference and were not dependent on the Mediterranean shipping route. In June 1941, as a result of the German advance, Greece and Yugoslavia were excluded. By the end of 1941 Turkey was no longer included; but Aden Colony and Protectorate and then Syria and Lebanon were added to the MESC area. Representatives of the British authorities in those countries became members of the General Committee, or Middle East Supply Council, as it came to be called. In March 1942 Iraq, Persia, Saudi Arabia, and the Persian Gulf Sheikdoms were added to the area; in December 1942, French Somaliland was added; and after the defeat of Rommel, Cyrenaica and Tripolitania were included, in February 1943, as the last additions to the list.

The functions of MESC were defined in agreement with London as follows:

*a*) to review and co-ordinate the joint resources and civilian requirements in essential commodities of the territories (including raw materials for their war industries), in order to make the group as self-supporting as possible; and to exchange relative information with corresponding control organizations in each territory;

*b*) to make recommendations accordingly to the authorities concerned in regard to local production, stocks, and distribution;

*c*) to estimate the balance of any essential requirements which must be imported from outside the group and make recommendations accordingly to the authorities concerned, with a view especially to the best possible use of available shipping;

*d*) to constitute reserve stocks; and

*e*) to facilitate the transport of essential supplies within and between the territories.

The General Committee decided that the business of MESC should be carried on by a small executive committee consisting of the members normally resident in Cairo. At this stage the Center was to be a solely British body.

The most important issue, on which the recommendations of the General Committee were not accepted by London, related to its executive powers. The General Committee proposed that MESC should have power to buy goods and hold stores, and on April 26, 1941, the deputy chairman, Keown-Boyd, cabled to London asking whether it was understood that MESC would be an executive body. He pointed out that if the Center was to ensure priority for military requirements over civilian needs and if the Middle East was to be treated as a single economic unit so as to become as self-sufficient as possible, MESC would need wide executive powers. It must not only have authority to call for information as to production, imports, and stocks in the territories, but must also be able to buy and accumulate stocks, to finance industrial enterprises, and to guarantee purchase of crops at given prices. It would also need power to control imports and to compel Middle East exporting countries to export any available surplus of essential goods to other territories in the area.

These views were considered in London and a reply was sent which narrowly restricted the executive powers conferred on the Center. It was pointed out that it would be politically impossible for a British authority to assume direct control of the imports and exports of independent sovereign states. Powers to buy and accumulate stocks could not be given to the Center but would rest with UKCC, which would be empowered to build up further stocks, in addition to those already held in Egypt, as recommended by MESC and approved by London. The power to guarantee purchase of local crops and to finance the development of local industry could only be exercised with the specific approval of the British Treasury, which preferred that UKCC should be its executive agency in such matters. The powers of the Center were to be limited to the collection of information, recommendations as to priority of imports, and co-ordination of the executive acts of the governments of Middle East territories and other authorities. The strict constitutional position was that neither MESC nor departments in London could require territorial governments to act on any given recommendation; they could only do their best to persuade or induce them to do so. Throughout its existence the influence of the Center rested not on any executive powers conferred on it but on the fact that the controllers of shipping and supplies in London and Washington relied on its recommendations as to the treatment to be accorded to the requests of Middle East governments for facilities. Apart from this indirect source of authority it had to depend on securing the voluntary co-operation of governments and establishing relations of mutual confidence with ministers, officials, and traders in the territories concerned.

As regards the procurement of essential imports, in accordance with an agreement reached between the Ministry of Food and UKCC, it was laid down that foodstuffs such as cereals, oilseeds, and sugar would be bought by UKCC from the Ministry of Food and released on resale to the territories on the recommendation of MESC.

These terms of reference and definition of functions, as agreed in June 1941, continued as MESC's charter, subject to minor amendments, until it came to an end in 1945. However, in July 1942 and again in December 1942 there were changes in the governing body because the Center had become an Anglo-American body by that time.

## CHAPTER 10

# THE MIDDLE EAST SUPPLY CENTER'S FIRST YEAR

Between June and December 1941 there was a critical period before the Middle East Supply Center (MESC) was able to find its feet and begin to operate under its wide terms of reference. In the three months April to June 1941, the Germans had overrun Greece and occupied Crete; the revolt in Iraq had been crushed by a narrow margin; and Syria had passed into Allied occupation. All this time Rommel was strengthening his position in the Western Desert. In the middle of June an unsuccessful attempt was made to drive him back from the frontier of Egypt. The shipping shortage, the closing of the Mediterranean, and the threat of invasion of Britain had prevented despatch of reinforcements to the Middle East on the scale needed for success on all these separate fronts. Above all, shortage of road transport and inadequacy and congestion of ports and railroads were hampering the effective use of such supplies as could be spared to build up an efficient armored force. A vast development of workshops, ports, and transportation facilities was needed if the expected flow of tanks, guns, armored cars, and trucks from the United States was to be handled in a prompt and orderly manner.

On June 4, 1941 the Prime Minister cabled to General Wavell informing him that he had decided to appoint Lieutenant General Sir Robert Haining to a new post with the title "Intendant-General of the Army of the Middle East" (*1*, pp. 347, 793). The object was to relieve General Wavell of some heavy responsibilities in the administration of supplies and transport, and to secure closer co-ordination between the supply organizations of the three services. But according to Wavell's biographer, the navy, army, and air-force supply systems, though in theory independent, were now closely interlocked through the Middle East Provision Office (MEPO) and the MESC over which General Hutchison presided. Moreover, since administrative factors were the limiting ones in all his campaigns, Wavell took the view that it was essential for him and his Deputy Quartermaster General to keep control of them. With little or no staff and "with no means of obtaining data as to the supply situation except through the administrative staffs of the three Services . . . the Intendant-General thus found himself somewhat of a fifth wheel to the Middle East coach" (*2*, p. 431).

A more fruitful and far-reaching decision was taken by the Prime Minister later in the month. On June 29, 1941 Captain Oliver Lyttelton, who had joined the government as President of the Board of Trade in October 1940, was appointed Minister of State in the Middle East with a seat in the War Cabinet. His principal task was to relieve the Commander-in-Chief of extraneous responsibilities and to settle promptly on the spot matters affecting several departments or authorities which had hitherto required reference to London (*1*, p. 349). While no specific mention of civilian supplies or MESC was contained in his instructions, the Minister of State was made responsible for economic and financial warfare and for supervision of the activities of the Intendant-General and of matters relating to Lend-Lease supplies from the United States.

The new Minister of State arrived in Cairo on July 5 accompanied by a senior civil servant, Sir Arthur Rucker, and a Foreign Office counselor, H. L. d'A. Hopkinson. In a few weeks he obtained the services of R. F. Kahn as economic adviser. Kahn, a lecturer in economics at Cambridge and a former pupil of Lord Keynes, had served under Lyttelton as a wartime official in the Board of Trade. Early in July a Middle East War Council was established, consisting of the three Commanders-in-Chief and the ambassadors or principal British authorities in the various Middle East territories with the Minister of State as chairman. The full Council met at infrequent intervals; but through its committees, the most important of which were the Defence Committee and the Supply and Transportation Sub-Committee set up early in August 1941, it acted as the central authority for strategic, political, and economic policy decisions in the Middle East theater of war. The office of the Minister of State functioned as a co-ordinating rather than executive department, analogous to the War Cabinet Offices in London.

Lyttelton was soon convinced of the need to overhaul and strengthen the existing supply organization. At first he proposed that a new supply council should be set up covering South and East Africa as well as the Middle East, with an executive organization under the Intendant-General which would deal with both civil and military supplies and incorporate MESC and the military MEPO. This plan was not favored in London for three reasons. First, it was felt that, though MESC might need strengthening, it had been constituted on the right lines and should be given a longer period of trial in its present form. Second, though closer contact was needed between MESC and MEPO, it would be impracticable to merge them since the supply of munitions and military equipment must remain under the Commander-in-Chief and the War Office. Third, the Middle East could not be autonomous and must continue to depend on the British government, India, or the United States for the great bulk of its requirements. In communicating this decision, the Lord President of the Council added that the most urgent need was to get the Middle East territories to estimate their essential requirements well in advance and to establish centralized control of their imports so as to reduce demands on shipping and ports to the minimum. This was particularly important in the case of Egypt, where civil imports were interfering with prompt and efficient handling of war stores at Suez.

Two steps were now taken by the Minister of State which went far to solve the administrative problem. Through the Supply and Transportation Sub-Committee of the Middle East War Council he was able, as chairman, to co-ordinate and stimulate the activities of the subordinate agencies. This important subcommittee, which met frequently throughout 1941 and 1942, consisted of representatives of the office of the Minister of State, the three fighting services, the British Embassy in Cairo, MESC, the United Kingdom Commercial Corporation (UKCC), the Petroleum Committee, and the local representative of the Ministry of War Transport. Jurisdictional disputes and crossing of wires were now more easily disposed of round the table under the Minister's chairmanship and a new spirit of co-operation and teamwork was engendered. MESC was strengthened by having a high-level policy-making body to direct it, backed by the personal interest and authority of the Minister and the Commanders-in-Chief. This was specially important in its relations with the British Embassy in Cairo and with the Middle East governments. It required a high degree of diplomacy and patience (in which Empson, the Commercial Counsellor, excelled) to bring to bear just the right amount of pressure on the Egyptian government to induce it to forego what it wanted or to take action that it did not want to take, without provoking a political explosion. On such issues the Ambassador and the Minister of State did not always see eye to eye.

The second contribution to the future MESC made by the Minister of State before the end of 1941 was the selection of Paymaster Commander R. G. A. Jackson as its future director-general. Jackson was a young Australian naval officer who found himself at Malta when Italy declared war in 1940, and had distinguished himself as Controller of Supplies under conditions of air bombardment and submarine blockade by sea. His experience had given him unrivaled insight into the problem of reducing civilian imports in an emergency and the need for detailed programing of imports, to ensure obtaining essential supplies on time, as and when ships could be spared to run the blockade. Representing Malta at one of the first meetings of the Middle East Supply Council, he had resisted the suggestion that MESC become responsible for provisioning Malta. In October 1941 he was invited by Lyttleton to examine the problem of provisioning the Middle East and to make suggestions for the reorganization of MESC. In his report he emphasized the need for three things: (*a*) forward planning and licensing of imports; (*b*) stimulation of local production in order to make the area more self-supporting; and (*c*) control of cereals collection and distribution. The Minister was favorably impressed with his report and action soon followed.

In December 1941 the post of Intendant-General was abolished, and in the following month Keown-Boyd resigned from his position as chairman and chief executive officer of MESC. Commander Jackson was appointed Director-General of MESC, and Kahn, economic adviser to the Minister, acted for some months as Deputy Director-General. In March 1942 Lyttelton himself returned to London to become Minister of War Production and was succeeded as Minister of State in the Middle East by R. G. Casey, the Australian Minister in Washington, who took up duty in Cairo in May 1942. During the early months of 1942 Jackson set about building up a staff to deal with MESC's growing burden of responsibilities. He had to face a critical cereals situation, particularly in Egypt and Syria, and to be constantly on the move visiting authorities in each territory, explaining the need for planning and control, and winning their confidence by offering all possible help. He had to exercise to the full not only his administrative powers of organization but his gifts of diplomacy and salesmanship. In a short time he had established good relations with the military authorities, which helped him to get needed staff and facilities with a minimum of delay and formality. They, for their part, looked to MESC to relieve them of the burden of dealing with civilian affairs and for help in clearing the lines of communication needed to reinforce the desert army.

For most of March, April, and May 1942, Jackson was left to act on his own initiative, with no minister in Cairo. During this period his main preoccupations were (*a*) the cereal shortage in Egypt and Syria; (*b*) the conversion of locomotives in Egypt, Palestine, and Sudan from imported coal to locally available oil; (*c*) the introduction or tightening up of import licensing, in order to replace all unessential civilian goods by munitions; and (*d*) the building up of MESC and the recruitment of suitable staff for its headquarters in Cairo and its representation in each Middle East territory. The story of cereals in Egypt and Syria is told in later chapters. The reduction in coal imports made possible by the substitution of oil as railroad fuel contributed an important saving of shipping. From a prewar annual level of 840,000 tons the annual import of coal was progressively reduced to less than 500,000 tons (*3*, p. 997). In addition, a drastic reduction, and for some months complete cessation, of fertilizer imports, which had been more than 500,000 tons before the war, was brought about. These two measures, combined with the cutting out of other nonessential imports, effected a radical improvement in the handling of military supplies. Normal civilian imports into Middle East ports had been about 5 million tons per annum, with a port capacity estimated at some 5.5 million tons. During 1942 more than a million tons of civilian cargoes had been replaced by munitions. By November 1943, at the time of the victory of El Alamein, the military program was running at a rate of more than 5 million tons per annum and civilian imports had been cut by nearly four-fifths to 1.25 million tons (*4*, pp. 171, 179; *5*, p. 204; *6*).

In the middle of May 1942 the new Minister of State in the Middle East, Mr. Casey, arrived in Cairo—none too soon. He came at a time when submarine activity was at its worst and losses of shipping were higher than at any time during the war. The cereal harvest of 1941 had been poor. In Egypt the government had exhausted its reserves of wheat and maize and had had to ask for 40,000 tons from British army stocks to avert famine in the towns. On May 18 the central wheat reserves under MESC control were down to 12,000 tons. In Syria the sale of 100,000 tons of imported wheat, which could ill be spared, had failed to check hoarding and the inflationary rise of prices; and it was widely believed that the new cereal-collection scheme, which the government was being pressed against its will to introduce, would break down through administrative weakness and opposition from the landowners. On May 27 Rommel launched his successful attack in the desert and it looked at one time as if he would advance to the Nile Delta and occupy Alexandria and Cairo.

In June 1942 preparations were made to evacuate Cairo and a

pall of smoke and charred papers from a holocaust of official documents rose over General Headquarters (GHQ). MESC transferred its staff and part of its most valuable records to Jerusalem and did not return to Cairo till October, just before the victory of El Alamein and the start of Montgomery's successful campaign to drive Rommel from North Africa. An eyewitness account of these critical days in Cairo is given by Major General Sir Francis de Guingand, who was at the time Director of Military Intelligence at GHQ (*7*, pp. 125–26):

> To start with, I should say that throughout this period the Egyptians and their officials behaved extremely well. They seemed to appreciate our difficulties and certainly did nothing to increase them, and as far as I know, we got very willing co-operation and help. There was no sign of panic as many had expected. There was a run on the banks, which was only natural. It was a severe test with the enemy within fighter range of Cairo, whilst his guns could be heard distinctly from Alexandria. I was a member of the Mohamed Ali Club, and I made a point of visiting the clubhouse as much as I could just then. I shall always recall, with very few exceptions, the extreme friendliness and the genuine sympathy which I encountered.
>
> The Navy, owing to the nearness of the enemy, were forced to abandon Alexandria as their naval base, only light forces being retained there.
>
> At G.H.Q. I'm afraid a pretty good "flap" did occur for a few days. Risks could not be taken with certain installations, organisations and documents. And so various moves into Palestine and elsewhere were started. In addition, documents were sent away, and departments were told to burn all unimportant papers, in order to make a move easier, if such a contingency ever occurred. It was inevitable that there was a certain amount of alarm and despondency, and the smoke from the various chimneys of the G.H.Q. buildings was an amazing sight. Wherever one walked bits of charred paper came floating past. Later, special incinerators were provided to help with the cremation of these relics. It was extraordinary how much was burnt, and more extraordinary how little any of these papers were missed. Afterwards we all blessed Rommel for making our lives that much easier! Plans were of course prepared for a move of G.H.Q., but luckily the necessity never arose.

By the end of 1942 the Director-General of MESC was able to look back on a year of crises surmounted and objectives realized. Imports had been cut down with growing co-operation from local governments. Replacement of coal by oil had gone well. The cereals situation was still critical, particularly in Persia; but bulk purchase and pooling of imports had been organized by UKCC and wheat-collection schemes had been launched in Egypt and Syria. Good relations had been established with departments in London, and with the army authorities in GHQ. There was an exceptionally close partnership between Jackson and General Sir Wilfred Lindsell, then Lieutenant General in charge of Administration, whom Wavell's biographer describes as "perhaps the best administrative brain produced by the Army in the Second World War" (*2*, p. 180). After Frederick Winant and his colleagues, William Rountree, Marshall MacDuffie, and Ben Thibodeaux, had joined MESC in the second half of 1942, there was growing understanding in Washington and London of the importance of MESC as an instrument of regional planning and Anglo-American co-operation.

MESC had now reached maturity. It had acquired a deserved reputation for what it had accomplished and for its promise of future performance. Valuable experience had been gained and the foundations of a sound organization had been laid. But greater efforts were now demanded to meet the growing shipping stringency. If the Germans were to be driven from North Africa and the Caucasus, every ship that could be spared was needed to carry munitions to the Red Sea and the Persian Gulf. In the 12 months from July 1941 to June 1942 over 600,000 tons of grain had been shipped to the Middle East. During the next 12 months imports of grain were reduced to less than half this amount. One of the factors that made this possible was the success of cereal-collection schemes in Egypt, Syria, Persia, and Iraq (described in later chapters). But meanwhile from London and Washington an insistent call came for more food production in the Middle East and for more effective control of rising prices. In 1943 and 1944 these issues were tackled by a strong combination of British and American talent. It will be seen from the sequel that the goal of expanding production and at the same time checking inflation was to pose some of the most interesting and most intractable of MESC's many problems.

## CITATIONS

*1* W. S. Churchill, *The Second World War: The Grand Alliance* (Houghton Mifflin Co., Boston, 1950).

*2* Major General R. J. Collins, *Lord Wavell* (London, 1948).

*3* Francis Boardman, "Civilian Requirements from War to Peace: The Middle East Supply Center," *Bulletin* (U.S. State Dept.), Dec. 23, 1945.

*4* Guy Hunter, in George Kirk, *The Middle East and the War* (London, 1952).

*5* Frederick Winant, "The Combined Middle East Supply Program," *Bulletin* (U.S. State Dept.), Feb. 26, 1944.

*6* MESC, *The Work of the MESC During the European War* (Cairo, July 1945).

*7* Major General Sir Francis de Guingand, *Operation Victory* (London, Hodder and Stoughton, Ltd., and New York, Charles Scribner's Sons, 1947).

## CHAPTER 11

# ANGLO-AMERICAN CO-OPERATION IN THE MIDDLE EAST SUPPLY CENTER

No official history of the Middle East Supply Center (MESC) has been published. The best short account of its activities written from the British point of view is to be found in a section of *The Middle East in the War*, contributed by Guy Hunter, former chief of MESC's Information Division (*1*, pp. 169–93). Winant (*2*) and Landis (*3*), who were the successive United States chiefs in MESC, published articles which throw interesting light on the American attitude; and Wilmington (*4*) contributed a scholarly piece of research on the Center.

In the spring of 1941 two events occurred which brought the United States into close association with the Middle East. On April 11, 1941, when Italy's naval forces in the Red Sea (nine destroyers and eight submarines) had been put out of action, President Roosevelt was able to declare that the Red Sea and the Gulf of Aden were no longer "combat zones" within the meaning of the Neutrality Act. Thereafter American ships were able to sail round the Cape to Suez at a time when they were still precluded from carrying goods to the United Kingdom or arming themselves in their own defense (*5*, p. 89).

The effect of this decision was soon felt in a growing volume of imports into Egypt not only of tanks, trucks, and munitions for the British armed forces, but also of civilian supplies of all kinds, including nonessential and luxury goods. There had been a growing scarcity of the latter, owing to the closing of the Mediterranean and the cutting off of normal sources of supply, first in continental Europe and then to an increasing extent in the United Kingdom. In order to ease the burden on shipping and supplies from the United Kingdom, it was decided in London in June 1941 that essential civil requirements for the Middle East should in future be obtained so far as possible from the United States. Under pressure of war needs Britain thus took the initiative in restricting her traditional exports to the Middle East of steel, engineering products, and textiles, which in spite of shipping shortage and licensing controls still amounted to about 20,000 tons per month. In October the United Kingdom Commercial Corporation (UKCC) mission in New York was asked to help in the supply of essential goods by putting Middle East importers in touch with United States suppliers and by finding space on ships controlled by the British Ministry of War Transport. But since there was no licensing or control of exports from the United States to the Middle East at that time, nonessential goods were carried without restriction in United States tonnage. This not only led to a drain on dollars from the sterling-area pool at a time when the United Kingdom government was coming to the end of its dollar resources and scraping the barrel to finance its own essential needs of munitions and food, but also intensified the congestion at ports on the Red Sea and hampered the speedy unloading of urgently needed munitions. One of MESC's first tasks was to regulate this flood of imports and to help reduce the huge and disorderly dump of civilian goods at Suez.

The second crucial event was the passing of the Lend-Lease Act in March 1941. Its application to the Middle East was first discussed in May 1941, when W. Averell Harriman came to London as Lend-Lease expediter with the rank of Minister and established his headquarters in Grosvenor Square. After talks with the Prime Minister at Chequers—he was there on the night that the *Hood* was sunk by the *Bismarck*—he flew to Cairo early in June (*5*, p. 308). Churchill cabled to Wavell on June 4 (*5*, p. 794) saying that he had asked President Roosevelt if Harriman could visit the Middle East because of "the great mass and importance of the American supplies, and the fact that the war in the Middle East cannot be conducted at its needful scale without them. . . . It would be disastrous if large accumulations of American supplies arrived without efficient measures for their reception and without large-scale planning for the future."

In the discussions that took place in Cairo, the question of military Lend-Lease supplies proceeded smoothly. Harriman's assessment of the strategic position in the Middle East and the stimulus he was able to give to the programing and procurement of munitions from the United States made an important contribution to the Eighth Army's first successful offensive against Rommel in November 1941. In December 1941, immediately after the United States entered the war, its War Department stopped 30 ships loaded with vital Lend-Lease supplies for the Middle East. Harriman intervened for their release by sending an urgent plea to Harry Hopkins at the White House (*6*, p. 440).

But the application of Lend-Lease to civilian supplies raised many complicated issues. Discussions on procedure continued with the American authorities for several months. Under the terms of the

Lend-Lease Act, Congress had authorized the President to deliver supplies to nations which in his opinion could best use them to ensure the defense of the United States and the defeat of aggressor nations. In the Middle East it was recognized that supply of essential food and other civilian goods was justified, even though the Middle East countries were not at war, on the strategic ground that maintenance of law and order and prevention of famine and civil unrest were vital to the success of the Allied arms. But, in order to screen demands and prevent abuses, a strict scrutiny of requirements and control of distribution would be necessary. Lend-Lease administrators had to be able to satisfy Congress that supplies were in fact used for the purpose intended and were not diverted to other ends or made a source of private profit. This opened up the prospect of detailed intervention in the internal economies of Middle East countries and attempts to prescribe measures of control which governments might be unable to enforce. Moreover, it was feared that if the Americans were to deal direct with individual governments, as they were fully entitled and indeed required to do, there was risk of duplicating existing arrangements and undermining the efforts of MESC to centralize the system of programing and supply for the whole area. This would be particularly serious in the case of such basic foodstuffs as cereals and sugar, where the principle of a single buyer and a central reserve had with difficulty been established by MESC.

It was soon clear to both sides that the best way to find a solution for these difficulties would be for the Americans to work in the closest contact with MESC, thus ensuring a co-ordinated supply program for the whole Middle East. On the British side, it was hoped that American participation in the Center would make it easier to ensure that United States shipping space was used to the best advantage by restricting less essential American exports to the Middle East, and, further, that requests for allocation to the Middle East of goods in short supply would carry more weight in Washington if they were backed by a joint body.

Early in 1942 an American mission headed by General Russell Maxwell arrived in Cairo to deal with military Lend-Lease supplies, and in February 1942 it was proposed that United States representatives concerned with civilian Lend-Lease should be associated with MESC. The proposal was accepted in principle both by the Office of Lend-Lease Administration (OLLA) and by the State Department; but action was delayed some weeks by a difference of opinion as to which department should nominate the senior American representative. Finally it was announced in May 1942 that Winant of the State

Department would be the chief American delegate with Rountree of OLLA as his principal assistant. The Board of Economic Warfare (BEW), as the agency responsible for licensing United States exports, nominated MacDuffie. Later, in response to a request from MESC for an agricultural expert, the State Department obtained the services of Thibodeaux of the United States Department of Agriculture.

Winant left Washington in July for discussions in London and took up his appointment in Cairo in August 1942. Meanwhile Mr. Kirk, the United States Minister in Egypt, attended meetings of the Middle East Supply Council at the invitation of Mr. Casey and arranged for preliminary American participation in the work of MESC. Shortly after the arrival of Winant in Cairo, it was arranged that he should serve as chairman of the Executive Committee of MESC and represent MESC on the Supply and Transportation Sub-Committee of the Middle East War Council.

In January 1943 MESC was listed along with the Combined Food Board (CFB) and other joint war agencies established in Washington and London. Its functions and composition as a joint Anglo-American body were officially described as follows (7, p. 76):

MIDDLE EAST SUPPLY CENTER

(United States and Great Britain)

LOCATION:

Cairo

ESTABLISHMENT AND PURPOSE:

The Middle East Supply Center was set up in Cairo in April 1941 to organize the provisioning of the Middle East with civilian supplies. Its main functions are (1) to review and coordinate the joint resources and civilian requirements in essential commodities of the territories (including raw materials required for their war industries), in order to make the Middle East as self-supporting as possible, and to exchange relevant information with corresponding control organizations in each territory; and (2) to estimate the balance of any essential requirements which must be imported from outside of the Middle East and make recommendations accordingly to the authorities concerned, with a view especially to the best use of available shipping. Its activities cover the following territories: Egypt, Sudan, Turkey (only as far as bulk commodities are concerned), Syria, Lebanon, Ethiopia, Palestine, Trans-Jordan, Malta, Cyprus, Aden, British Somaliland, Iran, Iraq, Eritrea, Saudi Arabia, and occupied enemy territory in East Africa. The British East Africa territories collaborate in furnishing supplies.

A policy committee functions in London known as the Middle East Supplies Committee.

MEMBERSHIP OF EXECUTIVE COMMITTEE IN CAIRO:

*United States*:

Frederick Winant, *Chairman and Principal Civilian Representative*

Gen. Russell Maxwell, United States Army, *Principal Military Representative*

Col. Samuel Claybaugh, United States Army, *Deputy for Military Representative*

*Great Britain*:

R. G. A. Jackson, *Director-General of the Center*

Sir Arthur Rucker, Secretary to the British Minister of State

E. H. Murrant, Representative in the Middle East of British Ministry of War Transport

MEMBERSHIP OF MIDDLE EAST SUPPLIES COMMITTEE IN LONDON:

*United States*:

W. Averell Harriman, Lend-Lease Coordinator

James W. Riddleberger, Second Secretary of American Embassy in London, *alternate*

*Great Britain*:

Capt. the Rt. Hon. Harry Crookshank, British Financial Secretary of the Treasury

MESC was thus recognized as a regional offshoot of the combined boards, and its activities were closely interwoven with the specialized agencies concerned with co-ordination of the war effort. Its work of programing Middle East imports and screening demands for tonnage brought it into relation with the control of shipping exercised by the Combined Shipping Adjustment Board, established in January 1942, with Rear Admiral Land and Sir Arthur Salter in Washington and Lord Leathers and Harriman in London as its members. For its supplies of food and agricultural requisites, such as fertilizers and seeds, MESC was dependent on allocations made or approved by CFB, set up in June 1942 with four American members (Claude Wickard, P. A. Appleby, L. A. Wheeler, R. B. Schwenger) and four British (R. H. Brand, Edward Twentyman, M. I. Hutton, Eric Roll).

In London the day-to-day work of dealing with MESC business was entrusted to a special office in the Ministry of War Transport under the direction of Max Nicholson. In March 1942 this was designated the Supply Section for the Middle East. Apart from high-level correspondence between the Minister of State or the Director-General with the chairman of the Middle East Supplies Committee all communications between MESC and London were handled by Nicholson and his staff. Co-ordination of policy on questions relating to civilian supplies for the Middle East was undertaken by an interdepartmental committee under the chairmanship of Captain Harry Crookshank.

In Washington it had been proposed by Winant as early as July 1942 that a joint Anglo-American agency should be attached to the

State Department, but this proposal fell through mainly because of the opposition from BEW, whose co-operation was necessary since it controlled licenses to export goods to the Middle East. Owing to the inability of the various departments in Washington to reach agreement on a combined agency, a British Middle East Supplies Committee (Washington) was set up under the British Supply Council in November 1942. Representatives of all the British supply missions sat on this committee and were often able through their contacts with United States departments to ensure that the claims of the Middle East put forward by UKCC mission in New York were not overlooked. But they soon found that the volume and complexity of Middle East business was such that stronger machinery was required, and early in 1943 they drew up a plan for a joint MESC agency in Washington with a liaison group in New York. For some months BEW continued to oppose this proposal and it was not till September 1943, when it was satisfied that its representation in the Middle East had been sufficiently safeguarded, that it agreed to join. On October 1, 1943 a Combined Agency for Middle East Supplies (CAMES) was set up in Washington. This body had a policy committee and an executive committee of which Winant, who had by then returned to the State Department, was chairman. The executive committee included representatives of OLLA, BEW, the British Supply Council, and the British Colonial Supply Mission; on the policy committee the War Shipping Administration and the War Production Board were also represented. It was some months before a liaison group was formed in New York and until then the UKCC Mission acted for CAMES there.

This brief account of the machinery of Anglo-American co-operation may be supplemented by some comments on the difficulties that arose in the working of MESC as a combined agency.

Since the British were always in the majority in MESC and had set it up under a British Director-General before the Americans arrived, both sides tended to regard it as primarily a British body with the British bearing the main burden of responsibility and their American colleagues watching and criticizing. Moreover, both British and American officials were accountable for their actions to departments in London and Washington with special interests which could not always be easily reconciled. These divergent interests were most marked in the field of exports to the Middle East.

Before the war Britain had been the principal supplier of manufactured goods to the Middle East. In Egypt and to a less extent elsewhere there were close commercial and financial ties with Britain, and the existence of British firms in Alexandria and Cairo gave Britain a predominant position both as exporter and importer. The United States was not a large importer of Egyptian products and, except for motor cars and agricultural machinery, had not been important as an exporter. It has already been mentioned that from 1941 onward British exports to the Middle East had to be drastically curtailed, partly to economize shipping and partly to enable British industry to concentrate on the production of munitions. As early as June 1941 MESC was warned by London that Middle East countries would have to look to the United States to provide essential requirements which they had hitherto obtained from Britain. Moreover, after the introduction of Lend-Lease Britain was precluded by the terms of the agreement from exporting goods manufactured from, or similar to, goods supplied under Lend-Lease. The necessity for this wartime switch in sources of supply gave American exporters an unrivaled opportunity for opening up new markets for their products in the Middle East.

From the very beginning of its activities MESC was bound to be a thorn in the side of American exporters for the simple reason that its main duty was to restrict and regulate Middle East imports. Very high prices were offered in the Middle East for American goods, and strong protests were lodged in Washington against what sometimes appeared to the private firms concerned to be unwarranted and high-handed interference by the British with their legitimate trade. Even when it had become a joint Anglo-American agency, the Center was sometimes accused of being a British tool used to discriminate against American goods and of employing Lend-Lease goods to strengthen British trade connections (*8*). The hostility of private traders was intensified when government procurement was adopted for many essential goods, including not only iron and steel, trucks and farm machinery, but foodstuffs, textiles, and medical supplies.

It was not until J. M. Landis succeeded Winant as senior United States representative in MESC in September 1943 that this issue came to the fore. Indeed, during 1942 there was considerable impatience in Washington with American merchants who tried to pre-empt cargo space or circumvent MESC licensing controls—at a time when Rommel was threatening to invade Egypt and force his way through the Middle East to join up with German armies in south Russia. But gradually, during 1943 and 1944, as Rommel was driven back and the shipping shortage became less acute, the American official attitude stiffened on the vexing questions of trade restrictions and discrimination against dollar imports. Most Middle East countries either belonged to the sterling area or drew on the Bank of England for conversion of their sterling balances into dollars; when the British Treasury asked them to restrict dollar imports on balance-of-payment grounds, a clash between the British and American viewpoints was only natural. Landis, who resigned early in 1945, publicly explained some of the difficulties he had experienced in defending the legitimate interests of American traders in his account of MESC (*3*, pp. 64–72).

Some difficulties also arose owing to the fact that Landis was appointed not only senior United States representative in MESC but also American Director of Economic Operations in the Middle East with the personal rank of Minister. The American Economic Mission to the Middle East, which he established in April 1944, served a useful purpose by co-ordinating all aspects of American economic policy in the area and substituting a regional approach for the traditional country-by-country approach. But the Mission also undertook supervision and criticism of the Center and reported its findings and recommendations direct to departments in Washington. This tended to bypass and sometimes to challenge decisions on policy reached either by the Combined Agency for Middle East Supplies in Washington, or by the Middle East Supplies Committee in London, or by the Supply and Transportation Sub-Committee of the Middle East War Council in Cairo. As a result, some friction and misunderstanding arose, which was sometimes accentuated by Landis' forceful personality and distinctive outlook. If Winant was regarded in some circles in Washington as being too pro-British, Landis gained a reputation among his British colleagues for being a consistent and outspoken opponent of British imperialism.

As Wilmington points out in his reappraisal of MESC (*4*, p. 162), the postwar problem of the dollar shortage cast its shadow before and hastened the dissolution of MESC. He even suggests that British officials, who favored some discrimination against American imports, "felt that they were acting in the United States' interest as well, since the latter's interests would not be served by a disastrous decimation of the dollar reserves of the Commonwealth . . . "; and he adds that it could "be claimed that by keeping down dollar purchases in British-controlled areas during the war an ultimate saving had been accomplished for the American taxpayer in his contribution to the European Recovery Program . . ." But these are the views of a disinterested historian writing eight years after what he calls the "prolonged internecine struggle which culminated in the resignation of

Mr. Landis early in 1945" (*4*, p. 164). It is doubtful whether anyone, British or American, could visualize the full extent of the postwar problem of dollar shortage and excessive sterling balances; and there were only a few, among whom can perhaps be counted Landis himself, who began to understand something of the significance of the sterling area and its relation to normal channels of world trade.

In retrospect the difficulties encountered in Anglo-American co-operation, mainly in connection with trade and payments, fade into insignificance compared with the teamwork and mutual understanding established in other spheres—particularly in the field of food and agriculture. It was here that MESC met its greatest challenge. The organization worked well mainly because its principal officers had a clear picture of what they were trying to do and were able to win confidence and make themselves listened to in London and Washington. Anyone who had experience of the friction sometimes generated by conflicts of jurisdiction and interdepartmental rivalry in the two capitals could not fail to be struck with the co-operative spirit and single-minded interest in the job that prevailed in Cairo. The importance of the work that MESC was doing appealed to the most crusty and disillusioned of its temporary officials, but the majority of its staff were neither. They were either experts engaged in a job which gave them greater scope than they had before or administrators with a sense of mission and a flair for getting things done. Each in his own way found that working together in MESC yielded a satisfaction that was enhanced rather than diminished by different national backgrounds. As an experiment in joint Anglo-American administration, MESC must be pronounced a success.

## CITATIONS

*1* Guy Hunter, in George Kirk, *The Middle East in the War* (London, 1952).

*2* Frederick Winant, "The Combined Middle East Supply Program," *Bulletin* (U.S. State Dept.), Feb. 26, 1944.

*3* J. M. Landis, "Anglo-American Cooperation in the Middle East," *Annals of the American Academy of Political and Social Science*, July 1945.

*4* M. W. Wilmington, "The Middle East Supply Center, A Reappraisal," *Middle East Journal* (Middle East Inst., Washington, D.C.), Spring 1952.

*5* W. S. Churchill, *The Second World War: The Grand Alliance* (Houghton Mifflin Co., Boston, 1950).

*6* R. E. Sherwood. *Roosevelt and Hopkins* (New York, 1948).

*7* *Bulletin* (U.S. State Dept.), Jan. 16, 1943.

*8* *Business Week*, Dec. 4, 1943.

CHAPTER 12

# THE STAFFING OF THE MIDDLE EAST SUPPLY CENTER

Meanwhile, important developments had been taking place in building up a joint staff in Cairo. In October 1941, when the total staff employed was only 28, with less than 10 senior executives, authority was sought by Keown-Boyd to double these numbers. On April 19, 1942, when the staff employed had risen to 94, Jackson put forward for approval in London a proposed new establishment consisting of a director, deputy director, secretary-general, 5 assistant directors, 36 executives, 22 assistant executives, and 92 clerks, stenographers, and messengers, making 158 in all. This was agreed to early in June. By July 1942 there were five divisions of the Middle East Supply Center (MESC), each under an assistant director: (1) Food Supplies, (2) Materials, (3) Shipping and Programming, (4) Industrial Investigations, and (5) Secretariat.

About the same time General Maxwell assigned Colonel Samuel Claybaugh as the first United States representative to work with the MESC, and the State Department announced that Winant and Rountree would be leaving Washington in July. The State Department was reported at the time to be undecided whether to send agricultural experts.

During the summer of 1942 the organization and staffing of the Center were examined by a Treasury expert, N. Baliol-Scott, who submitted his report with detailed recommendations to the Ministry of War Transport on October 3, 1942. He emphasized three factors that gave the work of MESC a degree of complexity that had not always been fully recognized in London. First, there was the distinction between the Middle East as a whole and the particular territories included in it: Egypt's problems were often more pressing and of greater military importance than those of other territories, but MESC had to hold the balance even and be equipped to look after the needs of all. Second, the differences in political status and relationship to the British government of the various territories had to be constantly borne in mind and added greatly to the work of the Center. Third, it was not possible to draw a clear distinction between military and civil affairs. Apart from the general strategic importance of civil security and political stability there was a direct military interest in questions of civilian supplies and transportation. Consultation with, and co-operation of, the military authorities were needed at every stage if MESC was to achieve its objectives. In addition to these difficulties, which required for their solution a rare combination of diplomacy and expertise, MESC had to meet the wishes and carry out the policies of several departments and agencies in London and Washington. Within a single organization were comprised what might be regarded as regional offices of the Ministries of Food, of Supply, and of War Transport, and the Board of Trade in London, and of the Office of Lend-Lease Administration, the Board of Economic Warfare, and the United States Department of Agriculture in Washington. To cap all, MESC had no executive powers of its own and could only get things done through the instrumentality of territorial governments or, in a limited field, of the United Kingdom Commercial Corporation.

Baliol-Scott paid a tribute to the efficiency with which MESC had organized control of imports and programing of civilian requirements; but he urged that in future more attention should be paid to development of local resources, equitable distribution of goods in short supply, and expansion of interterritorial trade. The function of the Center in these matters was to formulate plans after thorough investigation, to persuade governments to adopt them, and to help in their execution by providing technical advice. It could not itself undertake development projects or enforce schemes of collection, allocation, or rationing without encroaching on the jurisdiction of governments. In the first year and a half of its existence it had rightly concentrated on using control of shipping as a lever to persuade governments to regulate imports. The time had now come when increasing emphasis needed to be placed on expansion of production and more efficient mobilization of local resources. In such important matters as cereal collection and bread rationing this would involve bringing pressure on governments to change their policies on what they were bound to regard as their own domestic affairs.

To make progress in this difficult field, MESC had to be adequately represented in each territory. In Egypt, Persia, Iraq, and Saudi Arabia, the MESC staff was attached to the British embassies. In Syria and Lebanon, close liaison was maintained through the economic adviser of the Spears Mission and his staff. In Palestine, MESC had its own representative for some months in 1942, but later the government preferred to deal direct with the Center in Cairo. Similarly in Transjordan, Aden, and Sudan there was no local MESC staff. In the ex-enemy territories—Eritrea, Libya, and Cyrenaica—MESC officers were attached to the Civil Affairs Administration. The system had to be flexible and underwent changes from time to time; and—a most important point—it was supplemented by a frequent exchange of visits between the headquarters staff and territorial representatives.

Baliol-Scott's report was well received in London and within a few weeks general approval was obtained for a final reorganization and expansion of the staff. To relieve the Director-General, Jackson, of the heavy burden of administration and co-ordination and to act during his visits to London, Washington, and Middle East territories, a Deputy Director-General, Dr. E. E. Bailey, was sent out from London. In due course five directors were appointed: Keith Murray for Food and Agriculture, Marshall MacDuffie for Materials, Harold Elliot for Transport, and two others for Medical Supplies and Programming of Imports. The first two divisions were subdivided into supply and production sections each under an assistant director. The production sections were staffed by specialists who spent much of their time visiting the territories and promoting expansion of production. The Programming of Imports Division co-ordinated import requirements and loading programs, and supplied the Center with information and statistics. For a time there was a separate directorate for Interterritorial Trade but this was later merged with Programming.

By the time Winant left the Middle East in April 1943, the number of Americans employed was disappointingly small. It had proved difficult in 1942, when new wartime agencies were being rapidly built up in Washington, to recruit American personnel to go to the Middle East. Even when Winant returned to Washington, he had to reply to Jackson that a good economic statistician would be difficult to obtain, and he could do nothing to meet the request for a rationing expert from the United States to be attached to MESC. These posts had been suggested in view of the forthcoming conferences on statistics and rationing referred to later. It was not until Landis succeeded Winant in September 1943 that senior American staff began to be recruited in considerable numbers. A year later the American Economic Mission to the Middle East, of which Landis was Director, had a staff of 109 from the United States, of whom 27 had been assigned to work in MESC.

Landis was accompanied by Livingstone Short as special representative to deal with Lend-Lease supplies, which in 1944 consisted largely of medical supplies, tires, and agricultural machinery. It was agreed with Landis that, so far as possible, the senior posts in MESC would be equally divided; and eventually the divisions concerned with transport, medical supplies, and programs had American directors, while those concerned with food, materials, and administration had British directors. Early in 1945, an American Deputy Director-General, George Woodbridge, was appointed. Americans were also put in charge of MESC territorial offices in Persia, Iraq, Saudi Arabia, and Ethiopia.

For a year or more the important division concerned with food and agriculture had been undermanned. In the original setup the small staff available had as much as they could do to deal with Middle East food-import programs. In Egypt the long-drawn-out and difficult negotiations about fertilizers, cotton acreage, and cereal supply were largely conducted by Empson and Carver in the British Embassy; and it was not till Jackson took over at the beginning of 1942 that MESC began to look about for a man with wide enough experience to fill the post of director of the division concerned with food and agriculture. In this they were fully backed, indeed prompted, by Nicholson in London. In May 1942 Jackson and Kahn reported that they had made many enquiries in Egypt but that no one had been able to suggest an expert of the type needed. It seemed that the right man would have to be found in the United Kingdom or the United States. In June, Nicholson returned to the charge, expressing concern about MESC being so short of staff on the agricultural side. From the shipping angle it was essential to step up food production. He mentioned the names of two Americans in Persia and one British official in Cyprus; but after enquiries by Cairo none of these was found to be available. Then toward the end of July 1942 Nicholson was able to report that they had been able to secure the release from the Royal Air Force (RAF) of Flight Lieutenant Keith Murray to fill the vacancy of assistant director in charge of the food section.

Murray, who later became Director of the Food Supplies and Production Division of MESC and played a key role in wartime developments in the Middle East, had been one of Britain's leading agricultural economists in the Agricultural Economics Research Institute at Oxford. During the first year of war he had worked in the Economics Division of the Ministry of Food, and had specialized in working out with the agricultural departments the application of wartime controls of collection, distribution, and prices of farm products. He had been released at his own request at the end of 1940 to take a commission in the RAF. Seven months later, on the understanding that his appointment would be temporary, he was persuaded by Nicholson and Sir Arthur Street, Permanent Secretary of the Air Ministry, to go out to the Middle East.

Nicholson had in fact been successful in arranging that L. K. Elmhirst, Murray, and later Thibodeaux of the United States Department of Agriculture should tour the Middle East as a special agricultural mission and visit Egypt, Palestine, Syria, Turkey, Iraq, and possibly Persia. Elmhirst was due to return to London in November and Murray was to remain in MESC. During this three-month tour, Murray gained first-hand acquaintance with the urgent problem of collecting enough cereals off farms to feed the towns—a problem that was familiar to him, though not in so acute a form, in the British Ministry of Food. Murray's temporary release from the RAF expired on January 28, and MESC was told that if he remained in Cairo he would have to resign his commission. This he was not prepared to do, and the Air Ministry was persuaded to extend his release for six months provided they would be free to recall him at the end of this period.

Meanwhile Harriman had stated in London that there was likely to be a four-month delay before further American agricultural specialists could be found for MESC. Thibodeaux, who returned to the United States in January, undertook to obtain the services of an assistant director for food production, an agronomist, an agricultural economist versed in problems of farm management, and an agricultural statistician. In addition he agreed to try to find an agricultural adviser to work for MESC in Persia and an agricultural attaché for the United States Embassy at Ankara. It was hoped to fill the remaining posts in Murray's division with British personnel.

Here Murray had a piece of luck. During a visit to the Rehovoth Agricultural Research Station near Tel Aviv in Palestine he heard from its director, Dr. I. Elazari-Volcani, that a young RAF officer from the neighboring aerodrome at Lydda had shown a keen interest in the station's research. This officer turned out to be Dunstan Skilbeck, who had been lecturer in agriculture at Oxford University. Murray and Jackson soon got in touch with him, application was made for his release, and within little more than a month Skilbeck arrived in Cairo to fill the post of assistant director for agricultural development. Besides Murray and Skilbeck, three other commissioned officers with special agricultural background were obtained by MESC. Jock Fleming, who came from the Gezira Cotton Scheme in Sudan, and G. L. Bailey, who had had long experience in Egypt and Greece, also joined the agricultural section. It was not until the end of April 1943 that Jackson heard that Washington was planning to send out four or five agricultural specialists. Later in the year, after Landis had arrived, there were eight Americans, out of a total of 20 in MESC, posted in the division concerned with food supplies and agricultural production. The most outstanding of these was R. S. Kifer, who was made assistant director for agricultural production.

Finally, mention should be made of the distinguished scientists, Dr. B. A. Keen, of Rothamsted, and Dr. E. B. Worthington, director of the Fresh Water Biological Association, who came out as a scientific advisory mission to MESC, spent several months in 1943 and 1944 touring the Middle East, and attended the important Conference on Middle East Agricultural Development. The mission became Anglo-American when it was later joined by Dr. H. B. Allen, educational director of the Near East Foundation. Their reports constitute the first and most comprehensive regional survey that had ever been attempted of the main scientific and technical problems facing the Middle East, and have been useful not only to specialists and administrators in the area but also to United States, United Nations, and Food and Agriculture Organization experts concerned with technical-assistance projects. These postwar publications appeared in 1946 after MESC itself had been disbanded, and may prove to be its most lasting and fruitful legacy to the Middle East.

## CHAPTER 13

# CONTROL OF IMPORTS AND BULK PURCHASE

Control of imports was exercised in two ways: first, by the licensing of private traders; and second, by bulk purchase and pooling of imports through the agency of the United Kingdom Commercial Corporation (UKCC). The latter was the more important in the food field and the former in the case of textiles, engineering products, and a vast range of miscellaneous items—from refrigerators to surgical instruments—which fall outside the scope of this book.

When the Middle East Supply Center (MESC) started, it had to see that there was machinery set up for restricting imports. Palestine and Cyprus were already licensing imports; by August 1941, licensing was enforced in Sudan, and by November 1, import licensing was introduced in Egypt. Traders wishing to buy goods from overseas had to obtain an import license from their own government and had to show that the goods were in some way essential. If the license was granted, it was forwarded to MESC for further review. In some cases the importer would be told to buy from another source, either because the goods would be easier to obtain there or because the sea journey would be shorter. Approved licenses would be sent on to the supplying country with MESC approval stamped on them. In the early days of licensing, a steady stream of traders queued up at MESC's offices to press their cases; but soon a firm rule was laid down that applications for licenses must be made only to governments and not directly to MESC. Frequently an order placed in Britain had to be switched to the United States, or vice versa. Supply and shipping considerations often had to override private trade connections.

Soon it was found that a closer link was needed between MESC and the licensing authorities of the various governments; in some countries joint licensing committees were established on which MESC's representative would sit. MESC thus established contacts throughout the Middle East either by sending its own mission or by working through the British and American embassies. By this means British and American personnel came to know ministers and officials and to understand their special difficulties. At the same time the harassed officials realized that MESC was not simply out to prevent them getting what they wanted but was, in fact, acting as their advocate in getting a share of a controlled pool of supplies and tonnage. Much of the hardest and most fruitful work was done by joint licensing committees where both sides met to examine specific cases.

Soon there had to be grafted upon the licensing system the preparation of semiannual and annual import programs for controlling the total quantity of goods and tonnage allotted to the Middle East. These programs were built up from discussions in the territories and brought together in Cairo where they were compared, scrutinized, and frequently sent back for revision or further justification. Before being forwarded by MESC the combined civilian programs were discussed with the British and American military authorities in Cairo. Most civilian goods, apart from bulk cargoes of grain, came in ships carrying munitions and supplies for the armed forces, and every extra ton of civilian cargo, except in cases where careful stowage improved the loading of ships, meant one less ton with which to fight Rommel or to aid Russia. For wheat and other staple foods, military and civilian imports were combined in a single program.

In due course the military and civilian programs were sent to London and Washington to be combined into one worldwide shipping program. But before this was done the Ministry of War Transport, as MESC's parent body, scrutinized the program in relation to the latest shipping forecast and submitted it to the Combined Food Board and other supply authorities in London and Washington through the Supply Section for the Middle East (SSME) in London and the Combined Agency for Middle East Supplies in Washington. When the Middle East program had been screened, processed, and cleared by all these agencies, final figures were put forward in a supply-shipping program submitted to heads of states, who decided how many ships could be allocated for military operations. Thus, in October 1942 and again in February 1943, drastic cuts were imposed on programs already approved, in order to release required shipping for the North African campaign.

In all this complicated procedure the important point was that the Middle East had a powerful friend at court in the person of Nicholson and his SSME in the Ministry of War Transport itself. Throughout the war all telegrams to London from MESC went through SSME—housed not only in the same building but in the same corridor with the officials who were responsible for fixing the employment of all dry-cargo tonnage in the London shipping pool and who were in hourly contact with their opposite numbers in Washington. Thus every opportunity could be taken of dovetailing Middle East supplies with military and other shipping movements. This gave the Middle East something of a privileged position in the discussions that went on in the Combined Shipping Adjustment Board. While it was virtually impossible to import into the Middle East anything not included in an approved program, Middle East governments and traders were fortunate in having at their disposal machinery which ensured that facilities were nearly always granted for whatever imports were approved. If this had not been the case, it would have been almost out of the question for individual governments to undertake the burdensome and time-consuming task of processing their requirements through all the different bodies which might raise questions and objections.

The anomaly of having MESC attached to, and on the vote of, the Ministry of War Transport was often pointed out in London. Several times it was suggested that the Center should be taken away from the Ministry of War Transport and sponsored by some other department, but it never proved possible to find a more logical point of attachment or to find another department willing and able to take on the troublesome work involved. The fact that there was no breakdown in the flow of supplies to the Middle East, and that famine was averted, was in no small measure due to the fact that MESC was an offshoot of the department responsible for shipping, with close contacts with the various supply authorities both in London and Washington.

## BULK PURCHASE AND PRICE PROBLEMS

The task of feeding the Middle East, which meant primarily maintaining a regular daily supply of bread and flour for the towns, was complicated by the fact that MESC and the authorities in London and Washington had to deal with twenty or more different governments with separate administrations and independent fiscal and monetary systems. MESC was set up in the first instance to unify and co-ordinate the area's shipping requirements; but if the food supply of the towns was to be assured, control and programing of imported supplies could not be divorced from control over home-produced supplies. Policies adopted in regard to collection, distribution, and prices of cereals and other foods varied widely in the different territories, and it was beyond the power of MESC or of the authorities in London and Washington to do much more than offer advice and sometimes, as in the case of the Office des Céréales Panifiables (OCP) in Syria (see chapter 17), lend personnel to serve in the actual administration of control.

To round off the picture of MESC's operations, it may be useful to anticipate what is said in later chapters about particular countries by illustrating some of the complications that arose from the necessity of trying to impose a strait jacket of wartime control on a number of independent economies, bedeviled by shortage of supplies and varying degrees of inflation.

In principle MESC was compelled to treat the area so far as possible as a single unit. This meant that it had to aggregate total requirements, allocate supplies as fairly as possible, reduce demands on shipping to the minimum, make the area as self-supporting as possible, and arrange for surpluses in one country to be sent to neighboring countries where there was a deficit. In the case of cereals the first step was the organization of centralized buying of imported supplies through the agency of UKCC and the pooling of reserve stocks under the control of MESC. Next in importance were organized collection schemes, combined with efforts to increase the area under cereals and expand production in spite of a reduced supply of fertilizers. Last, and not least in importance or in inherent difficulty, were the complicated negotiations and maneuvers needed to transfer surpluses from one Middle East country to another, at prices that would be accepted by both parties. Since this often resulted in one or other or both governments having to bear a financial loss, or else in leaving UKCC or the British Treasury to provide a subsidy at the expense of the British taxpayer, the issues at stake more than once strained MESC's ingenuity and patience almost to breaking point. No satisfactory solution was ever evolved, fundamentally because it was politically impossible to devise any system of sharing the financial costs of the war or even to work out a rough-and-ready system of mutual aid between Middle East countries. As the Lebanese delegate pointed out at the Middle East Financial Conference in April 1944, the radical remedy for divergent price levels would have been economic and fiscal union. The alternative—free markets and free movement of exchange rates—was equally unthinkable. Inevitably, therefore, MESC's plans for saving shipping and checking inflation by pooling reserves and centralizing distribution of supplies encountered formidable obstacles, which were never wholly removed and at times even threatened a temporary breakdown in the supply of bread grain and flour to the towns.

Centralized buying developed gradually out of an early decision to build up reserve stocks in the hands of UKCC. In February 1941, even before MESC came into existence, stockpiling in the Middle

East had been advocated in a joint memorandum drawn up by the Ministry of Shipping (later to become the Ministry of War Transport), the Colonial Office, the Ministry of Economic Warfare, and UKCC. It was urged that a central stockpile of essential commodities was needed to ensure against nonarrival of cargoes due to losses at sea or diversion of ships, to meet unforeseen emergency demands, and to serve as a strategic reserve for use in any territory as the military or political situation changed. It was also intended to facilitate barter deals, which the Ministry of Economic Warfare was at that time trying to carry through in Balkan countries, and to meet the requirements of Greece and Yugoslavia without risk of enemy seizure in the event of invasion of those countries. Above all, it was felt that stockpiling would have great political significance in the Middle East in strengthening confidence in the British cause and promoting co-operation, or at least acquiescence, in the war effort. Public opinion and morale in the Arab world were recognized to be of primary strategic importance at a time when the fortunes of war were favoring the Axis powers.

Once the policy of building up reserves had been approved by ministers, UKCC was selected as the instrument to undertake purchase, storage, and sale of stocks. The commodities originally proposed were rubber, tin, copper, chemicals, medical supplies, and—among foodstuffs—sugar, tea, coffee, and preserved foods. The amount to be held in reserve was to be three months' requirements. Stockpiling of cereals was rejected at this date on the ground that no shipping could be spared for sending additional supplies over and above the minimum already provided for in the deficit countries' programs.

At the first meeting of the General Committee of MESC in April 1941, Keown-Boyd outlined the plans approved in London and invited representatives from the territories to submit detailed suggestions. In June a subcommittee on stockpiling was appointed which considered the list of commodities to be covered and urgently pressed for the addition of cereals. It suggested that the phrase "three months' reserve" should be defined as "the quantities which would have to be imported during the period of three months succeeding any given date during which a complete cessation of shipments might cut off all imports." This definition was designed to take account of seasonal variations in demand for certain imported commodities which depended on the harvest, such as cereals and gunny sacks. The subcommittee emphasized that stocks held by UKCC should be kept distinct from, and additional to, normal imports, which would continue to be handled by private trade. There was no idea at that time of replacing normal trade channels by an import monopoly in the hands of UKCC or of territorial governments. But as the result of growing scarcity both of supplies and of shipping during the second half of 1941 this conception was abandoned. Private buying became increasingly difficult and could not be relied upon as a regular and dependable source of supply. Moreover, the existence of UKCC as a competitor, buying for the stockpile and prepared to sell in the event of a shortage, introduced an element of uncertainty which discouraged private initiative. Reserve stocks thus developed into centralized pools to which all imports were directed and from which all demands from the area were met. This change came about soon after Lyttelton's arrival in July 1941. It was dictated first by increasing stringency of supply in world markets; second, by growing demands in the Middle East which private trade was unable to meet at reasonable prices; and third, by the urgent need to economize shipping of bulky cargoes like cereals and sugar and to reduce the size of stocks to the minimum through a single reserve for the area instead of through separate reserves in each territory.

The first detailed proposals for centralized supply of cereals came from London in August 1941 following representations from the Minister of State. For some months, however, the situation continued to be confused and unsatisfactory. Such imports as were being obtained by private trade were irregular and insufficient, and the prices at which they were being sold were exorbitant and constantly rising. Government action in Egypt, Palestine, Syria, Lebanon, Cyprus, and Turkey became necessary to assure supplies and ward off famine. Palestine and Cyprus were appealing to the Colonial Office for help; Egypt's and Turkey's requirements were being pressed by the British ambassadors in Cairo and Ankara and sponsored by the Foreign Office in London. Unco-ordinated attempts to buy by private traders and Middle East governments upset the markets and cut across the bulk purchase and loading arrangements of the British Ministry of Food, which complained of Palestine enquiries for wheat in Australia, Egyptian bids for maize in South Africa and for wheat in Canada, and Syrian attempts to buy wheat in India.

Meanwhile, such cargoes as were arriving in the Middle East were consigned to particular territories and therefore could not be allocated to meet the most urgent needs. At first the only wheat for emergencies at the disposal of MESC was a few cargoes that had been diverted from Greece and Yugoslavia after the German invasion of those countries. Small quantities of Lend-Lease flour were also beginning to arrive for the UKCC stockpile. MESC had as yet no precise knowledge of the level of stocks in each country, though a request had been made for monthly stock returns. The British forces were still buying cereals and flour locally, and some months elapsed before the War Office in London and General Headquarters in the Middle East agreed to obtain imported cereals and sugar through UKCC.

In August 1941 it had been agreed in principle that all cereal imports required for the services and for civilian consumption should be co-ordinated in a single program to be submitted by MESC to London and that the entire quantity required from outside the area should be purchased by the Ministry of Food. On arrival, cereals would be allocated by MESC in the light of its estimation of needs. To enable the system to work smoothly, it was agreed that a central reserve stockpile would be essential. But owing to the stringency of shipping at the time, the best that London could offer at the outset was to ensure that there would always be 50,000 tons of wheat or flour and 20,000 tons of barley or maize afloat in the form of cargoes already bought and consigned to the Middle East. This gave no insurance against delays or losses at sea nor against last-minute diversion of ships to other destinations, and thus was far from satisfying the need for an assured stockpile to be drawn upon as required. Indeed, throughout the winter of 1941 and the first six months of 1942 the flow of cereals to the Middle East was on a hand-to-mouth basis, and the greatest difficulty was experienced in allocating irregular and insufficient arrivals between the competing claims of Syria, Turkey, Palestine, and Egypt. MESC's efforts to satisfy the different governments are described in a later chapter. The final result was that between October 1941, when centralized buying first became fully effective, and June 1942, when the harvests began to come in, only 480,000 tons of wheat and flour had been delivered to governments and the armed forces, compared with an agreed program of 550,000 tons.

By the middle of 1942 the system was working satisfactorily and it was clear that the cereal crisis of the previous year could only have been dealt with by pooling imports. To avoid breakdown in the future it was essential to have adequate stocks; but the maintenance of a three-month strategic reserve in each Middle East country would have been wasteful and uneconomic. So long as each was able to share in a common pool, to meet both current needs and unforeseen emergencies, they were in effect enjoying a system of mutual insurance.

Centralized buying was gradually extended to sugar, fats, oils and oilseeds, tea and coffee, canned milk, meat, and fish as well as to rubber, tin, medical supplies, jute sacks, and some other items. As UKCC took over, private import came to an end or was prohibited. Monthly allocations were determined by MESC and deliveries were made by UKCC, sometimes from pool stocks and sometimes from cargoes as they arrived. An essential feature of the pooling system, which was only gradually accepted by governments, was that stocks held in any country were not earmarked for the use of that country but could be allocated by MESC to any territory that most needed them. Special agreement had to be reached whereby UKCC stocks were not liable to requisitioning by the governments of the countries where they were situated. Another important corollary of pooling was that the armed forces ceased placing orders independently for wheat and flour, sugar, rice, and other staple foods, and agreed to submit their requirements to MESC and buy from UKCC. Army supplies were programed along with civilian requirements and allocations were made by MESC; but demands from the armed forces were entitled to priority over civilian needs.

The development of bulk purchase and pooling of reserves placed a heavy responsibility on UKCC and its Middle East Board of Directors (MEBOD). Under MEBOD's able chairman, Colonel Gray, who was a leading figure in the British community in Egypt, UKCC grew into an efficient and flexible machine working harmoniously with MESC. It was natural that UKCC should wish to operate as independently as possible, particularly in the management and disposal of stocks and in negotiations for purchase and sale with local governments. But its dual responsibility—to its head office in London and to MESC in Cairo—fettered its freedom of action and gave rise to differences of opinion and sometimes to conflicting views on such matters as prices to be charged. UKCC, as a public concern set up and financed by the Treasury, could not simply aim at making profits nor could it afford to incur losses without express authority. It was laid down that it should sell at prices which would cover purchase price plus charges for storage, transport, overhead, and a small commission. This worked well enough in the case of bulk orders for cereals, sugar, oilseeds, etc., to be imported from overseas, which could be bought at controlled prices through the Ministry of Food in London. The benefit of the relatively low prices obtained by UKCC was then passed on to the territorial governments. But in later years, when UKCC was asked to buy high-priced cereals in Syria and Iraq for sale to Palestine, Cyprus, and the Sheikdoms of the Persian Gulf, difficulties arose as to the prices to be charged and the liability for losses incurred.

The problems involved may be illustrated by considering three occasions when the views of MESC backed by the Minister of State in Cairo clashed with those of UKCC and the Treasury in London. In each case UKCC's chief concern was to avoid taking a loss on their commercial transactions, while MESC was mainly interested in encouraging home production of grain and in saving shipping, and looked upon price considerations and the avoidance of financial loss as secondary. But there was also a different attitude toward the problem of inflation and the future course of prices: UKCC as a rule expected prices to fall, while MESC feared that they would continue to rise. The Treasury was anxious to check inflation and limit expenditure, and at first lent a ready ear to suggestions that UKCC's bulk purchase of grain at guaranteed prices encouraged inflation or at least prevented a fall of prices.

The issue first arose in Egypt in connection with negotiations for purchase of wheat and millet for export to Palestine, Cyprus, and other deficit countries. After MESC had with difficulty persuaded the Egyptian authorities to allow UKCC to buy for export, a last-minute hitch occurred when the London office instructed MEBOD that they must buy only what they had first been able to sell and that they must insist on receiving firm undertakings from the Palestine or other importing governments for reimbursement for the actual cost of specific consignments—which was always higher than the landed cost of Canadian or Australian wheat. In MESC's view, failure to buy the whole quantity offered would not only have risked the loss of Egyptian supplies but would have run counter to the system of pooling and allocation. There would have been delays in arguing about prices to be paid and no means of ensuring that supplies would be distributed to meet the most urgent needs. An appeal was made to the Treasury for reconsideration of UKCC's policy, and MESC's arguments prevailed. It was left to MESC to overcome the reluctance of governments of importing countries to bear the loss on Egyptian supplies allocated to them out of the common pool.

The second example comes from Iraq and is touched on in chapter 19. Here the question was a more fundamental one—whether bulk purchase and cereal collection at a fixed price was appropriate in the case of a crop, like Iraq barley, of which there was a large surplus for export. UKCC and its advisers tended to favor a free internal market for barley as the best means of obtaining it at a reasonable price; MESC argued strongly in favor of bulk purchase and control both to make sure of getting it and to prevent prices rising further.

After the collapse of Rashid Ali's *Putsch* in June 1941, an inflationary price rise set in and the wholesale index nearly doubled in six months. Barley exports were prohibited except under license, and it was not till February 1942 that UKCC was given an export license for 35,000 tons of barley, which it had been able to buy in the open market at prices ranging around 10 dinars per ton—or about double the prewar level. By this time there was a severe cereal shortage in the Middle East and Iraq barley was urgently needed to fill the gap. After Iraq's declaration of war against the Axis powers in January 1943, she was urged to do all in her power to assist the common war effort by instituting control of supplies and prices. By the middle of February the government with great difficulty was persuaded to act; stocks of barley were requisitioned, private trade was prohibited, and prices were fixed on a descending scale starting at 19 dinars per ton for uncleaned barley on the farm and falling to 10 dinars in April. UKCC, with British firms acting as agents, was granted an export monopoly, and before the next harvest 110,000 tons had been purchased and delivered under MESC's direction to Persia, Palestine, Turkey, and the British and American forces.

After meeting MESC's requirements, UKCC stopped buying and, when private trade was again permitted, the market price remained steady at about 25 dinars, equivalent to 19 dinars per ton on farms. Meanwhile some of the barley bought at high prices had been exported to the Sheikdoms of the Persian Gulf, where it had to be sold, by special arrangement with the British Treasury, at a loss of $64 a ton.

During May 1943 discussions began about the marketing of the new crop. There was every prospect of a good harvest but the Iraq authorities were reluctant to reduce the price. At first they proposed to fix the price at 17.5 dinars on the farm (equivalent to 23 dinars at collecting stations), or else to allow a free market. MESC was anxious to obtain 200,000 tons and considered that the price proposed was not unreasonable. It also maintained strongly that a free market, even with export control, would be an unjustifiable gamble in view of inflationary trends and the temptation to hoard. Agreement was finally concluded in July for the sale of 200,000 tons of uncleaned barley at 20.5 dinars per ton delivered to collecting centers. This corresponded to 15 dinars on the farm. By the middle of January 1944, 215,000 tons of uncleaned barley had been purchased by UKCC and 130,000 tons had been delivered, partly to neighboring countries in the Middle East but mainly to India to meet an unforeseen cereal shortage there.

A third example of differences of approach between MESC and UKCC was the controversy over the price to be paid for Syrian cereals in 1943. In the fall of 1943, partly owing to questions asked in Parliament about its financial activities, UKCC was more than ever reluctant to engage in operations liable to result in a loss. It asked that whenever a loss appeared likely, some government department should assume the responsibility and employ UKCC merely to act as agent. Thus in the case of seed potatoes shipped from Britain to the Middle East it was arranged that the Ministry of Food should purchase them and employ UKCC as agent. This was the result of rejection by the Egyptian government of some early shipments which had arrived in bad condition. UKCC objected to the purchase of Ethiopian cereals which were high-priced and of poor quality. As in the case of Iraq barley, UKCC was afraid of being caught with stocks bought at high prices which consuming countries would refuse to buy or only accept with the greatest reluctance.

In the case of the Syrian surplus of wheat, the price was nearly double the landed price of Australian wheat. This was of course mainly due to the inflationary situation in Syria, and was aggravated by high costs of transport and handling, plus the addition of a 15-percent charge levied by the Syrian government for administrative overhead. If UKCC purchased this wheat, it was bound to incur a loss unless the importing government could be persuaded to pay the full price and bear the loss itself. The Treasury had long been anxious to check the inflationary trend in Syria and had been advised by its financial representative in Beirut that one of the main causes of inflation was the excessively high price of cereals. Now that there was a substantial surplus of cereals for export the price should somehow be brought down. This view was strongly supported by UKCC, which maintained that it could buy more cereals more cheaply by normal commercial methods than by the existing system of fixed prices, government trading, and bulk contracts. In the case of Syria, it was recognized that it would be impossible to scrap OCP, which had been created with such difficulty by British initiative. The wheat was urgently needed; but the Treasury, backed by UKCC, insisted that an offer should be made to purchase it at a somewhat lower figure than had been proposed. If the Syrian government was not prepared to quote a lower price, it was hoped that the Free French authorities might be willing to supply the cereals as reciprocal aid. The result of these hesitations in London was that for about two months OCP's purchase of cereals virtually ceased.

MESC reacted promptly and vigorously to the threatened change of policy. It had been urged for many months to do everything possible to expand production and, now that substantial surpluses were in sight in Syria, Iraq, and Ethiopia, it had come as a shock to learn that London was reluctant to buy them. It was unsound to attribute the inflationary rise of prices mainly to the level of cereal prices. Iraq barley was in fact being bought below last year's prices, while the general price level had risen 50 percent, mainly because new money was still being injected into these countries at the rate of some $80 million of army expenditure each month. Any attempt to reduce cereal prices would endanger collection of the balance of this year's crop and might reduce next year's sowings. If cereal prices were to be reduced while prices of tea, sugar, and other consumer goods continued to rise, there could be only one result—a drop in output and a refusal to sell enough grain to feed the towns.

Part III

# CEREAL IMPORTS AND COLLECTION SCHEMES

## CHAPTER 14

# EGYPT: CEREALS, COTTON, AND NITRATES, 1941/42

In the early months of 1941 the cereal position in the Middle East appeared satisfactory. The wheat crops of 1940 had been good; in Turkey, Egypt, Syria, Transjordan, and Palestine they were above the average of 1934–38; and only in Persia was there a reduction of about 10 percent according to current estimates (later 20 percent). The important maize harvest of Egypt was 6 percent below normal, but in Turkey both maize and barley were well above prewar. For all grains, including rice and millet, production in the nine countries (including Turkey) for which estimates were available was about 17.5 million tons compared with a prewar average of 16.5 million and a high figure of 18.5 million in 1939. The position in Egypt was such that during the winter months of 1940/41 wheat was being exported, with the aid of a government subsidy, at the rate of several thousand tons per month. In addition the British armed forces had been buying wheat and maize in Egypt (20,500 tons of wheat and 7,300 tons of maize in the first seven months of 1941), and were being pressed to take more.

During April 1941 discussions took place about the Egyptian cropping program for 1941/42. It was agreed that the cotton acreage would have to be reduced to conform with arrangements then being made for the purchase of a reduced supply of cotton for the British Ministry of Supply. The Egyptian government at that time was concerned mainly with the problem of disposing of the surpluses of any alternative crops that might be grown in place of cotton. It offered to sell forward 200,000 tons of wheat from the crop to be harvested in May 1942, at a price of 12 Egyptian pounds (£E) per ton, and early in May 1941 the British government approved in principle the purchase of any exportable surplus up to a limit of 200,000 tons. But already the prospects of there being any large surplus of wheat for export was beginning to seem doubtful owing to the drastic cuts that had to be made in the use of shipping for fertilizer imports; and within less than six months Egypt was urgently demanding imports of wheat and maize to meet her estimated deficit from the harvest of 1941.

Before the war Egypt had imported annually about half a million tons of Chilean nitrates and other fertilizers. At the end of April 1941 stocks were officially estimated at no more than 80,000 tons, and no supplies were reported to be afloat. The Egyptian government asked for a minimum of 150,000 tons of nitrate imports in 1941—75,000 for the maize crop of 1941 and 75,000 for the wheat crop to be harvested in May 1942. It was not until the end of July 1941, as a result of urgent representations from the British Embassy, that shipping was made available for 63,000 tons. By the end of September stocks were down to 20,000 tons, and arrivals during the next six months to the end of March 1942 were only 142,000 tons. Total supplies during the preceding 12 months had been less than half of the normal prewar supplies.

Meanwhile reports coming in during May and June 1941 from many hundreds of threshing floors showed that the wheat harvest was going to be well below the level of the last two years. In view of this disappointing news and of the extreme unlikelihood of obtaining sufficient nitrates to ensure normal yields for the maize crop of 1941 and for next year's wheat harvest, the Egyptian government decided to introduce legislation restricting the acreage under cotton. It was hoped by this means to increase the area under wheat, maize, and millet sufficiently to offset the fall in yield due to shortage of fertilizers.

Before the war the Nitrates Corporation of Chile estimated that 425,000 tons of Chilean nitrates were used for the different crops: wheat, 160,000 tons; maize, 115,000; cotton, 115,000; and millet, 35,000. On the average 1 ton of nitrates was reckoned to produce about 2.5 tons of wheat or 3.7 tons of maize. This latter figure may be too high, but it was generally used in official discussions.

The normal maize crop was reckoned to be about 1.5 million metric tons from 630,000 hectares, with a yield of 24 quintals per hectare. In May 1941 the area under *nili* maize—sown in early summer and harvested in the fall—was officially forecast at 710,000 hectares. Without nitrates the production from this area was expected to be not more than 1.25 million metric tons, with a yield of only 17.7 quintals per hectare. On this assumption the shortage would be about 250,000 tons. If 1 ton of nitrates produced 3.7 tons of maize, this deficit would be more than made up by the application of 75,000 tons of nitrates, for which the government had asked. Actually the official figures for maize in 1941 were 1.28 million metric tons from an area of 642,000 hectares, with a yield of 20 quintals per hectare, representing a fall of about 16 percent from normal. About 60,000 tons of nitrates had been available, judging by the fall of stocks between April and September 1941. In the following year, 1942, in spite of a further fall in yield to 17.4 quintals per hectare, it was found possible to increase the area by 191,000 hectares and the total crop to 1.45 million metric tons, bringing it not far below the prewar average.

The problem of planning the area to be sown to wheat presented greater difficulty. The average area for 1934–38 was 588,000 hectares, yielding a crop of 1.18 million tons at 20.1 quintals per hectare. In 1940 and 1941 the area sown was 630,000 hectares. To produce a crop of wheat without nitrates, sufficient for the 1.35 million tons set for Egypt's requirements, it was estimated that an additional 250,000 hectares would be needed, with a yield of only 15 quintals per hectare. The minimum area required to be sown with wheat was therefore taken to be 880,000 hectares. If, in addition, the British authorities were to procure 200,000 tons of surplus wheat to meet the needs of neighboring territories and the armed forces, and if allowance were to be made for expected shortfalls in maize and millet crops, another 170,000 hectares would have to be sown, making 1.05 million hectares in all.

It appeared possible to obtain part of this large increase by restricting the cotton acreage; but at most it was thought that the area under wheat could not be increased by this means to more than 777,000 hectares, representing a transfer of 147,000 hectares from cotton. To make good the remaining deficiency the yield would have to be 20 quintals instead of 15 and, if 1 ton of nitrates produced 2.5 tons of wheat, over 200,000 tons of nitrates would have to be imported. In view of the worsening shipping position this was clearly out of the question. After urgent representations had been made by the British Embassy, the authorities in London replied that it would be impossible to spare ships for large shipments of nitrates and that they no longer counted on being able to buy 200,000 tons of Egyptian wheat for export.

Final official estimates for the 1941 and 1942 harvests were as follows:

| Year | Area (*1,000 hectares*) | Yield (*quintals per hectare*) | Production (*1,000 metric tons*) |
|---|---|---|---|
| 1941 | 631 | 17.8 | 1,124 |
| 1942 | 662 | 19.1 | 1,262 |

It was not till the following harvest that lack of nitrates caused the yield per hectare to fall to the low figure of 16 quintals. This was followed by a yield of 13.6 quintals in 1944, and by that time measures to restrict the area under cotton and expand wheat acreage had taken effect. In the fall of 1941 arrivals of nitrates had made it just possible to release 88,000 tons in time for the winter-sown crops, of which the greater part was available for wheat.

## COTTON RESTRICTION

On August 11, 1941 it was agreed to set up a joint Anglo-Egyptian Commission to buy up to 8 million kantars (360,000 tons) of cotton (virtually the whole crop) at prices similar to those paid in 1940. At the same time the Egyptian Prime Minister said that he would introduce a law to restrict the 1942 planting of cotton to 30 percent of the land in the northern Delta, where fine cotton is grown and the soil is less suitable for wheat, to 25 percent in the basinlands of Upper Egypt, and to 20 percent elsewhere. It was estimated that this would reduce the cotton crop by 37.5 percent to 5 million kantars. In explaining his proposals to Parliament he justified them on the grounds of an anticipated shortage in 1942 of 200,000 tons of wheat and 378,000 tons of maize. These figures seem to have been based on a comparison of the poor crops of 1941 with the good crops of 1940.

At the beginning of October 1941 a law was passed limiting the planting of cotton to 27 percent of the cultivated land in the northern Delta, and to 23 percent elsewhere. This was expected to lead to an increase of 126,000 hectares in the area under wheat, bringing it up to 757,000 hectares. In the absence of fertilizers the Ministry of Agriculture forecast a wheat yield of 15.3 quintals and a total crop of 1.16 million tons. Assuming Egypt's wheat requirements to be 1.35 million tons, this still left a deficit of 200,000 tons. Accordingly, in November 1941 a new law was passed designed to bring about a further diversion from cotton by the payment of a bonus for the cultivation of wheat, barley, or beans on land that might legally have been planted to cotton—at the rate of £E 1.5 a feddan ($15 per hectare) in the northern Delta and £E 2 elsewhere—with a limit for the whole of Egypt of £E 500,000. This set an upper limit of 126,000 hectares for further diversion from cotton acreage. It was hoped that 84,000 hectares of this might be planted to wheat, bringing the total area up to 840,000 hectares and providing even without nitrates a crop which should be sufficient for Egypt's own needs. As a further inducement the British government announced on November 7, 1941 that it would be prepared to buy any surplus wheat and would not buy more than 5 million kantars of the 1942 cotton crop.

Early in January 1942 a preliminary official estimate of wheat sowings gave a figure of 745,000 hectares. This was less than the Egyptian government had hoped to reach by cotton restriction alone, and indicated that the bonus law had had little or no effect. The final official estimate of the wheat acreage was only 662,000 hectares, and it was not till more drastic measures had been taken that it rose to the wartime peak of 805,000 hectares in 1943.

Following an instruction of the Middle East War Council, a report on "The Cereal Position in Egypt" was submitted to its Supply and Transportation Sub-Committee on January 10, 1942 by the Middle East Supply Center (MESC) and the Commercial Counsellor of the British Embassy. After reviewing the latest data on the poor maize crop and the disappointing wheat sowings, the report recommended that the Egyptian government should be urged to safeguard future cereal supply by enacting a second, more rigorous cotton-restriction law, by increasing the fixed price for cereals in order to encourage greater summer sowing of maize and other crops, and by enforcing dilution of wheat in bread with maize and/or millet; and that it should again be warned not to rely on any future imports of cereals. To the British authorities it recommended the creation of a Middle East reserve pool of wheat, from which releases to Egypt and other countries would be permitted only where real and urgent need had been proved.

The recommendations in the report were transmitted to the Egyptian government and promptly accepted. On January 26, 1942 two laws were passed, the first imposing a complete prohibition on the planting of cotton in the basinlands of Upper Egypt and a limit of 22 percent elsewhere; the other providing that all lands not planted to cotton must be sown during the coming year to maize, rice, and some other food or forage crop. At the same time the government undertook to purchase maize of such new cropping until the end of September 1942 at a special price of 225 piasters an ardeb ($66 a ton)—an increase of 50 percent on the current fixed price.

At the beginning of October 1941 the extraction rate for flour had been raised from 81 percent to 90 percent and admixture of 15 percent rice flour was made compulsory. On January 22, 1942 it was decreed that bread must henceforth be made only of a mixed flour containing 50 percent of wheat flour of 90 percent extraction, 25 percent of maize, and 25 percent of rice.

This compulsory admixture of maize in order to eke out supplies of wheat was bound to intensify the maize shortage. But it was hoped that the over-all cereal deficiency might be made up, in part at least, by imports of giant millet or sorghum (durra) from the Anglo-Egyptian Sudan. Prewar imports of millet varied widely from year to year—from virtually none to about 90,000 tons. In November 1941 the Sudan government told MESC that it expected to have 30,000 tons of millet available for export. This was later reduced to a possible 25,000 tons; and finally, on February 17, 1942, the Sudan War Supply Board reported that in the light of its review of the situation no export of grain could be permitted until local military and civilian requirements had been assured. From this time until the new wheat crop began to be collected toward the end of May, an increasingly critical cereal situation developed in Egypt, which could only be met by drawing on the small reserves of wheat and flour imported from overseas for the Middle East pool.

The cereal shortage in Egypt must therefore be considered in relation to the wheat position in the Middle East at the end of 1941 and to the difficulty in arranging an agreed program of overseas shipments.

CHAPTER 15

# MIDDLE EAST CEREAL IMPORTS, 1941/42

Until August 1941 the supply of cereals for other Middle East countries had given little cause for concern. After the good crops of 1940 little attention had been given to reports of less favorable harvests in 1941. Palestine, Cyprus, and Malta had notified the Colonial Office of their import requirements and had obtained their cereal supplies with the help of the Ministry of Food in London without the intervention of the Middle East Supply Center (MESC) or the United Kingdom Commercial Corporation (UKCC). But if MESC was to carry out its function of co-ordinating shipping programs and determining priorities, this system had to be changed. Accordingly MESC proposed to the Ministry of War Transport that certain standard commodities, like cereals, sugar, and newsprint, should be supplied in bulk for the Middle East as a whole and that purchase and distribution should be carried out by UKCC under directions from MESC. On August 13, 1941 London approved these proposals. For cereals, MESC was to act as the advisory body to determine requirements, the Ministry of Food would act as the purchasing agency for supplies needed from outside the Middle East, and UKCC was to be the central distributing agency in the area. This was agreed by the Executive Committee of MESC on August 20, with the rider that the final allocation of cargoes on arrival would be made on its advice.

Meanwhile demands for increased imports of cereals began to mount. Egypt, which early in August 1941 had asked for 75,000 tons of wheat and 70,000 tons of maize, a month later raised her figure for maize imports to 200,000 tons. In September Turkey made an urgent request for 50,000 tons of wheat in order to meet impending shortage brought about by a poor harvest, hoarding by peasants, and increased consumption due to mobilization of the army. London recognized the urgency of this need by giving it priority for the time being over other claimants. Cyprus reported that there was danger of impending shortage and asked for 33,000 tons of wheat. By the middle of September, Malta had put in a demand for 12,000 tons of wheat and flour and 2,700 tons of maize and barley. Palestine needed 74,000 tons of wheat. A new and unexpected demand for 80,000 tons of wheat imports came from Syria, strongly backed by MESC, the

Minister of State (Lyttelton), and the head of the British mission in Syria (General Spears), largely as a means of discouraging hoarding and speculation and of checking the alarming rise of prices.

The first cereal-import program for the Middle East for the period October–December 1941 put forward by MESC at the beginning of October 1941 was therefore as follows, in thousand tons:

| Country | Wheat, flour | Maize |
|---|---|---|
| Egypt | 150 | 200 |
| Turkey | 50 | — |
| Syria | 80 | — |
| Palestine | 74 | — |
| Cyprus | 33 | — |
| Total | 387 | 200 |

These figures left out of account the needs of Malta and the British forces in the Middle East, responsibility for which had not yet been transferred to MESC. A new cereal-loading program was at once prepared in London by the Ministries of Food and of War Transport covering 350,000 tons of wheat and flour, of which 90,000 tons were to be shipped in October and the balance in equal amounts of 130,000 tons in November and December. It was only with great difficulty that ships and supplies could be made available at such short notice and one of the immediate results was a reduction of over 100,000 tons of wheat imports into the United Kingdom.

The difference of 37,000 tons of wheat between the import requirements put forward by MESC and the loading program was left to be filled by "windfall" cargoes resulting from diversion of ships originally consigned to Greece. Tons of wheat and tons of flour were regarded for the purposes of programing as interchangeable; the extraction rate might vary from 70 percent for imported flour to 90 percent for flour milled from imported wheat as in Egypt.

In October 1941 MESC heard from Syria that 20,000 tons of wheat must be delivered before the end of November if it was to be distributed in the mountain villages of Lebanon before they became snowbound. The needs of Turkey were pressed with equal if not greater urgency; and as each cargo of wheat arrived in the Middle East, MESC had the difficult task of deciding which cargo should go to Turkey and which to Syria. In the middle of October the British Ambassador to Turkey was demanding immediate delivery of 25,000 tons and delivery of the remaining 25,000 tons before the end of the year. A month later he was again pressing for 50,000 tons of wheat and added a new request for 50,000 tons of barley. Before the end of the year he had obtained the consent of London for an increase in Turkey's wheat requirements to 100,000 tons to meet the needs of the Turkish army. MESC was in fact bypassed, and this led later to the virtual exclusion of Turkey from the MESC sphere of responsibility. During November the High Commissioner for Palestine called for further immediate deliveries to avert a threatened crisis. The British Ambassador to Egypt insisted that no grain shortage must be allowed to develop in Egypt, which might make it possible for the government to claim that the interests of Egypt were being sacrificed in favor of other countries. Full responsibility for the supply of wheat and fodder to Malta was now transferred to MESC and involved finding 32,000 tons of wheat before the end of March 1942. Finally, to complete their embarrassment, the Executive Committee of MESC was informed that Persia, which was at this time outside their sphere of operations, was facing a possible shortage of 200,000 tons and that, as a result, supplies of wheat intended for Syria might have to be diverted to meet this new and more menacing need.

Something of the atmosphere of crisis which prevailed in MESC at the turn of the year is conveyed in the following extract from a communication sent on December 4, 1941 by the Intendant-General Sir Robert Haining, as president of MESC, to the highest British authority or representative in each Middle East territory:

> 1. Chaotic state of cereal supply position in Middle East this year indicated necessity to assess general position well in advance for next year so that supplies may be properly co-ordinated with requirements.
>
> 2. Situation in Far East and possible further restriction of available shipping combined with probable increase in requirements of warlike stores makes it essential that Middle and Far East should as far as possible be self-supporting in cereals.
>
> 3. It is of utmost importance therefore that measures be taken to increase acreage under cereals and to increase yield. Please state what measures are being taken with these objects.
>
> 4. Grain economy will necessitate adulteration of wheat flour. Please state plans for this.
>
> 5. It is essential to prevent as far as possible hoarding and rigging of markets in respect of next year's crop. Please advise us what plans are so that desirability of centralized action may be considered in time to be effective.

### THE SHIPPING SHORTAGE, 1942/43

In the early months of 1942 losses of ships from submarine activity grew at an alarming rate. Up to December 1941 losses of British ships had been more than offset by acquisitions of almost 5 million tons of shipping belonging to enemy-occupied European countries. But this source of supply had now been exhausted. In 1942 losses of dry-cargo merchant shipping of 1,600 gross tons and over under British control were nearly 4 million tons—heavier than in any other war year. The total tonnage available fell from 22 million tons at the end of 1940 to 21.3 million in December 1941, and then to 18.8 million in December 1942—a drop of 2.5 million in one year (*1*, pp. 69, 293).

The whole Allied shipbuilding program at the time was little more than 1 million tons per annum. On top of these crippling losses the demands of the United States army and navy were increasing at an enormous rate. Civilian imports into the United Kingdom had to be progressively reduced until they were less than half their prewar volume.

The extension of U-boat warfare across the Atlantic and improvements in U-boat design constituted a formidable threat, while new methods being evolved to deal with this threat had yet to prove their efficacy. It had therefore become imperative to impose the greatest possible economy on the use of shipping for civilian imports into the Middle East. Every unnecessary cargo reduced the rate at which military stores could be sent to reinforce the desert army and postponed the date at which Rommel's forces could be outnumbered and driven back. But just at the time when the shipping shortage was at its worst and submarine sinkings reached their peak, harvests of Middle East countries proved insufficient to meet requirements and had to be supplemented by thousands of tons of imported grain.

## CEREAL REQUIREMENTS AND SUPPLIES, JANUARY–JUNE 1942

In a review of the Middle East wheat position prepared by MESC in the first week of January 1942, requirements and allocations were summarized as follows, in tons:

| Country | Requirements (Oct. 1941–May 1942) | Deliveries up to Dec. 31, 1941 |
|---|---|---|
| Egypt | 150,000 | 25,841 |
| Turkey | 100,000 | 15,958 |
| Palestine | 100,000 | 21,274 |
| Syria | 80,000 | 52,898 |
| Cyprus | 60,000 | 13,523 |
| Malta | 35,500 | 5,011 |
| Reserve | 43,000 | 1,000 |
| Total | 568,500 | 135,505 |

The requirements of the British forces in the Middle East, estimated at nearly 5,000 tons monthly, were not included in this table. Of the total deliveries of 135,505 tons, about 30,000 tons had been obtained as "windfall" cargoes diverted from Greece and other destinations, and 105,000 tons had been shipped from outside the area. Loadings reported up to the end of the year totaled 112,600 tons, and additional loadings not yet reported were expected to bring the total to 145,000 tons. This was 100,000 tons less than the original loading program, to the end of December.

During the first six months of 1942, until the 1942 harvests were gathered, the supply of imported wheat was barely sufficient to meet the most urgent requirements. In January arrivals were 30,000 tons below the programed figure of 97,500. News came from India that a shortage of wheat was developing there and that future shipments from that source could not be counted on. Meanwhile the army was requiring larger supplies, partly to feed the civilian population of Cyrenaica and Eritrea; and a further commitment had been entered into to supply wheat and flour to Greece. In a letter to London early in January the Minister of State in the Middle East wrote that "the position was such as to foreshadow an outbreak of famine which might imperil security in the Middle East." This warning had its effect; and actually, though a breakdown in the supply of bread to Egyptian towns was only narrowly averted, out of an approved program of 415,000 tons for the six months, it was found possible to find ships for just under 350,000 tons. The deficit of 65,000 tons was to a large extent met by drawing on the Middle East reserve-stock pool, which at one time reached 42,000 tons.

## CITATIONS

*1* C. B. A. Behrens, in her forthcoming volume, *Merchant Shipping and the Demands of War* (Hist. of the Second World War, U.K. Civil Ser.).

CHAPTER 16

# EGYPT: CEREAL COLLECTION AND DISPOSAL, 1942–45

In the early months of 1942 the Middle East Supply Center (MESC), under its new Director-General, was faced with a formidable series of problems. Syria, Turkey, and Palestine were clamoring for wheat imports. Against Middle East requirements of 750,000 tons from October to May, only 250,000 tons had arrived by the end of February 1942. Loadings were lagging behind schedule owing to the difficulty of finding ships at a time when monthly sinkings had risen greatly. Shipments of wheat from India ceased in February, leaving MESC to meet the needs of Aden and the Persian Gulf Sheikdoms. Maize shipments from the United States had been given a low priority in the vain hope that East Africa could supply 40,000 tons; and expected relief from the shipment of 30,000 tons of millet from Sudan had failed to materialize.

Added to these disappointments was the uncertainty as to the supply situation in each country. No territory had exact information on production, stocks, supplies on farms, or rate of consumption, and figures of import requirements might be very wide of the mark, generally but not always on the high side. In the absence of control of supplies, attempts to control cereal prices had had the usual result of forcing up prices in the black market and encouraging hoarding. In these circumstances there was a natural tendency for governments to look to increased imports as the only remedy for high prices and for the apparent, if not actual, shortage of home supplies.

One of the most urgent and difficult tasks of MESC was to persuade Middle East governments to establish control of collection and distribution of home-produced cereals. Only if this were done would it be possible to allocate supplies equitably and to avoid the risk of periodical crises. The first country to accept the need for compulsory cereal collection was Egypt, and this need was forced home by the threat of breakdown in the bread supply, which was only just avoided in May 1942.

Early in 1942 a Joint Supplies Committee of British and Egyptian officials was set up to consider the question of supplies for Egypt. At its first meeting on February 14, 1942, it was agreed that Egypt's monthly requirements of wheat were 75,000 tons, of which 20,000 tons were needed for the five principal cities—Cairo, Alexandria, Port Said, Suez, and Ismailia. At the second meeting the Egyptian Minister of Finance, in view of the rapid disappearance of stocks under the government's control, requested a loan of flour from British army stocks of one month's supply (20,000 tons) for the five principal cities. Two days later he was informed that the army would be willing to provide 10,000 tons of wheat during the first week of March and by the third week another 10,000 tons for release in an emergency.

At the fourth meeting on March 24, the Egyptian representative reported that their cereal-purchase scheme, described below, had brought in only 3,000 tons of wheat and 12,000 tons of maize during the last four weeks and that stocks would only last another week. It was agreed that an emergency had arisen justifying a further loan; accordingly, 20,000 tons were released—14,000 from Cairo stores and 6,000 from Alexandria.

A fresh crisis arose in the middle of April. The Egyptian Minister of Finance stated that he could no longer obtain sufficient maize for admixture in the grist and asked for a further 10,000 tons of flour. This was quickly arranged, but even this was not the end. Deliveries had been expected to begin from the new crop by May 20, but on May 18 MESC was informed that owing to cold weather no supplies could be counted on until June 10, which would leave a gap of 24,000 tons to be filled. By this time there were only 12,000 tons left in the central reserve with demands unsatisfied elsewhere. It was agreed to make a last loan but only to release 500 tons at a time. When 4,000 tons had been delivered, the new crop began to come in. The Egyptian officials had surpassed expectations in the speed with which they had operated their new collection scheme.

It was thus by the narrowest margin that bread riots and civil disturbance had been averted at a time when Rommel's offensive was starting—on May 27, 1942—leading to the capture of Tobruk, the advance to El Alamein, and the threatened invasion of the Nile Valley.

The wheat-control scheme introduced in June 1942 grew out of halfhearted and unsuccessful attempts to control prices and maintain supplies for the market during the preceding six months. As early as February Colonel Gray, the chairman of the United Kingdom

Commercial Corporation (UKCC) in Cairo, had stated that in his opinion there were considerable stocks of privately owned wheat, which the UKCC could acquire if authorized to offer a price in excess of the official maximum and more nearly corresponding to the cost of imported wheat and the price ruling in the black market. The official price was 200 piasters per ardeb for wheat, while imported wheat was costing about 50 percent more, the difference being met by a government subsidy on resale to the flour millers. The Egyptian government decided that it must make the offer itself and on February 18, 1942 issued an official announcement that up to the end of March it would buy all wheat and maize offered at prices of 300 and 200 piasters respectively per ardeb. This offer brought in only 650 tons of wheat and 2,100 tons of maize during the next week and only another 12,000 tons or so during the next four weeks. Much larger quantities had been expected, and the disappointing result may have been partly due to an unfortunate official statement, accompanying the offer to buy, that supplies might not hold out till the coming harvest. On February 25 UKCC was given authority to buy direct and not, as the government had done, through the agency of the Bank Misr and its associates. But by this time it was too late; the black-market price had soared well above the new official price and holders of such stocks as were left, on which no one had any precise information, were unwilling to accept less than they could get from private buyers. There were no visible stocks in the Cairo market. These had already been requisitioned in June 1941.

The shortage of cereals following the poor wheat crop of 1941 had led to high prices, speculation, and uneven distribution, which caused popular discontent and was a constant source of anxiety to the government. Attempts to combine government regulation of prices with maintenance of private trade had proved a failure. So in June 1942 the Egyptian government decided to control the collection and distribution of wheat by banning private trade and establishing a government monopoly. The scheme was designed to ensure supplies for the towns at fair prices without causing any reduction in rural consumption.

In Egypt the organization of a wheat-buying monopoly was facilitated by the concentration of production in the Delta and on the narrow ribbon of land along each side of the Nile. Every square meter was registered and supervised, and owing to irrigation there was less scope than elsewhere for hoarding grain in underground pits. It was also helped by the existence of a relatively strong Ministry of Agriculture, by the concentration of transport by road and waterway along a few well-defined routes which could be readily controlled, and by a system of government buying to maintain minimum prices through the agency of the Bank Misr, which had been in force during the years of depression before the war. A large proportion of the crop was brought to market by the growers and deposited for inspection and sale in wired-in enclosures called *shounahs*. These were usually controlled or owned by the Bank Misr, which would advance money to the seller or arrange credit for the buyer on the security of wheat under their control. In the dry climate of Egypt wheat could be stored in the open air, and once inside the locked gates of the *shounah* it was comparatively safe from pilfering. This method of marketing was well adapted for government purchase. All that was needed was to prohibit private purchase and transport of wheat from the *shounah* and to arrange with the banks to buy all that was brought forward at a fixed price on behalf of the government. The government then allocated supplies to the flour mills and sold them at a price related to the maximum price fixed for flour.

The original plan was for the government to acquire 5.5 million ardebs, or 825,000 metric tons. Compulsory quotas for delivery by the growers were fixed at varying rates in such a way as to leave at least 1.5 ardebs per acre (equivalent to about 550 kilos per hectare) for consumption on the farm and for seed. The highest quota for a grower with an average yield of 5 ardebs or over was fixed at 3.5 ardebs; if his yield was below 2 ardebs he was exempt. The quota had to be delivered to the nearest *shounah* or collecting center controlled by the Bank Misr. A permit to move the grain was issued in triplicate by the local mudir or headman of the village, and one copy was receipted by the Bank Misr and returned to the grower who presented it to the cashier for payment. If any surpluses were left after delivery of the quotas, the mudir was also responsible for supervising local distribution to families or villages which had a deficit. Wheat acquired by the government was issued to flour mills against permits to buy; and distribution of flour to bakeries and flour shops in the towns was regulated by permits based on an assessment of the number of customers normally supplied.

The Egyptian government also purchased compulsory delivery quotas of rice at fixed prices to meet the needs of the towns, and by special arrangement gave permission from time to time to UKCC, and later to the British Ministry of Food, to purchase rice from the Crédit Agricole for export and for army consumption. In the case of barley, maize, and millet there was no compulsory assessment of delivery quotas and private trade was permitted, subject to control of transport to ensure that the available supplies were satisfactorily distributed. In order to provide for admixture of coarse grains with wheat, the government undertook to purchase maize and millet for issue to the flour mills as part of their allocated supply. Purchase prices of wheat were fixed at 20 Egyptian pounds (£E) per metric ton for *Hindi* (Indian) wheat and £E 19 per ton for *Baladi* (native Egyptian) wheat. In order to keep down the price of bread, an important element in the cost of living and in the determination of wages, wheat was subsidized by the government and resold to flour millers at £E 13.33 per ton. The subsidy was later reduced but the government continued to pay the cost of storage and of transport from *shounahs* to city mills. The wheat-flour extraction rate was fixed for the year ending May 1943 at a minimum of 86 percent.

The estimated population of Egypt in 1941, based on the census of 1937 with an allowance of 1.2 percent annual increase, was about 17 million, of which 3.7 million lived in towns of over 20,000 inhabitants, with 1.4 million in Cairo and 700,000 in Alexandria. For consumption in the towns, on the basis of normal requirements of 450 grams of flour per head per day, it was reckoned that about 700,000 tons of wheat would be required with an extraction rate of 86 percent. But since the 1942 wheat crop of 1.26 million tons was below the average of 1939 and 1940 it was feared that there would be a considerable deficit in the country as a whole. In 1941 the maize crop had been 20 percent below average and about 300,000 tons short of requirements (see Appendix Table VI). This had caused an abnormally high consumption of wheat and barley in the agricultural districts during the first two months of the 1942/43 season before the *sefi* (summer) millet crop had begun to come forward. The reduction in the 1941/42 cotton acreage had been too late to allow of an increased wheat crop, but had resulted in a greatly increased acreage under millet, which, like cotton, is principally a *sefi* crop. In these circumstances it was clear that some admixture of barley or millet would be needed, possibly to the extent of 30 percent.

In view of the vital interest of the British authorities in maintaining the bread supply of the population in the towns and the responsibility that fell upon them for determining the amount of shipping which could be spared for nitrates and/or cereals, the Egyptian government agreed to the establishment of a Joint Anglo-Egyptian Wheat Control Committee. There were four Egyptian and four British representatives, with the Egyptian Minister of Supply as chairman. The Committee held its first meeting on June 3, 1942 and, at the request of the British members, the Egyptian government issued an official statement that they would maintain the system of compulsory purchase and the existing level of prices during the current year and that all growers' surpluses beyond their requirements for seed and consumption must be delivered to the *shounahs* without delay.

A difficult issue that arose at the outset was the question of coarse-grain admixture. It had been hoped to obtain substantial amounts of barley, which is the most suitable for mixing with wheat; but in July the Egyptian Minister of Supply reported that it had been found impossible to buy barley at the legal listed price. The Committee agreed that in the circumstances the policy of admixture should be deferred until the summer crops of maize and millet had come in. Meanwhile, experiments in the use of millet in bread were being carried out. This had never before been tried in the towns and it was feared that the resulting product would be unpalatable and disagreeably dark in appearance. The experiments showed that much depended on the type of millet used. The admixture of yellow millet or certain white millets resulted in a good bread of yellowish color, but dark millet and most white millets produced an inferior dark bread.

At the sixth meeting of the Committee on July 20, it was reported that deliveries were not satisfactory. Many appeals had been made by landowners asking for reduction in their assessments on account of poor crops and the aggregate figure for compulsory quotas had now been reduced from the original target of 825,000 tons to not more than 690,000 tons. The government agreed to put pressure on landowners with surpluses to sell their grain, and a target of 50,000 tons of barley was set for purchase in the market.

At their eighth meeting on August 15, a revised program was adopted which provided for the collection of 700,000 tons of wheat and 210,000 tons of millet. During the three months June–August, when the flour consisted wholly of wheat, consumption in the towns averaged 60,000 tons per month.

Admixture of other grains started on September 13, 1942, on the basis of two-thirds wheat and one-third millet, the extraction rates being 86 percent as before for wheat and 92 percent for millet. The final figures for consumption and disposal up to the end of May 1943 were as follows, in metric tons:

| | |
|---|---|
| Wheat: | |
| Urban and nonagricultural consumption from May 25, 1942 to May 31, 1943 | 583,000 |
| Seed issues | 29,000 |
| Deliveries for export | 13,000 |
| Stocks in hand (33,000 tons due to British Government; remainder sufficient till June 5, 1943) | 40,000 |
| Total | 665,000 |
| Millet: | |
| Urban and nonagricultural consumption | 103,000 |
| Deliveries to UKCC by Egyptian government | 11,000 |
| Stocks in hand (15,000 tons for export; remainder sufficient till June 10, 1943) | 20,000 |
| Total | 134,000 |

The surplus of the two grains collected thus fell short of the revised program by 110,000 tons. In terms of flour, urban consumption was 501,000 tons of wheat at 86 percent extraction and 95,000 tons of millet at 92 percent extraction, giving an average consumption per head per year of 160 kilos, or nearly 440 grams per day. The admixture of millet in the flour may have played some part in reducing the demand of the well-to-do as well as in eking out the supply, and thus made it unnecessary to introduce bread rationing in the towns.

The remainder of the crops not collected by the Egyptian government left 597,000 tons of wheat and 830,000 tons of millet for consumption by 13.3 million people on farms and in villages, in addition to 277,000 tons of barley and 1.45 million tons of maize, needed partly for animal feeding. Before the war, according to official estimates, about 10 percent of the maize and 90 percent of the barley were fed to livestock. On this basis of reckoning sufficient was left on farms to provide a daily ration of nearly 500 grams per head for the rural population. In addition the supply of rice was ample, sufficient to provide a surplus for export greater than before the war.

In August 1942 MESC estimated that the maize crop might be sufficient to meet requirements and that with normal rural consumption there might be surpluses of 315,000 tons of millet, 60,000 tons of barley after allowing for livestock feeding, and about 150,000 tons of paddy rice. On this basis negotiations were opened for the sale of surplus millet and rice for export and for repayment of the wheat loan. But the Egyptian government was reluctant to commit itself until the results of the collection scheme were assured and a sufficient carryover could be counted on to make good any shortage in 1943 or 1944. It feared that there would be a falling off in the yield of cereals in future years owing to shortage of nitrates, continuous cropping of cereals, and withdrawal of cotton from the crop rotation. It argued that if the Allies needed cereals from Egypt they must provide shipping for the import of more nitrates. The answer to this was that unless Egypt agreed to export cereals she could not expect to receive nitrates.

This argument continued unresolved for several months. Each side was in a strong bargaining position, and yet each recognized that there were risks in pushing its demands too far. Both the Prime Minister, Nahas Pasha, and the British Ambassador appreciated each other's arguments and were anxious to reach a reasonable compromise. Indeed, in an agricultural community so dependent on fertilizers as Egypt, the issue had grave political implications. The Wafd government and the Prime Minister were faced with growing opposition in the Egyptian Parliament and were naturally accused of being weak and subservient to the British. The Ambassador repeatedly warned London of the danger of undermining the authority of the Prime Minister and pushing the Egyptian people to a point where they would be unwilling to co-operate in the war effort and be driven into open opposition.

In December 1942 a firm decision was reached in London that in view of the shortage of shipping no undertaking could be given to supply any guaranteed quantity of fertilizers. It was argued that Egypt's needs of cereals, including rice, could be met from home production, even if no nitrates were imported; and the Allies were only prepared to use ships to carry nitrates if they could obtain an exportable surplus of crops which could be sent to neighboring countries. It was recognized that a mistake had been made in not making past imports of fertilizers conditional on the supply of surplus crops. The Ambassador was instructed to inform the Egyptian government that in future the shipping authorities would do their best to ship nitrates to Egypt but only on the following conditions: first, the immediate release of 46,000 tons of wheat in discharge of the loan from army stocks earlier in the year; second, the supply of at least 30,000 tons of millet for export; and third, the sale of any surplus from the current rice harvest at a fair price free of export tax. As regards the cereal crops to be harvested in 1943, nitrate imports would be related to cereal exports in the proportion of 1 ton of nitrate for every 2.5 tons of cereals exported. In the event of a shortage arising before the next harvest the deficiency would be made good by replacing any quantity of cereals exported.

The British Ambassador was told that, while no promise could be given, it was planned to ship up to 120,000 tons of nitrates during the coming year at the rate of 10,000 tons a month. This would be consigned to UKCC in Egypt and released to the Egyptian government only on the recommendation of MESC for allocation for particular crops under arrangements approved by the Anglo-Egyptian Fertilizers Committee. The decision reached by London was disappointing to the Ambassador and a shock to the Egyptian government. After difficult negotiations Nahas Pasha reluctantly agreed in February 1943 to repay the loan of 46,000 tons of wheat and to release for export 45,000 tons of millet and the equivalent in paddy of 75,000 tons of clean rice. By the end of June, mainly owing to transport difficulties, only 16,000 tons of wheat and 21,000 tons of millet had been exported; but the balance of the agreed amounts were obtained before the end of the year. The amount of clean rice exported before the end of June reached 74,000 tons and a further 75,000 tons was obtained in June in exchange for 30,000 tons of nitrates for the 1943 winter crops. The arrangements made by the British Ministry of Food for the purchase of the surplus rice crop are described in chapter 26.

In the summer of 1943 the improvement in the war situation and the opening of the Mediterranean to Allied shipping led to renewed appeals from the Egyptian government—backed this time by MESC and the Minister of State in the Middle East as well as by the British Ambassador—for larger imports of nitrates in 1944. The Minister of State estimated that during 1943 Egypt would have provided for export 150,000 tons of rice, 45,000 tons of wheat, and 45,000 tons of millet and barley. In addition, the British army had obtained 25,000 tons of rice, 17,000 tons of potatoes, and 25,000 tons of vegetables; and there was now a prospect of obtaining 50,000 tons of sugar. All these supplies of essential foods, as well as about 150,000 tons of long-staple cotton, had been made available, partly as the result of the application of 170,000 tons of nitrates for crops harvested in 1942 (one-third of the normal amount) and partly by drawing on reserves of soil fertility. Little or no surplus wheat for export was available from the 1943 harvest; and with the extremely small dosage of nitrates available for the maize and millet crops, total cereals would be barely sufficient to feed Egypt until May 1944. Unless soil fertility could be revived, prospects for the 1944 harvest were bad, and Egypt might be unable to feed herself in 1945 without imports. The Minister of State supported MESC's conclusion that at least 300,000 tons of nitrates would be needed between January and November 1944, if the 1944 crops were to equal those of 1942 and provide a surplus for export in 1945. Egypt had been able to live on her reserves of soil fertility during the period of most acute shipping shortage of 1942 and 1943. But now that this period was coming to an end, it was essential to bolster up Egyptian cereal production as the best source of export surpluses; these would be needed not only for the Middle East territories but later also for liberated countries in southeast Europe.

In August the Ambassador reinforced the Minister's plea by once more insisting on the political aspects of the problem. He went further and urged immediate increase in nitrate imports so that they would be available for the wheat and barley crops to be sown in the winter of 1943. He recognized that there were formidable shipping difficulties, but he believed that there was serious risk that cereals might have to be imported in the second quarter of 1944. Cereal imports would require far more shipping space than the nitrates needed to produce the equivalent cereals in Egypt. He asked whether it was really necessary to run this risk, and whether it did not make better sense to feed the goose that laid the eggs so badly needed. Would not surplus cereals from Egypt be needed in 1944 and 1945 even more than in 1943 in order to feed liberated territories in Europe? The present program of nitrate imports would provide for an allocation for the wheat and barley crops sown in 1943 of barely one-third of a sack per acre, compared with a normal supply of one sack. To provide less than half a sack per acre would mean, first, no cereal exports in 1944; second, the probability of having to import cereals in the early part of 1945; and third, aggravation of political discontent already caused by shortage of nitrates.

These arguments were bound to carry great weight in London, all the more because of the dramatic change that was now taking place in the battle of the Atlantic against the U-boats. The turning point in the campaign came in June 1943, when "shipping losses fell to the lowest figure since the United States had entered the war. The convoys came through intact, and the Atlantic supply line was safe" (*1*, p. 10). From that time till the end of hostilities new construction exceeded losses at the rate of approximately 1 million gross tons per month. In the Mediterranean also the U-boat menace had been overcome and the long haul round the Cape, which had added six or seven weeks to the voyage of each convoy to the Middle East, could now be discontinued. Some relaxation of the tight control of fertilizer imports into Egypt was now possible, and with some misgiving it was agreed that the target for 1944 should be raised to 300,000 tons.

In October 1943 negotiations were opened for release of surplus grains for export from Egypt in exchange for increased imports of nitrates. Agreement was eventually reached in January 1944 for export of 125,000 tons of paddy rice (87,500 tons clean), 20,000 tons of wheat, and 10,000 tons of barley or millet to be set against an import program of 300,000 tons of nitrates in 1944. It was agreed, as in 1943, that the wheat would be replaced in the event of any deficiency occurring before the 1944 harvest.

Meanwhile, collection of cereals from the harvest of 1943 proceeded with gratifying success. By the end of December, 762,000 tons of wheat, 95,000 tons of barley, and 173,000 tons of paddy rice had been collected as compulsory quota deliveries and in addition 133,000 tons of millet had been purchased at controlled prices in the open market.

By careful management of flour extraction and admixture no deficiency in fact arose. At the beginning of the season, when stocks of millet ran out, it was decided to replace the 30 percent millet admixture by a 10 percent admixture of barley. On May 29, 1943 the flour-extraction rate for wheat was raised to 95 percent and for barley was fixed at 62.5 percent. These rates continued till February 1944, when the wheat extraction rate was reduced to 92 percent and the admixture of barley with extraction unchanged was increased from 10 to 20 percent. Then in April 1944 the Egyptian government reintroduced a one-third admixture of millet with an extraction rate of 88 percent for both wheat and millet. By this time the bread supply for the towns was assured until the end of June 1944.

By that time there was growing concern about the exceptionally poor wheat harvest of 1944. The final estimate of the 1944 wheat crop was only 946,000 tons. The Joint Anglo-Egyptian Wheat Control Committee described it as "the worst wheat crop within the statistical memory of the Egyptian Government." It was 20 percent below the 1934–38 average and 30 percent lower than the bumper crop of

1940. Compared with 1943 there was a reduction of 112,000 acres, or 14 percent in the area sown, and a fall of 15 percent in the yield from 16.0 to 13.6 quintals per hectare. The official figures from 1939 to 1945 compared with prewar are shown in Appendix Table VI. According to MESC experts, the 1943 area of 806,000 hectares was probably an overestimate and the yield of 16 quintals was somewhat too low.

The catastrophic reduction in yield was due to a combination of factors beyond the control of the authorities: black rust; hot winds when the wheat was in the milk stage; fertilizer deficiency; and continuous cereal cropping in place of the usual rotation of berseem, cotton, wheat, fallow, and maize. But the sharp fall in acreage after the record area of over 800,000 hectares in 1942/43 may be attributed, partly at any rate, to a deliberate change of policy on the part of the Egyptian government. Following the poor harvest of 1941, a Wheat Acreage Law had been passed in 1942 under which a compulsory percentage of the arable area had to be planted with wheat and barley in the winter of 1942 for harvesting in 1943. The required minimum percentages were:

| Item | Northern Delta | Basins | Rest of Egypt |
|---|---|---|---|
| Wheat and barley...... | 45 | 60 | 60 |
| Wheat only .......... | 20 | 40 | 50 |

In addition it was forbidden to let any arable land lie fallow. The result of this was an increase of 140,000 hectares under wheat and 40,000 hectares under barley. In May 1943 the principle of compulsory cereal planting was extended by military proclamation to maize, rice, and other food crops. The compulsory percentages for these crops were 70 percent in Lower Egypt and the publicly irrigated lands of Upper Egypt, and 45 percent in the basinlands. At the same time, the prohibition of fallow was repealed: 15 percent fallow was permitted in areas where 15 percent of the area was under cotton; 8 percent fallow was permitted where 22 percent of the area was under cotton.

Then in July 1943, in spite of vigorous protests by the British Embassy and MESC, the Egyptian government issued revised percentages for wheat and barley. These new minimum percentages were as follows:

| Item | Northern Delta | Basins | Rest of Egypt |
|---|---|---|---|
| Wheat and barley...... | 35 | 50 | 50 |
| Wheat only .......... | 20 | 35 | 40 |

Another factor that may have contributed to the fall in wheat acreage was the delay in raising the controlled price of wheat, which in 1942/43 was £E 3 per ardeb or £E 20 per ton. On this issue there was room for some difference of opinion. As early as May 1943 the Egyptian authorities had proposed to raise the price of wheat sold for export to UKCC. This had been successfully resisted by MESC on the ground that it would have encouraged growers to hold back for higher prices and thus jeopardized the success of the collection scheme. In August 1943, at a time when it was agreed to raise the controlled price of yellow millet from £E 16 to £E 17.5 per ton, the Egyptian government wished to raise the price of wheat from the 1943/44 crop by one-third. The arguments in favor of the increase were two: first, the rise in the estimated cost of production, and second, the claim that unless a higher price was offered the full acreage aimed at would not be sown to wheat. Strong representations were made by MESC and the British Embassy in an effort to prevent what they regarded as an excessive rise likely to have inflationary effects both in Egypt and in neighboring countries. For two months no decision was taken, but finally the increased price of £E 4 per ardeb (£E 27 per ton) was officially announced by the Egyptian government. Some increase in price, or possibly an acreage bonus for wheat was needed; but the question of timing was important. An earlier announcement, even if a lower price had been chosen, might have had a greater influence in checking the fall in the wheat acreage. But this is uncertain, and there was as usual no clear criterion for judging the rightness of the price fixed. In 1943 and 1944 the problem of price fixing became increasingly baffling, and it was found almost impossible to reconcile the conflicting objectives of stimulating expansion of production and at the same time combating inflation. This problem will be discussed in later chapters dealing with rationing, price control, and inflation.

In September 1944 the official target for wheat collection, originally set at 637,000 tons, was reduced to 525,000. The minimum required for urban consumption was put at 600,000 tons and in addition 75,000 tons were required for seed. The deficit for the year to mid-June 1945 was therefore estimated at 150,000 tons, equivalent to three months' urban consumption. Fortunately the millet and *sefi* maize crops were expected to be up to the previous year's level; but in order to provide a safe margin the Egyptian authorities asked for 180,000 tons of imported wheat.

Before agreement could be reached the disposition of the rice crop again came to the forefront. The crop was better than in the previous year—815,000 tons compared with 685,000 in 1943—and the Egyptian government stated that its maximum target for collection would be 234,000 tons. If it was unable to obtain its requirements of imported wheat it would be compelled to use rice for admixture with flour for the bread supply. MESC therefore proposed that, since rice was urgently needed for Ceylon and was in shorter supply than wheat, London should obtain the agreement of the Combined Food Board (CFB) to an allocation to Egypt of 150,000 tons of imported wheat in exchange for an undertaking to release for export 225,000 tons of paddy, equivalent to 150,000 tons of white rice. This proposal was eventually accepted. In November 1944 preliminary agreement was reached for the release for export of 30,000 tons of white rice during the three months November–January against imports of an equivalent amount of wheat. Then in February 1945, in exchange for a further 120,000 tons of rice, 50,000 tons of imported wheat were handed over to the Egyptian authorities out of a total of 150,000 tons allocated to Egypt by CFB in Washington at a meeting on December 19, 1944; and by the end of May 1945 delivery of the full 150,000 tons from pool stocks had been completed. For the second time during the war the risk of a bread shortage in Egypt had been successfully surmounted.

## CITATIONS

*1* W. S. Churchill, *The Second World War: Closing the Ring* (Houghton Mifflin Co., Boston, 1951).

# CHAPTER 17

# SYRIAN CEREALS

## THE STORY OF OCP[1]

"Born in convulsions and nurtured in adversity." This was the apt description applied by General Spears (*1*), head of the British mission, to the scheme for cereal collection launched in Syria and Lebanon in 1942.

Before the war the two countries had supplied their own needs and normally there had been a net export of cereals. In 1939 and 1940 there had been good crops. In 1941, owing to hot weather in the spring, there was a poor crop; and just when the harvest was being gathered, in June and July 1941, fighting broke out when British and Free French forces invaded Syria and Lebanon to prevent establishment of a base by the Germans aided by the pro-Vichy authorities.

Military expenditure and a budget deficit precipitated a sharp inflation. In January 1942 the cost-of-living index had risen to two and a third times prewar, and wholesale prices nearly fivefold. The local currency, consisting of notes of the Banque de Syrie et du Liban bore the inscription "*Remboursable en Francs à Paris*"; and Axis radio propagandists from Bari made every effort to destroy confidence in its value by announcing that it had now no legal backing. It was not surprising, therefore, that a strongly bullish market for cereals quickly arose. The price of wheat at Beirut, which had been about 50 Syrian pounds (£S) per ton before the war and £S 175 in the spring of 1941, started rising—first slowly and then, under the influence of shortage of supplies, hoarding by producers, bad war news, and monetary expansion, at a runaway rate. In November 1941 the price had reached over £S 600 per ton—more than three and a half times the price six months earlier.

In the middle of September 1941 Keown-Boyd, then deputy chairman of the Executive Committee of the Middle East Supply Center (MESC), with the approval of the Minister of State (Lyttelton) and the head of the British mission (Spears), cabled to London from Syria urging that 80,000 tons of wheat be shipped as soon as

[1] Office des Céréales Panifiables.

possible. This figure was included in the first program of Middle East import requirements, aggregating 387,000 tons, forwarded to London early in October. By the end of the year over 50,000 tons of wheat on its way to the United Kingdom, mostly from Australia, had been diverted to Syria.

The plan was to break the market and induce speculators and hoarders to unload their stocks. Imported wheat was to be offered for sale at well below the ruling market prices on a descending scale. At first all went well. The price was forced down from £S 600 to £S 400 and then to £S 350. But a revival of bullish sentiment was brought about by the entry of Japan into the war on December 7, involving a potential threat to shipments from Australia, and some slowing down in the rate of arrivals. MESC could not afford to flood the market without limit and the Levantine merchants rightly guessed that there would continue to be a shortage. Prices stopped falling and the stocks landed were readily absorbed into private hoards. It had been hoped at first that 30,000 tons would be enough to bring prices down and keep them at a reasonable level. This expectation underestimated the absorptive capacity of the market under conditions of growing inflation. After the first 50,000 tons had been sold, prices resumed their upward trend, and although total imports were increased from 80,000 to 103,500 tons the market price continued to rise, until it reached nearly the same height as at the beginning of the operation.

As a means of bringing down prices and beating the speculator the operation could only be regarded as a failure. But as a gesture of good will it enhanced British prestige at a time when propaganda and dislike of French rule were undermining support for the Allied cause. Above all it taught a lesson which bore fruit in the ambitious plan for complete control of the marketing of the 1942 crop which now began to take shape.

The objectives were clear enough. They were to ensure that the two countries should be fed without calling for a single ton of imported cereals, and that the whole surplus, above what was needed for seed and for feeding the producers and their dependents, should be collected by an official agency for distribution at controlled prices to the rest of the population. But the difficulties to be overcome were immense. Apart from the purely administrative problem of creating in two or three months a brand-new organization which could be counted on to work with reasonable efficiency, there was an awkward constitutional and political issue. The local governments had been given a promise by the British and Free French authorities that they would be independent and they were increasingly resentful of the exercise of supreme power by the Free French *délégué général* (delegate general), then General Catroux.

When General Catroux issued a decree on April 21, 1942 creating an Office du Blé with statutory powers to monopolize the purchase and transport of wheat and flour, there was violent opposition from the government of Syria. They protested that the decree was an infringement of Syrian sovereignty and would give the Free French complete control of their wheat. As a compromise General Spears proposed the creation of a wheat commission of four members—Syrian, Lebanese, French, and British—with a Syrian chairman. This plan was accepted by Catroux with two provisos—first, that the commission might apply to him for army support; and second, that decisions of the commission would need his approval. But again the Syrian authorities objected. During May protracted negotiations took place, in which General Spears, backed by the Minister of State and General Auchinleck in Cairo, eventually succeeded in bringing the contending parties together.

The protocol finally adopted set up a Wheat Commission of the four powers with a Syrian chairman. Its decisions were to be taken by a majority vote and would have the force of law, provided they were ratified by a higher committee consisting of Catroux and Spears in their official capacities. The Commission's decisions would be implemented by decrees of the French *délégué général*; but they would contain a statement that they were issued with the concurrence of both members of the higher committee. Even after the amended protocol had been signed by the Syrian Prime Minister and Minister for Foreign Affairs, there was a last-minute refusal to ratify by the Syrian government; and General Spears had to insist that, if they refused to collaborate, the British would have no choice but to join with the French in enforcing the scheme without them. The protocol was finally signed and ratified on May 23 just as the new crop was beginning to be harvested.

But before the scheme could be got under way there were formidable difficulties, many of which were never fully overcome. First there was the natural opposition of merchants and large landowners to the abolition of private trading. This deprived them of the large profits which they had been obtaining in the past year and upon which they had been counting in the future. One of the first decisions of the Commission was that it would be impracticable to employ private grain merchants to act as government agents, either individually or as a pool; and that it would be necessary for the Wheat Commission, or OCP (Office des Céréales Panifiables) as it was now called, to recruit its own staff of British and French army officers, with subordinate local officials, to do the actual buying in the villages and to be responsible for transport and distribution. This was a regrettable necessity. It had the disadvantage of encouraging evasion and contributed to the black market which continued to exist to a greater or less degree throughout the operation of the scheme.

The second main handicap was the administrative weakness resulting from divided authority at the top and the lack of efficient and reliable organs of local government in the towns and villages. The French authorities exercised supreme administrative power since, by agreement with the British, they retained responsibility for matters of common interest to the two states, including customs, currency, and wartime control over prices and distribution. The British had no legal administrative authority but were vitally concerned as the occupying power, responsible for defense and the prevention of civil unrest. As such, the British army and General Auchinleck in Cairo could in the last resort act independently. They were thus able to exercise a strong influence both on the French and on the Syrian and Lebanese governments, and on several occasions General Spears was able to act as mediator between them. The two governments, particularly the Syrian government, were increasingly anxious to assert their independence, which had been promised by the French and guaranteed by the British. It was inevitable therefore that serious differences should arise as to the best methods to be adopted in enforcing decisions made by the Commission and the higher committee.

But even if complete harmony had existed at the center, the scheme ran the risk of failing through local opposition. This was the rock on which it was always in danger of foundering. As General Spears observed (*1*), "for nearly fifty centuries of Syrian history armies and foreign rulers had set themselves the task of collecting grain and the peasants had developed traditional ways of concealing the stocks on which their livelihood and frequently their survival depended." The poorest families would dig a hole under the earthen floor of their hut, pour in the grain and stamp down a covering of earth. Others would dig a pit under a road or an ancient burial mound, or hide their wheat under a heap of chopped straw. The larger farmers would dig a pit in one of their fields, cover the grain with soil, sometimes even sow a new crop on the top.

On one occasion when a British officer visited a village in search of hidden hoards, the *mukhtar* (headman of a village) blandly disclaimed all knowledge and at first refused to help. But finally he gave way and said, "Well, if there is any wheat, perhaps my donkey will help you to find it." As he untethered the donkey he pretended to whisper something in its ear. It led the officer straight to its stable and there under a pile of straw was some hidden wheat. With oriental courtesy he had hit on a way of responding to the officer's friendly attitude without openly admitting that he had lied to him.

The tendency to hoard was strengthened by a widespread expectation, fostered by merchants and landowners, that the scheme was bound to fail, as the attempt to break the market in 1941 had failed. In 1942 hoarding was almost impossible to prevent, owing to the late start of the scheme. To ensure success it would have been necessary to collect wheat on the threshing floors, as was done in later years. Once the grain was taken away by the producers, it could easily be hidden or disposed of in the black market. Moreover, the peasants were often indebted to merchants or big landowners and were under pressure to repay their debts in cash or in kind as soon as possible after the harvest.

One of the most important and difficult issues, which had to be settled at the outset, was the official buying price for wheat. Toward the end of the 1941/42 crop season the market price of wheat had been at times above £S 600 per ton, equivalent to about $270 per ton at the pegged rate of exchange. This was more than ten times the prewar price of £S 55 per ton, whereas wages and salaries were in general little more than twice the prewar level. Bread and flour were the staple food of the masses and the high prices ruling in the first six months of 1942, a time of great scarcity, had given rise to widespread unrest. After much debate, it was agreed that a price of £S 340 per ton for wheat of first quality delivered to the nearest collecting center would be fully remunerative and would provide an incentive to produce more and to make increased profits.[2] Given the inflationary conditions prevailing it would probably have been a mistake, even if it had been politically possible, to have fixed the

[2] Two years later, when the cost of living had risen considerably, it was reckoned that the average cost of living for a family of four persons (taken as three adults) for one year was about £S 1,500 and that seed and farm expenses for an area of six hectares under wheat might be put at about £S 350. In order to cover this sum of £S 1,850 the producer would need to sell 5.5 tons of wheat at a price of £S 340 per ton. On an area of six hectares under wheat he could expect to obtain a crop of about 6 tons.

price at a lower level. An important point that had to be borne in mind was that across the frontiers in Turkey and Transjordan prices in the free market were high enough to encourage smuggling. Actually a large part of the crop grown in Jezira found its way across the frontier into Turkey.

It was not surprising that the scheme got off to a bad start, with so little time to build up the organization and complete preparations for assessment and procurement. By the end of June the threshing floors in most districts were bare and only 5,000 tons had been collected. Almost everything needed was lacking—cars, trucks, sacks, weighing machines, and personnel. The maps available were out-of-date and particulars of areas taken from the official cadastre proved to be unreliable. The declarations of *mukhtars* about areas sown, average yields, and quantities required to be retained on farms were inaccurate and often deliberately misleading. In July a crisis was reached and for a time it seemed that the original plan, based on the voluntary co-operation of the Syrian government and the local authorities, would have to be given up and replaced by a more drastic scheme of wholesale requisitioning of stocks through the agency of the armed gendarmerie and garde mobile. The situation was saved by the appointment of new directors of OCP combined with a fresh appeal for help to the Syrian government.

At the critical moment MESC and the Minister of State in the Middle East in Cairo were able to find the right man for the job—Leonard Aldridge, who had built up an extensive business in Egypt and the Middle East. He had had no previous experience of the grain trade or of government service; but he was well known as a resourceful man of business fully able to hold his own with the cleverest traders of the Middle East. More important still, he was willing, and indeed anxious, to volunteer for war service and to stake his reputation on carrying through a tough assignment. It was at first feared that the fact that Aldridge could speak neither French nor Arabic would be a serious handicap; but it was soon evident that his ability to get things done and inspire confidence were in no way diminished by the need to use an interpreter. On July 25 he was appointed economic adviser to the Spears Mission. His first action was to insist that, if he was to serve as British representative in the administration of the wheat scheme, he must be appointed a codirector of OCP with powers equal to those of his French colleague. The former French director resigned and was succeeded by Colonel Valluy, who proved a most co-operative and loyal colleague. This

Anglo-French partnership worked with gratifying smoothness which did credit to both parties. The harmonious relations established between the two codirectors, neither of whom spoke the other's language, saved the scheme from collapse in its early stages and paved the way for its ultimate success.

But for some weeks the issue remained in doubt. During the early summer of 1942 the war news had been almost consistently bad. After a succession of disasters in Southeast Asia, ending with the fall of Singapore, Rommel had seized the initiative in North Africa and on June 21 had captured Tobruk. The British army had been driven out of Libya and Cyrenaica and had retreated 400 miles to the Egyptian frontier with the loss of 50,000 men, mostly taken prisoner, and vast quantities of munitions. Alexandria and Cairo were expected to fall in a few days or weeks. Mussolini flew to Libya in the hope of joining in a triumphal entry into Egypt. These unexpected misfortunes had taken place while Mr. Churchill was in Washington, and on his return he faced a vote of censure in the House of Commons. In the debate, which lasted two days and ended on July 2 in a vote of 475 to 25 against the motion of "No Confidence," the Prime Minister used these words (*2*, pp. 401–02): "The evil effects of these events, in Turkey, in Spain, in France, and in French North Africa, cannot yet be measured. We are at this moment in the presence of a recession of our hopes and prospects in the Middle East and in the Mediterranean unequalled since the fall of France."

During the critical month of July the government of Syria began to lose confidence in the scheme, and the local authorities and village *mukhtars* reported that they were unable to fulfill their quotas. Prices in the black market rose and the tendency to hoard as a hedge against the risk of inflation and of renewed disturbances was intensified. Early in July Australian officers loaned by the army to help in operating the scheme were recalled to join their units fighting in Egypt.

On the top of all these troubles there was a temporary shortage of bank notes for making payments. Consignments of new notes from London had been unexpectedly delayed. One lot that eventually got through were of such low denominations as to be almost useless for buying wheat in bulk. Another lot was reported to have arrived at Port Sudan in the *Queen Elizabeth* and to have been taken back to South Africa, because enemy bombing of the port had prevented discharge of the cargo. To help meet the shortage of cash special promissory notes (*bons de caisse*) were issued, but the peasants had little confidence in them and they soon fell to a discount.

At the end of July the government of Syria insisted that if it was to continue to co-operate, the targets must be drastically reduced. The original target for the whole of Syria was 250,000 tons of wheat out of a total harvest conservatively estimated at 370,000 tons. (Later revised official estimates for the 1942 crop given to the International Institute of Agriculture were 464,000 for Syria and 43,000 for Lebanon, or a total of 507,000 tons.) Requirements for consumption in the towns (including those of Lebanon) were roughly calculated to be about 250,000 tons. On the other hand it was estimated that the producers needed to retain 280,000 tons—about 90,000 for seed and 190,000 for feeding their families and other village households. The two figures added together exceeded the Syrian government's cautious estimate of the crop and left a deficit of 160,000 tons without making any allowance for losses by smuggling and leakage into the black market. It therefore proposed that the target for collection by OCP should be reduced to a more realistic figure, and that district quotas should be revised and reallocated in the light of the later information that had now been received. After difficult negotiations, revised targets were set at 180,000 tons of wheat, 40,000 of barley, and 40,000 of sorghum from Syria, and 8,000 of wheat and 3,000 of barley from Lebanon, making a total of 271,000 tons. (Actual deliveries for the 12 months to June 15, 1943 were 201,500 tons.) In 1943/44, the second year of the scheme, when there was a crop of 624,000 tons of wheat, the amount collected reached 227,000 tons of wheat and 177,000 of barley and sorghum. Recorded net exports of wheat in 1944 were 15,000 tons, mostly to Palestine and Cyprus.

On August 6, 1942 some of General Catroux's advisers once more proposed forceful action. Four battalions of *Groupes Spéciales* (special groups), under Free French officers, were to be sent to the four principal wheat-growing areas; and if the required deliveries were not made by a given date, all wheat on farms and in store was to be seized. Though the majority of General Catroux's advisers favored this course, there were a few who agreed with General Spears that force would fail, as it had always failed in Syria. During World War I both the Turkish and later the German military authorities had tried to requisition wheat supplies by force and had encountered stubborn resistance. General Spears agreed that the situation was critical but pleaded for a final appeal to the Syrian authorities to co-operate. With General Catroux's agreement he was able to persuade the Syrian Prime Minister, Husni Barazi, to tour the disaffected areas and to bring pressure on the local authorities to see that the revised quotas were delivered. The next day the Prime Minister, accompanied by Aldridge and Colonel Valluy, began his tour and visited the districts of Homs and Hama where, it was said, he owned as many as 20 villages.

This was the turning point. The results of the tour were even better than General Spears had hoped. A visit in person by the Prime Minister of Syria, bringing with him the French and British codirectors of OCP, succeeded where decrees and threats of force would have been largely ignored. By the end of August, wheat began to come forward at the rate of 3,000 tons a day, faster than it could be handled and transported. By September 25, there had been collected 113,500 tons; and on October 31 the total reached 136,000, consisting of 95,000 tons of wheat and 41,000 of barley and sorghum. At this date—one week after Rommel's defeat at El Alamein—OCP was able to report to MESC that it had in store 55,675 tons of cereals, equivalent to three months' reserve, and that no call would be made on Allied shipping for imported wheat and flour during the first six months of 1943. During the rainy season, from the second half of November to the end of February, roads in the north of Syria became almost impassable, and movement of cereals from villages to railhead by camel and pack transport was seriously restricted. The total of 201,500 tons collected from the 1942 crops up to June 15, 1943, consisted of 124,700 tons of wheat and 76,800 of barley and sorghum. This amount just sufficed to avert any major breakdown of supplies to the towns; but the greatest care had to be taken to regulate monthly releases and to eke out the scarce supplies of wheat by raising the milling extraction rate to 90 percent and introducing compulsory admixture of other grains. The system of rationing flour and bread in Syria and Lebanon is described in chapter 23.

### PROCEDURES OF COLLECTION AND DISTRIBUTION

During the first six months of the scheme, while the organization was being built up, the main concern was to collect the wheat and find the means of transporting it to OCP depots for delivery to the municipal authorities in Syria and to the *Ravitaillement* (food supply) authorities in Lebanon. In the early months of 1943 the chief preoccupation was to improve distribution. A brief account of the procedures adopted will illustrate some of the difficulties that had to be overcome.

First came the assessment of surpluses. Each producer was allowed to retain 13 kilos per head per month for his family and dependents together with enough seed for next year's crop, and was required to sell the remainder to OCP at the official prices. Responsibility for assessment of the crop was at first placed on the village *mukhtar*, who was required to furnish a declaration, countersigned by the village council of elders and two of the principal producers, giving the names of the producers, the areas sown, the amount of seed sown, and the number of persons in each producer's household. District commissions were set up to examine these declarations and to fix the quota of grain to be collected from each village. The quotas so fixed were then divided among the producers by the *mukhtar* and the village council. At the same time the *cadastre*, or cadastral survey department, supplied its preliminary estimate of the Syrian and Lebanese crops for the purpose of checking the village declarations. Unfortunately these official figures were no more reliable than the *mukhtar's* declarations. Owing to the disturbances in 1941 there had been no proper survey of 1941 sowings, and estimates were largely based on intelligent anticipation of what the crops should have been in a normal year. After the loss of valuable time, during which there was plenty of leakage to the black market, it was decided to fix a quota for the whole country and apportion it between the *mohafezats* or regions. Special regional commissions were appointed to split up the quotas by districts, and the district commissions were then instructed by the state governments to divide these assessments between the villages. This still left the final allocation among producers to the *mukhtars* and village councils—an arrangement which allowed plenty of scope for favoritism and evasion, since the *mukhtars* were often under the influence of the leading landowners.

For the second year of the scheme it was found possible to make a satisfactory assessment of the crop by organizing teams of OCP estimators to visit the villages during the winter months and obtain individual declarations as to areas sown, quantity of seed sown, and the number of dependents and animals on each farm. A second visit was paid shortly before the harvest for the purpose of obtaining an agreed estimate of the probable crop which was then signed by the OCP estimator, the *mukhtar*, and the farmer. The completed cards were then sent to the regional inspectorate of OCP. Since yields in any given district are fairly uniform, a practiced estimator could readily make a reliable estimate of the production per hectare. This procedure conformed with local custom, as it was usual before the war for merchants to purchase the standing crop on the basis of an agreed estimate of yield. After completion of the card with the necessary particulars, the producer received a notification of the quantities of cereals to be delivered to OCP and of time and place of delivery, together with an official warning of the penalties for nondelivery. This system proved more satisfactory to all concerned than the former arrangements, since it brought OCP into direct contractual relations with producers and reduced to a minimum the arbitrary decisions of *mukhtars* and village councils.

The procedure for actual purchase was made as simple as possible. On delivery at the collecting centers the cereals were weighed, tested for impurities, and bagged on the site. OCP had to purchase sufficient new sacks to cover its needs and secondhand sacks were recovered from the *Ravitaillement* authorities. After being filled, the sacks were sewn up and sealed with the distinguishing mark and number of the collecting center. Special importance was attached to prompt payment in cash on delivery, and for this purpose the purchasing officer had to be supplied with large quantities of bank notes of the right denominations, neither too large nor too small. In the early days of the scheme, as mentioned above, it was not always easy to arrange a regular supply of notes to match the delivery of cereals.

OCP was financed by an arrangement between the British Treasury and the Caisse Centrale de la France d'Outre Mer of the Free French in London. Funds were provided by the Banque de Syrie et du Liban, which discounted bills drawn by OCP; these bills were endorsed by the Caisse Centrale, which was given a guarantee by the British Treasury against any eventual loss. Money was transferred from the bank's head office to seven regional offices which supervised and accounted for the supply of cash to the collecting centers. Apart from exports, which were considerable in the second year of the scheme, the cereals bought by OCP were for the most part sold to the *Ravitaillement* or other official bodies. Payment was due in 60 days, which allowed time for the purchasers to collect the proceeds of resale to retailers.

The basic prices (in £S per ton) set out below were fixed in the first year of the scheme for wheat and other cereals delivered to the nearest main consuming center—Damascus, Aleppo, Homs, and Hama in Syria, Latakia in the Alaouites (northwest of Syria), and Beirut and Tripoli in Lebanon:

| Cereal | Seed | First quality commercial | Second quality commercial |
|---|---|---|---|
| Wheat . . . . . . . . . . . | 350 | 340 | 320 |
| Barley . . . . . . . . . . . | 250 | 240 | 220 |
| Maize . . . . . . . . . . . | 275 | 275 | — |
| Sorghum . . . . . . . . . | 250 | 250 | — |

From these prices deductions were made for transport charges by road or rail from the collecting centers, and also from the village to the collecting center in cases where OCP undertook collection from the village. Differential prices to producers, varying with distances from the nearest important market, accorded with the usual commercial practice and were more readily accepted than a lower uniform price for the whole country would have been. The prices for wheat and barley were paid for grain with what were said to be the normal commercial impurities, amounting to 8 percent. For each additional 1 percent impurities, up to 12 percent, there was a deduction of £S 5 per ton, after which the grain was rejected. For wheat and barley containing only 5 percent impurities, a premium of £S 5 per ton was allowed. Maize and sorghum had to contain not more than 4 percent impurities.

During the second year of the scheme, the basic prices remained the same but the conditions about impurities were tightened up. The prices for wheat and barley were paid for grain containing no more than 3 percent impurities and a deduction of £S 10 per ton was made for each additional 1 percent impurities between 3 and 5 percent. Above 5 percent there was a deduction of £S 10 per ton for cleaning and an additional £S 5 per ton for each 1 percent by which the impurities exceeded 5 percent.

The problem of storage and safe custody raised special difficulties. Satisfactory storage space was hard to find, particularly in the country districts. As a rule it was found advisable to keep a stock of wheat at or near the collecting centers, partly to reassure the villagers against a possible shortage later in the year. The fear of famine was a very real one as a result of bitter experience in two world wars. The bulk of the supply was sent by truck to the nearest consuming center or to railhead for transport to Lebanon. Storage in town depots was never completely satisfactory. Warehouses were apt to be damp and not properly ventilated. There were no grain silos in Syria and storing had to be in sacks, stacked crisscross in separate piles for ventilation and ease of handling. No steps could be taken to combat infestation by insects and rodents, and losses from this cause, as well as from pilfering, were far from negligible.

When OCP was launched, one of the most baffling handicaps to be overcome was lack of transport facilities. OCP's task was to collect cereals grown in an area of about 200,000 square kilometers containing upwards of 7,000 villages. In both countries, and especially in Syria, there were relatively few hard-surfaced roads suitable for heavy transport, and facilities for repairs and upkeep of motor transport were almost nonexistent outside the large towns. One single-line railroad runs south from Jezireh via Aleppo to Lebanon, and a second narrow-gauge mountain railroad connects Beirut and Damascus. The British military authorities were in control of the railroads and had spent considerable sums in repairing and improving them after the fighting of 1941. Arrangements were soon made for the fullest use of rail transport and for a supply of freight cars to be put at the disposal of OCP. This worked smoothly, the chief difficulty being to anticipate the probable flow of grain to the collecting centers and to avoid wastage of freight cars standing idle. Far more difficult was the supply and organization of road transport. At the outset OCP had no trucks of its own. It was able to borrow 70 new trucks recently imported by the Free French authorities; but for the most part it had to rely during the first year of its operations on local transport contractors and their Syrian drivers. This resulted in constant troubles and friction. Contractors and drivers were extremely independent and often dishonest and could not be relied on to carry out instructions. It was difficult to get them to work on a fixed schedule and they objected not unnaturally to their trucks being used on bad roads. As wear and tear increased and spare parts became scarcer, trucks were laid up for months. Then in the spring of 1943 Lend-Lease trucks began to arrive. By July 1943 OCP itself owned a fleet of 250 trucks, about half the number required during the period of heaviest deliveries; and in order to move as much as possible of the bumper wheat crop before the winter rains made transport impossible, the British army loaned the services of a General Transport Company with 176 heavy vehicles of 4.5-ton capacity. A British officer was put in charge of all transport of cereals by road and rail, and in course of time built up an organization that worked with a satisfactory degree of efficiency. One of the chief difficulties that was never surmounted was the high cost of operating road transport in Syria largely because of the excessive cost of maintenance and repairs. Additional burdens, against which OCP protested in vain, were the increased tax on motor spirit and the import duty levied on tires supplied under Lend-Lease.

## CITATIONS

*1* General Sir Edward Spears, unpublished memorandum.

*2* W. S. Churchill, *The Second World War: The Hinge of Fate* (Houghton Mifflin Co., Boston, 1950).

CHAPTER 18

# CEREAL COLLECTION IN PERSIA

## THREAT OF FAMINE IN TEHERAN

It was not until March 1942 that Persia was included, along with Iraq and the Persian Gulf, within the sphere of operations of the Middle East Supply Center (MESC). At that time Egypt was facing a cereal crisis and the first steps were being taken to introduce a cereal-control scheme in Syria; but no special ground for anxiety had arisen in Persia. At the first Middle East Agricultural Conference, held in Cairo on May 14 and 15, 1942, under the chairmanship of R. F. Kahn, economic adviser to MESC and to the Minister of State, it was reported from Teheran that there was already in force a system of government purchase of wheat for the towns at a fixed price of 1,000 rials or $31 a ton; the price had recently been raised to 1,400 rials, but this had now been canceled and the former price restored. This was less than half the official price of $80 per ton in Iraq; and at least $100 per ton was expected to be fixed for the 1942 crops in Palestine and Syria. No reliable forecast of the 1942 cereal crops in Persia was possible, but there was little reason to suppose that supplies would be insufficient, provided a reasonable price was fixed before the coming harvest. It was provisionally concluded that no cereal imports into Persia would be needed during the coming cereal year.

In less than six months the position had become extremely critical. In December 1942 riots broke out in Teheran, caused largely, though perhaps not entirely, by a bread shortage; and virtual breakdown of internal collection and distribution of wheat necessitated prompt measures of relief. The reasons for this rapid change for the worse were similar to those that had operated the year before in Syria: a crop less than average coincided with increased demand for supplies, transport, and labor, resulting from Allied military expenditure. Insecurity and rising prices stimulated hoarding; and mistaken efforts of the government to check inflation by holding down the official price of wheat, in order to prevent a rise in the price of bread, had discouraged the marketing of supplies through official channels.

During the three years 1936–38 wheat production according to official estimates averaged 1.87 million tons and the 1939 crop was probably about 1.70 million. During the war there was more than usual difficulty in getting an accurate assessment of the crop, but there seems no doubt that both the 1940 and 1941 crops were below normal. The published estimates of 1.50 million tons in 1940 and 1.20 million in 1941 may be too low. In 1940/41, 15,000 tons were exported, compared with 22,500 in 1936–38.

Allied military intervention in August and September 1941 had had an unfavorable influence on sowing in the south, where for a time fighting took place, and Russian occupation of the northern provinces cut off supplies from Azerbaijan, whence the capital, Teheran, normally drew about a third of its requirements. MESC at the time estimated the 1942 crop at about 1.4 million tons, but later estimates gave a lower figure of just under 1.2 million. The barley crop, variously estimated at 560,000 or 600,000 tons, was also below the prewar average of 793,000. Barley is little used in Persia for human food and to a large extent is fed green to livestock. Rice is produced and consumed mainly on the shores of the Caspian Sea, which came within the Russian zone of occupation. Prewar production of paddy was about 425,000 tons and the crop was estimated to have been 25 percent lower in 1942.

Wheat is the traditional bread grain of Persia in both towns and villages. The risk of occasional crop failures, leading to shortage of bread and social unrest, had induced the government in recent years to intervene in the marketing of wheat and the distribution of flour. Under the system prevailing in 1940/41, landlords, whose rent usually took the form of a share in the crop, were required to sell their assessed surplus to the government, which itself assumed responsibility for feeding the towns and maintaining central reserves. Riza Shah Pahlevi, who overthrew the Kajar dynasty and assumed dictatorial powers in 1926, had erected on the outskirts of Teheran a large concrete grain elevator, called in Persian the "Silo," with a modern flour mill equipped with machinery imported from the USSR. The Silo had a storage capacity of about 60,000 tons, sufficient for more than half a year's supply for the capital. In a country where the supply and price of wheat could make or unmake governments the establishment of a reserve stock in the capital was a prudent measure. But in the fall of 1941, after two poor crops, the Silo was all but empty and the supply of wheat to Teheran was on a hand-to-mouth basis.

In 1940 and 1941, before the entry of the Allied armies, the official price of 1,000 rials per ton (equivalent to $58 per ton at the rate of exchange prevailing before October 1941) was above the price ruling in the free market and in neighboring countries. But when the rial was devalued on October 1, 1941 and the rate rose from 17 to 35 rials to the dollar, the fixed price became less attractive. Riza Shah Pahlevi refused to raise the price for fear of arousing discontent in the towns. Until his abdication in September 1941, his orders were obeyed and collection of the new crop proceeded with little difficulty. But early in 1942 with the removal of his authority, insecurity and fear that inflation would get out of control led to hoarding and a rise of price in the free market. In March 1942 an antihoarding act was passed by the Majlis (Persian national assembly) but had little effect. In May the official price, which had been temporarily raised to 1,400 rials, was again fixed at 1,000 rials. Meanwhile the open-market price had risen to 4,000 rials per ton and landlords refused to sell to the government at the official price. Merchants in the towns competed with one another to obtain supplies and wheat was smuggled into Turkey and Iraq. The government's control of collection and distribution of wheat was in danger of imminent collapse. The Persian government complained that wheat requirements of Persian labor employed by the Allies on road and railway work conflicted with the requirements of Teheran and other towns, and asked for wheat to be imported from abroad.

Enquiries showed that although the current harvest would be a partial failure in some parts of the country, there was, or should be, no serious shortage provided that hoarding could be checked and government collection of wheat could be organized with some degree of honesty and efficiency. G. F. Squire of the British Legation made the suggestion that if British officers were stationed in the principal wheat-producing areas they might be able not only to induce farmers and landowners to sell their surplus grain to the government but to see that government officials on their part really paid for it. The Persian Minister of Finance, M. Bader, who was at that time the minister responsible, accepted the proposal and the scheme was launched in June 1942.

The officers appointed were called consular liaison officers, and played an important part in the ultimate success of cereal collection in Persia. They worked directly under the control of the British Legation and had no executive authority. But since they were officially introduced to the local governors by the Persian Ministry of Finance, they were able to make their own investigations and to estimate whether there was or was not any surplus grain in their districts that should be delivered to the government. Later, in some places, they were allowed to do a great deal more, not only in cereal collection, but also in seeing that the larger towns were properly supplied with their requirements. In the first year, however, they could do little to effect any radical improvement in the situation.

In August a Food Department was established in the Ministry of Finance and in September a separate Ministry of Food was created. In October J. K. Sheridan, an American businessman who had lived most of his life in the Middle East, was appointed adviser to the Persian Minister of Food and began to infuse a new spirit into the administration. About the same time Dr. A. C. Millspaugh was invited by the Persian Prime Minister, at the suggestion of the British government, to return to the post of Administrator General of the Finances from which he had been dismissed by Riza Shah Pahlevi in 1927. Millspaugh, in his frank and revealing book (*1*, p. 45), summarizes as follows the conditions which prompted the government and Majlis to invite him once again to do what he could to cope with the financial crisis: "Armed forces of Britain and Russia occupied the country. Insecurity prevailed. Prices were skyrocketing. Trade was in a slump and administration in chaos. Bankruptcy and famine, perhaps revolution, threatened. Constitutional government, restored, betrayed its impotency; but in the reaction from Pahlevi's tyranny the dream of 1906 seemed to have another chance for fulfillment."

Before Millspaugh arrived, the riots in Teheran in December 1942 became front-page news in the American and British press. Mobs attacked and burned the house of Qavam Salteneh, the Persian Prime Minister (*2*, pp. 192, 195). For some months the supply of bread had been insufficient and of bad quality. Isolated cases of starvation had occurred and large numbers were suffering from shortage and high prices of food. The poor harvest was not the only, or indeed the principal, cause of the shortage. More important were the indirect and unintended consequences of armed intervention. Millspaugh refers to the disintegration of the Persian army and the demoralization and partial paralysis that affected the bureaucracy when Riza Shah abdicated. The tribal chiefs, whom Riza Shah disarmed and kept in check, were now, he says (*1*, p. 40),

> again armed, and resumed their banditry. Protected by the general anarchy, government officials stole the revenues, while other classes of extortioners

made free use of the opportunity that chaos presented. War already had cut off much of the country's foreign trade. Internal insecurity now aggravated the hoarding of goods, accelerating inflation and stimulating speculation. The Persian government made elaborate but futile efforts to deal with spiraling prices. The swollen bureaucracy suffered demoralization and partial paralysis.

Above all, grain collection depended on transportation. In September 1941, when British and Russian forces met at Teheran, the Trans-Persian Railway passed into Allied hands, the British army taking control of the southern part and the Soviet army of the northern. Ports on the Persian Gulf were taken over by the British; ports on the Caspian Sea by the Russians. The Treaty of Alliance with Persia concluded by Great Britain and the USSR on January 29, 1942 gavc to the Allied powers the unrestricted right to use and control all means of communication including railways, roads, rivers, airfields, ports, and telegraph, telephone, and wireless installations. The Persian government also undertook to furnish help in obtaining material and recruiting labor for the maintenance and improvement of these means of communication.

Under these clauses of the Treaty an enormous effort was at once put in hand to develop the supply line to Russia (*3*, p. 93). In October 1941 Persia's one single-track railroad, completed only four years before at a cost of $120 million, was able to carry 200 tons a day; later it was to carry 2,400 tons daily. By the end of 1942 the carrying capacity had been vastly expanded, not by doubling the whole track which would have been almost as big a task as the original construction, but by building new lines from Ahwaz to Khorramshahr and Tanuma, doubling the tracks in the marshaling yards at Ahwaz and Teheran, and constructing 40 new crossing stations. The permanent way had to be kept in sound repair with gravel ballast and timber, both difficult to buy locally. A large building program of sheds, workshops, storehouses, offices, and hutted camps was undertaken. All this involved heavy expenditure of local currency for men, materials, and supplies, including food for railroad personnel. "A special officer was appointed to get food which Persian employees at remote stations could buy at prices within their slender means" (*3*, p. 99).

But the development of the railroad alone could never cope with the vast amount of tonnage to be carried to Russia. Increased carrying capacity on the highways assumed equal importance and involved even greater expenditure on locally recruited labor. The total length of roads included in the program of development was 3,000 miles—

the distance from New York to San Francisco. Three different routes were finally put in order and largely rebuilt—in the west from Khanaqin on the Iraq border to Kazvin in the Russian zone; in the center from Bushire on the Persian Gulf to Isfahan to Teheran; and in the east from Mirjawa near the southwest frontier of Afghanistan, connecting by rail with India, to Meshed near the northeast border of Persia. In the west the road had been metaled from time to time but for some years past had been allowed to fall into shocking disrepair. In the east and center the roads were gravel tracks alternating with stretches of sand and salt mud. The reconstruction and maintenance of these roads was entrusted to contractors and subcontractors, working under the supervision of British officers and of engineers of a Danish company which had acted as consultant to the Persian government in railroad construction. At one time the number of Persian laborers employed reached 67,000 (*3*, p. 108). By 1943 the road from Khanaqin had been entirely remetaled and surfaced with bitumen. In April 1943 responsibility for operating the railroad was taken over by the American army. By the middle of 1945 nearly 5 million tons of munitions and supplies of all kinds had been carried by road and rail into the USSR.

It had been agreed with the Persian Prime Minister that the essential needs of the Persian population were to come first. Nevertheless all this activity was bound to have disturbing effects on the civilian economy. First, it aggravated the inflation which had already started before the Allies' intervention, for it put into circulation a large amount of new currency obtained from the National Bank in exchange for sterling and dollars. Second, it made heavy drains on existing transport facilities and dislocated internal distribution of civilian goods. Third, it increased the demand for food and civilian supplies and encouraged speculation and hoarding. The only grain bought by the British in Persia was for feeding the laborers employed on roads and other public works, and even this was abandoned toward the end of 1942 when imported supplies were brought in. But in the first year of operation the feeding of laborers on rail and road construction was a difficult problem, and the high prices that had to be paid to attract supplies interfered with official collection of grain for the towns. The net effect was to divert a considerable part of the productive resources of the country from normal peacetime activity into a vast program of public works financed not by taxation or loan issues but by expansion of currency and bank credit.

In 1942 Allied military expenditure was about 1,300 million

rials. During the same twelve months the volume of notes in circulation nearly doubled, with an increase of 1,550 million rials. The cost-of-living index (April–August 1939 = 100) rose from 191 in December 1941 to 390 in December 1942. After rising 100 percent in 1942 and again in 1943 (from 390 in December 1942 to 774 in December 1943) when military expenditure reached 4,200 million rials, the index fell from 774 to 684 in 1944. This result was partly due to a reduction of Allied expenditure in 1944 to 3,400 million rials and partly to the successful efforts of Millspaugh and his American mission to check inflation by controlling supplies and prices and by increasing taxation. Between April 1942 and April 1943 the cost-of-living index rose 179 percent; in the next twelve months to April 1944 it rose only 17 percent. After May 1944 the turning point was reached, and as military expenditure declined the index began to fall.

This reference to the inflationary impact of Allied intervention, a topic which is discussed more fully in chapter 20 below, supplies a necessary background to the cereals crisis in the early months of 1943 with which Sheridan, the American food adviser, and later Millspaugh, were called upon to deal. The crisis was unexpected and the extent of the shortage which was to develop was unforeseen. At a meeting in Cairo of the Supply and Transportation Sub-Committee of the Middle East War Council on October 21, 1942, shortly after Sheridan had been appointed, the Persian cereal-supply position was reviewed. In view of the prevailing scarcity of wheat and the growing difficulty of obtaining supplies at reasonable prices, the conclusion was reached that the quantity needed for feeding civilian labor employed by the British army and by the Anglo-Iranian Oil Company, estimated at 3,000 tons monthly, should be met from imports.[1] If this were done, it was estimated that the towns could be fed by supplies from Azerbaijan in the Russian zone of occupation and from other surplus districts. Fears were expressed that transport facilities might be inadequate; but it does not seem to have been appreciated that the Russians were counting on drawing supplies from Azerbaijan and were preventing the normal movement of wheat to Teheran.

Meanwhile in Teheran the Persian government had decided, on Sheridan's advice, to abandon the previous system under which a free market was allowed to operate alongside government purchase

[1] The Anglo-Iranian Oil Company received permission to bring grain back from Australia in its tankers and it provided wheat and flour not only for its employees but for the other inhabitants of the oil area.

of officially assessed "surpluses," and to replace it by government monopoly and prohibition of private trade, as in Syria and Egypt. The Persian Ministry of Food became the sole legal purchaser of wheat, and prices were fixed which varied from 3,000 to 3,800 rials per ton according to the district—the highest price being paid in frontier districts where smuggling into Turkey or Iraq had been prevalent. But these changes came too late in the cereal year to ensure sufficient supplies for the towns, and after the outbreak of disorders in December 1942, which led to the fall of Qavam Salteneh's government, an urgent plea was sent to London and Washington for 10,000 tons of imported wheat to be sent monthly until the next harvest. The two governments recognized the urgency of the need and the Combined Food Board (CFB), recently set up in Washington, recommended allocation of 25,000 tons during the next six months. At the same time the government of the USSR offered to release 25,000 tons from Azerbaijan in the Russian-occupied zone. In addition it was arranged that the United Kingdom Commercial Corporation (UKCC) should import 18,500 tons of barley into Persia from Iraq. Admixture of barley in the loaf had already been introduced in the towns, and on one occasion early in 1943 the bread in Teheran had to be made entirely from barley flour.

Many difficulties had to be overcome before supplies could be assured in sufficient quantities. Shipment of cereals from India, which had been the normal source of supply to the Persian Gulf Sheikdoms and to ports on the Red Sea, came to an end late in 1942. Loadings of wheat from North America to the Middle East had been reduced in recent months and from November 1942 a cut of 50 percent in shipping to the Middle East had been imposed for operational reasons. MESC had had to take over responsibility for supplying the Persian Gulf territories, involving 6,000 tons of wheat and rice monthly, as well as 3,000 tons for the British forces in Persia and Iraq (Paiforce) and the Anglo-Iranian Oil Company. To this was now added 25,000 tons for the Persian government, delivery to start as soon as possible.

For some months the supply position in Teheran remained extremely critical. In February and again in March 1943 supplies were reduced to a few days' requirements. Special priority had to be given to the railing of barley from Iraq, and the army more than once came to the rescue by providing trucks to move supplies by road. From April onward the stock position began to improve and by the end of June 24,000 tons of barley had been sent from Iraq and

22,000 tons of imported wheat had arrived from overseas. Only 4,500 tons of wheat from Azerbaijan had been delivered by the Russians before the end of June and the remainder of the 25,000 tons they had promised did not arrive till July and August. These deliveries from Azerbaijan would not of course be recorded as imports; nor, it seems, were the deliveries of barley by UKCC. According to the Persian government's published trade returns, net imports of wheat were 32,500 tons in the 12 months ended March 1943, and 30,100 tons in the following year, most of which arrived before December 1943.

The necessity of diverting grain ships to feed Teheran served to focus attention, not only in MESC but in London and Washington, on the need for improved cereal collection in the coming crop year. Owing to the disturbed state of the country and partial paralysis in the machinery of government, no reliable estimate could be made of the probable size of the crop. MESC officers in Teheran reported that 1943 cereal crops were expected to be about one-fifth larger than those of 1942. This would mean about 1.68 million tons of wheat and 700,000 tons of barley. The Persian Ministry of Food reckoned that 318,000 tons of cereals would be needed to feed the towns, and of this amount Teheran alone would require 92,500. The original plan was to acquire by government purchase 280,000 tons of wheat and 70,000 tons of barley, and thus provide a carryover of 32,000 tons.

In April 1943 the Persian ministries of Supply and of Food made public their first proposals for cereal collection as follows:

1. Landowners would be invited to undertake to sell to the government at fixed prices all their surplus wheat and barley. In most provinces the prices were fixed at 3,000 rials ($94) a ton for wheat and 2,250 rials ($70) for barley. For the purpose of assessing the surplus, landowners were entitled to deduct their tenants' share of the crop, their seed requirements, and two tons for their own use plus a percentage of the remainder varying from 5 percent to 20 percent according to the size of the crop.

2. From November 23, 1943 to February 21, 1944 the price would be reduced by one-third, and from February 21 any surplus not delivered would be liable to confiscation.

3. Peasants would be free to sell any part of their share in the open market and likewise landowners who had fulfilled their undertakings.

This scheme left obvious loopholes. Landowners' surpluses could not be accurately or expeditiously assessed and the existence of a free market made it difficult to check evasion. Lack of trained personnel led to a request for help from British consular liaison officers. In certain areas contracts were made with dealers under the supervision of these consular liaison officers, who also helped local officials in the assessment and collection of surpluses where this system could be adopted.

In July 1943 Sheridan resigned his post as food adviser and the Persian Prime Minister, Mr. Soheily, persuaded Millspaugh to take responsibility for the operation of the Persian Ministry of Food. The latter writes (*1*, p. 100) that, before he took over, "the political direction of the Ministry of Food kept the whole operation in a state of uncertainty, inefficiency, and gross corruption; while in some of the most important grain-growing regions governors interfered with and in some cases completely controlled local operations, paying little attention to the needs of the country as a whole or to the orders of the central government." He also says (*1*, p. 100) that grain collection "would have been in an even worse state had it not been for British help in collection and British and Soviet assistance in transportation." From the Persian standpoint it was of course equally true that grain collection would not have been in such a bad state if so much of the country's transport facilities had not been required for the vast operation of sending aid to Russia.

On August 3, 1943, control of cereals was tightened up by declaring wheat and barley to be government monopolies. Private trading was made illegal; transport of grain was to be carried out only on behalf of the new Cereals and Bread Department of the Ministry of Finance. Cereals sold privately or hoarded were to be confiscated, and export was prohibited. Existing arrangements for the purchase of landowners' surpluses were to continue, including the reduction of one-third in the price on November 23, 1943; but the date for confiscation of surpluses not delivered was extended from February 21 to March 23, 1944. Collection of grain during the first few months after the harvest lagged far behind schedule. Up to August 10, 1943 only 16,000 tons had been collected. It was fortunate that there was now in Teheran a stock of imported wheat and a carryover of supplies tardily released by the Russians from Azerbaijan. But in Ahwaz in the south there was an acute shortage in August which led to violent public demonstrations. Rationing had to be temporarily suspended and the price of bread rose from 4 to 12 rials per kilo.

The chief difficulty to be overcome was the shortage and disorganization of transport. There was also a scarcity of sacks. In many provinces there was insufficient cash available to pay for cereals offered; in others tribal disturbances and banditry brought buying to a standstill. Communications were poor and lack of passenger cars and tires was a serious handicap.

After Millspaugh took control in August 1943 conditions began to improve. A credit of 100 million rials was opened with the National Bank. Rex Vivian, one of Sheridan's American assistants, was put in charge of the road transport administration; and in September Colonel Speake of the United States army was appointed director-general of cereals and bread. Supplies remained barely sufficient in September and October, and at one time stocks in Teheran were down to 1,250 tons, or five days' supply. In September 1943, although no official request for imported wheat had been made, MESC feared that deliveries would be insufficient and ordered 8,000 tons to be shipped for arrival early in 1944.

Meanwhile Millspaugh was under constant pressure from deputies in the Majlis to relax his prohibition of private trade. He writes (*1*, p. 108):

> In order to ensure continuous and effective control, the government had prohibited private transportation of grain into the cities. About a dozen deputies met with me in two conferences, each of which lasted some three hours. They proposed that we lift the prohibition of transport in order to permit householders to lay in their own supplies of flour, as had been the custom in the past. They had plausible arguments; and, if we had an ample reserve in the Silo, it would have been quite safe and eminently politic to free the trade in grain and flour, as we did a year later. At the time, we had no reserve, and no assurance that we could feed Teheran during the next winter. It appeared also that a partial freeing of transport and sale would hamper our collection work, since the black market price in the capital was then considerably above the government price outside the city.
>
> The pressure for flour permits appeared trifling in comparison with the agitation that followed over bread. This and the anxiety over the prospects of food during the coming winter stimulated a highly emotional newspaper propaganda, led to an interpellation of the government, and prompted the deputies to discuss in secret session a proposal to annul my economic powers.

Before the end of the year the situation had been greatly improved through the loan of trucks and the provision of transport facilities by the Allied military authorities. Paiforce made 500 trucks available for the transport of up to 10,000 tons of grain from Kermanshah; the Russians loaned 200 trucks for deliveries from the north; and the

United States army arranged for backloading of grain in trucks carrying Lend-Lease cargoes for the Red army. Total collections and arrivals of cereals at Teheran were as follows, in tons:

| 1943 | Total collections | Arrivals at Teheran |
|---|---|---|
| July 1 to September 22..... | 40,000 | 6,540 |
| September 23 to October 23 | 32,000 | 9,045 |
| October 24 to November 22.. | 68,000 | 8,295 |
| November 23 to December 22 | 90,690 | 15,740 |
| Total ................ | 230,690 | 39,620 |

On November 11, 1943, just before the opening of the Teheran Conference of Roosevelt, Churchill, and Stalin, a new regulation was issued permitting householders in Teheran to buy grain from peasants and landowners who had fulfilled their obligations to the government, and to transport it at their own expense to the Silo in Teheran, where it could be exchanged for flour or bread on surrender of bread-ration cards. The story of bread rationing in Persia is told in chapter 25.

During the winter months, when the reduction of one-third in the official buying price came into effect, a new inducement scheme was introduced by which landowners who had fulfilled their undertakings, and also peasants who had any grain to spare, were offered part of the purchase price in sugar valued at the controlled price, which was much below the market price. In the first month the terms offered were 15 percent sugar and 85 percent cash, in the second 10 percent sugar, and in the third 5 percent. Purchase on these terms was to be limited to two tons from any one seller. About 5,000 tons were bought in this way in the difficult area round Ahwaz.

At the end of 1943 six American transport experts headed by Floyd Shields joined the Millspaugh mission and took over the direction of the road-transport administration. As more imported trucks, cars, tires, and spare parts became available, grain collection ran more smoothly. By the end of April 1944, 311,500 tons had been collected and total stocks had reached the record figure of 152,000 tons, equivalent to a six-months reserve for the towns. On July 1, stocks in Teheran were 35,000 tons, sufficient for more than four-months consumption. MESC decided that the emergency reserve of 8,000 tons of imported wheat which had been earmarked for Persia was no longer needed and it was able to cancel a cargo of wheat due to be loaded in Australia for the Middle East.

In the following year, 1944/45, the organization of cereal collection was much improved. Millspaugh wrote (*1*, p. 117): "With the help of American provincial officials and their British assistants and under the direction of Dr. Black and his American and British colleagues at Teheran, grain collection marched on to an achievement unprecedented in this land of famines." By the end of January 1945 total stocks reached 273,000 tons, sufficient to feed the towns for ten months; and the Silo at Teheran was almost filled to capacity with a seven-months reserve of 56,000 tons (*1*, p. 130). In April 1945 MESC was able to negotiate for the export of 50,000 tons of wheat from Persia to other Middle East territories.

On February 28, 1945, when Millspaugh left Persia, he had been for nearly two years subjected to venomous attacks in the Majlis for doing what he could to prevent famine, inflation, and civil unrest. If only he had been appointed a year or eighteen months earlier, immediately after the Allied intervention, many of the misfortunes and hardships for which he was wrongly blamed might have been avoided or greatly reduced. But unfortunately it was not at the time foreseen, and perhaps it was impossible to foresee, what grave impacts all-out aid to Russia was to have on the Persian economy. That the situation was not worse was to a large extent due to Millspaugh's indefatigable and at times almost desperate efforts to restore order in the Persian administration.

## CITATIONS

*1* A. C. Millspaugh, *Americans in Persia* (Brookings Inst., Washington, D.C., 1946).

*2* George Lenczowski, *Russia and the West in Iran* (New York, 1949).

*3* Gt. Brit., War Off., Cent. Off. Inf., *Paiforce . . .* (1948).

CHAPTER 19

# IRAQ CEREAL SUPPLIES

## WHEAT

Up to and including 1940, Iraq had been a wheat-exporting country as well as a large exporter of barley. Net exports of wheat before the war averaged 50,000 tons, and were 33,000 tons in 1940. In the cereal year, July 1941–June 1942, widespread damage was caused by the sunn pest and some local shortages were reported. In 1941, 24,000 tons were imported, and 26,000 in 1942. Production and trade figures for the war years are shown in Appendix Tables IV and V respectively. Production estimates for Iraq are particularly uncertain; current estimates were considerably lower than the revised figures shown (25 or 30 percent lower in some years).

Up to July 1942 the grain trade was free and uncontrolled, except for the traditional tax of 10 percent on grain brought into Istikhlak markets and some requisitioning of stocks on farms in Mosul province. Toward the end of the season wheat prices had risen to more than twice the prewar price and a maximum price of 25 dinars ($100) per ton was established. The price of bread in the towns was fixed at 24 fils (10 cents) per kilo, made possible by a government subsidy which permitted the price of flour to be brought down to 18.5 dinars per ton.

In March 1942 Iraq's Central Supplies Committee introduced a compulsory admixture of 10 percent of barley. In November of the same year the admixture was 30 percent barley in Basra, and in Baghdad 15 percent barley plus 15 percent maize. The extraction rate of wheat was fixed at a minimum of 95 percent, of barley at 65 percent. The introduction of bread rationing was considered but was rejected as impracticable or at least unnecessary.

On July 1, 1942 the Iraq Ministry of Finance planned to purchase 100,000 tons of the 1942 wheat crop at prices not exceeding 25 dinars per ton to meet the estimated consumption of the urban areas. At the same time the United Kingdom Commercial Corporation (UKCC) started negotiating on behalf of the Middle East Supply Center (MESC) to build up a reserve stock of wheat in Iraq for the purpose of meeting any unexpected shortage that might develop, thus avoiding further imports. Rumors got about that the British were planning to export wheat on a large scale and these rumors, combined with the fact that in June the Syrian wheat price had been fixed at $156 a ton, sent the market price soaring well above the official maximum price. The government then announced that its buying program would be reduced to 60,000 tons. On July 21 all purchasers of more than one ton of wheat were required to be licensed, and on August 1 stocks of wheat in rural areas, except those belonging to the fellahin, had to be registered. One-fourth of the stocks so declared had to be delivered to the government or to a licensed merchant within one month. At the end of August, Judge H. I. Lloyd, President of the Court of Cassation, was appointed to the new post of director-general of cereals.

In November 1942, 50,000 tons of wheat had been acquired and at a conference of *mutasarrifs*, or provincial governors, it was decided that stocks would be sufficient to last until the end of the cereal year. No imports of wheat and flour, in fact, took place in 1943.

### BARLEY

Before the war, Iraq was a large exporter of barley, mainly to the United Kingdom for animal feeding, the average for the five years 1934–38 being over 200,000 tons. Revised figures of production and exports for the war years are shown in Appendix Tables IV and V respectively. As for wheat, the production estimates are uncertain.

At the outbreak of war, the price of Iraq barley touched a low point of less than 5 dinars ($20) per ton. During the disturbances of 1941, when inflation got under way, the price of barley rose in sympathy with wheat and other commodities. During the six months June–December 1941, prices nearly doubled. In October the government decided to regulate exports and UKCC was granted the sole license to export barley of the 1941 crop. In February 1942 the government granted permission to export 35,000 tons of barley, partly in exchange for import of wheat. Net exports for the year 1942 were 54,000 tons.

For the 1942 crop the Iraq government was urged by the British to institute more drastic measures of control, and in September 1942 was warned that it could not expect to have its import requirements for sugar and textiles favorably considered if it failed to co-operate in making surplus barley available for export.

After the Iraq declaration of war on the Axis powers on January 16, 1943, the long-drawn-out negotiations resulted in a scheme satisfactory to both parties. In February the government ordered registration of all stocks of barley above personal requirements and prohibited private trading. Prices for uncleaned barley on the farm were fixed on a descending scale beginning at 19 dinars per ton (with 10 percent impurities) and falling to 10 dinars per ton on April 1. Three British firms established in Iraq were appointed purchasing agents for export; in turn they resold to UKCC, charging 5 percent commission for expenses. With a further weakening of prices and the prospect of a good crop in 1943, it proved possible to remove the prohibition on private trade at the end of May.

Measures taken were sufficient to fulfill the original MESC program for deliveries of Iraq barley during the period September 1942–June 1943. Actual deliveries compared with the original program were as follows, in thousand metric tons:

| Country | Original program, 1942/43 | Deliveries, Aug. 1, 1942–Aug. 31, 1943 |
|---|---|---|
| Palestine and Syria (British 9th Army | 25,000 | 13,200 |
| Palestine (civil) | 35,000 | 18,100 |
| Turkey | 35,000 | 31,000 |
| Syria | 25,000 | — |
| Persia | — | 23,800 |
| British and American armies and Anglo-Iranian Oil Company | — | 20,800 |
| Arab states | — | 3,100 |
| Total | 120,000 | 110,000 |

Some millet was also purchased for export during the first six months of 1943.

It was hoped at one time to obtain part of the rice surplus, estimated at 30,000–40,000 tons, but the prices, $280 per ton for first-quality rice and $140–$160 for second-quality, were considered too high. Net exports as shown by customs returns averaged 1,360 tons in 1934–38, 600 in 1939, 1,890 in 1940, and 5,890 in 1941. In 1942, net exports were only 260 tons; but to these must be added a considerable and unknown quantity smuggled into Turkey and Syria by animal transport which did not pass through the customs.

### 1943 CEREAL COLLECTION

For the 1943 wheat and barley crops an organized collection scheme was prepared under which sowings had to be registered. Local committees were appointed to estimate standing crops and the results of threshing, and British political advisers were called in to assist locally. Farmers were given the right to appeal for reassessment before October 1, 1943, in the event of crop failure or for other reasons. Under the original scheme the government was to purchase compulsorily one-half of the wheat crop and one-third of the barley crop, and a contract was made to sell 200,000 tons of barley for export to the British government at a price of 20.5 dinars ($82) per ton. The original program for collection and disposal of the 1943 crops, as given in a report dated October 28, 1943 by the director-general of local products, was as follows, in thousand metric tons:

| Item | Wheat | Barley |
|---|---|---|
| Estimated total crop[a] | 390 | 581 |
| For delivery to Iraq government | 195 | 193 |
| For consumption by noncultivators | 100 | 40 |
| Reserve | 50 | 20 |
| For sale to UKCC by Iraq government | — | 200 |
| Estimated surplus (available for purchase) | 45 | 128 |

[a] Current estimates; some years later the estimate for wheat was raised to 480,000 tons, for barley to 899,000 tons.

The official maximum prices were 32 dinars per ton, including tax, for first-grade wheat at collecting centers and 25 dinars on the farm. In September 1943 the open-market price of wheat had exceeded 50 dinars per ton. For barley, first-grade, the corresponding maximum prices were 20.5 dinars and 15 dinars per ton. UKCC was permitted to buy additional quantities at lower prices on the open market if it could do so.

These high prices were a matter of serious concern, and some authorities in London urged the desirability of holding off the Iraq market in order to force prices down. But pressure of continued shortage of shipping, large demands for imported cereals from India, necessity of replacing Indian wheat with Iraq barley in the Arab states after September 1, 1943, and need for meeting requirements of Palestine, Cyprus, and the Ninth British Army and making some provision for a Balkan reserve, rendered this policy impracticable. The level of prices in Iraq was already out of line with world prices, largely owing to the inflationary expenditure of Allied armies, which included Polish troops brought through Persia from the USSR. Notes issued doubled between December 1941 and December 1942 and by December 1943 reached six times the prewar level. If proper control all along the line had been exercised and some means had been found for withdrawing the surplus purchasing power by increased taxation and savings, the rise of prices might have been checked; but any attempt to force down the price of a single commodity like barley, particularly when it was urgently needed for war purposes and to save shipping, was unwise and doomed to failure. It was true that by holding off the market and prohibiting private trade, the price of barley had been reduced from about 30 dinars in November 1942 to a nominal 15 dinars on April 1, 1943; but meanwhile, between November 1942 and November 1943, cotton had risen 56 percent, wool 25 percent, dates 25 percent, rice 33 percent, and the general level of wholesale and retail prices by about one-third.

These arguments put forward by MESC were reluctantly accepted in London. But the high cost and poor quality of Iraq barley created serious embarrassment for the deficit countries to which it was sent. To induce the independent Persian Gulf Sheikdoms to accept it, it proved necessary to lower the price by means of a subsidy of $64 per ton paid by the British government. India also experienced difficulty in absorbing her full allocation of 100,000 tons owing to the poor quality and high prices.

Collection of crops on the whole proceeded smoothly, except in the north, where there were transport difficulties and a tendency to withhold supplies. Supplies were scarce in Basra during October, but the crisis was overcome by improved distribution and transport. In September it was necessary to stop the movement of Iraq barley over the Baghdad–Aleppo railway in order to permit the maximum use of rail transport by OCP (Office des Céréales Panifiables) for collecting the large crop of wheat in Syria.

In April 1944 it was reported that 120,000 tons of wheat had been collected under the new collection scheme, with 20,000 tons more expected—sufficient to last to the next harvest. At the end of the cereal year the carryover of wheat in government hands amounted to 40,000 tons.

Collection of barley was equally satisfactory. By the end of 1943 the original program of purchase by UKCC had been achieved. By January 15,1944 some 215,000 tons of barley had been obtained and plans were being made to continue purchasing on the open market at prices below the official ceiling of 20.5 dinars per ton. In May 1944 barley stocks at Basra reached 50,000 tons, and since no more could be stored UKCC had to stop buying. In spite of the transport difficulties on the Syrian railway it was found possible to move 6,800 tons of barley from Baghdad to Haifa by rail. Stocks of wheat and barley in Palestine were at the time only sufficient for ten days' consumption. One of the chief problems still facing MESC was to move barley by rail or sea from Iraq to Palestine and Cyprus. In September 1944 a new contract was made for the purchase of 200,000 tons of new-crop barley at a price of 19.5 dinars f.o.b. Basra—a substantial reduction on prices paid during the previous year. This barley was still needed for supply to other countries in the Middle East, mainly for purposes of admixture with wheat. By January 1945 UKCC had bought 81,000 tons; stocks in Baghdad were 6,900 and in Basra 37,800 tons. Exports of Iraq barley from July to December 1944 were 100,000 tons, two-thirds by sea and one-third by rail transport through Syria. As in the previous year, transport by rail through Syria of Iraq barley for Cyprus and Palestine was held up from June until the end of October owing to the need for lifting the Syrian harvest.

By July 1945 conditions had so far improved that the UKCC monopoly of export was discontinued and the export trade in barley was restored to private enterprise. Net exports during 1945 reached the high figure of 243,000 tons, 20 percent above the prewar average.

The story of Iraq barley has been referred to earlier in chapter 13 as an illustration of conflicting objectives. All parties wanted to maintain and, if possible, increase production; but the Iraq authorities had to bear in mind the interests of consumers and the need to check the wage-price spiral, and the British Treasury was anxious to stop inflation and the piling up of sterling balances. From the standpoint of shipping and supply, maximum exports of Iraq barley were needed; but the easiest way to keep down the price was to limit exports and allow a free internal market. The British Treasury was reluctant to authorize a bulk contract at the high price asked by Iraq ministers; and UKCC urged that if the weight of supplies were left to bring down prices in a free market, it would be able to buy all that was needed without any bulk contract, so long as it was given the sole right to export. MESC was unable to agree with the Treasury and UKCC; if the full surplus was to be obtained for export, it was convinced that a bulk contract was essential, combined with compulsory collection at fixed prices which must take account of the inflationary rise in the general price level. So long as inflation was rampant and shortage of shipping was the dominant consideration MESC's arguments were difficult to rebut and in fact prevailed. But the participation in the scheme of UKCC and, in 1943, of three British firms acting as its purchasing agents, was never popular in Iraq and was only reluctantly accepted by the government and by UKCC itself as a temporary wartime expedient.

After the experience of 1941 and 1942, when barley exports had fallen to 55,000 tons (27 percent of the prewar average), exports in 1943 and 1944 reached 170,000 tons. This was a satisfactory outcome of the bulk contracts, which had been negotiated with so much hesitation and hard bargaining on both sides, and provided a useful addition to Middle East supplies at a time when it was worth while to pay a high price in order to save shipping.

PART IV

# THE MENACE OF INFLATION

## CHAPTER 20

# MONEY, PRICES, AND MILITARY EXPENDITURE

During the first two years of the war little attention had been given in the Middle East to questions of finance, currency, and inflation. When the Middle East Supply Center (MESC) was set up in April 1941, its main purpose was to cut down imports and clear the ports and lines of communication for military supplies; nothing was said in its terms of reference about the need for controlling prices and checking inflation. At that time, indeed, there had been few signs of inflation. In 1940 wholesale prices in the Middle East had risen less than 25 percent above the prewar level in Egypt and Persia and about 25 percent in Sudan, Palestine, and Iraq. In Syria and Lebanon the collapse of France had shaken confidence in the local currency, which was based on the French franc, and prices had risen more than 50 percent. From the spring of 1941 onward the economic climate was increasingly disturbed by military operations, by cuts in imports, and by steadily mounting Allied expenditure. Then in the summer of 1941 there were poor crops throughout the Middle East and threat of food shortage in the towns led to hoarding of grain and a growing flight from money into goods. From the beginning of 1942 until the end of the war, the problem of feeding the Middle East became increasingly mixed up with the issue of checking runaway inflation. Before coming to grips with this complex issue, it may be useful to marshal some of the data and show what happened to money and prices in each country. For a fuller account of wartime inflation in Middle East countries (excluding Persia) the reader is referred to the excellent study by Prest (*1*).

### EGYPT

The Egyptian pound (£E) is divided into 100 piasters and is worth slightly more than the pound sterling (£1 equals 97.5 piasters). During the war the currency was backed partly by $53 million in gold but mainly by British Treasury bills. This system had its origin in World War I. Before 1914, when Egypt and Britain were both on the gold standard and gold sovereigns circulated in Egypt, there was an annual movement each fall of gold coins imported by the banks to pay for the cotton crop. On the outbreak of war in August 1914, shipments of gold ceased and there was a run on the banks. Notes of the National Bank of Egypt were made legal tender, and in September 1916 British Treasury bills became legal cover for the note issue. This issue, which was £E 8 million in December 1914, rose to £E 67 million in December 1919; and in February 1920 the price of wheat had risen to four times the prewar level, and of coal to ten times (*2*).

In World War II the increase of money and prices was not dissimilar. Wholesale prices and the cost of living rose to three times their prewar level, and notes in circulation increased fourfold and bank deposits fivefold. As in the previous war, cotton acreage was restricted and the price of bread was subsidized. Administration of wartime controls of production, prices, and distribution was developed earlier and more effectively than in World War I, partly owing to the experience then gained.

The inflationary impact of the war was neutralized in the early months by the collapse of the market for Egyptian cotton. In October 1939 the British government agreed to support the cotton market by buying the surplus that would normally have gone to Germany; and again a year later it undertook to buy any cotton offered from the 1940 crop at somewhat higher prices. The British government was to bear any eventual loss but offered to share equally with the Egyptian government in any profit. *The Economist* commented (*3*) at the time that Egypt had "been rescued from one of the worst crises in her history . . ." and General Wavell is reported to have said (*4*, ch. ix) that the cotton agreement was worth at least three brigades to him.

The development of wartime inflation in Egypt is shown in the following tabulation of indexes of money and prices:

| End of year | Currency[a] | Deposit money | Total money | Wholesale prices | Cost of living | Food, fuel,[b] and soap |
|---|---|---|---|---|---|---|
| 1939...... | 100[c] | 100[c] | 100[c] | 100 | 100 | 100 |
| 1940...... | 138 | 134 | 137 | 118 | 113 | 112 |
| 1941...... | 190 | 175 | 183 | 150 | 144 | 141 |
| 1942...... | 274 | 234 | 254 | 207 | 200 | 194 |
| 1943...... | 339 | 334 | 337 | 242 | 238 | 263 |
| 1944...... | 406 | 497 | 452 | 273 | 267 | 312 |

Sources: United Nations, *Statistical Yearbook, 1953* (New York, 1953), and National Bank of Egypt, reports.

[a] Excluding holdings of the National Bank of Egypt. [b] Average for each year.

[c] Currency in circulation, £E 31 million; deposit money, £E 32 million; total money, £E 63 million.

The above figures show that prices did not rise as fast as the increase in money. This was partly due to government control of prices and distribution and partly to the time lag in raising wages and salaries to keep pace with price increases. But the degree of control varied greatly with different commodities. Examples of the rise in retail food prices from unofficial sources are given below (August 1939 = 100):

| Food | June 1943 | June 1945 |
|---|---|---|
| Bread and flour | 127 | 200 |
| Sugar | 185 | 219 |
| Rice | 194 | 236 |
| Tea | ... | 260 |
| Meat | ... | 364 |
| Edible oil | 352 | 420 |
| Onions | 500 | 1,000 |
| Beans | 750 | 1,000 |

Sources: A. R. Prest, *War Economics of Primary Producing Countries* (Cambridge, 1948), p. 139; and, for bread and flour, unpublished data of MESC.

Bread, flour, and sugar were kept at a low level by subsidies and tea was more strictly controlled than other commodities.

## SUDAN

Since 1898, when the Anglo-Egyptian Condominium was established, the monetary unit of Sudan has been the Egyptian pound. The currency consisted of notes of the National Bank of Egypt and of Egyptian coins. English shillings and florins, reckoned at 5 and 10 piasters respectively, also circulated. There was a smaller increase in the supply of money than elsewhere in the Middle East, partly because Allied military expenditure was relatively moderate and partly because the government took successful measures for controlling prices and insulating the Sudanese economy from price rises in

| End of year | Currency[a] | Bank deposits | Total money | Wholesale prices | Cost of living |
|---|---|---|---|---|---|
| 1939 | 100[b] | 100[b] | 100[b] | 100 | 100 |
| 1940 | 104 | 108 | 105 | 123 | 110 |
| 1941 | 152 | 207 | 169 | 149 | 130 |
| 1942 | 170 | 275 | 203 | 182 | 151 |
| 1943 | 190 | 357 | 241 | 195 | 177 |
| 1944 | 154 | 400 | 231 | 202 | 160 |

Source: Sudan government returns, quoted in A. R. Prest, *War Economics of Primary Producing Countries* (Cambridge, 1948), p. 166.

[a] Currency and notes issued. No exact figure of currency and notes *in circulation* are available. Part of the Egyptian note issue circulated in Sudan.

[b] Currency and notes issued, £E 2.7 million; bank deposits, £E 1.2 million; total money, £E 3.9 million.

Egypt and India. The cost-of-living index at the end of 1943 had risen only to 177 at a time when import prices were about three times their prewar level (*1*, p. 173). This was mainly brought about by holding down prices of home-produced goods and subsidizing imported goods out of profits on exports.

Indexes showing the increases in money and prices are given on the preceding page.

### PALESTINE

The currency of Palestine under the British mandate was the Palestinian pound (£P), equivalent to £1 sterling. Notes were issued by the Palestine Currency Board and were covered by a reserve of bank deposits, British Treasury bills, and securities in London. Local currency for military expenditure during the war was obtained by crediting the Palestine Currency Board with sterling at par. Total disbursements for goods and services required for war purposes were disproportionately heavy in Palestine. Though there was a rapid expansion of industrial output to replace imports and to supply the armed forces with a wide range of goods, the increase of money in circulation led to inflationary pressures which were kept under control only with difficulty. Net military expenditure absorbed a higher proportion of the current production of Palestine than of other countries in the Middle East and in 1943 reached about one-third of the national output. In spite of this major contribution to the war effort, control of production, prices, and distribution by the government was carried out with a considerable measure of success, and inflation was kept in check more effectively than in neighboring countries which contributed proportionately less to the military requirements of the Allies.

Indexes of money and prices are shown below:

| End of year | Currency[a] | Bank deposits[b] | Total money | Wholesale prices | Cost of living |
|---|---|---|---|---|---|
| 1939...... | 100[c] | 100[c] | 100[c] | 100 | 100 |
| 1940...... | 124 | 102 | 110 | 126 | 118 |
| 1941...... | 158 | 150 | 153 | 184 | 150 |
| 1942...... | 282 | 226 | 248 | 245 | 190 |
| 1943...... | 424 | 382 | 400 | 277 | 207 |
| 1944...... | 488 | 502 | 496 | 297 | 227 |

Source: *General Monthly Bulletin of Current Statistics* (Palestine, Dept. Stat.), various issues.

[a] Some part of the Palestine currency was in circulation in Transjordan.

[b] Excluding co-operative and savings-bank deposits.

[c] Currency in circulation, £P 8.5 million; bank deposits, £P 12.8 million; total money, £P 21.3 million.

### CYPRUS

The monetary unit is the Cyprus pound (£C), divided into 20 shillings of 9 piasters each, and the currency reserve consists of sterling investments and cash on deposit with the Joint Colonial Fund in London. During the war the increase in the supply of money and the rise in prices were similar to those in Palestine and Egypt. By the end of December 1944 the index of money in the form of notes and bank deposits was 468 in Cyprus, compared with 496 in Palestine and 452 in Egypt, while the cost-of-living index, reflecting controlled and subsidized prices and not black-market prices, was only 229 in Cyprus, compared with 227 in Palestine and 267 in Egypt. The main cause of the expansion of money and money incomes was Allied military expenditure, which averaged $16 million a year during the three years 1942–44, or about $40 per head of the population.

The following tabulation includes indexes of import and export prices, which illustrate the problem of divergent price levels in Middle East countries; high prices for wheat imported from Syria in 1943/44 had to be partly offset by a subsidy:

| End of year | Currency | Bank deposits | Total money | Import prices[a] | Export prices[a] | Cost of living |
|---|---|---|---|---|---|---|
| 1939...... | 100[b] | 100[b] | 100[b] | 100 | 100 | 100[c] |
| 1940...... | 138 | 96 | 109 | ... | ... | ... |
| 1941...... | 239 | 131 | 165 | 266 | 132 | 192 |
| 1942...... | 385 | 198 | 257 | 302 | 220 | 246[d] |
| 1943...... | 497 | 335 | 386 | 541 | 307 | 235 |
| 1944...... | 581 | 416 | 468 | 473 | 286 | 229 |

Sources: Cyprus, *The Cyprus Blue Book, 1939,* and Treas., *Cyprus: Financial Report,* various issues, for currency and bank deposits; and A. R. Prest, *War Economics of Primary Producing Countries* (Cambridge, 1948), pp. 186, 195, for prices and cost of living.

[a] Annual average.

[b] Currency in circulation, £C .85 million; bank deposits, £C 1.9 million; total money, £C 2.7 million.

[c] August 1939.

[d] January 1943.

### SYRIA AND LEBANON

The Lebanese-Syrian pound, which was sometimes designated £LS took the place of the Turkish pound, or lira, which was the legal money before World War I. The Turkish gold pound circulated along with the gold sovereign, gold 20-franc piece, and other gold coins. Till 1914 the only notes in circulation were those of the Imperial Ottoman Bank. During the 1914–18 war the country was flooded with notes of denominations as low as one piaster, which soon fell to a discount. Under the French mandate the Lebanese-Syrian pound was linked to the French franc and in 1939 its exchange value was fixed at

20 francs or about 45 cents (£LS 8.83 equaled £1 sterling). After the pro-Vichy forces had been defeated in June 1941 and Syria and Lebanon had been promised independence, the link with Paris was broken, and the local currency came under the control first of the Free French Office des Changes, and later of the Caisse Centrale de la France d'Outre Mer in London. The British and French authorities credited the exchange authority with sterling or francs and obtained local currency from the Banque de Syrie et du Liban. The issue of new notes was thus covered by foreign-exchange reserves in London, as in the case of Egypt, Palestine, and Iraq.

Distrust of the future value of the currency and a tendency to hoard goods and gold were more pronounced in Syria and Lebanon than elsewhere in the Middle East, partly owing to doubts spread by Axis radio propaganda as to the future value of the franc. This was countered in May 1943 by making Syrian-Lebanese pounds freely convertible into sterling and sterling-area currencies. Funds were transferred to Egypt on a considerable scale and this tended to slow down inflation in Syria and Lebanon.

The course of inflation is illustrated by the following indexes:

| End of year | Currency | Deposit money | Total money | Wholesale prices | Cost of living (Beirut) |
|---|---|---|---|---|---|
| 1939...... | 100[a] | 100[a] | 100[a] | 100 | 100 |
| 1940...... | 165 | 156 | 161 | 153 | 147 |
| 1941...... | 212 | 138 | 183 | 361 | 211 |
| 1942...... | 388 | 372 | 382 | 568 | 332 |
| 1943...... | 549 | 681 | 600 | 672 | 455 |
| 1944...... | 686 | 806 | 733 | 812 | 540 |

Sources: *International Financial Statistics* (Internatl. Monetary Fund, Washington, D.C.), various issues, for money; and Syria and Lebanon, Conseil supérieur des intérêts communs, Services d'études économiques et statistiques, *Recueil de statistiques de la Syrie et du Liban* (Beirut), various issues, for prices.

[a] Currency in circulation, £LS 51 million; bank deposits, £LS 32 million; total money, £LS 83 million.

Neither the wholesale nor the cost-of-living indexes give a reliable measure of price movements since both were based on ceiling prices rather than black-market prices. The wholesale index covered only 57 commodities and the cost-of-living index included charges for rent, education, and services that lagged behind retail prices. Moreover, the latter index was influenced by the subsidized price at which bread and flour for poor people were sold in the towns.

Such information as was available to MESC about wage rates suggests that they rose less during the war than the cost of living. In April 1943 at the Cereals Conference in Damascus, when MESC tried to bring down the official prices for wheat and barley paid to the cultivators, it was stated that salaries and wages in the towns had only risen about 2.5 times. Wages of unskilled workers employed by an oil company at the end of 1943 had increased about threefold (*1*, p. 231). The reduction in the supply of consumer goods, particularly of cotton piece goods, inflicted hardship on all except a small class of merchants and landowners who were able to profit from inflation. Imported cotton piece goods fell from an average of 9,000 tons in 1938 and 1939 to less than 2,000 tons per annum in the three years 1941–43. Though there was some expansion of local output (cotton yarn production rose from an average of 1,300 tons in 1938 and 1939 to 2,150 tons per annum in 1941–43), this was insufficient to replace imports (*1*, pp. 224, 226). Failure to control prices and distribution of textiles meant that the effects of the shortage fell disproportionately on the low-income groups and the poorer peasants. In 1941, during the period of Vichy control, the volume of imports was lower in relation to the prewar level than in any other Middle East country except French Somaliland.

## IRAQ

Iraq's monetary unit is the Iraq dinar, equivalent in value to £1 sterling. During the war the issue of notes was managed by a currency board with offices in London and Baghdad, and issue of additional currency was limited to an equivalent amount of pounds sterling in London. As in Palestine and Cyprus there was no fiduciary issue and no provision for loans and advances to be made by the currency board to the Iraq government. Indexes showing the expansion of money and prices during the war are tabulated below:

| End of year | Currency[a] | Bank deposits | Total money | Wholesale prices |
|---|---|---|---|---|
| 1939...... | 100[b] | 100[b] | 100[b] | 100 |
| 1940...... | 110 | 142 | 115 | 126 |
| 1941...... | 186 | 500 | 239 | 235 |
| 1942...... | 371 | 533 | 399 | 440 |
| 1943...... | 600 | 1,067 | 679 | 526 |
| 1944...... | 692 | 1,292 | 793 | 431 |

Sources: United Nations, *Statistical Yearbook, 1951* (New York, 1951), for money; and A. R. Prest, *War Economics of Primary Producing Countries* (Cambridge, 1948), p. 205, for prices.

[a] Currency and notes issued.

[b] Currency issued, 5.9 million Iraq dinars; bank deposits, 1.2 million Iraq dinars; total money, 7.1 million Iraq dinars.

The index of wholesale prices can only be taken as a rough guide. Wholesale prices of rice, wheat, and barley in August 1943 were about four, six, and eight times their prewar levels. Owing to drastic curtailment of imports, prices of consumer goods, other than tea and coffee, rose still higher. The price of white cotton shirting had risen in August 1943 to 15.5 times its prewar price. In 1943 the yardage of cotton piece goods imported was 40 percent of the prewar quantity, and woolen piece goods were reduced to less than a fifth (*1*, pp. 206, 216).

### PERSIA

Persian currency has had a checkered history. Before World War I Persia had a variety of gold, silver, nickel, and copper coins, the principal monetary unit being a silver coin, the kran, worth about 10 cents. In 1939, after the reorganization of Persian finances by the American mission headed by Millspaugh, the new rial currency consisted mainly of notes issued by the National Bank, though gold and silver coins continued to circulate at fluctuating values in rials. The note circulation, which had been increasing before the war as a result of Riza Shah Pahlevi's prewar schemes of economic development, amounted to just over 1,000 million rials at the outbreak of war.

An act of November 1942 prescribed that any increase in the note issue should be backed as to 60 percent in gold and as to 40 percent in sterling or dollars. This provision enabled the National Bank, when selling local currency to the Allies, to obtain 60 percent in gold at the official rate. In the four years 1941–44 the Persian National Bank acquired $108 million gold in addition to an increase of $104 million in its holding of sterling and dollar balances.

In 1942 the exchange rate was fixed at 32.50 rials to the dollar and 128–30 rials for the pound sterling. In the course of 1942, the

| End of year | Note circulation | Bank deposits[a] | Total money | Wholesale prices[b] | Cost of living | Retail food prices |
|---|---|---|---|---|---|---|
| 1939...... | 100[c] | 100[c] | 100[c] | 100 | 100 | 100 |
| 1940...... | 114 | 128 | 122 | 113 | 113 | 113 |
| 1941...... | 157 | 219 | 192 | 143 | 184 | 210 |
| 1942...... | 300 | 268 | 282 | 252 | 375 | 446 |
| 1943...... | 504 | 338 | 410 | 461 | 745 | 845 |
| 1944...... | 634 | 340 | 468 | 500 | 644 | 681 |

Sources: *Bank Melli Iran Bulletin* (Teheran), various issues, for notes in circulation, cost of living, and food prices; *International Financial Statistics* (Internatl. Monetary Fund, Washington, D.C.), various issues, for bank deposits defined in Appendix Table IX; and *Monthly Bulletin of Statistics* (United Nations, Secretariat, Stat. Off., New York), various issues, for wholesale prices. [a] March of year following. [b] Average for the year.

[c] Notes in circulation, 1,010 million rials; bank deposits, 1,320 million rials; total money, 2,330 million rials.

first year of aid to Russia, the note circulation nearly doubled and rose to 3,000 million rials, and by the end of 1944 it had reached 6,400 million. The course of wartime inflation is illustrated by the indexes given on the opposite page.

The price indexes, as in Iraq and Syria and Lebanon, cannot be regarded as reliable and probably underestimate the price inflation that took place in Persia. The wholesale-price index tended to reflect official ceiling prices and first-hand prices charged by government monopolies, rather than the prices at which transactions took place in the bazaars. Reduction of imports, interruption of transport, budgetary deficits, and Allied military expenditure, which in 1943 was adding to the money in circulation at the rate of 250 million rials a month, combined to cause a speculative fever. Millspaugh writes (*5*, p. 58) that, on his arrival early in 1943 to take charge of Persian finances, "it looked as if inflation had reached the sky-rocketing stage."

Lastly, to complete this roundup of Middle East currencies, there were three countries which had no paper money and consequently no problem of inflation. These were Saudi Arabia, Ethiopia, and Yemen.

### SAUDI ARABIA

As the Saudi Arabian delegate, Sheik Izzadine Bey Shawa, said at the Middle East Financial Conference (*6*): "Inflation was practically non-existent in Saudi Arabia because the monetary system was based on silver coin." The legal currency of Saudi Arabia is the riyal, a silver coin with the same silver content as the Indian rupee of 1933. English gold sovereigns are also current and are used as the recognized standard of value for important transactions. During the war the exchange rate of riyals and sovereigns fluctuated under the influence of local supply and demand and of market prices for gold and silver in India.

The gold sovereign rose in value from about 26 riyals in 1939 to 75 in the middle of 1946, largely as the result of an increased supply of riyals minted from several million ounces of silver obtained under Lend-Lease.

The main source of revenue to the government before the war came from dues for the annual pilgrimage to Mecca, and amounted to about $5 million. This was much reduced during the war, and before oil revenues became important after the war, financial aid had to be provided by the British and United States governments.

Some attempts were made to control prices even in Saudi Arabia, but they had little effect and were soon abandoned. Owing to the restriction of imports, consumer goods—particularly textiles—were in short supply and prices rose to more than twice their prewar level in terms of gold sovereigns and to five or six times in silver riyals. On the other hand the staple grains—wheat and millet in the west and rice in the east—were maintained in fairly regular supply and, though their prices in silver riyals rose, there were times when prices in gold sovereigns were little above the prewar level, particularly in 1942 when the number of pilgrims bringing gold into the country was much reduced. A considerable part of the government's imports of food and textiles was distributed free in the form of subsidies to tribal chieftains.

## ETHIOPIA AND YEMEN

The traditional currency of Ethiopia and Yemen is the Maria Theresa dollar, a silver coin first struck in Vienna in 1780, which has the same silver content as the riyal. The Yemen riyal is divided into 40 buqsha, and small silver and copper coins are minted locally. In Ethiopia there was a silver coinage of talari worth about fifty cents. After their conquest of Ethiopia the Italians introduced lira notes. In 1943 the governor of the State Bank of Ethiopia, G. Blowers, said it was impossible to determine whether or to what extent the currency of Ethiopia had increased. Italian lire had been taken out of circulation and had been replaced by East African shillings. Maria Theresa dollars had been specially minted for use in Ethiopia and the East African shilling had depreciated. According to Cheesman (7, p. 184), in remote parts of Ethiopia salt bars were used as currency and bits would be broken off to make payments of small amounts. Salt is preferred to silver dollars since, as the tribesmen explained, "We cannot eat dollars."

## ALLIED MILITARY EXPENDITURE

Figures of Allied military expenditure made available to delegates at the Middle East Financial Conference of April 1944 showed that over $1,800 million had been spent up to the end of 1943. Expenditure by Middle East governments during the four years of war had been about $1,200 million; and apart from some borrowing from the National Bank by the government of Persia, their expenditure had been covered by revenue. If the two forms of public spending were added together, about 40 percent had been offset by taxation and loans and the remaining 60 percent had been met by expansion of currency and bank deposits.

Later figures, tabulated below in million dollars, show that up to December 1944 there was a fairly close correspondence in each country between increases in the supply of money in the form of currency and bank deposits and the amount of Allied military expenditure during the years in question:

| Country | Years | Increase of total money[a] | Allied net military expenditures [b] |
|---|---|---|---|
| Egypt | 1940–44 | 900 | 1,100 |
| Sudan | 1940–44 | 20 | 53 |
| Palestine | 1940–44 | 350 | 364 |
| Cyprus | 1941–44 | 40 | 57 |
| Syria and Lebanon | 1940–44 | 240 | 307 |
| Iraq | 1941–44 | 200 | 256 |
| Persia | 1941–44 | 250 | 275 |
| Total | ... | 2,000 | 2,412 |

[a] For sources, see Appendix Table IX.

[b] "Net" military expenditure means that receipts of local currency from various sources (such as canteen receipts, remittances by the troops, and sales of salvage to civilians) have been subtracted from gross outgoings to show net acquisition of local funds in exchange for sterling or francs and, in the case of the United States army, for dollars.

The figures illustrate the importance of Egypt as the principal base of military operations; but in relation to population military expenditure was heaviest in Palestine and Cyprus. In most countries Allied military expenditure was somewhat greater than the increase in deposits and currency—particularly where there was an import surplus to help in absorbing purchasing power. But in Persia, where there was both an export surplus and a series of budget deficits, the increase in means of payment exceeded military expenditure in 1943. In Syria and Lebanon a substantial import surplus in 1942 and 1943 and sales of gold in 1943/44 helped to keep expansion of credit and currency to only four-fifths of the Allies' military expenditure. Moreover, some part of the payments to contractors in Syria and Lebanon was remitted to banks in Palestine and Egypt. Subject to these qualifications, the figures above serve to illustrate the extent to which Allied military expenditure brought about an expanded supply of money in each country.

The impact of monetary expansion on prices varied in different countries. The following indexes summarize the changes from December 1939 to December 1944 (December 1939 = 100):

| Country | Currency and deposits | Wholesale prices | Cost of living |
|---|---|---|---|
| Egypt | 452 | 273 | 267 |
| Sudan | 231 | 202 | 160 |
| Palestine | 496 | 297 | 227 |
| Cyprus | 468 | 286[a] | 229 |
| Syria and Lebanon | 733 | 812 | 540 |
| Iraq | 793 | 431 | 611[b] |
| Persia | 468 | 500 | 644 |

[a] Export prices.
[b] December 1945.

The above figures illustrate the problem of divergent price levels in Middle East countries which created serious obstacles to interterritorial trade. Sudan was in a class by itself, with prices only about 30 percent higher than in the United Kingdom, where the cost-of-living index in 1944 stood at 126 and the wholesale-price index at 160. This was partly because military expenditure in Sudan had been moderate and of short duration, and partly because effective anti-inflationary measures had been adopted.

In Egypt, Palestine, and Cyprus wholesale prices were between two and three-quarters and three times prewar, while in Persia and Syria and Lebanon the rise was from five to eight times. No great accuracy nor comparability can be attributed to the price indexes, since they were largely based on official ceiling prices and made no allowance for changes in the quantity of goods available for purchase. The rise in the cost-of-living index mainly reflected conditions in the capital cities, and was less than that of wholesale prices partly because of the inclusion of controlled rents. But in Teheran excessively high rents were the chief factor in raising the cost-of-living index above the wholesale-price index.

Owing to the absence of reliable statistics of national income it is impossible to estimate with any accuracy what proportion of the total resources of Middle East countries were absorbed by military expenditure. But a rough approximation may be attempted.

In Palestine the government statistician, G. E. F. Wood, from New Zealand, estimated that the armed forces in 1943 had by their purchases appropriated about a third of the total amount of goods and services produced (*8*). At the same time there had been a substantial increase in production, of the order of 20 percent since

1939. The net result was that the level of consumption in real terms had been reduced by about 18–20 percent. This was also the estimated fall in consumption in the United Kingdom; but a reduction of 20 percent was obviously a greater burden for a country like Palestine to bear. In 1944 the ratio of military expenditure to national output in Palestine had fallen to about 18 percent (*9*).

INDEXES OF MONEY SUPPLY AND COST OF LIVING IN SELECTED COUNTRIES, 1939–45*

(*Logarithmic vertical scale*)

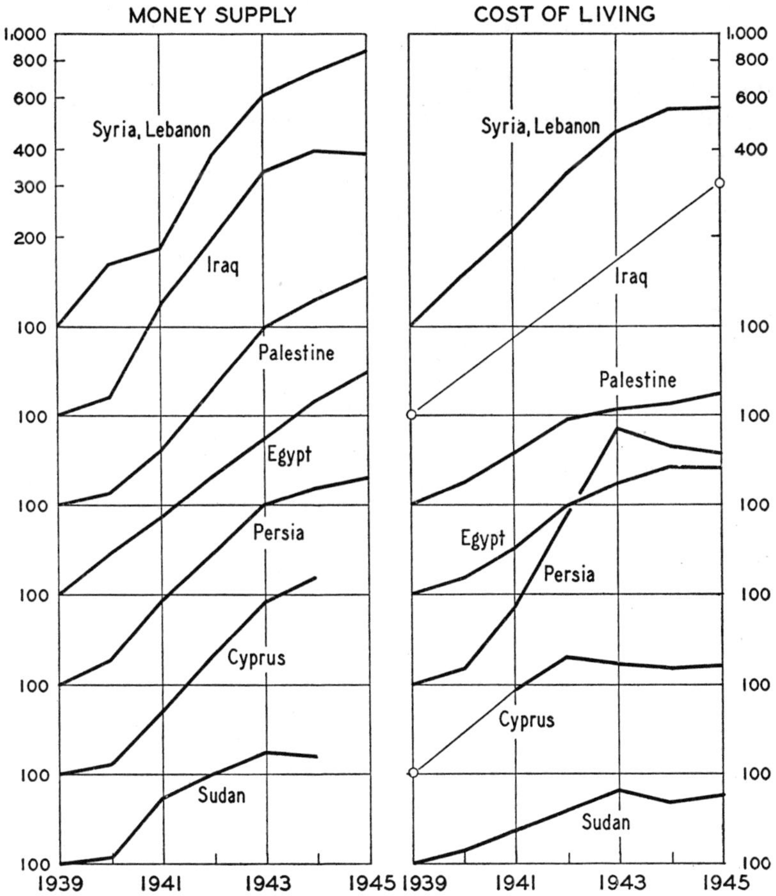


* Data in Appendix Table IX. The full scale shown for Syria-Lebanon may be applied to any part of the chart.

In Egypt, where national income per head was about half that of Palestine, the proportion of military expenditure to the total value of goods and services on the basis of estimates by Anis (*10*), may be reckoned at about 20 percent in the three years 1941–43 and between 8 and 12 percent in 1940 and 1944. In other Middle East countries, where estimates of national income are even more uncertain, the greatest impact of Allied expenditure was probably felt in Iraq. Here the proportion of national income—estimated by Bonné (*11*, p. 21) at $48 per head in 1936/37—which was appropriated for military purposes may have been between 15 and 20 percent in the three years 1941–43. In the Levant states the proportion in the peak years 1942 and 1943 may be roughly estimated at about 10 percent. In Persia, where military expenditure per head was lower than in the above countries, the effects of military intervention were intensified by reduction in national output, transport difficulties, and food shortages in the towns.

The broad conclusion that emerges is that in the six years 1940–45 the Middle East received about $2,500 million for goods and services worth approximately $1,000 million at 1939 prices. After allowing for a rise of world prices of about 50 percent during the war, price inflation in the Middle East accounted for nearly a billion dollars of the postwar sterling balances.

If at the outbreak of war it had been possible to foresee the consequences of financing the war in the Middle East by multiplying the total amount of currency and bank deposits nearly fivefold—from $540 million in December 1939 to $2,540 million in December 1944—a different policy might have been followed. What more might have been done to obtain the money required by taxation and loans will be discussed in the next chapter.

## CITATIONS

*1* A. R. Prest, *War Economics of Primary Producing Countries* (Cambridge, 1948).

*2* A. E. Crouchley, *Economic Development of Modern Egypt* (London, 1938).

*3* *The Economist* (London), Oct. 5, 1940.

*4* R. S. Sayers, in his forthcoming volume, *Financial Policy 1939–45* (Hist. of the Second World War, U.K. Civil Ser.).

*5* A. C. Millspaugh, *Americans in Persia* (Brookings Inst., Washington, D.C., 1946).

*6* Unpublished proceedings of the Middle East Financial Conference, Cairo, April 24–29, 1944.

*7* Major R. E. Cheesman, *Lake Tana and the Blue Nile* (London, 1936).

*8* G. E. F. Wood, in *General Monthly Bulletin of Current Statistics* (Palestine, Dept. Stat.), August 1944.

*9* P. J. Loftus, *National Income of Palestine* (Palestine Govt., 1946).

*10* M. A. Anis, in *L'Egypte contemporaine* (Société khédiviale d'économie politique, de statistique et de législation, Cairo), March 1945.

*11* A. Bonné, *The Economic Development of the Middle East* (London, 1945).

CHAPTER 21

# THE MIDDLE EAST FINANCIAL CONFERENCE (*1*)

One of the difficulties in fighting inflation was to find agreement on the meaning of the word and to distinguish between symptoms and causes. This naturally led to uncertainty about appropriate remedies. The commonest view was that rise in prices was due primarily to a shortage of goods, and secondarily to the rapacity of traders and producers who took advantage of the shortage to make unreasonable profits. The obvious remedy was to obtain more goods; but if that was impossible, it was still the duty of governments to prevent profiteering by fixing prices. Those who took this view tended to ignore or minimize the importance of the increase in the supply of money and the rise in money incomes; and the suggestion that governments should take drastic steps to reduce the amount of money in people's pockets by heavier direct and indirect taxation was regarded as irrelevant or at least inopportune. Even in Anglo-American circles there were those who thought that to impose indirect taxes on goods in short supply was undesirable since this would result in raising prices. In any case it would be inconsistent with the policy of the Lend-Lease Administration, which stipulated that goods should be sold at prices based on landed cost and not at prevailing market prices.

Even in financial circles there was some doubt as to what was the right policy to pursue. This doubt arose partly from the different senses in which the word "inflation" was used. Some central banks and ministries of finance refused to admit that there was any inflation in the strict sense; for, they held, inflation meant the issue of fiduciary currency with no backing of gold or foreign exchange. This had not happened in the Middle East. Except in Persia budgets were balanced and there were no inflationary deficits. All Middle East currencies were fully covered by gold or foreign exchange and there had been no depreciation of their exchange value. The increase in the supply of money represented a gain in each country's foreign assets, which would be available after the war for importing consumer goods and capital equipment. It was only natural that prices should rise during the war owing to shortage of goods and heavy expenditure by the Allies; but so long as this did not get out of control and confidence was retained in the stability and future value of Middle East currencies, there was no reason why Middle East governments should wish to put any limit to the increase in their foreign assets. For political and social reasons they were anxious to obtain more imported goods and were willing to co-operate with the Allies in preventing a runaway inflation; but they were convinced that it would be impossible to persuade their parliaments to tax themselves and create a budget surplus in order to finance Allied military expenditure.

In September 1942 an Anti-Inflation Conference was held in Cairo, attended by British representatives in Middle East countries and by two United States observers, for the purpose of exchanging views and formulating policies. They agreed that the main attack must be directed against increase of spendable incomes, and called for measures on a wide front—higher taxation, loan issues, savings campaigns, control of prices and distribution, and rationing. But they recognized only too clearly that these measures were extremely difficult to introduce and administer effectively in the Middle East. They therefore urged upon the authorities in London and Washington a radical new proposal—namely, that gold should be sent for sale in the open market. Gold like other goods had risen in price. In December 1942 the gold sovereign was quoted at over £5 in Teheran and six months later it was worth £6 15*s.* in Beirut. After much debate and hesitation the proposal was adopted in June 1943, with results which will be described in the following chapter.

Meanwhile, renewed efforts were made to persuade Middle East governments to take remedial action on orthodox lines. Suggestions that heavier taxes should be imposed to absorb spendable income and provide budget surpluses that could be lent to the Allies fell on deaf ears, but greater readiness was shown to control prices and distribution and to enforce rationing. In particular, most Middle East governments were willing to help by organizing collection of cereals at fixed prices.

Early in 1944 Lord Moyne, British Minister Resident in the Middle East, who had succeeded to the post formerly held by Casey as Minister of State, decided to hold a conference of Middle East governments in order to try to concert measures to stop inflation. The Middle East Financial Conference which was held in Cairo from April 24 to 29 was attended by five ministers of finance and about 70 senior officials from 15 countries, including representatives of the United States and British treasuries.

Lord Moyne, in his opening remarks, referred to the different senses in which the word "inflation" was used. He understood that in the French language the word "inflation" meant expansion of currency based on government borrowing from the bank of issue; but a less restricted definition implied an increase of prices accompanied by an increase of money in circulation. It was in this sense that inflation existed in the Middle East. The problem arose from heavy Allied expenditure which could not be offset immediately by imports.

Professor G. Leduc, the French financial adviser to the Syrian and Lebanese Interêts Communs, explained that in his view inflation did not exist in the Middle East in its strict sense—that is to say, an increase in the note issue caused by government borrowing from the issuing authority. The expansion of money in Middle East territories was due not to budgetary deficits but to very substantial margins on the credit side in their balance of payments. These large foreign balances could not find their natural outlets—the purchase of imports from abroad—until after the war. The crux of the problem was thus what to do between now and then. Effective state intervention in the field of finance must aim at transferring from individuals to the government, by taxation or by public loans, a part of the individuals' cash holdings which, though expressed in local currency, consisted in the last analysis of foreign-exchange assets—in particular, sterling.

Mr. Ebtehaj, governor of the Bank Melli of Iran, hoped that the Conference would find some other terminology to describe the present situation in the Middle East. He had seen the harm caused in Iran by the use of the word "inflation." This point was to some extent met by the statement in Paragraph (2) of the resolutions of the Conference (see Appendix Note I) that monetary inflation, "in the restricted sense of fiat money," had not taken place in the Middle East, and by the use of the expression "price inflation" in Paragraph (6) to describe the consequences of military expenditure combined with a reduced supply of goods. The remedy, it was added, was to reduce the flow of money and to increase the supply of goods.

Resolutions passed by the Conference for consideration of Middle East governments fall under four headings: (1) General, (2) Taxation, (3) Loans and Savings, and (4) Price Policy and Price Control.

Under the first heading it was recorded with satisfaction that after a critical period in the spring and summer of 1942 there had been growing confidence during the last twelve months in the stability of Middle East currencies; that there had been no monetary inflation in the restricted sense, since all Middle East currencies were fully backed by gold or foreign exchange; and that these assets would be available for the purchase of imports after the war. The Conference took note of statements that the policies of the British and United States governments aimed at stabilizing the purchasing power of sterling and the dollar after the war; and welcomed the discussions then in progress on the establishment of machinery for international monetary stabilization and convertibility of currencies. The price inflation which had occurred in the Middle East had been caused by increase of money in circulation resulting from military expenditure with no corresponding increase in supply of goods. Under war conditions supply of goods for civilian consumption had had to be reduced and this made it essential to neutralize excess purchasing power by all possible measures including taxation, loans, and control of prices.

### TAXATION

Under the heading of taxation, the Conference emphasized the need for increased taxes both to reduce the superabundance of money and to enable governments to build up reserves for postwar development schemes. An excess-profits tax should be introduced where it was not already in force; income tax should be progressively increased at higher levels of income and profits; and a compulsory-savings element in the form of postwar credits should be introduced into the tax system. Evasion and delays in payment of taxes must be energetically tackled; and lack of experienced income-tax officials, in countries where direct taxation had only recently been introduced, pointed to the need for improved training facilities for technical staff. Of special interest in its bearing on the problems of price control, which are discussed later, was the recommendation that "indirect taxes and railway freights on non-essential commodities should be increased. The funds obtained by such increased taxation might assist the subsidizing of essential consumer goods."

### LOANS AND SAVINGS

The resolutions about loans and savings referred to the fact that certain Middle East countries—notably Egypt and Iraq—had been able for the first time to float internal government loans during the war, and the Conference urged others to do the same. The development of a capital market would be of particular value after the war, when governments would need to obtain control of foreign-exchange balances by internal rather than external borrowing. The particular methods of promoting savings varied in different countries and included premium bonds, lottery loans, post-office savings, and savings certificates. The Conference noted with special interest the schemes adopted or proposed for a compulsory-savings levy on incomes or war profits to be repaid in whole or in part after the war as a means of absorbing surplus purchasing power and providing reserves for meeting problems of postwar adjustments. A paper submitted by the Syrian government advocated a scheme of this kind; and J. W. Cummins, assistant financial secretary to the Sudan government, referred to the compulsory-savings element included in the Sudan business-profits tax, which was intended to provide traders with funds for repairs and renewals after the war. Another form of compulsory savings in Sudan was the arrangement whereby cash distributed to cotton growers was limited to an amount sufficient for a reasonable level of consumption and the balance obtained from bulk sales of the crop was held in reserve for the benefit of the cultivators after the war.

### PRICE CONTROL

The fourth session of the Conference was devoted to discussing problems of controlling prices and distribution. This was the most interesting and fruitful session. There was little new to say about taxation and loans; but in debating price policies the delegates were expressing divergent views on matters of some theoretical, as well as practical, importance. The discussion was opened by Keith Murray, Director of the Food and Agriculture Division in the Middle East Supply Center (MESC), who echoed Sir Theodore Gregory's remark that the key to anti-inflation lay in control of food prices.

In its resolutions on price policy and price control the Conference agreed that "every effort should be made to reduce essential food prices to the lowest practicable level since this is a fundamental condition to the successful adoption of other anti-inflation measures." It recommended that the Middle East grain-collection schemes should be continued as a means of discouraging hoarding and ensuring supplies to the towns and to deficit areas, and urged that the resolutions of the recent Damascus Cereals Conference should be taken into account by the countries which took part in it. It also drew attention to the resolutions adopted by the Middle East Conference on Control of Distribution and Rationing held in Cairo in August 1943 (see Appendix Note II). It added an important rider containing an exception to the general principle of controlling prices in the following terms: "The Conference recommends that in the case of luxuries and of any articles the prices and distribution of which cannot be effectively controlled, the differential between the cost price (including reasonable profit) and the open market price should be appropriated by the Government for the public benefit."

This resolution represented a compromise between two alternative, and sometimes conflicting, methods of attacking inflation: the first, keeping prices down by regulation in order to prevent wages and incomes rising; the second, raising prices by indirect taxes, in order to mop up purchasing power and appropriate for the state profits due to scarcity value. No one at the Conference dissented from the view that luxuries should be taxed even if it meant raising their price; on the other hand there was general agreement that the bare necessities of life must be controlled and kept within the reach of everyone, if necessary by rationing and subsidies. But it was not so clear what was the right course to follow with the fairly wide range of less essential goods, which were neither luxuries nor necessities. Where was the line to be drawn?

Murray, in his introductory remarks, referred to the danger that if a government acquiesced in or fixed high prices for less essential goods, allowing the trader only a reasonable profit and appropriating the balance for itself, this would conflict with equitable distribution; and he suggested that the confidence inspired by equitable distribution might in practice prove more anti-inflationary than a policy of high prices. W. A. B. Iliff of the British Treasury pointed out that in the United Kingdom essential commodities were subsidized and strictly rationed while semiluxury and luxury goods were sold at what the market would bear, the excess profit being taken by the government. Thus tea, sugar, butter, and meat were cheap; but the price of whisky had trebled and that of beer and cigarettes had doubled. By this means the alternatives suggested by Murray could be reconciled.

But this still left open the extent to which control of prices in the Middle East did in fact lead to equitable distribution. The Conference recognized that in order to make price control effective it was important to establish close control of supplies and distribution, and urged governments to strengthen and, if necessary, extend their organization for doing this. But Leduc pointed out that price control was extremely difficult to enforce, especially if it were limited to only one section of the national economy. In Syria and Lebanon it had first been applied to imported commodities, since it was much easier to control goods at the port of entry than in the interior and there was no difficulty in discovering the cost of goods from overseas. But controlling the price of imports was not anti-inflationary, since it did nothing to absorb surplus purchasing power. On the contrary, he pointed out that, paradoxical though it might seem, one means by which inflation could be reduced would be for the Middle East to have to pay higher prices for imports since this would create a larger outflow of money. He paid a tribute to the British and United States governments for their policy of selling for export at prices ruling in their home markets. Even with higher freights and insurance, c.i.f. prices of British and American goods were well below those ruling in the Middle East; and in the absence of price control very large profits were obtained by importers and middlemen. When attempts had been made to ensure that the benefit of low import prices was passed on to consumers by controlling distribution and prices at each stage, the greatest difficulties had been encountered. For the full benefit to reach the consumer it would have been necessary to fix prices and control distribution of all commodities made from imported materials—and, he might have added, of all raw and semifinished materials entering into the finished products. Partial control was ineffective and tended to lead to everwidening state intervention. In any case it did not cure inflation; to some degree it gave it an added stimulus. Similarly, in regard to home-produced products, it was difficult to limit the area of control. In Syria and Lebanon cereal prices had been fixed at what was generally considered to be a very generous level; but when, following the Damascus Cereals Conference, a reduction had been suggested, the growers had demanded that similar reductions should be brought about in the prices of goods they bought. It was thus extremely difficult to limit control to foodstuffs and essential agricultural commodities. Leduc agreed that in so far as prices were controlled, the volume of military expenditure, and hence the rate of monetary expansion, was kept down. One method of keeping prices in check was to stimulate local production and that was being done in Syria and Lebanon.

The Lebanese Deputy Prime Minister, Habib Bey Abi Chahla, said that in Lebanon the prices of only a few commodities—such as kerosene, benzene, and cereals—had been controlled, but other prices had been left free. Imports had been licensed and enormous profits had been made by importers and local industrialists owing to restriction of supplies. At one time it had been proposed by the French authorities to introduce a wider control based on a system of "just" prices, but no one had been able to decide what just prices were. Special courts had been set up to deal with profiteering but only small men had been prosecuted while big merchants and producers had not been disturbed. However, his government was now hoping to introduce a system of controlling prices of imported goods at the source, since the right to import was a privilege granted by the authorities and ought not to be a source of illicit profit.

G. H. S. Pinsent, representing the British Treasury, acknowledged Leduc's tribute to the United Kingdom and the United States for selling exports to the Middle East at landed cost and said that he was not sure whether or not that was really the correct policy. He did not, however, advocate a change at the present time; rather he hoped that the Middle East governments would be able to reduce their internal-price levels so that the problem of import prices would disappear. So long as imports were sold at landed cost it was essential that they should reach the consumer at a corresponding price; thereby the cultivator might be compensated for reduction in internal prices. Pinsent hoped to see this happen when military expenditure began to fall off and goods became more freely available. R. F. Mikesell for the United States Treasury agreed that imports ought to be sold to the Middle East at world prices so as to facilitate the reduction of Middle East price levels; but it was essential that governments should exercise strict control over their distribution and prevent profiteering. He emphasized the importance of restoring a better equilibrium between Middle East prices and world prices. If nothing were done, exports would fall, imports would rise, and there would be unemployment and severe dislocation. To institute high tariffs and exchange control would be in direct opposition to the policy of the United Nations. One way of restoring equilibrium would be to devalue the currency, but devaluation had many undesirable repercussions. The best line of action to follow was to begin a progressive deflation now and to reduce wages and costs by reducing the cost of living.

The Syrian Minister of Finance, Khaled Bey el Azm, said that it was the policy of the Syrian government to reduce prices progressively so that at the end of the war prices in Syria would be at world levels. It was not practicable to fix all prices and control should be limited to basic necessities. The government should own these commodities and should possess sufficient stocks to ensure their equitable distribution to the whole population. Producers' prices would have to be lowered and the government must be prepared to sell its own stocks at a loss. But substantial help from the Allies would be needed. After the war Syria must be in a position to export and to compete in world markets. For that purpose imports of machinery were required—agricultural machinery to reduce the cost of wheat, and textile machinery to increase the production of cotton yarn. A larger volume of imports of all kinds would make the biggest contribution to reduction of prices.

Amine Fikri Bey, undersecretary of state in the Egyptian Ministry of Supply, gave an interesting summary of price control in Egypt. He said that his own staff had expanded from 100 before the war to 600 in 1942 and to 850 in 1943; it was expected to reach 1,250 in the future. This large number was necessary if control was to be properly enforced. The mere fixing of prices by legislation or decree was not enough. Various systems of control, ranging from licensing and supervision of private traders to government purchase and allocation, had to be applied to ensure that price regulations were observed. Consumers were rationed in the case of tea, sugar, edible oil, and kerosene. He thought partial control tended to push up uncontrolled prices. It was a mistake to try to fix all profits by law, and he agreed that some goods which realized inflated prices ought to be taxed and the proceeds used to subsidize essential commodities. For instance, in the case of cotton goods the better qualities of cloth should be taxed in order to subsidize the yarn needed for cheaper types.

He claimed that Egyptian cereal policy had been outstandingly successful. Cereal collection was based on accurate assessment of production and requirements for consumption; growers had been allowed to retain sufficient for their own needs, and the whole surplus had been bought at fixed prices by the government and then transported and sold at uniform prices to the millers. The price of cereals was of the utmost importance, since 50 percent of the expenditure of the poor was devoted to bread and flour. Two and a half million Egyptian pounds had been spent on subsidizing bread and, as a result, prices of wheat and bread had been kept steady for two and a half years. Recently, however, there had been a rise in prices because yields had fallen due to shortage of fertilizers. He agreed with the Syrian delegate that the main problem was to provide Middle East countries with the means for increasing production. Egypt required above all else fertilizers and textile machinery.

The delegates for Persia and Iraq stressed, among other difficulties which had delayed or prevented effective price control in their countries, the shortage of administrative personnel and the long land and sea frontiers which facilitated smuggling. H. D. Gresham, director-general of customs in Persia, referred to the new pattern of demand created by military requirements and the acute scarcity of transport. These factors caused wide regional variations of prices and a flourishing black market in freight rates and transport charges. Where the official transportation rate was 3.5–4 rials per ton, or about 7.5 rials inclusive of the contractor's commission, the black-market rate averaged 20 rials per ton. A year ago there had even been a black-market price of some 5,000 rials for the use of a railroad car, in addition to the official transportation charges. The recent check to the rise in wholesale prices had been partly due to the elimination of black-market baksheesh for rail carriage of goods north from the Persian Gulf. Control of prices and of distribution had been applied to only a few commodities; and neither attempts at control nor the prosecution of hoarders had had any effective influence on the general level of prices. According to the official price indexes, food and clothing had risen more than had the general level of prices; but great caution was needed in using these indexes. Both the wholesale-price index and the cost-of-living index included commodities which were not in fact available.

L. M. Swan, financial adviser to the Minister of Finance in Iraq, drew a similar picture of frustration and discouraging results in attempts to control prices. The key problem was to create an efficient organization. They had tried to obtain additional staff from abroad and that had not been easy. In the early stages of control there had been premature issue of a spate of rules and regulations, which for lack of administrative machinery could not be enforced. Many different methods of controlling imported goods had been tried. Some—mainly sugar, tea, and soap—had been rationed; some had been allocated to licensed consumers; and a few had been distributed at controlled prices through reliable importers. Many articles, however, could not be successfully passed on to consumers at moderate fixed prices. Swan was convinced that in such cases the best policy was to keep prices somewhere near their precontrol level and to take any profit for the government, either by taxation or by levying a special charge. Surplus money could thus be withdrawn from circulation and goods could be prevented from disappearing into the black market.

The Iraq government fully realized the importance of reducing food prices and had introduced effective control of barley and wheat at the beginning of the 1943 harvest. The prices then fixed had been criticized as overgenerous; but they had been largely determined by prices ruling in neighboring countries. In such a matter Iraq could not act alone; any reduction in cereal prices would have to be part of a general Middle East policy. Moreover there was the difficulty of meeting the cultivator's urgent demand for sugar, tea, and clothing. Sugar presented no problem. But the clothing situation was catastrophic and the tea ration amounted to only 30 grams (1 ounce) per head per month. Until the government could offer the cultivator more of such goods, it would be extremely difficult to reduce the prices of his crops. In the case of tea, there had been a general reduction of imports to 40 percent of their prewar level, imposed by MESC and the Combined Food Board on grounds of supply and shipping; but Swan thought it unreasonable to apply the same flat rate of reduction to prosperous countries with a high prewar consumption and to countries in the Middle East where consumption before the war had been extremely low. If the British Commonwealth and the United States would give up a minute quantity of their rations, perhaps 50 or 70 grams a month, Middle East rations could be considerably improved.

J. A. C. Cruickshank, deputy controller of supplies in Cyprus, had some interesting comments to make on the administrative problems of making controls effective. In his experience the kernel of the whole matter was the central organization itself; unless that could be made to work reasonably well it was almost useless to proceed with controls at all. In Cyprus they had found that it could be made to work by careful planning and in particular by not wasting the time of senior staff on routine tasks. For example, the entire supply of fruit and vegetables for urban markets was bought, transported, and sold by the government. The producers had been assured remunerative prices; the cost to the consumer had been reduced by 20 percent in six months; and all this had been done by a single high-grade officer who had been careful not to put his scheme into operation until it was ready in all its details. Soap and shoes were for some time mismanaged by committees representative of the trades concerned. They were then placed under a local businessman, not connected with either trade, and, after an intensive period of detailed organization, control of these commodities now took only part of Cruickshank's time. In other spheres control had been less successful; but that was because the principle had not been applied. He was convinced that it was possible effectively to control almost all commodities with little or no increase in senior staff. Control was most successful when it extended from the first stage of production or manufacture to the final sale to the consumer. Prices and distribution of home-produced goods were fully controllable; but imported goods could only be controlled from port of entry, a fact that raised the vital problem of divergent price levels in the Middle East. Owing to restriction of imports from the outside world and growing importance of interterritorial trade, the problem of divergent price levels was becoming acute in all Middle East countries; in Cyprus it was of major importance. He urged that the whole question of divergent price levels be considered as soon as possible by some suitable body in order that concrete proposals might be made for its solution.

M. J. Flanagan, price controller in Palestine, said that they had not suffered from lack of staff, though some senior officers held more than one post as controllers of different commodities. Nor did they suffer from any lack of experts; Palestine probably had more experts per square mile than any other country and they all offered their opinions through the press. He did not share the view that price control was futile unless the goods in question were owned by the government. As in Cyprus, it had been found possible to fix prices and margins at each stage of distribution, and traders could be relied upon to police each other and inform the government about unfair profiteering. He believed that the best policy was to control as many prices as possible even if complete success could not be assured.

On the question of divergent price levels, which particularly affected Palestine as a country with relatively low prices, H. Wolfson emphasized that goods exported from Palestine had to be sold at the same restricted prices as were permitted in the home market and no producer or exporter was allowed to make more than a limited profit. Similarly the prices of imported goods were controlled at every stage from importer to consumer. But Palestine had no control over the price she had to pay for essential imports from other Middle East countries; and of course it was not possible to prevent excessive profits being made in other countries on resale of Palestine's exports. In recent months the landed cost of some Middle East cereals had been as high as 70 Palestinian pounds (£P) a ton; but the controlled price of flour had been kept at £P 23.5 a ton. This involved a very heavy loss to the government. Out of a total budget of £P 14 million, £P 5 million was being spent on subsidies and nearly four-fifths of that was being used to subsidize imported cereals. The high prices paid by Palestine for food imports were an inflationary factor in the economies of other Middle East countries. Wolfson suggested that all countries should adopt the policy of using subsidies to stabilize wage rates and should consider how far they could assist each other in making such policies effective.

The pleas advanced by the delegates from Cyprus and Palestine that some agreed solution should be found for the problem of divergent price levels received no support from other delegates and no mention was made of this thorny subject in the resolutions of the Conference. The Egyptian undersecretary for supply said that he did not favor the suggestion for a Middle East pool for the stabilization of prices, and implied that the only remedy was to be found in increased production and larger imports. But it was left to the Deputy Prime Minister of Lebanon, Habib Bey Abi Chahla, to draw the logical conclusion. After referring to the enormous profits made by Lebanese importers, which the Free French authorities had been unable to check but which his government was now hoping to deal with by controlling prices, he concluded with an eloquent passage in favor of economic union. Behind this whole question of prices, he said, lay the political anarchy of the Middle East. If the present situation, in which each country went its own way, was allowed to grow worse, the Conference would have failed to yield the hoped-for results. Egypt, Palestine, Syria, Lebanon, and Iraq ought to form an economic union to pool their resources and to share according to their needs. When such a pool had been created and that degree of economic unity had been achieved, reasonable imports would be obtained and distributed rationally. "At present," he added with a glance at J. M. Landis in the chair, "the Middle East Supply Center often produces excellent excuses rather than supplies." He appreciated that such a scheme would raise political difficulties but it was essential that it should be carried out if the economic situation was not to get out of control. Once economic union had been established, the Middle East countries would have done their part and would be able to demand that MESC do its share and provide the imports for which they asked.

Hassan Moukhtar Rasmy Bey replied for Egypt that he doubted whether the system suggested by the leader of the Lebanese delegation would be easy to create and thought it might take some time to produce results. He proposed instead that a joint standing committee of Middle East governments and MESC should be created to draw up import programs, to assess the needs and potential output of each country, and, having obtained the necessary machinery and fertilizers, to distribute the increased supply among the different countries according to their respective needs.

## CITATIONS

*1* Unpublished proceedings of the Middle East Financial Conference, Cairo, April 24–29, 1944.

## CHAPTER 22

# SELLING OF GOLD

The story of gold sales in the Middle East in 1943–44 deserves a chapter to itself, not only for its intrinsic interest but because of its bearing on food prices and cereal collection. It was only after much hesitation and careful weighing of the possible advantages and disadvantages that Sir John Anderson (now Lord Waverley), the British Chancellor of the Exchequer, decided to authorize the novel experiment of selling gold to the public at open-market prices, not only in the Middle East but also in India. In his history of British financial policy during the war Sayers writes (*1*, ch. 9) that, as far as India was concerned, the experiment may be claimed as "one of the most successful in war finance." In the Middle East it also had a considerable measure of success while it lasted; and it would have had more important results if it could have been started earlier and continued longer.

Sales of gold to the public began in Persia in June 1943; in Iraq, Palestine and Transjordan, Syria and Lebanon, early in August 1943; and in Egypt in November 1943. Sales in Persia continued till January 1945, but in the rest of the Middle East they ended in June 1944.

### ORIGIN OF THE EXPERIMENT

At the first Anti-Inflation Conference held in Cairo in September 1942, which was attended by British officials in Middle East countries and by two American observers, a resolution was passed advocating the import of gold for sale in the open market on three grounds: (1) that a supply of gold in the form of coins and jewelry would be likely to absorb surplus purchasing power which would otherwise be invested in commodities; (2) that the proceeds of sale of gold would provide some of the currency required for military expenditure and thus slow down the rate of expansion of the note issue; and (3) that a fall in the price of gold in Middle East markets might have the effect of bringing down other prices in sympathy.

This recommendation was largely inspired by Kahn, who had followed the abortive attempt to bring down the price of wheat in

Syria in 1941 by the sale of 80,000 tons of imported wheat in the market (see ch. 17, p. 145). He saw clearly that inflation was bound to continue so long as the supply of money was constantly being increased by military expenditure without any corresponding increase in goods. But since imports were being drastically cut owing to shipping shortage, there were bound to be fewer goods available for purchase. The problem therefore was to find some commodity of high intrinsic value which would take up the minimum of shipping space and absorb the maximum of purchasing power.

The recommendation of the Conference attracted considerable interest both in London and Washington. In London there were two schools of thought. In some quarters, particularly in the Bank of England, it was feared that the import of gold—especially gold coins—for sale in local markets would undermine confidence in the paper currency and lead to a demand for payment in gold for all purposes; that thc Middle East could not be treated differently from other parts of the world, especially India, where the capacity to absorb gold would be very much greater; and that Middle East governments might refuse sterling in exchange for local currency and might demand shipment of gold up to the full amount of their sterling balances. In the limit this might involve having to find gold to meet all of Britain's overseas financial requirements. Since the central gold reserve of the sterling area held in Britain at that time was only about a billion dollars, this was unthinkable. For countries in the sterling area the gold held by the Bank of England constituted a common pool of reserves only to be used as a last resort for meeting deficits with the outside world. There were also the skeptics who argued that sales of gold would have little or no effect on price inflation. As one Bank of England official put it (*1*, ch. 9), "Sales would have as much effect on the Indian market as a pea-shooter would have on an elephant."

The views of the Bank of England were bound to carry weight in the British Treasury; and even those, including Lord Keynes, who favored the proposal, were concerned about the possible drain on the sterling-area gold reserves. This led to some discussion of the use that might possibly be made of United States gold. The writer remembers Lord Keynes making a rough calculation that the financing of Allied military expenditure in India, China, and the Middle East might cost about a billion dollars of gold per annum. The United States had a reserve at Fort Knox of over $22 billion and if it could be shown that sale of gold at this rate would serve to shorten the war, its use could be abundantly justified. Indeed, he added in one of his characteristic quips, it might be the last chance that the United States would ever have of finding any use for its gold reserves.

This idea of mobilizing the gold in Fort Knox for financing the war in Asia never got beyond the realm of speculation. There was no provision in the Lend-Lease Act whereby gold could be supplied to finance British military expenditure in India and the Middle East. At a later date the United States Treasury followed the example of Britain in selling gold to meet part of its own expenditure in India, Persia, and Egypt; and Saudi Arabia—which had no paper money and needed silver to increase its riyal currency during the war—received several million ounces of silver from the United States on Lend-Lease terms. The Chinese government also was granted facilities to use part of its dollar loans to import gold for sale in the open market in China. But the United States government was never persuaded to mobilize its gold reserves as an instrument of war finance. Special legislation would have been required to amend existing laws restricting the minting and sale of gold; and it would have been next to impossible to expect that Congress would agree to the sale of gold coins over the counter in Asia while American citizens were not allowed a similar privilege at home .

As regards the second objection, it was evident that gold could not be sold in the Middle East without repercussions in India; and the government of India had naturally raised the strongest objection to the Middle East receiving preferential treatment. Since there were two schools of thought in India as well as in London about the policy of selling gold, the Minister of State invited Sir Theodore Gregory, economic adviser to the government of India, to visit Cairo and discuss the matter. Sir Theodore Gregory was himself in favor of the scheme and regarded it as a potentially useful anti-inflationary measure. As a result of his visit it was agreed to suggest to London that any gold that could be made available should be divided in the ratio of two for India and one for the Middle East. It was recognized that there was some risk that sale of gold in India and the Middle East might strengthen demands for convertibility of rupees and sterling into gold at the official price; but it was felt that this demand could be resisted without difficulty.

To be set against the doubts and objections discussed above were arguments calculated to carry weight with the shipping authorities. It was pointed out that the Allies, and in particular the British, were responsible for seeing that the towns in the Middle East were fed. Indeed, prevention of civil unrest and bread riots was recognized to be of the highest political and strategic importance. In order to save shipping it was vital to see that the towns were fed to the maximum possible extent on home-produced cereals; but cutting down imports of consumer goods made it difficult to provide the producer with an incentive to sell his grain. The villagers were having to reduce their consumption of sugar, tea, textiles, hardware, tools, and utensils. Experience in Persia and Syria had shown that the problem of inducing landowners and peasants to part with their grain in exchange for rapidly depreciating paper money was a real one. Gold in the form of coins or jewelry was an article that from time immemorial had appealed to the acquisitive and hoarding instincts of the people, and was traditionally used both as a form of savings and for personal display. In good times, when prices were high, producers bought necklaces of gold coins, bangles, and other jewelry of solid gold to adorn their womenfolk; and in bad times they would sell these to meet the claims of the moneylender.

There was no tradition of hoarding paper money and still less of investing in government bonds. A gold sovereign could indeed be regarded as the Middle East equivalent of a British war-savings certificate. Owing to its high intrinsic value gold could be shipped to the Middle East with the minimum call on transport. At prices ruling in Syria a ton of wheat was worth about two fine ounces of gold. At this rate, 50 tons of gold (nine-tenths fine) would be equal in value to 672,000 tons of wheat, which was greater than the total tonnage of cereals imported into the Middle East in 1942. There was thus a prospect of making a major economy of tonnage, if gold could be shipped to the Middle East to extract home-produced wheat for feeding the towns instead of having to divert shipping for imported wheat.

At the time, this argument may have carried greater weight than did the theory that sale of gold would check inflation and slow down the formidable increase in military expenditure. In 1943 the immediate threat to the Allied cause and in particular to Britain was the submarine attack on shipping. The postwar balance-of-payments problem and the rate at which sterling balances were being piled up were at that time of secondary importance.

It was finally decided in London that the experiment should be tried. Gold was to be made available for sale on account of the British Treasury at the rate of 750,000 fine ounces per quarter in India, and 375,000 fine ounces per quarter in the Middle East outside Egypt.

When the Minister of State submitted his plan for selling 375,000 ounces per quarter, he made a shot in the dark and estimated that he would be doing well if he could sell 3 million sovereigns (equivalent to 706,000 fine ounces) during the following six months for about $40 million ($57 per fine ounce). Considering the uncertainty of the market, this guess proved to be surprisingly near the mark. In fact, he was able to do rather better than this in the first six months. The total amount of gold sold (1.2 million fine ounces) during the 11 months August 1943 to June 1944 was probably not large in relation to the total quantity in circulation and in hoards. The best guess that could be made at the time was that there might be as much as $800 million worth of gold in the whole Middle East, or about 11 million fine ounces. Total sales on behalf of the United Kingdom and United States governments for the whole period are estimated to have amounted to rather more than 10 percent of this quantity.

The adverse repercussions which had been feared never materialized. There was no evidence that confidence in the local currency had been undermined by the sale of gold coins, or the small 5-tola bars (1.87 fine ounces) which were supplied when coins ran out. If anything, confidence had been strengthened. No government had refused to take sterling in exchange for local currency; and the sale of gold had not undermined exchange control nor facilitated export of capital to any noticeable extent. Export of gold was prohibited in Middle East countries, but a certain amount of smuggling had always taken place across Middle East frontiers and into Turkey.

These negative conclusions were reassuring. As to positive results, it was more difficult to draw precise conclusions. As might be expected, experience varied in each of the four countries. Since the chief cause of the increase in the note issue was the amount of military expenditure less the amount of any import surplus, the significance of gold sales can best be measured by relating the proceeds of sale to net military expenditure, increase in note circulation, and import surplus during the same period.

Gold sales yielded about enough during these five months to cover 22 percent of the total military expenditure; they absorbed an amount equal to 38 percent of the total increase in notes; and they represented an addition of 50 percent to the total surplus of imports (excluding gold) into these countries. The percentages were highest in Syria, where inflation had been intensified by the need for expanding the note issue to purchase the wheat crop. Syria and Lebanon were more gold-minded than the other territories and there was a keen demand there for gold coins and jewelry. Moreover, political disturbances in November 1943 led to an increased demand. For these reasons both the volume and price of gold sold were highest in Syria and Lebanon. During the two months November and December, gold sales actually exceeded military expenditure, and notes in circulation declined.

In Persia the results of gold sales were relatively less important. A high level of military expenditure and a chronic budget deficit had combined to raise prices to five or six times their prewar level. One of the reasons why Persia, with a population of about 15 million, bought so much less per head than the other countries is that the mass of the people are traditionally silver-minded. Some silver was in fact imported from India and sold, along with gold coins, by the Bank Melli; but figures of the amount are not available.

According to an official report from Baghdad the sale of gold in six months contributed more than the annual yield of all the deflationary measures taken by the Iraq government. In Palestine, where military expenditure per head of the population was much higher than elsewhere, gold sales per head were also higher. Judging by the course of prices shown below, gold sales may have been almost as important as in Syria in preventing further inflation.

### COURSE OF PRICES

In all these countries prices continued to rise during the five months August–December, but the rate of increase was noticeably less than in the corresponding months of the previous year. Increase of wholesale-price indexes as percentages during these months are shown below:

| Country | 1942 | 1943 |
|---|---|---|
| Iraq | 30 | 17 |
| Persia | 55 | 13 |
| Syria and Lebanon | 17 | 7 |
| Palestine | 20 | 1 |

Other factors besides gold sales contributed to the slowing down of price inflation. There was some falling off in military expenditure in all countries except Palestine. In Persia there had been an extremely sharp rise of prices during the last five months of 1942; but in the corresponding months of 1943 the energetic measures taken by Millspaugh to control prices and improve distribution were having a noticeable effect. In Syria, where the peak of the inflationary trend was reached in May 1943, the removal of the ban on free purchase of sterling and some reduction in military expenditure helped to slow down the rate of inflation. In Palestine during the latter part of 1943 stricter control of prices and distribution, including rationing, was imposed.

### SELLING POLICY

In the early stages, some difference of opinion existed as to the best selling policy to adopt in order to counter inflation. One school of thought attached chief importance to bringing down the price of gold in the expectation that other prices would fall in sympathy; the Governor of the Banque de Syrie et du Liban went so far at one time as to urge that gold be sold at a low price even if the market price were well above it. The opposite view was that, with a limited amount of gold to sell, the object should be to sell "at best" and absorb the maximum amount of purchasing power. This policy was approved by the British Treasury. It meant in practice feeling the pulse of the market and judging when to raise or lower the price in such a way as to dispose of the supply available for the best return. Since the market was highly sensitive and subject to speculative influences, it was not easy to judge the probable reaction to price changes. The launching of the scheme led to expectation of large sales and falling prices. But when it was evident that supplies were limited, the market soon reacted. Delays in transit sometimes made it impossible to meet demand, and to tide over temporary shortages a system of rationing was introduced. In Persia buyers whose demand could not be met at once were given vouchers entitling them to purchase next day at the price ruling on the day of purchase.

In the initial stages, sovereigns only were on sale and it was feared at one time that there would be little demand for the small bars (weighing 5 tolas) that had been specially prepared for retail sales. During the transition period, when bars were being introduced on the market, sovereigns were rationed, and in Palestine and later in Iraq it was stipulated that with every five sovereigns one 5-tola bar must be bought. In this way the market became accustomed to deal in small bars, although sovereigns continued to enjoy a substantial premium, especially when their sale was stopped.

In all the territories except Iraq, gold was put on sale to the general public over the counter at more than one bank. In Baghdad sales were made only to a few brokers or dealers at the head office of the Eastern Bank; and, though the public were free to buy in small quantities, no steps were taken to encourage them to do so. Instead of fixing uniform prices for sale over the counter the practice in Baghdad was for the bank manager or his deputy to interview the dealers and negotiate the best price for each transaction. An attempt was made at one time to introduce this system in Syria and Lebanon, but it was abandoned after a short trial, partly because it appeared to favor the few selected dealers.

### PREMIUM ON SOVEREIGNS

Gold coins enjoyed a substantial premium over gold bars. King's-head sovereigns were generally quoted at a premium of about 10 percent. The premium on the Queen's-head sovereign was less, the price being about 2.5–5 percent below the price of the King's-head; in Saudi Arabia it was quoted at 15 or 20 percent below. Gold coins were still used to some extent in trade, particularly in Arabia, Transjordan, and parts of Syria; but they were also popular as ornaments and for hoarding. Five-tola bars valued at about $130 were rather large units for investment by small savers and if more coins, or even discs of smaller weight, had been available, they would have met with a ready sale.

### PRICE FIXING

No attempt was made to maintain a uniform price for gold throughout the Middle East and considerable discretion was left to representatives in the territories to fix prices in the light of local conditions. Co-ordination was obtained by exchange of telegrams and periodical conferences. In view of differences in the degree of inflation and in price levels it might have been expected that the market price of gold would vary more widely than it did, particularly since export was prohibited in every country. In practice, however, smuggling and freedom to make remittances between the various territories provided scope for arbitrage and kept prices from varying by more than 10 percent between the highest and the lowest. In Syria, where the wholesale-price index was about eight times prewar, the price was the highest, and in Persia one of the lowest. This created difficulties in Baghdad, where it was necessary to fix prices which would as far as possible discourage smuggling from Persia and to Syria.

Except in Baghdad, where a separate price was negotiated for each transaction, frequent changes in price were the exception and changes were only made in the light of market conditions. Demand fluctuated widely from day to day and from week to week, partly because the market for bars was a restricted one and partly because of the operations of speculators. Favorable war news tended to reduce sales. A political crisis in Lebanon and disappointing news from the Allied front in Italy stimulated sales. Demand was also seasonal and was naturally greatest at the time when cultivators were selling their harvest. This was particularly marked in Syria, where the value of the wheat crop was about one-third of the currency in circulation and the note issue had to be increased by about 20 percent to finance the purchase of the crop. During Moslem festivals, which are fairly frequent, it is customary to buy gold ornaments, and jewelers were specially busy at these times.

In the case of sales over the counter at a fixed price the most difficult problem was to decide when to raise or lower the price and by how much. When sales first started, prices fell sharply and so long as the market price was below the official selling price no sales took place. Experience confirmed the view taken at the outset that it would be a mistake to follow the market down each day, quoting the price of the previous day. To do so would merely have strengthened the expectation that the price would fall and buyers would naturally hold off. As a general rule reductions of price were fairly substantial when they were made and were followed where possible by gradual increases of small amounts.

Larger quantities might have been sold, particularly in Egypt, if the price had been drastically reduced. But it is doubtful whether the demand would have proved sufficiently elastic to make this worth while from the point of view of absorbing the maximum amount of local currency. The demand from jewelers was limited by their capacity for turning out gold ornaments, and investment demand was more likely to be influenced by views as to the future value of money than by the price of gold. In any case, at its current price gold was a good deal cheaper than most commodities, compared with its prewar price.

### SAVING TO EXCHEQUER

The sale of gold provided local currencies for Allied military expenditure at a cheaper rate than through the sale of sterling or dollars. About half the proceeds of sale represented a saving which went some way to offset the high cost of goods and services obtained locally. But this result was secondary and of less importance than the indirect effect of gold sales in absorbing purchasing power, slowing down the expansion of the note issue, and checking the rate of inflation.

Before the experiment started, no one could say how much gold would be bought at what price in the Middle East. Actually it was found that for carrying out the plan it was not necessary to lower the price as much as was originally expected. The sale of gold, estimated at about 1.2 million fine ounces, can be regarded as a satisfactory achievement, and its contribution to slowing down the rate of inflation was by no means inconsiderable.

## CITATIONS

*1* R. S. Sayers, in his forthcoming volume, *Financial Policy 1939–45* (Hist. of the Second World War, U.K. Civil Ser.).

## CHAPTER 23

# RATIONING IN THE MIDDLE EAST

The Middle East Conference on Control of Distribution and Rationing which met at Cairo in August 1943 under the chairmanship of E. M. H. Lloyd, economic adviser to the Minister of State in the Middle East, was attended by 35 experts from 15 territories, ranging from Morocco and Algeria in the west to Saudi Arabia and Persia in the east, and by 15 British and American officials. It was a remarkable gathering. Delegates had met to discuss a technical problem of baffling complexity which was giving concern to governments not only in the Middle East but throughout the world. Millions of workers and their families depended for their daily bread on the efforts of these administrators to ensure that limited supplies were fairly distributed. It was their primary responsibility to prevent bread riots and civil unrest. Nearly every territory had found it necessary to adopt some form of rationing of food and bare necessities; but the variety of methods that had been evolved by each, generally after much trial and error and for the most part independently of one another, was one of the most striking features brought out by the Conference.

In August 1943 the outlook was reassuring. The enemy had been driven from North Africa in May, and from Sicily just before the Conference met. The invasion and collapse of Italy was imminent and the submarine attack was being mastered. Harvests had been good nearly everywhere and in some territories, particularly Syria, above the average. Successful efforts had been made to organize cereal-collection schemes. But governments were increasingly concerned with the problem of controlling prices and distribution, not only of food but of consumer goods. Inflation had placed a growing volume of money in the hands of the public, but owing to diversion of resources to war purposes there was a growing world shortage of consumer goods. Restriction of consumption was inevitable. The crucial question which all governments had to face was whether consumption should be restricted by allowing prices to rise, or whether prices should be controlled and distribution regulated by some system of allocation.

In his introductory remarks the Chairman said (*1*):

There is no easy solution to the problem we are to discuss at the Conference. Government control is always unpopular. It requires a sufficient and reasonably competent staff; and above all it needs to win general acceptance and, in particular, a fair measure of support from traders who have to be controlled. In no country is it wholly satisfactory. In Britain I can only claim that it is a good deal more satisfactory than in the last war. Indeed conditions in the United Kingdom in 1916 and 1917 resembled in some ways those now prevailing in the Middle East—widespread profiteering and natural hesitation on the part of the Government to launch out on the uncharted and perilous waters of State interference.

These considerations make it all the more remarkable that Middle East Governments should have attempted to do as much as they have done. We all know that rationing and control of distribution can never be 100 percent perfect; but if the need is sufficiently great, there is some force in the view that even an imperfect attempt at rationing and control is better than doing nothing. Hence we who have had some experience in other countries welcome the response which has been made to the invitation to attend this Conference.

The Conference appointed two vice-chairmen: Hussein Enan Bey, undersecretary for agriculture in Egypt, who had just returned from the Hot Springs conference where the Food and Agriculture Organization of the United Nations was brought into being; and Dr. Mocharraf Naficey, ex-minister of finance from Persia. A valuable feature of the Conference was the full documentation about rationing and control in each territory which had been prepared for delegates.

At the first session Keith Murray, Director of the Food and Agriculture Division in the Middle East Supply Center, introduced the subject of control of supplies and wholesale distribution, and summarized the common principles which experience had shown to underlie the successful working of Middle East cereal-collection schemes. His address is given below (*1*):

The Middle East Supply Council, which met in May 1943, noted the growing trends towards inflation and stressed the need for more effective control of the distribution of essential commodities in the various Middle East territories. It recognized that the introduction of control schemes presented great difficulties but that it would be necessary, none the less, to introduce such schemes owing to the impossibility of securing fair distribution through any system of price control. Even if supplies were ample, the wide divergence in income under present inflationary conditions would prevent the price mechanism acting as an efficient and fair distributor of essential goods.

In the Middle East, it is an obvious truism to say that the possibility of effective rationing depends entirely on the extent to which the Rationing Authority is able to gain control of the supply and this, in turn, depends to a great extent on whether the supply is mainly imported or mainly home-produced. So far as imports are concerned, the problem would appear to be relatively simple; through control of shipping and internal transport, it is not difficult to ensure that these supplies pass into the hands of the authorities concerned. There are few essential foods coming into the Middle East today, which are not consigned, directly or indirectly, to the central Government or its agents.

But the control of home-produced supplies is a more difficult matter and here we have not advanced so far. The first problem is the control of grains, followed by oils and fats, and sugar. If a fair distribution of cereals can be assured, other food problems, from a short term point of view, become less serious; somewhere between 80 and 90 percent of the diet of the various countries is made up from these three sources, of which bread grains are far and away the most important.

So far as grain is concerned, the greater part of the supply in these territories is produced locally, mainly by small producers, and the first essential to ensure a sufficiency for the towns and deficit rural areas is to gain control of the whole surplus above the cultivator's own needs; over 2,000,000 tons of cereals a year must be collected from cultivators in the Middle East countries to satisfy the needs of other consumers.

In the last two years we have gained considerable experience in the working of the collection schemes designed and operated by the various Governments. These have differed in extent and function, but it may be useful if I summarize one or two common principles which our experience indicates as necessary for successful working.

1. Free markets cannot be depended upon to produce the necessary quantities of grain under present conditions either where they are needed most, or at reasonable prices. Hoarding, due to fear of famine or expectation of higher prices, is too strong a factor under war-time conditions.

2. The Government should be the sole purchaser of the grain and, with minor exceptions, private trade should be forbidden. Any increase in the number of purchasers on the market starts competitive bidding and price rises. Partial monopoly, i.e. purchase of only a portion of the crop, will fail so long as there is any free market left, since the cultivator will be unwilling to deliver his quota to the Government at the official price, which is invariably below the free market price.

3. Maximum prices should be fixed well in advance of the harvest season and, when once fixed, should not be varied during the season. Any weakness on the part of the Government and suggestion of possible higher prices stops the collection of cereals.

4. The price to the cultivator must be a reasonably fair one; if fixed too low, then the grain will not be forthcoming and production in the ensuing year will be seriously affected.

5. Cash payment to the cultivator should be made promptly on purchase of the grain.

6. An accurate assessment of production is essential and should be made in the first instance while the crop is still growing, and, in the second instance, when threshed. Without such assessments it is impossible to allocate the share of the crop to be given up to the Government, and upon the setting of these quotas the whole collection scheme is dependent.

7. It is important to leave ample grain with the cultivator to satisfy the needs of his family, his livestock and his seed. Unless this is done and confidence established, he will be unwilling to produce any of his surplus.

8. Cereal collection schemes in the different territories are closely related. Prices and policies must be co-ordinated if the schemes are to be properly controlled. Developments in one country affect those in neighboring territories.

9. Control of means of transport and of movement of cereals is a useful complement to control of cereal markets and prices. Confiscation of the means of transport, as well as of any grain which is being moved illegally, is a very great deterrent.

The control of other indigenous products may not be as difficult as control of cereals, since the number of producers is smaller; moreover, where products have to be processed or manufactured before reaching the consumer, there is often a bottle-neck where control can be achieved. The control of the supplies of edible oils is probably one of the most urgent needs at the present time.

So much then for the first of the two major rationing problems of the Middle East—securing control of supplies of home-produced commodities primarily for distribution to non-producers.

The second point, very closely related to the first problem, is the question of getting supplies of other consumer goods, both food and industrial products, out to the rural workers. This concerns chiefly supplies of tea, sugar, clothing, and fuel. I stress particularly the problem of distribution of these goods to the rural districts, because this is going to be the main problem of internal distribution in the immediate future. Unless the cultivator can be assured of something to buy with the money he gets for his produce, the grain surpluses will not be forthcoming, and we shall not succeed in getting the town populations adequately fed.

In the discussion of Murray's paper Hussein Enan Bey said that he was glad that Murray had mentioned the necessity of offering cultivators a reasonable price. It was useless to expect the cultivator in Egypt to be satisfied with a price of £3 per ardeb of wheat when it was worth £10 in other countries. Prices in one country must be co-ordinated with those in neighboring territories; otherwise smuggling and illicit dealing were encouraged. He agreed that prices should be fixed before the harvest, but in certain circumstances (for instance weather conditions) it might be necessary to change them. In Egypt, another important factor influencing the collection of grain was the supply of fertilizers. If bigger quantities could be made available the grain-supply position would be eased and prices brought down to a reasonable level.

The need for improving the supply of consumer goods to the cultivators was stressed by delegates from Syria and Lebanon. Murray mentioned the obligation on the part of the grain-collecting organization to ensure that the cultivator should be able to buy what he needs with the money received from the sale of his crops. The system of direct barter was considered unsound, but it might have to be considered for a country like Syria, where the bulk of the harvest was grown away from the large towns. Commodities like cotton piece goods and paraffin oil should be made available to the producer, otherwise he could not be expected to deliver his grain. It was useless to fix a maximum price for grain for the farmer, if, at the same time, another man was allowed to make enormous profits on cotton piece goods. The control of cereals would have to be linked up with a general system of control.

The Sudan delegates asked whether it would not be possible to stabilize the cost of living since, at present, prices of grain sometimes were fixed low in relation to living costs. The question of inflation raised problems outside the scope of the Conference. Unfortunately the increase in price levels had been markedly different in the different territories. The Sudan government had managed to keep its price level lower than that of most countries in the Middle East; in countries farther to the east, the increase in prices was becoming a very difficult problem. It was agreed that prices should be kept as much as possible in line in neighboring countries; but if the cost of living was already widely divergent between different territories, the right policy was to prevent the price of cereals rising beyond the increase in the cost of living. At the Cereals Conference in Damascus an attempt had been made to co-ordinate prices of wheat in the adjoining territories. But in view of the very considerable divergence between the general level of prices in Palestine and Transjordan, the attempt to co-ordinate prices of wheat alone in the two countries had proved impossible.

The resolutions adopted by the Conference are printed in Appendix Note II. Many of them are elementary and obvious enough, though often overlooked by members of the public and by some political spokesmen. But even what appear to be truisms may be misleading if they are taken out of their context and applied in different circumstances. Thus the doctrine laid down in Resolution (3) about the need to combine price control with some form of allocation or rationing is carefully phrased so as to permit of exceptions. In fact it is not easy to lay down hard-and-fast rules about the conditions necessary for successful price control.

In World War I, before the introduction of price control in Britain, it was widely held that it was impossible, or at least contrary to economic laws, for the government to fix prices. Proposals for preventing profiteering were met by the retort: "You cannot get away from the laws of supply and demand." In Britain the idea that the government could fix prices by statute was regarded as an exploded fallacy going back to Tudor times and earlier. The medieval doctrine of the "just" price figured in economic textbooks as a museum curiosity having no relation to the modern world. This attitude of mind and the difficulty of finding any legal or constitutional basis for giving the executive power to fix prices explains the hesitation and delay in introducing wartime controls in Britain. It was not till 1918 that food rationing and control of food prices was fully enforced, and then only under strong pressure from public opinion that something must be done to check the rising cost of living.

When the experiment somehow worked not too badly, it was natural that in World War II public opinion should expect the government to be able, in Lord Rhondda's phrase, "to suspend the laws of supply and demand" (*2*, p. 31), at any rate for the period of the war, and to fix the price of anything at will. But as many price controllers found to their cost, fixing prices is a ticklish business; and there is no well-defined technique for ensuring success. As in all government planning, so much depends on factors that are imponderable and incalculable.

One fairly safe generalization is that prices cannot be fixed just by writing down on paper what they should be and publishing the paper as a decree. If nobody pays any attention, the law is merely brought into disrepute, for proceedings cannot be taken against everyone. This is an important point in the Middle East, where the phrase "black market" does not carry with it the dishonorable connotation that it does in the west. The most natural reaction of both buyers and sellers is to ignore government price fixing, unless the price fixed happens to suit both parties. Indeed, freedom for all to buy and sell at their own price is regarded in the Middle East as one of the elementary human rights.

But if the government can deal with an organized group of traders, able to police themselves and anxious to keep on the right side of government and public, the group may be willing to observe a statutory regulation as to the price at which they must sell. Then if the price fixed is much below the level which would be determined by supply and demand, the familiar troubles begin; for the holding of prices at an artificially low level—below what they would be in a free market—stimulates demand and by itself creates a shortage of supply in relation to that demand. If the demand can be met, no problem arises and rationing is unnecessary. Thus bread was not rationed in Britain until after the war, because the supply was sufficient to meet the demand even at the low subsidized price. But usually the price is controlled just because the free-market price is high owing to insufficient supplies, in which case it will be quite impossible to meet the demand of consumers if the price is reduced. Price control, if it is to be effective, must then be accompanied by rationing. Otherwise it leads to queues of dissatisfied housewives, to excessive purchases by early or favored customers, or to virtual disappearance of the goods under the counter or into the black market. For these reasons goods that are difficult to ration, like fruits and vegetables, are not easily brought under effective price control.

It is not quite correct therefore to say that "Price control without rationing is not only ineffective but in some cases harmful," as was stated in a paper submitted to the Conference by the Syrian delegation. Resolution (3) adopted after discussion was more guarded. It read (*1*):

> Control of prices, by removing the free play of market forces and keeping prices at a level at which demand exceeds supply, needs as a general rule to be accompanied by some form of allocation or rationing if it is to prove just, efficacious and practicable. Price control without allocation or rationing cannot by itself achieve fair distribution.

Even this guarded statement may seem contrary to the experience of wartime control of prices in the United States and Canada, where stabilization of prices was established over most goods and services and only a few had to be rationed. But there is no real contradiction. If measures can be taken to peg the existing level of prices and wages at a time when supply and demand are in equilibrium, and if supplies remain fairly adequate to meet the stabilized demand, no serious problem will arise. But when there is a reduction of supply or an increase in demand, as happened in the United States in the case of tires and meat, then some form of rationing of consumers, or allocation of supplies based on a percentage of past trade, becomes necessary.

In general, there is much to be said in favor of the general stabilization of all prices, wages, and profits, as in Germany, the United States, and Canada, rather than the policy of selective price control adopted in Britain. But the methods of the Office of Price Administration for fixing price ceilings and profit margins for practically everything would have been quite out of the question in the Middle

East. It was difficult enough to control prices and distribution of the most essential goods. In most Middle East territories, rationing and price control never extended much beyond bread and flour, sugar, tea, fats, soap, kerosene, and to a less extent clothing.

### RATIONING IN EGYPT

Rationing was first introduced in Egypt for kerosene toward the end of 1940. A family census was carried out by the statistical department in much the same way as the general census last taken in 1937. Family cards were then prepared by local supply boards giving the name and address of the head of the family, the number of persons in the family, and the quantity of kerosene normally consumed during a two-week period. Under the rationing regulations, the local boards had to be notified of change of address and movement from one district to another, so the total quantity of kerosene allocated to each district could be adjusted. This was particularly important at the time when enemy air attacks caused a considerable displacement of inhabitants from Alexandria to the interior of the country.

When kerosene rationing came into force each family was given a ration equivalent to 100 percent of its normal consumption. The ration per head and per family thus varied with purchasing power and the extent to which kerosene was normally used for different purposes. At a later date, owing to shortage of supply, rations were reduced by a uniform percentage. For example, on May 1, 1942, household consumption was cut by 25 percent and on September 1, 1942, by a further 12.5 percent.

This system of rationing kerosene was called "Social Standard Rationing," since the households were rationed according to their size and social standing. When later it became necessary to ration sugar in the city of Cairo it was found convenient to use the kerosene cards as a basis for sugar rationing. The result was that, when consumption of sugar had to be reduced, households with the smallest consumption per head were subjected to the same percentage cut as households who could normally afford a much higher consumption per head. Given the extreme inequality of income in Egypt this system, which in Western eyes appears contrary to the principle of "fair shares," may have been unavoidable. It was explained in an official memorandum of the Egyptian Ministry of Supply that, if a uniform system of rationing had been adopted, some classes of the population would have been undersupplied and some unjustifiably oversupplied. The explanation is more valid in the case of kerosene, especially if it is used for lighting and heating as well as cooking; but the principle seems less justifiable in the case of sugar, since the need for it varies with a person's capacity to consume rather than with the size of the house in which he lives.

Apart from kerosene, sugar, and in 1944 fats and oils, there was no direct consumer rationing in Egypt; but in order to ensure equitable distribution of cereals the Egyptian Ministry of Supply controlled the collection of wheat, barley, millet, and rice and their transport to the towns. Flour mills received wheat, barley, and millet at fixed prices, transport and storage charges being met by a government subsidy. In 1943 the standard rates of extraction were 95 percent for wheat flour and 62.5 percent for barley flour. The rate of admixture varied from time to time. At the time of the Conference the standard flour consisted of 90 percent wheat and 10 percent barley. In 1942 the admixture had been two-thirds wheat and one-third millet. Flour mills received their requirement of wheat and barley on the basis of cards showing the amount of flour needed for distribution to controlled bakeries and flour shops, which in turn received permits based on the number of customers normally supplied by them. No consumer rationing was necessary for bread and flour, since the required degree of restriction of wheat consumption was enforced by the higher extraction rates and admixture of other cereals.

In the case of tea the Ministry of Supply controlled the monthly distribution of Egypt's aggregate import quota among the recognized tea importers. Each importer received an allocation based on his share of total imports during the three years 1939–41. Importers were responsible for rationing their customers on the basis of their purchases in normal times. A special allocation of tea was made to co-operative societies for distribution to their members.

No complete system of rationing meat was introduced in Egypt but an attempt was made to deal with wartime shortage and high prices by enforcing meatless days. It was made illegal to sell or offer for sale fresh or frozen meat on Monday, Tuesday, and Wednesday of each week; during the other four days of each week the number of cattle and sheep to be slaughtered in public abattoirs was regulated in proportion to the average number of cattle slaughtered each day during the corresponding week in 1940.

Maximum prices were fixed for the most important foods under Decree Law No. 101 of 1939. A central price-regulation committee was responsible for formulating price regulations, and subcommittees were formed in each governorate or province to fix prices in their respective areas. The following foodstuffs were subject to price regulations: wheat, barley, maize, rice, lentils, beans, bread, flour, meat, sugar, coffee, tea, and vegetable oils. By Military Order No. 214 of January 1942, power was taken to fix prices in catering establishments. In February 1943 the maximum price of a lunch was fixed at 25 piasters and of a dinner at 30 piasters. Under Order No. 99 of 1943, public establishments were forbidden to serve to any person at any meal more than one dish of meat, fish, hare, or poultry, or to serve two dishes of the same course. Decree Law No. 128 of 1939 prohibited hoarding and excessive purchases of certain commodities including cereals, cottonseed, cottonseed oil, and tea. Manufacturers and traders were required to make returns of the quantities of these commodities in their possession. A military order required manufacturers and traders to keep special books showing their transactions in these commodities, and under further orders only persons inscribed in the Commercial Register of the Ministry of Supply were permitted to deal in goods manufactured locally or imported from abroad without a license.

### SYRIA AND LEBANON

Syria and Lebanon were closely linked by common institutions set up during the French mandate. Hence the principles and methods of rationing were similar in the two countries; but their administration and detailed application were separate. Rationing in the main was limited to bread, flour, and sugar, with occasional issues of rice when it was available. In addition some other items were distributed on a ration basis to government officials and railroad employees through their respective co-operative societies.

One of the chief difficulties experienced by the Office des Céréales Panifiables (OCP) in the distribution of cereals was the absence of a reliable census of the population. In Lebanon a special census was made by the state *Ravitaillement* (food supply) authorities in December 1942 with the help of a young British captain borrowed from the army by OCP. It was carried out by supplying every house with declaration forms on which each member of the household gave the numbers of his identity and ration cards, and declarations were checked by collectors who verified the number of persons present. A similar system was adopted in the large towns of Syria, but for small towns and villages estimates of the population had to be based upon the normal *État Civil* (civil-status) registrations, and were only approximate. When the census had been completed, family ration cards were made out on the basis of household declarations and in Lebanon were distributed on one day during which curfew was imposed and the whole population were confined to their houses. This system made possible a double check and brought to light certain errors in declarations. During the first day 90 percent of the cards were distributed; during the next 12 days, 7 percent; and the remaining 3 percent, which required further checking, were distributed over a period of 12 months. The population of Lebanon was found by the census to be 1.06 million. Ration cards for each district in Lebanon were different in color in order to facilitate treatment of persons moving from one district to another. This was particularly important, for in Lebanon there was a big migration to mountain resorts in the summer and a considerable movement in and out of the city of Beirut.

In Lebanon a uniform system of rationing was applied to the whole population, but in Syria ration cards were only issued in towns. Villages and nomadic tribes received bulk allocations and the distribution to households was left to the village *mukhtars* (headmen) or to the head of the tribe. In Syria the Bedouin tribal population was estimated at 108,000. Their summer and winter movements are fairly regular and arrangements were made in advance for them to obtain supplies of cereals and sugar. One ration card, valid for a limited period, was issued to cover a whole tribe. Prisons, hospitals, and other public institutions received allocations based on the number of inmates. A certain amount of double rationing for individuals was unavoidable, since it was difficult to ensure that names of individuals entering institutions or joining the army were removed from the family card.

In Lebanon the distribution of cereals and sugar was in the hands of the *Ravitaillement* service, which obtained cereals from OCP and sugar from the United Kingdom Commercial Corporation. Depots were set up in towns and villages where the rationed foods were distributed direct to a representative of each family, who could normally obtain a month's ration at a time; but it was difficult to ensure a regular flow of supplies especially during the winter months, and frequently issues were spasmodic and irregular. Families in Lebanon drew a ration of flour in the towns and of grain in the villages. In Syria the villages received grain, which they had milled locally, but towns received an allocation of flour based on the total population and issues were made to bakers who baked and sold bread to the public. No attempt was made to tie customers to particular bakers and many irregularities occurred, particularly in Damascus, which at times gave rise to serious unrest. Sugar was distributed in the towns at *Ravitaillement* depots, and when consumers purchased their rations they surrendered a coupon which was detached from their cards. Officials in charge of the depots had to deposit a sum of 2,500 Syrian pounds with the *Ravitaillement* service as a guarantee of integrity. In the villages a bulk issue of sugar was made to the *mukhtar* who was responsible for distributing rations to each family.

Rations ruling in Syria and Lebanon in the summer of 1943 were reported by OCP to be as follows, in kilos per head per month:

| Commodity | Syria | | Lebanon | | Normal consumption |
|---|---|---|---|---|---|
| | Towns | Villages | Towns | Villages | |
| Bread | 13 | — | — | — | 12–15 |
| Flour | — | — | 10 | — | 12–15 |
| Cereals | — | 12 | — | 11 | 15–20 |
| Sugar | 1 | .5 | .5 | .5 | 2 |

The difference between the quantities of sugar issued in the towns and villages of Syria was explained by the fact that certain sweet fruits such as dates and raisins were in adequate supply in the villages but not in the towns.

## CITATIONS

*1* Unpublished proceedings of the Middle East Conference on Control of Distribution and Rationing, Cairo, August 21–23, 1943.

*2* E. M. H. Lloyd, *Experiments in State Control at the War Office and the Ministry of Food* (Econ. and Soc. Hist. of the World War, Brit. Ser. . . . , Humphrey Milford, Oxford, 1924).

CHAPTER 24

# POINTS RATIONING IN PALESTINE

Rationing in Palestine developed from a simple regulation cutting sales of sugar to 50 percent of normal to one of the most ambitious schemes of points rationing to be found in any country.

Palestine was wholly dependent on imports for its supplies of sugar, and 45 percent of its wheat and flour was normally derived from imports. From the early days of the war, records had been kept of stocks of sugar, wheat, and flour held by importers and wholesalers. In April 1941 an order was made restricting the sale of sugar, wholesale or retail, to a quantity not exceeding 50 percent of the quantity normally sold weekly during a datum period. Restriction of sales was later strengthened by an order prohibiting any sale of sugar, except from retailer to consumer, without a permit. The same system of control was later applied to flour.

Limitation of retailers' supplies combined with fixed maximum prices left the responsibility on the retailer for rationing his customers; this led to queues and waste of time on the part of customers and retailers. Consequently, though any attempt to enforce consumer rationing was regarded with many misgivings, it soon became clear that some form of coupon rationing or of tying consumers to particular retailers would have to be introduced. The main difficulty was to ensure a reasonably accurate registration of the population.

In addition to the usual obstacles to taking a census of population in Arab countries, there were in Palestine special difficulties arising from recent political disturbances and illegal immigration. The government decided against attempting to take a uniform census for the whole country, but instead empowered district controllers to carry out registration in their areas under the Food and Essential Commodities (Registration) Rules of January 1942. Each district was given discretion to devise its own method of enumeration. In Jerusalem, Tel Aviv, and Jaffa registration was made on a family basis; but in Haifa from the outset it was on an individual basis. At a later date all four of these town areas were assimilated, so that ration cards could be issued to individuals rather than households and different rations could then be given to children up to seven years of age and between the ages of seven and twelve.

In rural districts, villages, and settlements registration was undertaken by the *mukhtars* under the supervision of district officers. Neither the normal census estimates nor the results of registration for food rationing could claim a high degree of accuracy. But it is interesting to compare the results. The government statisticians' estimate of the total population was 1.62 million and the food-registration figures added up to 1.86 million. If the former was too low, the latter was almost certainly too high. A combination of the two yields an estimate for the total population of 1.74 million with a margin of error roughly of 7.5 percent.

The rationing of sugar by coupon was introduced on February 1, 1942 and under the Food Control (Commodity Linking) Rules of 1942, consumers were required to select the retailer of their choice. This system of tying consumers to a particular shop provided the key to the distribution of sugar, since retailers obtained an allocation based upon the number of consumers on their books. Contrary to the expectations of the skeptics, registration and linking of consumers was carried out fairly smoothly, and within a few weeks the coupon rationing of sugar was working successfully.

The rationing of bread and flour met with more serious difficulties owing mainly to the wide variation in consumption by different sections of the population. Thus an Arab laborer engaged in hard manual work was said to consume as much as one kilo of bread per day, while a European Jew with a much more varied diet might eat only 200 grams, or one-fifth as much. If flour had been rationed in the same way as sugar, on a per capita basis, the Jew would have received more than he needed and the Arab a great deal less. Fortunately supplies of flour in 1942, though insufficient to meet all demands, were never so low as to make it necessary to fix a low ration per head. Nevertheless supplies were not sufficient to meet all demands, and complaints of unfair distribution were reinforced by the appearance of bread queues. This situation was first met by extending to bread and flour the principle of tying consumers to particular shops. Retailers then received an allocation of flour or bread on the basis of an average ration per head for the members of families on their list. This gave the retailer a certain latitude to adapt his sales to meet the varied requirements of his customers. It was of course easier for the larger retailers, especially those with shops serving mixed populations, to satisfy their customers. To meet the case of small retailers in Arab quarters a special allowance had to be made. Even so, there was considerable discontent about the inequality of the ration and the extent to which customers were at the mercy of their retailers.

All that could be claimed for this system was that it eliminated the bread queues and ensured that all bakers and retailers got a regular allocation. In the autumn of 1942, however, because of dwindling stocks and increasing uncertainty about future imports, it became more and more evident that other foodstuffs, such as meat and fats, would have to be rationed and that with so mixed a population no system of "straight" rationing would be practicable. What was needed was some new method of limiting the demand and restricting the consumption over a fairly wide range of different foodstuffs. Only thus would it be possible to achieve anything like fair shares in a country with such varied food habits as Palestine.

The Palestine points-rationing scheme was introduced by an order of October 17, 1942, entitled "Food Control (Points Restrictions) Rules, 1942." The Palestine government's report on the scheme submitted to the Middle East Conference on Control of Distribution and Rationing (*1*) in August 1943 may perhaps be quoted as giving the best summary of the doubts and hesitations with which the scheme was launched and the comparative success which was in fact realized:

> To those who gave any thought to the matter, the underlying principles of the scheme were generally accepted, since it was realized that restriction of consumption of essential foodstuffs had become imperative and the "straight" or coupon rationing applied to individual commodities would not suit the somewhat peculiar circumstances of Palestine. At the same time, although the scheme was regarded as a courageous attempt to grapple with the situation, there was much scepticism in regard to its successful application; the illiteracy of a section of the population, their individualistic outlook, the astronomical number of points involved, the impossibility of applying the scheme to rural areas, the difficulties of exercising a moderately efficient check over operations, and the complicated nature of the scheme itself all giving rise to misgivings. However, the principles of the scheme received Government's approval and it was launched. Of deliberate intent the number of points issued to the individual (based on a "nutritional ration") was generous; and, after a month of apprehension on the part of the housewife, points expenditure was faced with equanimity if not complaisance. Several important primary objectives had been gained by the launching of the scheme. The housewife took a far more lively interest in her expenditure on foodstuffs than was formerly the case, points were a favorite topic of conversation, and their implications became increasingly clear particularly as Food Control had issued a blunt warning that the scheme would be tightened up in due course and consumption was in fact restricted, although the restriction was not yet sufficiently severe. As regards the last point, restaurants, hotels, and cafes had been brought under control in the matter of charges for meals and this in conjunction with the points system (which applied to restaurant meals) had an important effect on consumption.
>
> With the second issue of Points Books, the tightening up process began. The number of points per individual was reduced and the practical effect of

the scheme as a restriction scheme became increasingly evident. There was considerable opposition from the trade, even to the threat of open sabotage by the closure of business premises; but a counter threat to open Government shops for the sale of Government owned commodities effectively disposed of this particular difficulty.

The officers responsible for the formulation of the Points Scheme had had no practical experience of the operation in the United Kingdom. In fact, none of them had visited the United Kingdom since the outbreak of the war, and available literature on the subject was meagre. By a fortunate circumstance, however, Mr. E. M. H. Lloyd visited Palestine and was able to give invaluable advice on the subject as he had a wide experience of this form of control. As a consequence, commodities not under complete Government control were dropped from the scheme, Points Banks operating directly under Food Control were established in all the main consuming centers, and a periodical balance as between availability and total points values was struck—issues of Government controlled commodities included in the scheme being made dependent on the surrender of sufficient points to cover the issues. These were matters of high administrative importance, since the onus of obtaining points was thus transferred to the retailer, who very rapidly realized that without points he could not remain in business. The consuming public knew little of these alterations in the administrative machine, but felt their repercussions in the changed attitude of retailers towards the collection of points. This latest modification came into effect on May 1, and since that time it may be said that the scheme has operated with reasonable and increasing efficiency.

The following table gives a list of the commodities on ration in June 1943, showing the average quantities consumed monthly per head in pointed and unpointed areas together with estimates of average monthly consumption in the three years 1937–39, in grams:

| Commodity | Pointed areas | Unpointed areas: Arab: Villages | Unpointed areas: Arab: Semi-urban areas | Unpointed areas: Jewish: Settlements | Unpointed areas: Jewish: Semi-urban areas | Special issues | Entire country average: 1943 | Entire country average: 1937–39 |
|---|---|---|---|---|---|---|---|---|
| Flour | 6,979 | 7,500 | 7,500 | 7,500 | 7,500 | 358 | 7,382 | 8,520 |
| Sugar | 1,187 | 300 | 600 | 600 | 600 | 118 | 801 | 1,497 |
| Macaroni | 99 | 0 | 0 | 200 | 200 | 6 | 55 | 46 |
| Margarine | 314 | 0 | 50 | 200 | 200 | 17 | 149 | 88[b] |
| Edible oil | 533 | 0 | 100 | 600 | 600 | 22 | 261 | 530 |
| Jam | 150 | 0 | 50 | 180 | 180 | 9 | 82 | 66[b] |
| Tea | 6 | 2 | 6 | 8 | 8 | 1 | 6 | 14 |
| Coffee | 82 | 40 | 60 | 40 | 40 | 10 | 68 | 109 |
| Cocoa | 6 | — | — | — | — | 1 | 3 | 12 |
| *Halawa*[a] | 108 | 40 | 40 | 20 | 20 | 1 | 70 | 44[b] |
| Meat: | | | | | | | | |
| Beef | 86 | — | 17 | — | — | 17 | 30 | 600 |
| Mutton | 77 | — | 30 | — | — | 30 | 27 | 750 |

[a] A sesame-seed product.
[b] Figures for local production are very uncertain.

The extremely low figures for tea and cocoa are explained by the fact that they were drunk by only a small proportion of the European population. On the other hand coffee is the traditional drink of the Arabs and of most European Jews. It will be noted that no butter was included in the ration. Before the war average imports in 1937–40 were 2,179 tons. This had to be wholly replaced during the war by home-produced margarine.

The special feature which distinguished points rationing in Palestine was the inclusion of bread and flour within the scheme. The value of points to be spent on bread and flour represented more than 50 percent of the total. In practice the Arab laborer could obtain almost all the bread he was accustomed to consume, if he was willing to spend all or nearly all his points on bread. On the other hand, those accustomed to a European diet had to economize on their bread and flour consumption if they were to get anything like a fair supply of meat, fats, and sugar. It would of course have been much easier to work the scheme if it had not been necessary to ration bread, or if bread could have been rationed separately. As it was, the chief criticism of the scheme arose from the fact that it was not comprehensive enough. Thus one of the deficiencies, particularly in the early stages of the scheme, was that home-produced olive oil was not included. The Arabs, who prefer olive oil to margarine or other edible oils, were able to purchase it on the free market without having to surrender points and were thus able to buy extra flour or sugar or to sell some of their points in the black market; indeed trading in points on a small scale took place, the market price at one time being as much as 1.5 Palestinian pounds per thousand. Olive oil could not be included in the early stages because it was difficult to establish control of home-produced supplies at the source. Consequently the Arabs complained because they had to buy olive oil at a high price outside the points-rationing scheme, whereas the Jews complained that, since the Arabs could get olive oil without points, they had more points left for obtaining more than their share of flour and sugar.

The points system only applied to the larger urban areas, Jerusalem, Tel Aviv, Haifa, Jaffa, etc., comprising a population of about 650,000. In the rural areas, where the population was either wholly Arab or wholly Jewish, it was found more suitable to apply bulk rationing combined with the tying of consumers to a single shop. The combination of the two systems, points rationing in the towns and bulk rationing in the villages, gave rise to fewer difficulties than might have been expected. Movement of population was in any case discouraged during the war owing to the need for economizing transport.

Books of points were issued to each registered person through the retailers, and were valid for a period of three months. For the period beginning August 1, 1943 the books contained thirteen pages, one page for each week. An adult's book contained 168 points for each week with coupons of different denominations varying from one to twenty. Each page was differently colored, and there were different designs for the first four, the second four, and the third five weekly pages. The weekly allowance of 168 points constituted in effect a supplementary currency, and point prices were set and changed from time to time in such a way as roughly to balance demand with supply. To enable the scheme to work it was essential that the points available for use each week should be backed by a supply of goods in the shops; and it was important to ensure that if possible the total point value of the goods available in the shops should be equal to, and if possible slightly greater than, the total points to be spent during each week. A points balance sheet was drawn up at frequent intervals showing the point value of the estimated supplies against the probable total demand. When necessary, points prices had to be adjusted either to stimulate or to reduce the demand, and thus make it balance the supply. There was no guarantee that any consumer would necessarily be able to obtain any given quantity of each particular food. All that he was assured was that he would get an equal share of the aggregate supplies, measured in point prices, and a reasonable degree of consumer's choice in deciding how to spend his weekly ration of points on the different foods included in the scheme.

A weekly statement was received by the rationing section of the Food Control headquarters giving returns of stocks and distribution of rationed commodities from importers, manufacturers, and wholesalers. Weekly and sometimes daily advices were received from district rationing offices giving particulars of the state of demand and the number of points surrendered compared with those issued. The function and duties of the rationing sections at the headquarters were (1) co-ordination of issue and collection of points coupons, (2) maintenance of stock accounts for manufacturers and importers of rationed commodities, (3) direction of supplies of rationed commodities by allocations to districts, and (4) maintenance of equilibrium between supply and demand by adjustment of point prices.

In pointed areas hotels and restaurants were required to collect points from civilian customers and point prices for meals were fixed.

Exception was made in the case of tea and coffee, which were allocated free of points to each establishment on the basis of assessments by inspectors of their normal usage. Meals in restaurants cost seven points each. It was reckoned that purchases of bread and flour on the average accounted for about 50 percent of points expenditure, with one kilo of bread costing 32 points.

## CITATIONS

*1* Unpublished proceedings of the Middle East Conference on Control of Distribution and Rationing, Cairo, August 21–23, 1943.

CHAPTER 25

# RATIONING IN IRAQ, SUDAN, AND PERSIA

## IRAQ

Control of prices and distribution in Iraq was scarcely attempted before 1943. In August 1943, at the time of the Middle East Conference on Control of Distribution and Rationing, sugar was the only commodity subject to ration. Bulk supplies were imported and distributed by the United Kingdom Commercial Corporation on the basis of import quotas and shipping space allocated by the Middle East Supply Center. Under the original scheme introduced in Baghdad in 1942, the ration was one kilo per person per month. Each householder received a ration book containing a number of coupons corresponding to the number of persons in his household. When a man had purchased all his sugar for the month, he surrendered his book at the retail shop. The books were then returned to the supply department of the Ministry of Finance, where a fresh set of coupons was inserted for the following month, and the books were distributed through the *mukhtars*. The collection and return of books each month proved unsatisfactory and difficulties arose both through books getting mislaid and through bribery of officials. New books were therefore issued containing twelve coupons, each valid for one month, but the coupon value varied according to the number in the household, so that a man with a family of 10 could only buy 10 kilos of sugar at a time—if he could afford to do so.

In 1942 under the original scheme sugar was sold in shops run by the director-general of supply and at a limited number of private stores for the foreign population; but at the end of 1942 the shops run by the supply department were closed. The reason given was that employees were giving short weight or adding water to the sugar, and could not be adequately punished, since they had no financial resources and were not permanent civil servants. Instead, 85 retailers in Baghdad were allowed to distribute sugar on a commission basis. The sugar books were marked for supply at a certain shop. At the start, each retailer was allowed to buy 25 bags of sugar from the customs department. In order to get more the retailer had to present an equivalent quantity of coupons to the supply department. Coupons had different colors according to the month in which they were to be used. Inspectors were appointed to supervise retailers, but did not make checks to see that the sugar in stock plus the coupons in hand were equivalent to 25 bags. In August 1943 rations per head per month were 750 grams in towns and 500 grams for tribes. The price was 85 fils per kilo.

Apart from sugar rationing, in 1943 there were special arrangements for distributing scarce commodities, such as soap and utility cloth, to government employees, oil-company personnel, and other organized bodies. Special rations of vegetable oil and rice were issued to government servants. In January 1944 schemes for rationing tea and coffee to the whole population were introduced. The combined tea and coffee ration in June 1944 was three ounces per head per month for the towns and two ounces for the rural population.

Neither price control nor rationing could be successfully applied in Iraq owing to administrative inexperience and lack of adequate control of supplies. Long land frontiers and shifting population made smuggling and evasion of regulations all too easy. No complete census of the population was taken.

### SUDAN

Early in 1942 the Sudan government appointed a rationing committee under the chairmanship of the director of customs, who had had many years of experience in the operation of the Sudan government's sugar monopoly which had been started in 1919 to control supplies, prices, and distribution after World War I. In its report the committee agreed that no national system of coupon rationing could be operated in a country so large as Sudan with small, scattered townships and a large proportion of nomad and illiterate tribes.

On the other hand the war supply board exercised complete and effective control of the distribution of imports and, in addition, went a long way to ensure equitable distribution of home-produced foods by controlling transport and wholesale distribution. The distribution of sugar, durra or millet, wheat, and cotton piece goods was controlled by the government through the agency of local boards, local pools of merchants, or authorized wholesalers. Individual rationing was left to the discretion of district commissioners.

The most outstanding example of successful local rationing was the scheme introduced at Omdurman, a town of 104,000 inhabitants. This scheme, devised and administered by John Hillard, district commissioner at Omdurman, aroused considerable interest at the

Cairo conference. The commodities rationed were: sugar (2 pounds per head monthly, started in September 1942), kerosene (.5–1.5 gallons per household monthly according to size of household, started in November 1942), cotton piece goods (10 square yards per adult male yearly, started in January 1943), durra (28 pounds per head monthly, started in May 1943), and coffee beans (.5 pound per head monthly, started in July 1943). In addition, imported white flour was issued to regular customers under permit in February 1943, supplemented later by local wheat. A special ration of wheat was given to 80 Europeans and also to Copts and other non-Sudanese who were not accustomed to eat durra. This concession was unanimously agreed to by the town council, consisting of 14 Sudanese and two non-Sudanese, and was the only case of differentiation on the grounds of nationality.

The system of "straight" rationing adopted meant that all persons, rich and poor, educated and illiterate, young and old, were treated alike. Any attempt to ration on the basis of a normal level of consumption, apart from the single exception noted above, would have involved great administrative difficulties and might have provoked civil unrest. Actually, since the rations gave the poor a surplus above what they were accustomed to get, they were able to sell part of their ration to the rich and thus get more cash to meet the general rise in the cost of living. Rationing thus introduced not only greater equality of consumption but some redistribution of income.

In spite of the strict control which the government was able to maintain over supplies, transport, and wholesale distribution, it was found as difficult as in other Middle East countries to prevent dishonest practices by the majority of retailers. There were nearly 600 retailers of basic necessities in Omdurman, and attempts to use them for rationed goods by tying consumers to particular shops had to be abandoned. The administrative staff available, which had been reduced rather than increased during the war, could not cope with the degree of control involved. Gross favoritism was practiced and the widespread exploitation of poor and illiterate customers led to discontent and threatened civil disorder. It therefore became necessary to take away the distribution of rationed goods from private retailers. Sugar, which had been a government monopoly since 1919, was sold direct to householders from 18 government shops (one in each of the 18 subdivisions of the town) on four days in the first week of the month. Each householder presented his ration card for endorsement and received his whole ration for the month at one time. These 18 shops were managed by government pensioners; at the end of each day administrative officials checked the books, collected the cash, and paid it over to the town treasury. In the case of durra, coupons were issued at the sugar shops during the last four days of the month and supplies were obtained on any day during the following month at special grain shops. These were generally small courtyards rented for the purpose and were operated by authorized grain retailers, who sold at the fixed price paid by them to the wholesalers, their only profit being from the empty sacks which the government bought back from them at the end of each month.

Coffee beans were distributed through 18 town-council shops operated by 25 approved merchants, with a paid servant of the council standing by to endorse the ration cards presented by the customers.

Special attention was paid to publicity for rationing regulations. In addition to notices inserted in the vernacular press, which only reached a small percentage of the population, monthly leaflets were printed for distribution in boys' schools. The leaflet would be read out by the master to each form, and every boy would be given a copy to take home to read aloud to his family and neighbors. This system, which gave the adults information they wanted and the boys an opportunity of showing how well they could read, seems to have been well received by parents and children.

## PERSIA

The information supplied to the Cairo conference about rationing in Persia was not so complete as for other countries. According to Dr. Naficey, chief delegate from Persia and ex-Minister of Finance, rationing of sugar started in Teheran in 1941 in order to prevent queues in the retailers' shops. The system of rationing was based on the distribution of individual cards after presentation of identity cards. At the beginning, before supplies became scarce, the scheme worked satisfactorily; but soon afterward it was found that identity cards were being forged or copied, and peasants from the surrounding villages would present themselves as inhabitants of Teheran with a borrowed identity card or one belonging to a dead person. To put an end to these abuses, it was decided to take a new census in Teheran. As in Lebanon, all inhabitants were required to remain in their houses from dawn to dusk, while groups of three or four officials visited each house and examined the identity cards of the residents. After a declaration had been signed by the head of the household, a new ration card was handed to each holder of an identity card. The same procedure appears to have been followed in the other main towns.

These new ration cards were issued in September 1942 by the recently created Ministry of Food. They contained sheets for sugar, tea, bread, and cotton piece goods of twelve coupons—one for each month. Cards numbering 17.5 million were printed and 11.5 million were issued. In the provinces bulk supplies of ration cards were issued to the senior official of the town or district.

In Teheran the ration of sugar was at first 500 grams per month per head; elsewhere, only 400 grams. As in other countries the capital city tended to be favored for political reasons. In July 1943 the sugar ration was raised to 800 grams per month. The tea ration was nominally 50 grams per month per head. In Teheran most coupon holders drew their supplies, when they were available, but in the provinces it was believed that many poor consumers sold their rations and went without sugar and tea altogether.

Coupons in Teheran could be used for buying at any shop authorized to retail sugar and tea, and there was no tie of consumers to particular shops. There were a few government depots for supplying sugar and tea direct to hospitals and institutions. Hotels and restaurants were not included in the rationing system and had to obtain their supplies in the free market.

Owing to holdups and delays at ports and on railroads, distribution was irregular, and in 1943 the piling up of sugar, tea, and textiles in customs warehouses led to some reduction or postponement of imports. The scarcity and irregularity of supplies meant that the rations frequently could not be honored in full, and the fraud and bribery to which this gave rise undermined the success of the scheme and led to an agitation against the efforts of Millspaugh and his American colleagues to control prices and distribution. In Millspaugh's words (*1*, p. 139): "Grafters, large and small, wanted license to steal, and looked hungrily and impatiently at our tempting stocks of grain, sugar, tea, piece goods, and tires." Dr. Naficey said in Cairo in August 1943 (*2*): "Experience has proved that where rations have been fixed in sufficient quantity it is easy to make a proper organization of rationing, but when rations are too small, many attempts at fraud make the organization inefficient. For the time being the great difficulty which the Rationing Department encounters is that of forging ration cards. No efficient remedy to this has yet been discovered."

But the defects of sugar and tea rationing were of minor significance in comparison with the weaknesses and occasional breakdowns of bread rationing. The bread riots in Teheran in December 1942, and the political disturbances which led to the collapse of bread rationing in Ahwaz in August 1943, have been mentioned in chapter 18. When supplies of wheat ran short, drastic measures of adulteration had to be adopted. At one time the bread in Teheran was being made entirely of barley flour.

Normally the ration of bread in Teheran was 400 grams per day for adult consumers, with 800 grams for heavy workers and 200 grams for children under seven. A separate bread-ration card was issued monthly.

In the early days of bread rationing there were widespread complaints about the quality of bread supplied by private bakeries. To some extent this was due to the high extraction rate and adulteration of the standard flour produced in the government flour mill, called the Silo; but many of the bakers made matters worse by carefully sifting the flour supplied by the government and obtaining from it two grades of flour—one which they sold to their favorite customers at black-market prices as a passable imitation of white flour, and the other, containing the bran and impurities, which they used for baking rationed bread. The typical private bakery was frequently an underground cellar with an entrance open to the street. In April 1943 the writer was shown one such bakery, where the baker would turn from kneading the flour to put a handful of sawdust in his oven and then resume kneading his next batch of loaves. Any sawdust clinging to his hands would be incorporated into the flour.

It was partly to deal with these and other malpractices of private bakers that Sheridan, the American food adviser, decided to install an improvised modern bakery in the Silo. As Millspaugh says (*1*, p. 100), his object was to "break the power of the bakers, who retained insanitary methods and an age-old reputation for skulduggery. . . ." The bakery consisted of a large warehouse in which a row of a dozen or so brick ovens were fired by petroleum fuel. The operative bakers were recruited from among the former employees of closed-down private bakeries. Most of the bread produced in this modern bakery, which was designed by a Danish engineer, was of the rectangular American type. Unfortunately the Persian is accustomed to flat, thin, unleavened bread and, though the new bread was a great improvement, it was not thought to be better than the best loaves which private bakers could produce with reasonably pure flour.

Early in 1943, at a time of acute shortage, when the new bread was first put on sale at a government shop, a crowd of hungry customers stormed the shop and broke the plate-glass windows. Colonel Ata-Ulla, an Indian Moslem army doctor who was Sheridan's assistant in charge of the bakery, complained that the police had not done their job. The next day, when the police again failed to turn up, Ata-Ulla himself got the crowd to form a queue and issued 1,000 numbered tickets corresponding to the number of loaves he had. At the same time he gave instructions that no bread should be delivered to the police barracks. The Persian chief of police, when he heard this, went to complain to the Minister of Food; but the Minister had just resigned as a result of a cabinet crisis. He was received by the Permanent Secretary, who rang up Ata-Ulla, saying that the chief of police threatened to resign if he didn't get any bread. Ata-Ulla replied, "Well, Sir, it's your bread and, if you give orders that the police must have it, I will see that they get it. But in that case I regret that I shall have to resign myself." The Permanent Secretary arranged a conference at which a compromise was reached. The police got their bread and in return undertook to control the crowd at the bread shop.

At a later date when Millspaugh himself took over direct responsibility for the Ministry of Food, the mass-produced Silo bread itself became almost uneatable. He says in his book (*1*, p. 108) that the "Silo bread was of disgracefully poor quality—heavy, soggy, with a cement-like crust, containing not only a more than ordinary percentage of barley, but also bits of straw, small stones, and sand. Every day I received samples of this stuff, with appealing or threatening letters." He adds in a footnote, "One day I went to the Majlis and met with the President and a score of excited deputies. One advanced toward me talking too fast for much interpretation, and gesticulating with a loaf of bread. 'See what you give us to eat!' he shouted. About all that I could do was to admit the bad quality of the bread and to assure them that, if they would give me time, I would do my best to bring about improvement."

The causes of the bad bread, apart from heavy adulteration, were to be found in the wearing out of the milling machinery, poor screening of the flour, and incompetence, sabotage, and lack of inspection at the Silo bakery. Millspaugh appointed an exceptionally able and honest man, Colonel Saffari, to deal with the situation. By heroic efforts he was able to obtain spare parts and replacements for the flour mill, and conditions in the bakery were gradually put right.

At any rate, by the end of 1943 public complaints and criticisms in the Majlis had practically ceased.

When Roosevelt and Churchill met Stalin at the Teheran conference in November 1943, the quality and quantity of the bread left little to be desired. It was even possible for Millspaugh to relax his prohibition of private trade by a regulation permitting householders in Teheran to buy grain from farmers in the neighborhood and to exchange it at the Silo for flour or bread on surrender of bread ration cards. From this time onward the nightmare of bread rationing in Persia was over.

## CITATIONS

*1* A. C. Millspaugh, *Americans in Persia* (Brookings Inst., Washington, D.C., 1946).

*2* Unpublished proceedings of the Middle East Conference on Control of Distribution and Rationing, Cairo, Aug. 21–23, 1943.

# PART V

# RICE, SUGAR, AND OTHER FOODS

CHAPTER 26

# RICE

Rice is an important grain for human consumption in Egypt, Persia, Iraq, and Arabia, but is of minor significance compared with other bread grains in the Middle East as a whole. During the war the occupation of Burma by Japan cut off four-fifths of Ceylon's rice imports and the movement of Egyptian rice to fill this gap became a major operation in Allied food strategy.

Annual consumption of rice before the war was about 17 kilos per head in Egypt, 13 in Palestine, 5 in Syria and Lebanon, and 4 in Cyprus. These figures compare with 79 kilos in India, 124 in Ceylon, and 134 in Japan (*1*, p. 25).

Egypt had an average annual export of 95,000 tons and Persia exported just under 30,000 tons. Syria and Lebanon imported an average of 19,000 tons, Palestine 16,000, and Cyprus and Sudan 5,000 between them. There was thus a net export from the seven countries included in Appendix Table V amounting to 85,000 tons.

Rice production and trade fluctuated widely during the war. Net exports rose to a record level of 174,000 tons in 1940; but in 1942, following an exceptionally low crop in Egypt, they fell to 13,000 tons. After a record harvest in Egypt they rose again in 1943 to 108,000 tons; and in 1945 they reached 156,000 tons—80 percent above the prewar average. Figures of production and net trade for seven countries are to be found in Appendix Tables IV and V. Prewar imports of some other countries not included in the appendix tables were: Transjordan, 3,000 tons; Saudi Arabia, 17,000; British Somaliland, 11,000; and Libya, 5,000 tons (*1*, p. 72; *2*).

## EGYPT: NEGOTIATIONS FOR RICE EXPORTS

In 1939 Egypt had a bumper crop, and the outbreak of war led, as in the case of sugar, to some stocking up and hoarding, with a cessation of net exports from Persia and an increase in imports elsewhere. In 1940 net exports from the area were more than double the prewar average; this was due to exceptionally high exports from Egypt and Persia and to a sharp drop in imports into Syria and Lebanon after the fall of France. In 1941 supplies in the four chief importing countries reverted to their prewar level, while exports from Egypt and Persia declined.

It was not till toward the end of 1941 that the supply of rice began to cause concern to Middle East governments and the Middle East Supply Center (MESC). The first six-month import program for January–June 1942 submitted to London for the Red Sea and Mediterranean area contained provision for 11,000 tons of milled rice from India and Burma. Apart from this small amount it was hoped that the Middle East would be self-supporting. The second six-month program included 11,000 tons for Aden, later reduced to 5,500, and 17,500 for Saudi Arabia. There was some doubt whether these quantities were likely to be available from India, but in August 1942 the government of India agreed to allow exports of 15,200 tons to Saudi Arabia.

Meanwhile the government of Egypt had been restricting exports of rice to neighboring countries owing to rising prices following the poor crop of 1941. Palestine, Syria and Lebanon, Cyprus, and Sudan between them showed recorded imports of under 4,000 tons in 1942, compared with average imports of 40,000 tons before the war. Had it not been for some carryover of stocks from the previous year, MESC would have been under even stronger pressure to obtain imports from the outside world. In August 1942 the prospects of the coming rice crop in Egypt were reported to be exceptionally good, but MESC and the British Embassy expected difficulty in persuading the Egyptian government to release large supplies for export. At the same time the government of India found it necessary to divert to Ceylon rice intended for Saudi Arabia. Iraq was asked, as a matter of urgency, to release 3,000 tons but was unable to comply.

In view of the shortage that was now apparent it was decided that either the United Kingdom Commercial Corporation (UKCC) or the British Ministry of Food would have to buy as much as possible of the Egyptian crop. In October 1942, UKCC was authorized by the Minister of State in the Middle East to start buying up to 100,000 tons. The crop was at the time forecast at about 660,000 tons, out of which it was hoped to secure as much as 200,000 tons of paddy for export. Unless action was taken promptly it was feared that the surplus would rapidly disappear. The requirements of the armed forces for six months were 30,000 tons, mainly to feed Indian regiments fighting in North Africa or stationed in the Middle East. In November 1942 the government of Palestine asked for 40,000 tons to make up for the shortage of cereals and potatoes; and the government of Syria insisted that, if they were to obtain their requirements through UKCC, they would have to be assured 16,000 tons. At the beginning of 1943 the Egyptian government imposed an export tax of 50 Egyptian pounds (£E) per ton on milled rice, which they justified on the ground of the wide difference between the controlled price in Egypt and the free-market prices in other Middle East countries such as Syria and Lebanon.

Import requirements into the Red Sea and Mediterranean area in the six months January–June 1943 were originally put at 12,600 tons—8,800 tons for Saudi Arabia and 3,800 for the remaining countries. For the Persian Gulf area, requirements were given as 6,400 tons. Then in the early months of 1943, after two severe cuts in shipping had been imposed, it was agreed in London and Cairo that it was difficult to justify any import of rice into the Middle East in view of Egypt's large surplus. Indeed, it had become urgent to ship rice from Egypt to Ceylon, which before the war had drawn four-fifths of its supplies from Burma and French Indochina, now occupied by the Japanese.

In March 1943 the Director of Rice in the British Ministry of Food, Sir Harold Sanderson, was sent out to Egypt to negotiate terms for the purchase of Egyptian rice. Provisional agreement had already been reached between the Egyptian government and MESC for the release of 125,000 tons of paddy, equivalent to 75,000 tons of milled rice, besides 30,000 tons of wheat and 20,000 tons of millet, in return for an undertaking to supply 55,000 tons of nitrates for the millet and maize crops. Already 45,000 tons of nitrates had been shipped when Sanderson arrived, and the balance of 10,000 was due to be loaded in April. Before the end of March he had bought 25,000 tons in the open market, in addition to another 25,000 obtained for the British army. By the middle of April he had bought more than 83,000 tons of white rice, mostly in the form of paddy to be milled by Egyptian millers. Serious transport difficulties were encountered in moving the paddy to the mills, but these were gradually overcome with the help of MESC's Transport Division. Out of the first 75,000 tons, 31,000 were exported to Ceylon, 24,000 were allocated for the needs of the army, and the balance of 20,000 tons was held in reserve. The question of the price to be paid was settled without too much difficulty at £E 25 per ton and the Egyptian government agreed to waive the export tax.

In June 1943 Sanderson was able to report the conclusion of a further contract for 75,000 tons out of the balance of the 1942 crop.

The rice was to be acquired by the Egyptian government through the Crédit Agricole, which received payment in cash on delivery to Cairo. To avoid disturbance of the market while the rice was being acquired, the army was supplied from stocks at the disposal of MESC. Total purchases out of the 1942 crop, including supplies for the army, amounted to 194,000 tons of paddy. Early in the year the crop had been estimated at only 660,000 tons, but later official figures showed it to have been 940,000 tons. Since normal consumption was reckoned at about 310,000 tons, larger supplies might have been available for export had it not been for the shortage of cereals and the desire of the Egyptian government to check the rise in price of this important element in the cost of living. This policy tended to encourage consumption and substantial amounts disappeared into private hoards.

By the end of October only 53,000 tons had been delivered against the second contract for 75,000 tons of white rice and it seemed unlikely that the balance of 22,000 would be secured from the 1942 crop. In these circumstances MESC put forward a strong plea that no further shipments should be made to Ceylon. The army required 3,500 tons a month, and both on supply grounds and for political reasons MESC felt that it would be difficult to reduce allocations to neighboring countries, especially Palestine. At the time, the 1943 crop was expected to be no better than the prewar average of 609,000 tons; but the official figure, published later, gave a total production of 685,000 tons. No deliveries of white rice from the 1943 crop were likely to be available until January 1944, and MESC felt it would be unwise to count on getting more than 75,000 tons from the new crop. But after London had drawn attention to the seriousness of the position in Ceylon, MESC agreed to postpone civilian allocations in order to release another 8,000 tons to Ceylon. The following figures illustrate the extremely critical position in Ceylon at this period, in thousand tons of milled rice (*3*):

| Year | Production | Imports | Total |
|---|---|---|---|
| Average 1934–38 | 180 | 529 | 709 |
| 1942 | 184 | 263 | 447 |
| 1943 | 179 | 141 | 320 |
| 1944 | 158 | 114 | 272 |
| 1945 | 98 | 182 | 280 |

Meanwhile the Egyptian government had decided to raise the price of rice and to requisition 150,000 tons of paddy from the 1943 crop, from which they said they would be willing to sell any balance that remained after their own requirements had been met. A compulsory collection scheme for rice was brought into force and 173,000 tons were in fact acquired by the end of December 1943. MESC and the British Embassy informed the government that they would need 225,000 tons of paddy from the 1943 crop if nitrates rather than cereals were to be shipped in 1944; but it was finally agreed that 125,000 tons of paddy would be delivered before the end of the year. The claim for the balance of 100,000 tons was left open but was dropped when the result of the maize harvest was known. Recorded exports in 1944, mostly from the 1943 crop, were only 65,000 tons of white rice, which nearly all went to Ceylon.

The 1944 crop was 815,000 tons, 20 percent higher than in the previous year and a third higher than prewar. In October 1944 the Egyptian government decided to make compulsory purchases of 260,000 tons of paddy, sufficient to produce about 156,000 tons of white rice. The British Ministry of Food undertook to buy any surplus supplies above Egypt's needs for export to Ceylon and other Middle East territories. Actually 100,000 tons of rice were shipped in 1945 to Ceylon, and special arrangements were made to send supplies to Saudi Arabia at the time of the pilgrimage to Mecca.

### PERSIA AND THE PERSIAN GULF SHEIKDOMS

Early in 1944 it became impossible to supply normal requirements of rice for the Persian Gulf Sheikdoms, mainly owing to the cessation of imports from India and Persia. Stocks of rice in the Persian Gulf Sheikdoms fell to a dangerously low level, and in January there was an acute shortage in Muscat and the Trucial Coast. The Arab states on the Gulf would only accept flour with reluctance, and it was not till March 1944 that it was found possible to send 1,500 tons of rice from Iraq. This was the first consignment that had been sent for some months. In May it was reported that Iraq rice was still in great demand in the Sheikdoms, especially for the pearling fleet, which starts operations in May and continues for four or five months. The normal diet of the pearl fishers is rice, dates, and fish; and wheat, barley, and millet were said to be unsuitable. In Bahrein the pearling season gave employment to 15,000 men or about 17 percent of the population. Their demands for rice could only be met to a limited extent and at very high prices by smuggling from India and Iraq. In June complaints were again received by MESC and permission was at last obtained for the Sheikdoms to obtain supplies through ordinary trade channels from Iraq. When the Sultan of Muscat visited Cairo that summer he was able to inform the Director of Food in MESC that he was satisfied with the existing arrangements. In September 1944 the Anglo-Iranian Oil Company complained that they were unable to obtain rice either from Iraq or from Persia, and with the approval of the Ministry of Food in London a supply of Egyptian rice was sent to Abadan in tankers. In November 1944 it was reported that the rice harvest in northern Persia had been good and was expected to produce a substantial surplus for export. In March 1945 negotiations took place which resulted in supplies being sent to the Persian Gulf Sheikdoms through private trade channels. Recorded rice exports from Persia in 1945 exceeded 40,000 tons, the highest level reached during the war.

The wartime story of rice may be summarized in a few words. By careful planning, which involved not only diversion of cotton acreage but an assured market at satisfactory prices, the government of Egypt was able to expand the area under rice from 1942 onward by 100,000 hectares over the prewar level and to increase output of paddy rice by 35 percent. This increased supply was used largely to raise consumption per head, and exports were only allowed to rise by 5 percent during a period of acute world shortage. Most of the export surplus, in 1943–45 averaging 100,000 tons, went to Ceylon to meet the critical shortage there, and neighboring countries in the Middle East had to go short.

Imports into the four importing countries shown in Appendix Table V fell from an average of 40,000 tons in 1934–38 to 36,000 in 1940–41, reached their lowest point of 4,000 in 1942, and averaged only 12,600 in 1943 and 1944. Consumption per head in Palestime fell sharply in 1942 and 1943, recovered somewhat in 1944 and 1945, but remained considerably below the prewar level. The experience of Cyprus, Syria, and Lebanon was similar.

## CITATIONS

*1* Food and Agriculture Organization of the United Nations, *Rice Bulletin* (Commod. Ser. 7, Washington, February 1949).

*2* MESC, unpublished estimates for Saudi Arabia.

*3* Internatl. Inst. Agr., *International Yearbook of Agricultural Statistics, 1941–42 to 1945–46* (Rome, 1947).

CHAPTER 27

# SUGAR

Consumption of sugar in the Middle East is low by Western standards. The prewar average was about 8 kilos per head, ranging from 4 in Sudan to 20 in Palestine, compared with 40 kilos or more in highly industrialized countries. Egypt and Persia were the only sugar-producing countries. Before the war Egypt produced about 150,000 tons of cane sugar, and Persia's production of sugar beet yielded an average of 17,000 tons of raw beet sugar. Egypt was a net exporter, but Persia was a net importer like all other Middle East countries. In Egypt a considerable quantity of cane juice and molasses was used for human consumption. Near Cairo it is no unusual sight to see a fellah chewing a piece of green sugar cane as he takes his load to the factory on a camel's back. Honey, grapes, dates, and other fruits are the traditional substitute for sugar in the Middle East, dates being particularly important among the nomad tribes of Arabia and Iraq.

During the war consumption fell owing to severe restriction on imports, and sugar had to be rationed in most Middle East countries. Figures of production of refined sugar in Egypt and Persia are tabulated below, in thousand tons (*1*):

| Country | Average 1934–38 | 1940 | 1941 | 1942 | 1943 | 1944 | 1945 |
|---|---|---|---|---|---|---|---|
| Egypt | 146 | 175 | 159 | 190 | 167 | 173 | 180 |
| Persia | 15 | 36 | 24 | 12 | 20 | 23 | 22 |

Net imports into the Middle East countries before the war (1934–38) and net exports of Egypt, as published by the International Institute of Agriculture, are tabulated on the following page, in thousand metric tons. For the war years figures for the seven countries shown in Group I are given in Appendix Table V. For most of the countries in Group II published figures are incomplete or not available.

Prewar net imports into the whole area averaged 211,000 tons, of which half were taken by the Red Sea and Mediterranean countries and the remainder by Persia and Iraq. Aden's imports probably included some supplies sent inland to Yemen and Saudi Arabia.

| Group I | | Group II | |
|---|---|---|---|
| Cyprus | 3.4 | Malta | 9.5 |
| Egypt | −22.3 | Libya | 10.3 |
| Sudan | 27.0 | Transjordan | 3.4 |
| Palestine | 24.6 | Eritrea | 3.0 |
| Syria and Lebanon | 31.9 | British Somaliland | 5.1 |
| Persia | 68.4 | French Somaliland | 1.2 |
| Iraq | 37.2 | Italian Somaliland | 5.3 |
| | | Aden | 3.1 |
| Total | 170.2 | Total | 40.9 |

In 1939 there was a rush to buy sugar as insurance against war shortage. Recorded net imports into the seven countries in Group I reached 236,000 tons, and total Middle East imports were probably not far short of 290,000 tons. In Egypt, which was the only net exporter before the war, gross imports in 1939 rose to 2.5 times the prewar average and, in spite of larger exports to Sudan, there was a small import surplus.

During 1940 net imports into the countries in Group I reverted to a more normal level of 175,000 tons. Most countries received more than their prewar supplies, the chief exceptions being Syria and Lebanon, which were faced with supply difficulties after the fall of France and were only able to import about half their normal requirements.

In 1941 shipping and supply shortages became more pronounced, and recorded net imports into the seven countries fell to 138,000 tons. The British Ministry of Food was buying the exportable surplus of many of the potential supplying countries, and private importers in the Middle East were finding it increasingly difficult either to buy sugar or to ship it. Attracted by rising prices, Egyptian production had increased since the war, and net exports in 1941 rose to a wartime peak of 39,000 tons; but demand was also growing, and shortage and high prices in the towns were causing the government growing concern.

Arrivals in the Red Sea area fell to a critically low point in the second half of 1941. During the last four months of the year, against agreed requirements amounting to 70,000 tons, only 23,000 tons were delivered from outside the area, the figures for each month, according to records of the Middle East Supply Center (MESC), are shown on the opposite page, in tons.

This shows how the procurement machinery was creaking at the time. General Haining said in his telegram of December 4, 1941,

| Month | Agreed requirements | Deliveries | Deficit |
|---|---|---|---|
| September | 15,000 | — | −15,000 |
| October | 21,000 | 7,000 | −14,000 |
| November | 17,000 | 16,000 | − 1,000 |
| December | 17,000 | — | −17,000 |
| Total | 70,000 | 23,000 | −47,000 |

quoted in chapter 15, that the cereal-supply position in the Middle East was in a "chaotic state." He might almost have said the same about sugar. As so often in wartime administration the problem was largely a matter of correct timing. MESC, as it was then organized, was too slow off the mark, and its staff was too small, to keep abreast of its growing responsibilities. Middle East governments were dilatory and ill equipped in assessing supplies and requirements, and private traders were reluctant to recognize the necessity of giving information and accepting government control. All this made for delay, and little or nothing had been done to anticipate future shortages or to plan before the emergency arose.

The result was that in the second half of 1941 urgent requests were put forward spasmodically and too late, and usually without the full statistics of stocks and consumption that were needed to carry conviction. Another defect in the organization was that allocation of sugar had become too highly centralized in London. In 1941 the British Ministry of Food had been procuring supplies for Middle East countries at the request of the United Kingdom Commercial Corporation (UKCC), and had itself been responsible for allocating supplies between civilian and military requirements. MESC was not yet being used, as had been intended, to aggregate all Middle East demands from the armed forces as well as from governments and traders. There was no long-term program for the whole Middle East, and no reserve pool under MESC's control to be drawn upon in an emergency, so as to ensure fair allocation when shipments fell short of the program.

These shortcomings were brought to light and gradually corrected when Jackson was appointed Director-General. In his report to the Minister of State in the Middle East in December 1941 he had emphasized the need for forward planning of imports, for more systematic procedures of screening and procurement, and for correct timing of the various stages involved. In January 1942 a first six-month sugar-import program was drawn up covering military and civilian requirements for the Red Sea and Mediterranean area; and in March the needs of Iraq, Persia, and the Persian Gulf Sheikdoms, known for shipping purposes as the Gulf area, were included in MESC's program.

The program for the Red Sea and Mediterranean area provided for a monthly rate of just under 12,500 tons—7,500 for civilian needs and 5,000 for the armed forces, including under the latter heading the requirements of Malta, Eritrea, Ethiopia, and the Somalilands. This represented a reduction of about 10 percent on prewar civilian imports.

For a time the outlook appeared favorable. MESC was told that loadings would be 8,600 tons in January and would be stepped up to 11,200 tons in February; and for the next three months loadings were planned at the rate of 20,000 tons per month to the Red Sea area in the hope of gradually building up a reserve stock of 30,000 tons by the end of the year. Until March 1942 the supply position remained satisfactory. Some stocks of Javanese sugar were available in India, and there were supplies to be drawn upon from Mauritius, Natal, and Queensland.

When Persia and Iraq were added to the program, the provisional allocation for six months was raised to 15,000 tons monthly for the Red Sea area and 11,000 monthly for the Gulf area. Deducting 6,000 per month for the armed forces and assuming normal exports from Egypt, this would have given civilians a rate of consumption exceeding the prewar level. But this was soon to prove much too optimistic. In the first four months of 1942 there was a shortfall of 38,000 tons in loadings to the Red Sea area and of 14,000 to the Gulf area.

Middle East governments were now being urged to introduce sugar rationing and to tighten up control of supplies and distribution. In Persia, control of imports and distribution was unsatisfactory, and uncontrolled imports overland and by dhows from India long continued to hamper efforts at control. The government of India was reluctant to interfere with private exports to the Gulf area and this hampered attempts in Persia and Iraq to centralize imports and introduce rationing. In Egypt MESC hoped that, if an additional 10,000 tons of nitrates and sugar-making machinery could be imported, local production of raw sugar might be stepped up from 209,000 tons in 1942 to 300,000 in 1944. It was also hoped that it might be possible to reduce consumption by about 25 percent from 165,000 to 125,000 tons; but MESC warned London that this would involve difficult negotiations with the Egyptian government. Sugar rationing was in fact introduced in 1942. To meet the pressing claims of Palestine, Cyprus, Syria, and Lebanon it was planned to get a loan of 50,000 tons from Egyptian stocks against an undertaking to replace them from Mauritius in August.

For the second six months of 1942 a more realistic program was drawn up—60,000 tons for the Red Sea area (including 25,000 for the armed forces and 4,000 for Aden) and 60,000 for the Persian Gulf area (including 12,500 for the armed forces). The main sources of supply were to be Mauritius and Natal. In addition Saudi Arabia was to get 2,700 tons from stocks of Javanese sugar in India, and Persia was expected to get about 10,000 tons overland from India.

Again actual shipments fell short. By the end of the year there was a shortfall of about 20,000 tons in loadings for the Red Sea and Mediterranean area; and owing to congestion in the Persian Gulf ports one ship carrying 9,300 tons for Persia had to be diverted to Ceylon, and another with 6,200 tons had to be discharged in the Bahrein Islands, where it remained as a reserve stock.

Recorded imports in Appendix Table V show that in 1942 Persia and Iraq received only 58,000 tons, compared with MESC programed requirements of 95,000 tons and prewar imports of 105,000 tons. In addition there were shipments to the armed forces, not included in the customs returns, amounting to nearly 25,000 tons, as well as the 15,500 tons referred to above which had been shipped but could not be discharged. Countries in the Red Sea area, including Aden and Transjordan in addition to those shown in Appendix Table V, show net imports of nearly 60,000 tons, compared with the revised civilian program of 70,000 tons.

In spite of this reduction in supplies, the year 1942 ended with the sugar position fairly well under control. In Egypt the production of sugar from the 1942 harvest was expected to beat all records and it was hoped at one time that there might be a sugar surplus of about 100,000 tons. Rationing was in force in most of the Middle East and, except in Persia where there was a holdup of sugar at the ports, distribution appeared to be working smoothly. The basis of allocation adopted by MESC was an allowance of 600 grams per head per month, which later had to be reduced to 500 grams. Average prewar consumption had been about 640 grams.

Estimated stocks at the end of the year were 30,000 tons, which suggested to London either that the import program had been too high or that private imports had been larger than expected. Part of these stocks was immobilized in Persian ports through failure to organize control of distribution, while an unknown quantity of sugar, which may have been of the order of 10,000 tons, had arrived overland or by dhows from India.

But the temporary improvement was short-lived. Hopes of buying Egyptian sugar were frustrated by long-drawn-out negotiations conducted by the Ministry of Food in London and the British Embassy in Cairo with Abboud Pasha, head of the Egyptian Société des Sucreries, and the Egyptian Prime Minister, Nahas Pasha. For the six months January–June 1943, MESC put in requirements of 67,500 tons for the Red Sea area (27,000 for the armed forces and 40,500 for civilian needs) and 26,000 tons for the Persian Gulf area. But by the time this request reached London there had been a sharp worsening in the shipping situation. Civilian shipments from the United States and the United Kingdom in October 1942 had already been reduced below normal "minimum" requirements and put on a "siege" basis, on the understanding that the cuts would be restored as soon as possible; and in January still further restrictions had to be made for operational reasons. In February MESC had to protest that the present scale of imports was "below the level required to maintain security." Loadings to the Persian Gulf in January had been only 1,200 tons in broken stowage from the United States, and nothing was loaded in February. UKCC in Persia pressed strongly for a full cargo to be loaded in March, but this was rejected on the ground that stocks were available in the Persian Gulf which could be drawn upon.

Meanwhile MESC found it difficult to justify imports into the Red Sea area on the scale originally proposed, while negotiations for the purchase of Egyptian sugar were taking place. Agreement between Abboud Pasha and the British Ministry of Food for the purchase of 55,000 tons of sugar was not finally reached until June 1943. Abboud, who had originally stood out for £37 a ton, finally agreed to sell at £27 a ton, on the understanding that an equivalent amount at the same price would be placed at his disposal at the cessation of hostilities.

During the first six months of 1943, 58,450 tons were loaded for the Red Sea area against requirements originally put at 67,500 tons. The July–December program for sugar imports for the Red Sea area was 97,500 tons, to be reduced by the amount of any Egyptian surplus made available. Provision was also made for a reserve of 20,000 tons. For the Gulf area, requirements were put at 30,000 tons for Persia and 24,500 tons for Iraq.

In July the effect of the double cuts, the stopping of regular supplies from Mauritius, and the delay in implementing the Egyptian purchase brought reserve stocks for the Red Sea area down to a very low level. For two or three months the position remained difficult. Supplies overland from East Africa to Sudan were temporarily stopped because of a breakdown in one of the East African refineries, and in October 4,000 tons of Egyptian sugar had to be sent to Sudan. In the Persian Gulf area the figures of stocks and requirements were still not clear. It was reported that on September 1, 1943, 14,000 tons still remained to be cleared from the Persian ports and at Basra there were fair stocks on hand. In the light of this information MESC directed that a cargo of sugar destined for the Persian Gulf area should be discharged at Bahrein. In the following month a representative of MESC went to Persia to examine the position. Meanwhile MESC continued to emphasize the importance of maintaining supplies of sugar to this area as a contribution to checking inflation and helping the collection of cereals.

By the end of the year 1943 the supply situation was more satisfactory. Sugar production in Persia was expected to be 20,000 tons with a small carryover of 5,000 from the previous year. With the improvement that had taken place in internal transport, stocks at the ports were now being distributed and supplies in sight were sufficient to last until July 1944. In Sudan, imports from East Africa by land and down the Nile had been resumed after an interval of six months, at the rate of 800 tons per month. The Egyptian surplus was moving freely, mainly to Sudan and for consumption by the forces. Stocks in Palestine were heavy, and no difficulties were being experienced in supplies to other countries in the Middle East.

Published figures of wartime imports show that 1942 and 1943 were the years in which net imports of sugar reached their lowest point. In 1943 Palestine was the only country which received nearly its prewar figure, while Persia and Iraq imported only one-third. The total for the six countries in Group I of the tabulation on page 254 excluding Egypt was 92,500 metric tons, or less than half the prewar quantity. In 1944 the reopening of the Mediterranean and some improvement in the supply and shipping situation raised the level of imports from the outside world to 157,000 tons (Appendix Table V); but it was not till 1946 that the average consumption of sugar reached its prewar level.

MESC records of sugar loadings and arrivals show that total supplies, including sugar for the armed forces and liberated territories, were 40 percent higher in 1944 than in the previous year. The Persian Gulf area received 35,300 long tons in 1943 and 67,300 in 1944; while the Red Sea and Mediterranean area received 135,500 long tons in 1943 and 168,000 in 1944. Deducting 72,000 tons each year for the armed forces and 19,000 for imports into other countries not included in the table, the MESC figures are broadly consistent with recorded imports as shown in Appendix Table V. But the figures for Persian imports in 1943 may be understated by the amount of unrecorded imports, which may have been as much as 10,000 tons sent overland or in dhows from India.

Wartime restriction of supplies lowered Middle East sugar consumption from a prewar figure of about 8 kilos per head to 5 or 6 kilos per head in 1942 and 1943.

## CITATIONS

*1* Food and Agriculture Organization of the United Nations, *Yearbook of Food and Agricultural Statistics—1947* (Washington, 1947).

## CHAPTER 28

# OILSEEDS, FATS, AND OILS

The supply of fats and oils was a minor source of anxiety to the Middle East Supply Center (MESC) compared with maintenance of the cereals supply. But in the absence of reliable statistics of production and consumption, assessment of supplies and requirements of fats and oils involved a disproportionate amount of work.

Before the war the Middle East was able to produce enough to meet its requirements and to provide a net export of about 54,000 tons of vegetable oils, including the oil equivalent of seeds, mainly cottonseed, exported from Egypt and Sudan (Appendix Table V). Palestine was the only deficit country, with average net imports in 1934–38 of 9,100 tons of vegetable oils (including oilseeds and nuts in terms of oil) and 2,000 tons of butter. Out of an average cottonseed production of 771,000 tons, Egypt exported 353,000 tons (equivalent to 55,000 tons of oil) and 9,700 tons of cottonseed oil.

The big problem that had to be faced by MESC during the war was the reduction of 60 percent in Egypt's output of cottonseed resulting from the diversion of 450,000 hectares from cotton to cereals. In spite of increased exports of cottonseed from Sudan to Egypt, the net result was that the Middle East became a deficit area; and instead of having a net export of 54,000 tons of oil equivalent it had to draw on the outside world for imports, averaging 14,000 tons in the four years 1942–45 (see Appendix Table V).

After Pearl Harbor world trade in fats and oils was severely reduced, partly by the cutting off of major sources of supply in southeast Asia, and partly by increased consumption and some falling off of production in producing countries. Imports into Britain were reduced below the prewar level, and margarine, butter, cooking fat, and soap had to be rationed. In these circumstances it was not easy to persuade the Ministry of Food in London, or the Oils and Fats Committee of the Combined Food Board (CFB) in Washington, that imports into the Middle East were a wartime necessity; and the uncertainty and unreliability of estimates of production and consumption in Middle East countries made it extremely difficult for MESC to make out a convincing case for any given level of imports.

The degree of uncertainty in the Middle East estimates of fats and oils consumption may be illustrated by comparing the Food and Agriculture Organization of the United Nations' (FAO) first and second world food surveys for prewar consumption (*1*). A third column has been added to the tabulation below giving an alternative set of proposed figures based on MESC's wartime estimates. The figures are all estimates of prewar consumption of fats and oils in kilos per head per year:

| Country | First survey | Second survey | Alter-native |
|---|---|---|---|
| Cyprus | 8 | 7 | 8–9 |
| Egypt | 6 | 3 | 5–6 |
| Palestine | 12 | 9 | 10–12 |
| Syria and Lebanon | 4 | 3 | 5–6 |
| Transjordan | 1 | .. | 3–4 |
| Iraq | 1 | 3 | 4–5 |
| Persia | 1 | 1 | 3–4 |

Part of the discrepancy between FAO's estimates results from uncertainty as to whether animal fats are included. The third column is intended to include butter and *samne* or ghee (clarified butter). The first column includes them for Egypt and Palestine but probably not for the rest. The figures in the second column are derived from estimates prepared for FAO's Near East regional conference held in Syria in August 1951, which cover vegetable fats and oils but exclude animal fats, "tentatively estimated to represent about one-third of the region's aggregate output of fats and oils" (*2*, p. 17). Egypt's prewar consumption of vegetable fats and oils (mostly cottonseed oil) is given in FAO's *Food Balance Sheets* (*3*, p. 285) at 2.8 kilos per head and of butter and ghee at 2.6, giving a total of 5.4 kilos. If oils used for technical purposes are added, this would become 6.6 kilos, which was the figure adopted by MESC during the war. The figures for other countries are more conjectural. Like other estimates presented at the Near East meeting they are no more than rough "approximations and indicate merely the order of magnitude of the consumption levels" (*2*, p. 60). But it seems unlikely that prewar consumption of edible oils in Persia and Transjordan should have been only a third of that in Iraq.

In May 1943 MESC, faced with similar uncertainties, made a rough estimate that in 1943 supplies of locally produced vegetable oils were about 145,000–150,000 tons, compared with requirements of about 160,000 tons, including technical oils for soapmaking. (This estimate excluded seeds consumed as such, consumption in Sudan, and production in Iraq and Persia, about which little was known except that they were nearly self-supporting.) This left a balance of 10,000–15,000 tons of oils (or the equivalent in oilseeds) to be imported from the outside world into the Red Sea and Mediterranean area. As will be seen later, this was challenged in London; but in fact recorded net imports into the area in 1943 came to 9,200 tons of oil. Most of this went to Palestine and helped to give her rather more than her prewar imports.

In January 1942 MESC's first six-month program included a request for 3,300 tons of peanuts from India. This was rejected in London on the ground of shortage of supplies, and MESC was told that the Middle East should meet its requirements from locally produced cottonseed, sesame, etc. Later, Persia and Iraq each asked for a few hundred tons of copra or coconut oil from East Africa, but this too was refused on the ground that both countries had been net exporters of vegetable oils before the war. The British Ministry of Food agreed to forego any claim for cottonseed or cottonseed oil from Egypt; but MESC was not satisfied with this and claimed a share of the exportable surplus of copra, peanuts, and sesame from East Africa, mainly to meet the needs of Palestine and of the British forces stationed there and in Syria.

MESC's second program, for July–December 1942, included a provisional figure of 12,270 tons of oilseeds from East Africa for the Red Sea and Mediterranean area. This was later reduced under pressure from London to 1,800 tons of sesame and 750 tons of soft oil. Iraq was allotted 1,000 tons of coconut oil and 250 tons of soft oil. Persia was given no allocation partly because of her failure to control imports from India by dhows.

Toward the end of 1942 the prospective shortage of Egyptian cottonseed began to cause MESC growing concern, and the Palestine government complained that it was not getting enough to maintain a reasonable level of stocks. Owing to the drastic cuts in shipping that were made during the winter months, the Middle East had to go short, and the plan for building up stocks in Palestine by importing copra from East Africa had to be postponed. The program for January–June 1943 provided for 5,780 tons of oilseed imports, mostly for Palestine, including 3,000 tons earmarked for the armed forces.

In May 1943 MESC drew up a two-year program giving the best forecast it could make of Middle East import requirements in the light of a 50 percent reduction in Egyptian cottonseed and increased demands for the British army. It asked for 128,000 tons of oil to be spread over the next two years—80,000 tons for the army and 48,000 for civilian needs. To this London countered with a critical analysis arguing that prewar imports into the area, after deducting cottonseed and oil imported from Egypt, had only been about 10,000 tons for two years. They agreed that allowance must be made for the reduced cotton acreage in Egypt and for the additional 80,000 tons required for the army. But as regards civilian requirements it was thought reasonable to suggest a reduction in consumption of the order of 20 percent in view of world shortage of supplies and shipping. They therefore proposed an annual program of 18,750 tons to meet civilian needs instead of 24,000, and a total of just under 118,000 tons instead of 128,000 over the two years. Questions were raised about the level of stocks in Egypt, where consumption appeared to have been running in excess of crushing capacity; and further information was asked about prospective production, consumption, and stocks in Cyprus and Palestine.

This discouraging reply led MESC during June and July to undertake a further enquiry into possible ways of bridging the gap between prospective supplies and requirements. In August 1943 a more detailed statement was submitted which, with minor reservations, was accepted by departments in London and later by CFB. First, it was proposed to meet the total import requirements of Egypt, and the army in Egypt, from Sudan where there was now a fair prospect—provided transportation could be arranged—of getting substantial supplies of cottonseed formerly used as fuel for locomotives. This would meet an estimated deficiency of 33,000 tons up to the end of September 1944. In addition 32,000 tons would be needed up to the end of 1944 to supply Palestine (16,000), Syria and Lebanon (8,000), and other countries (8,000). Total requirements were therefore put at 65,000 tons for the next year, of which only half would need to be shipped from overseas. The army's needs could not be reduced and might have to be increased. Civilian consumption of fats and oils was everywhere low, the highest being in Palestine where it was estimated at 14 kilos per year. In Syria it was reckoned at less than half this amount—only 6.5 kilos per year. These were regarded by MESC as absolute minima. In the light of estimates of prewar consumption given above, these figures may appear to be on the high side. But unlike FAO's estimates they include technical oils used for soapmaking.

MESC's figures were finally accepted subject to further enquiries about stocks in Egypt and Aden. It was agreed to leave Sudan cottonseed to meet the estimated deficit of 15,000 tons in Egyptian civilian requirements of oil, and to ship 10,000 tons of peanut-oil equivalent from India for the army. In addition, MESC was to get for other territories, mainly Palestine, exports from East Africa amounting to 23,600 tons of oil equivalent, together with 14,000 tons of Zanzibar copra (equivalent to 8,400 tons of coconut oil), making 32,000 tons in all.

During the next two years Palestine received rather more than her programed supply of 16,000 tons of oil equivalent; but Syria and Lebanon, which had bumper olive crops in 1942 and 1943, received practically no imports until 1945. Supplies to Cyprus also appear to have been negligible in 1943 and 1944. Total recorded net imports into the seven countries in 1944 and 1945 were the equivalent of about 20,000 tons of oil each year. These figures are not easy to reconcile with MESC records, which give shipments of 7,540 long tons of oilseeds in 1943 and actual arrivals of 126,850 long tons of oilseeds in 1944. The latter figure, but not the former, includes substantial supplies, probably 25,000 tons, for the armed forces.

## EGYPT

The principal oilseeds produced in Egypt were cottonseed, linseed, peanuts, and sesame. Of these, cottonseed was by far the most important, its oil accounting for 90 percent of the vegetable oil produced. Peanuts are not generally crushed for oil in Egypt, but are mainly eaten as roasted nuts. Most of the sesame seed is used to produce two native foods called *tahina* and *halawa*; the latter was also a staple food in Iraq and of the Arabs in Palestine.

In the five years 1934–38, out of a total cottonseed production averaging 771,000 tons, Egypt exported 350,000 tons of seed and nearly 10,000 tons of oil, leaving a net supply of cottonseed oil for domestic consumption of about 55,000 tons. She imported about 13,000 tons of sesame and 4,550 tons of peanuts from Sudan. In addition, she imported for industrial purposes, particularly soapmaking, 10,700 tons of coconut oil, 1,500 tons of palm oil, 2,900 tons of olive oil, and small quantities of copra, linseed, and other oils. In terms of oil equivalent, net exports of cottonseed and oil were 64,000 tons, and net imports of other oils about 25,000 tons.

In the three years 1939–41 the supply of cottonseed averaged

710,000 tons and was sufficient to meet domestic consumption of about 60,000 tons of cottonseed oil; but exports of oil were progressively reduced, both to meet the growing requirements of the British army and to build up reserve stocks.

In 1942/43 the reduction of cotton acreage by 60 percent more than halved the production of cottonseed; but owing to drastic reduction of exports there was an estimated carryover of about 40,000 tons of oil at the beginning of the cottonseed year in October 1942. This, combined with 55,000 tons of home-produced oil, was barely sufficient in 1943 to meet Egyptian civilian requirements, now estimated at 72,000 tons, and 16,000 tons required by the British army.

In October 1943 the outlook became critical. There was virtually no carryover from the previous year and production of seed had reached the lowest point touched during the war—296,000 tons. This was reckoned to produce about 44,000 tons of oil, which would only go halfway to meet the requirements of 88,000 tons. This deficit was a constant source of anxiety to MESC in the first six months of 1944. It was only met by exceptional efforts to overcome transport difficulties in the movement of surplus cottonseed from Sudan. Imports of seed from Sudan, which had been 40,000 tons in 1942/43, rose to a wartime peak of 140,000 tons in 1943/44 and 112,000 tons in 1944/45.

Approximate estimates of apparent consumption during the war years are tabulated below, in thousand metric tons:

| Year | Cotton-seed oil | Other oils | Total |
|---|---|---|---|
| Average 1934–38 | 55.1 | 32.6 | 87.7 |
| 1939 | 74.1 | 29.1 | 103.2 |
| 1940 | 95.2 | 21.2 | 116.4 |
| 1941 | 69.3 | 18.1 | 87.4 |
| 1942 | 70.2 | 14.4 | 84.6 |
| 1943 | 67.2 | 14.2 | 81.4 |
| 1944 | 79.1 | 15.8 | 94.9 |
| 1945 | 71.9 | 14.7 | 86.6 |
| Average 1940–45 | 75.5 | 16.4 | 91.9 |

## SUDAN

There was little information about the consumption of fats and oils in Sudan, but reasonably accurate figures were available about the production of cottonseed, which averaged 103,400 tons in 1934–38. Prewar exports had averaged 85,000 tons, but fell to 22,000 tons in 1941 and 31,000 in 1942. During these years cottonseed largely supplanted coal as fuel for locomotives, at a rate estimated in May 1943 at 2,000 tons a month. Special efforts were made to step up exports of cottonseed to Egypt in 1943 with the result that they averaged 125,000 tons for the three years 1943, 1944, and 1945. By this means it was possible to meet both the Egyptian deficit and the requirements of the British army. Included in the British army's offtake of 16,000 tons of oil were Malta's annual requirements of 1,620 tons of cottonseed oil, 1,800 tons of soap, and 1,920 tons of margarine.

## PALESTINE

Official estimates of prewar and June 1943 per capita consumption of fats and oils have been given in chapter 24. In addition to the products rationed, prewar consumption of butter and *samne* were estimated at 126 and 44 grams per head per month, respectively. This gave a prewar total of about 10 kilos per head per annum of fats and oils, excluding technical oils and slaughter fat, and not including olive oil and olives, which were largely consumed in Arab villages.

Before the war Palestine's net imports of oilseeds averaged 22,600 tons, of which about half consisted of peanuts and the balance of sunflower seed, copra, sesame, and linseed. Imports of vegetable oils averaged only about 300 tons, two-thirds of which consisted of linseed oil. Total imports of oils and oilseeds as oil averaged 9,100 tons, and average home production of olive oil and sesame oil was 8,500 tons, making a total supply of 17,600 tons. MESC reckoned Palestine's requirements for 1943 at 24,000 tons of vegetable oils plus 1,000 tons of hardened peanut fat. An additional 1,000 tons was required for the manufacture of soap and margarine for the British army's use outside Palestine. The 1942 olive crop of 65,000 tons was better than usual and was estimated to yield about 9,400 tons of oil. This was followed by another record crop of 75,000 tons in 1943; but in 1941 and 1944 the olive crop was exceptionally poor. On top of the crop failure in 1941 imports of oilseeds and nuts fell to the lowest point, and the deficit was made good only in part by imports of 2,500 tons of cottonseed oil from Egypt. Substantial imports exceeding 25,000 tons were received in 1942 and 1943, and imports of oilseeds in 1944 were stepped up to about 40,000 tons—equivalent to over 19,000 tons of oil. Estimates of apparent consumption are given below, in thousand metric tons oil equivalent:

| Year | Production | Net imports | Consumption |
|---|---|---|---|
| Average 1934–38 | 8.5 | 9.1 | 17.6 |
| 1940 | 13.5 | 11.5 | 25.0 |
| 1941 | 5.0 | 8.8 | 13.8 |
| 1942 | 12.2 | 13.7 | 25.9 |
| 1943 | 12.5 | 11.8 | 24.3 |
| 1944 | 5.6 | 19.4 | 25.0 |
| 1945 | 12.8 | 15.1 | 27.9 |
| Average 1940–45 | 10.3 | 13.4 | 23.7 |

## SYRIA AND LEBANON

Apart from *samne* or ghee, for which no estimate is available, olive oil is the principal source of Syria's edible fats and oils. Olive-oil production averaged about 12,000 tons before the war and rose to 14,000 in 1940. As in Palestine, there was a poor crop in 1941 (variously estimated to yield 10,000 or 6,600 tons) followed by two bumper crops in 1942 and 1943 with yields of 26,000 and 27,000 tons. Production of sesame seed averaged about 4,000 tons. During the five prewar years an average of 2,500 tons of cottonseed was exported, 4,800 tons in 1939. About 6,000 tons of oil were normally derived from imported oils and oilseeds; this was exceeded by exports of olive oil, resulting in a small net-export balance. In 1941 net imports fell to a low level of 1,300 tons after the high olive-oil production of 1940, but recovered in 1942 with the arrival of over 7,000 tons of cottonseed from Egypt. In 1942 and 1943 Syria was able to export soap and vegetable oil to Iraq. In 1943 and 1944, owing to their record olive-oil output, Syria and Lebanon were almost self-supporting, with net imports averaging less than 500 tons of oil equivalent. The poor olive crop of 1944 was offset by imports of 3,500 tons of peanuts and sesame in 1945.

Efforts were made in 1943 to extend cultivation of peanuts in Syria and 50 tons were sent from Egypt for distribution to farmers who had undertaken to grow them, but little success was achieved and production has remained negligible.

Apparent consumption of vegetable oils in Syria and Lebanon, in thousand metric tons oil equivalent, is as follows:

| Year | Production | Trade | Total |
|---|---|---|---|
| Average 1934–38 | 15.5 | − .8 | 14.7 |
| 1940 | 16.7 | +2.9 | 19.6 |
| 1941 | 8.9 | +1.1 | 10.0 |
| 1942 | 30.4 | +5.1 | 35.5 |
| 1943 | 29.8 | + .9 | 30.7 |
| 1944 | 7.1 | + .1 | 7.2 |
| 1945 | 27.9 | +1.6 | 29.5 |
| Average 1940–45 | 20.1 | +2.0 | 22.1 |

## IRAQ

No reliable estimates of Iraq's supplies of fats and oils were available. According to official figures, production of sesame in Iraq averaged 18,000 tons and of cottonseed 4,300 tons during 1937–38. Production of sesame declined during the war to 3,000 tons in 1942 and 5,000 in 1943. Cottonseed rose to 10,500 tons in 1940 and fell to less than 5,000 in 1942. Production of 3,000 tons of linseed was also recorded in 1942. There was no recorded production of olive oil.

Cottonseed exports during 1934–38 averaged 3,000 tons but fell to 1,500 in 1941 and thereafter ceased. Exports of linseed, which averaged 1,740 tons before the war, rose to 3,400 in 1940 and thereafter were negligible. Iraq's principal import requirements during the war were for soap from Syria and for ghee and peanuts from India. Coconut oil imports rose from about 600 tons before the war to 1,740 in 1940. Vegetable oils were of relatively minor significance in Iraq, supplies of animal fats being of greater importance. An oilseed crushing mill was erected in 1942/43, which led to a more economical use of cottonseed and sesame, part of which had formerly been used for stock feeding or exported.

In general there appears to have been little evidence of wartime shortage of fats and oils in Iraq. There is reason to believe that estimates of supplies for human consumption are too low, particularly the estimate in FAO's first *World Food Survey* of one kilo per head per annum (*1*). It seems more likely that a considerable part of the sesame seed, though not crushed for oil, was in fact used as in Egypt and Palestine in making the Arab food called *halawa.* The revised FAO estimate (*1*) of 3.1 kilos per head for vegetable oils is to be preferred to the previous low estimate; and if ghee and animal fats are included an estimate of 4–5 kilos per head seems reasonable.

## PERSIA

During the war MESC had insufficient data for accurate appraisal of the fats and oils situation in Persia, but it was generally believed in Teheran and Cairo that requirements were covered by local production. From the scanty official figures published it appears that in 1939 there were exports of 8,870 tons of cottonseed, 1,610 tons of sesame, and 840 tons of linseed. In 1944 there were no exports of any of these seeds, and imports of about 120 tons of oils and seeds were recorded.

## EFFORTS TO EXPAND PRODUCTION

In Palestine, Syria, and Libya the olive crop, which is consumed by the Arab population both as a fruit and as olive oil, fluctuated sharply during the war with poor crops in 1941 and 1944 and exceptionally good crops in 1942 and 1943. As regards animal fats, no figures were available; but there was some demand for livestock, particularly in Iraq, to provide meat for the armed forces, and this not only forced up prices but probably reduced the supply of animal fats below the prewar level.

Opportunities for expanding oilseed production to offset the reduction in cottonseed were found to be very limited. Crops such as peanuts, sesame, sunflower, soya beans, and linseed had as a rule to

| Item | Egypt[a] | | Palestine[b] | |
|---|---|---|---|---|
| | Nut yield | Fat yield | Nut yield | Fat yield |
| Oilseeds: | | | | |
| Peanuts | 700 | 230 | 1,600 | 500 |
| Cottonseed | 240 | 40 | — | — |
| Sesame | 300 | 120 | — | — |
| Linseed | 360 | 120 | 480 | 160 |
| Sunflower | — | — | 600 | 150 |
| Soya beans | — | — | 480 | 90 |
| | Grain yield | Flour yield | Grain yield | Flour yield |
| Grains: | | | | |
| Wheat | 600 | 540 | 600 | 540 |
| Barley | 800 | 500 | 800 | 480 |
| Millet | 800 | 700 | 600 | 540 |

[a] Based on average yields.

[b] Experimental results on irrigated land.

be grown on irrigated land owing to insufficient rainfall. But since so large a part of Middle East agriculture consists of farming for family subsistence, production of bread grains had to be given priority over cash crops. Moreover, grains give more food per acre than most oilseeds, though peanuts may be an exception in some parts of the Middle East. The figures on the opposite page, obtained during the war in Egypt and Palestine, illustrate the comparative yields of oilseeds and grains, in kilos per acre (*4*).

The possibilities of increasing production of peanuts in Egypt were examined by a special committee, and peanut seed was sent from Egypt to Palestine, Syria, and Iraq. In Sudan efforts were made to economize in the use of cottonseed for fuel; locomotives were converted to oil burning, which released about 25,000 tons of cottonseed that had been used in place of coal. In Cyprus it was decided that since any extension of the area under sesame would have to be at the expense of dry beans, it was more important to maintain the maximum area under pulses. The Iraq Department of Agriculture carried out experiments with a view to the development of peanuts, castor seed, and sunflower seed. At one time it was hoped that 7,000 hectares might be used for growing peanuts in Palestine. They were to be grown in the citrus groves, either between the trees or on areas to be cleared of old trees. But objections were raised to this proposal and less than 800 hectares were planted to peanuts in 1943/44, mainly in substitution for sesame, the yield of which was unduly low. Shortage and high cost of labor was an additional argument against increased production of peanuts. Possibilities of increased production in Syria, Eritrea, and Ethiopia were also examined, but under war conditions it was not possible to make any significant progress.

The general picture of Middle East fats and oils supplies during the war is that there was no such acute threat of shortage as occurred with cereals, even though supplies were restricted and prices rose sharply in sympathy with other food prices. Outside Iraq and Persia, which were virtually self-supporting, the reduction in cottonseed output in Egypt was the chief source of anxiety, particularly after the summer of 1943; but this was made good partly by cessation of exports of cottonseed to Europe and partly by movement of larger quantities of cottonseed from Sudan. According to MESC records total tonnage of oilseeds consigned to the Middle East in controlled shipping came to 38,370 tons in 1942, 7,540 in 1943, and 126,850 in 1944. The last figure includes substantial supplies for the armed forces.

Average per capita consumption during 1940–45 of vegetable fats and oils (including soap and industrial uses) shows little change from the prewar average (see p. 262) for Egypt, Palestine, Syria and Lebanon, but a decline for Cyprus. There appears to have been little annual fluctuation for Egypt, a low year for the other three countries in 1941, and another low year for Syria and Lebanon and Cyprus in 1944.

## CITATIONS

*1* FAO, *World Food Survey* (Washington, July 5, 1946), and *Second World Food Survey* (Rome, November 1952).

*2* FAO, *Current Development and Prospects for Agriculture in the Near East. Second Near East Meeting on Food and Agricultural Programs and Outlook, Bloudane, Syria—28 August 1951* (July 12, 1951).

*3* FAO, *Food Balance Sheets* (Washington, D.C., April 1949).

*4* Unpublished MESC, Agricultural Report No. 2, May 1943.

CHAPTER 29

# POTATO SUPPLIES AND PRODUCTION

Potatoes are not part of the normal diet of the Middle East except to some extent in Cyprus and Palestine. This is mainly for climatic reasons. Potatoes grow best in temperate zones and special care is required in hot and dry climates to get good crops free from disease.

Before the war potatoes were produced in Egypt, Palestine, Cyprus, Syria, and Lebanon, but total production averaged only about 129,000 tons. Below are given figures of production and net trade in the years 1934–38 and approximate estimates of food use per head:

| Country | Area (*1,000 hectares*) | Production (*1,000 tons*) | Net trade (*1,000 tons*) | Food use per head (*kilos per year*) |
|---|---|---|---|---|
| Egypt | 4 | 47 | +18 | 3 |
| Cyprus | 3 | 24 | −13 | 21 |
| Syria | 3 | 18 | − 5 | 6 |
| Lebanon | 6 | 24 | | |
| Palestine | 1 | 6 | +16 | 16 |
| Others | 5 | 10 | + 7 | .. |
| Total | 22 | 129 | +23 | .. |

Since consumption in Egypt was mainly confined to the towns, the amount consumed by the urban population of about 4 million may be estimated at 12 kilos per head. In Palestine prewar consumption by Jews was estimated by the Jewish Agency for Palestine at 22 kilos per head.

During the war great efforts were made by the Middle East Supply Center (MESC) to help departments of agriculture in these countries to increase potato production, partly for civilian consumption and partly for the Allied forces. During the peak year 1944 local production was stepped up to nearly 250,000 tons—almost double the prewar figure. This was not as much as had been planned; but in view of the many difficulties encountered it represented a considerable achievement. Special credit is due to Major Charles Bennett of MESC's staff, who was responsible for the seed-potato enterprise and for the successful outcome of the campaign to expand production of ware (marketable) potatoes.

The main problem to be overcome, apart from lack of experience and technical knowledge on the part of growers, was to prevent degeneration of potato stocks through disease, infestation, and unsuitable storage of seed. In the past, varieties had been mixed and crops had been heavily infested with virus diseases and insect pests. Yields rapidly declined with successive crops from the same stock, and the third generation would often yield no more than what had been planted. In Egypt and Palestine, where there are two crops in a year, it was found difficult to obtain satisfactory seed from local sources. The seed from the winter crop is apt to become dried up during hot weather; and the seed obtained from the summer crop has too short a period of dormancy before it is required for winter planting. It is also probable that too much intense sunlight has an adverse effect on growth.

In peacetime these difficulties were partly met by importing seed potatoes, mainly from the United Kingdom and Italy. The imported supplies used for seed were between 10,000 and 15,000 tons, and it was easy to obtain them through the Mediterranean at the right time for winter or summer planting without risk of deterioration. But when the Mediterranean was closed in 1940, the longer voyage around the Cape, which involved a double passage of the equator, necessitated cold storage in refrigerated tonnage.

In addition to the need for increasing civilian supplies, there was a large demand from the British forces, amounting to over 100,000 tons per year for the whole Middle East. This alone was sufficient to justify the provision of special tonnage to maintain and, if possible, to increase the import of seed potatoes. The army launched special production schemes in Egypt, Palestine, Cyprus, Syria, and Iraq. In Egypt contracts were made with the government under which the army supplied the seed free and bought back, for each ton of seed supplied, five tons of ware potatoes at 9 Egyptian pounds (£E) per ton. In addition to this government contract, which was implemented through a co-operative society of growers, two private contracts were made under which seed was sold at £E 30 per ton and the produce bought back at £E 13.50. Open-market prices, in December 1942, had risen to £E 30 per ton and at the end of January 1943 to £E 50. The advantage of the contract system was, therefore, considerable. Altogether about 15,000 tons were obtained from Egypt during 1943.

In Palestine contracts were made with the Jewish settlements, the seed being sold at 20 Palestinian pounds (£P) a ton and the produce purchased at £P 24. Out of 1,000 tons of seed supplied, it was hoped to obtain 4,000 tons from the first crop and 6,000 from the second, making a total of 10,000 in 1943. The market price for potatoes in January was about £P 40 a ton. In Syria and Lebanon the target was 18,000 tons from the two crops, and in Cyprus ware potatoes were sold to the army. Requirements in Iraq, originally put at 25,000 tons, had to be reduced to about 5,000, and contracts were placed providing for free seed and purchase of the produce at 26 Iraq dinars per ton; but owing to the difficulties in obtaining seed only a quarter of this amount could be obtained.

In 1940 Egypt obtained about 10,000 tons of seed potatoes and in 1942/43 about half this amount. The most suitable varieties were found to be "Up-to-date" and "Arran Banner." Early in 1944, 3,000 tons were received, and a considerable quantity of locally produced seed was collected and distributed under the supervision of the Egyptian department of agriculture. The result was that in 1944 and 1945 production exceeded 125,000 tons.

Palestine normally imported about 1,000 tons of fresh seed which arrived early in January. During the early years of the war, production was stepped up to over 20,000 tons and reached 23,000 in 1942. After a moderate crop of 15,000 tons in 1943 special efforts were made to increase the acreage planted, with seed specially imported from the United Kingdom. The result was that in 1944 production reached a record figure of 52,000 tons. During the summer months there was a temporary glut of potatoes in Palestine; but this was met by increasing the maximum price for later months and thus encouraging farmers to hold back supplies. Palestine was thus able to make an important addition to her supplies in 1944 of more than 45,000 tons of ware potatoes. The Palestine agricultural department was able to buy local seed potatoes for planting in the fall of 1944, but the 1945 crop fell to 33,000 tons.

In Cyprus, where production before the war averaged about 24,000 tons, 4,500 tons were required for seed and about 8,000 for local consumption. The remainder was exported to neighboring countries for seed or for consumption. Cyprus is climatically well suited for potato production and partly owing to high winds it is relatively free from virus disease. Cyprus seed is well liked in Egypt and Palestine, and, given a renewal of stock from the United Kingdom, it should be possible to increase exports of seed potatoes to about 10,000 tons a year. During the war the peak years' production was about 29,000 tons (in 1944) and 31,000 (in 1945).

In Syria little interest was shown in potato production. Before the war production was about 18,000 tons, and declined to less than 13,000 tons in 1942–45. In Lebanon, on the other hand, there was a fair crop in the Bekaa Valley, which averaged 24,000 tons before the war. In 1942 production reached 58,000 tons, but fell back to 35,000 in 1945.

No potatoes were grown in Transjordan before the war, but excellent returns, ranging from sixfold to tenfold, were obtained by planting "Epicure" potatoes in the Jordan Valley. Production reached 1,350 tons in 1943 and rose to 3,000 in 1944.

Prewar production in Iraq was relatively unimportant, probably less than 5,000 tons. There was a small increase during the war, mainly to supply the armed forces. There are two crops a year—the first planted in April and lifted in July, the second planted in November and lifted about February.

About 600 hectares were planted with potatoes in Eritrea in 1943; but prevalence of disease, high cost of production, and difficulties of transport made the country unsuitable for potato growing on a large scale.

In the summer of 1944 MESC was able to inform the shipping authorities in London that no seed from the United Kingdom would be required for the autumn planting. Egypt was able to obtain supplies of imported seed from Cyprus and Malta, and another large crop of 125,000 tons was obtained in 1945. In other territories, the harvests in December and January 1944/45 were satisfactory with the exception of Palestine, where yields were low owing to excessive rains in the autumn of 1944.

Acreage under potatoes in the Middle East was considerably increased during the war. The seed-potato trade was developed in Cyprus and Malta. Plans were made to start a seed industry in Lebanon, where conditions in the Bekaa Valley had proved suitable. Much had been learned about the most suitable varieties, treatment of disease, and best methods of storage. The war thus gave a definite stimulus to the introduction and development of this crop.

In Egypt potatoes have now become a staple crop. In 1946 the area planted was 13,000 hectares and the crop rose to 163,000 tons with a yield of 126 quintals per hectare. In 1948 on an area of 18,000 hectares the yield rose to 134 quintals and the crop reached 242,000 tons, more than five times the prewar average of 47,000 tons. In Palestine a fivefold increase in area and improved yields raised local production from an average of 5,600 tons in 1934–38 to 47,000 tons in 1946 and 38,000 in 1947. In Syria the area has remained constant at 3,000 hectares, with a crop in 1946 of only 15,000 tons. In Lebanon the wartime increase in yields has been well maintained; with an area of 5,000 hectares, production in 1949 was 40,000 tons compared with 24,000 in 1934–38. Production in Cyprus since the war has been about 50 percent higher than prewar.

CHAPTER 30

# COFFEE AND TEA

Coffee and tea are not essential foods, but in the Middle East as elsewhere they are virtual necessities. This led to their being given a high priority in wartime import programs. Moreover they were recognized by the Middle East Supply Center (MESC) as having a special value as "incentive" goods. Incentive goods were anything that helped to bring food to the towns by inducing producers to accept paper money and sell, rather than hoard, their cereals and other crops.

To the Middle East we owe coffee and to China, tea. The use of tea in China was known to the Arabs as early as the ninth century, but it is only during the last hundred years that tea, mostly from India and Ceylon, has come to rival coffee as a popular drink in Arab countries. The use of coffee was recorded in the fifteenth century in Ethiopia, where the tree grows wild in the province of Kaffa, from which its name is derived. By the end of the sixteenth century its use had spread to Egypt and in the seventeenth century to neighboring countries. Coffeehouses had already become popular in Constantinople and Venice before London's first coffeehouse was established in 1652. Until the end of the seventeenth century, Yemen in southern Arabia, through the port of Mocha, supplied the entire world's requirements, probably less than 1,000 tons, of the original Mocha coffee. Shortly after 1700, coffee plants were introduced from Arabia to Java, and in 1718 they were taken to Ceylon by the Portuguese and to Jamaica by the British. In the nineteenth century coffee cultivation spread rapidly in Central and South America, until, in the 1930's, out of total world exports of 1.6 million tons 70 percent came from Brazil and other tropical parts of Latin America and only about 2 percent was supplied by Ethiopia and Yemen.

Production of coffee and tea in the Middle East is confined to three countries. Coffee is produced in Ethiopia and Yemen, and tea in Persia. The annual exportable production of Ethiopian coffee in the decade before the war was about 16,250 tons. Coffee grown in Yemen in 1934–38 has been roughly estimated by the Food and Agriculture Organization of the United Nations (FAO) at 7,800 tons, but there are no official statistics of output. In Ethiopia the best coffee for export is grown in the highlands of the province of Harrar, which is connected by rail with the port of Djibouti in French Somaliland. Exports of Ethiopian coffee, which averaged 12,000 tons in 1934–38, declined to 300 tons in 1940 and ceased entirely during 1941 and 1942. After the restoration of Emperor Haile Selassie there was rapid recovery and Ethiopia became one of the principal sources of supply to the Middle East; 6,300 tons were exported in 1943, 6,000 in 1944, and 8,200 in 1945.

In Yemen coffee is mainly grown on the steep mountainsides of the western highlands at altitudes between 4,000 and 7,000 feet (*1*, p. 234). Wartime shortage and high prices stimulated production; no figures of exports are available, but in 1947 FAO estimated that the output of coffee in Yemen had increased to 9,000 tons.

Tea production in Persia was introduced under Riza Shah Pahlevi. In the early 1930's there were about 1,200 hectares under tea, and the estimated output averaged less than 900 tons in 1934–38. In 1943 the crop was estimated by MESC to be about 1,700 tons, but since tea growing was confined to the northern area under Russian occupation there was considerable uncertainty as to the supply that was likely to be available. The International Tea Committee (*2*, p. 7) gives an average of 5 million pounds or 2,270 tons for the war years 1940–44.

As consumers of coffee and tea Middle East countries fall into three categories. Persia and Iraq, like China and India, are predominantly tea-drinking countries. In Egypt before the war consumer preferences were about equally divided, with coffee just leading. In Sudan, the Levant States, and Arabia there was a marked preference for coffee, the traditional drink of the Arabs; and the same is true of Ethiopia, where coffee drinking originated. Consumption of tea in Ethiopia was negligible.

Net imports of coffee into Middle East countries, the United Kingdom, and the United States (*3*) are shown on the following page, in metric tons.

The tabulation shows that during the war the coffee-drinking countries were able to increase their consumption. Average coffee supplies for the Middle East in 1940–44 were 30 percent higher than in 1934–38 and in no year during the war did imports fall below the prewar average. This was mainly due to the fact that ample supplies were available from Ethiopia, Yemen, East Africa, to some extent from Madagascar (which exported to Syria and Lebanon), and from

| Country | Average 1934–38 | Average 1940–44 |
|---|---|---|
| Middle East countries: | | |
| Egypt | 7,730 | 8,860 |
| Sudan | 7,250 | 8,430 |
| Palestine | 1,600 | 2,210 |
| Syria and Lebanon | 1,160 | 2,610 |
| Cyprus | 480 | 390 |
| Transjordan | 290 | 750 |
| Aden | 190 | 610 |
| Iraq | 800 | 1,870 |
| Persia | 200 | 10[a] |
| Total | 19,700 | 25,740 |
| United Kingdom | 14,130 | 32,740 |
| United States | 788,050 | 981,980 |

[a] 1944 only.

the Belgian Congo (which supplied part of Sudan's imports). Coffee from these countries made little call on tonnage controlled by the Allies; some of it was transported by land and some came in dhows or in uncontrolled ships. Owing to the cutting off of the European market there was no world shortage of supplies. The United States, the United Kingdom, and the Commonwealth countries were able to obtain more than their prewar imports, though total world exports fell from 1.6 million tons in 1934–38 to just over a million tons in 1942. This was the year when rationing in the United States brought about a cut of 25 percent in consumption (*4*, p. 111). In Britain coffee never had to be rationed.

The story of tea was very different. Both supplies and shipping space were limited and MESC had to exercise strong pressure at times to maintain a reasonable flow of imports into the Middle East. The tabulation below shows that in 1943, when both world supplies and available shipping space reached their lowest point of the war, the Middle East obtained less than half its prewar imports of tea. This cut fell with special severity on Persia owing to its dependence on tea rather than on coffee as the staple beverage; if the official trade returns can be trusted, imports of tea in 1943 were only 1,642 tons, or less than a quarter of the prewar supply. However, this was sandwiched in between two good years; and if the five years 1940–44 are taken, tea imports into Persia averaged nearly 85 percent of the prewar five-year average. For the whole area, tea imports in 1940–44 averaged 17,000 tons compared with 20,000 tons in 1934–38, but there were wide variations from year to year and from country to country, as shown below. The figures are of net imports in metric tons (*3*):

| Year | Egypt | Sudan | Pales-tine | Syria and Leb-anon | Cyprus | Trans-jordan | Aden | Iraq | Persia | Total |
|---|---|---|---|---|---|---|---|---|---|---|
| Average 1934–38 ..... | 7,130 | 2,602 | 284 | 175 | 16 | 73 | 150 | 2,741 | 6,769 | 19,940 |
| 1939....... | 7,065 | 2,504 | 324 | 141 | 13 | 98 | 123 | 3,091 | 8,773 | 22,132 |
| 1940....... | 6,455 | 2,464 | 320 | 156 | 8 | 93 | –36[a] | 3,233 | 7,433 | 20,126 |
| 1941....... | 6,595 | 3,158 | 202 | 81 | 16 | 86 | 102 | 2,272 | 2,091 | 14,603 |
| 1942....... | 6,890 | 2,336 | 540 | 291 | 5 | 133 | 405 | 2,880 | 9,110 | 22,590 |
| 1943....... | 2,971 | 1,216 | 128 | 122 | 0 | 17 | –256[a] | 2,835 | 1,642 | 8,675 |
| 1944....... | 5,526 | 1,736 | 129 | 12 | 0 | 83 | 66 | 1,471 | 7,631 | 16,654 |
| 1945....... | 4,359 | 1,738 | 158 | 68 | 5 | 58 | 180 | 2,321 | 1,778 | 10,665 |

[a] Net exports.

In 1939 and 1940 supplies were at a satisfactory level, with some increase in imports into Persia, Iraq, and Palestine and a slight falling off in Egypt and Sudan. In 1941 Middle East supplies were reduced by 25 percent, the chief reduction being Persian imports, which fell by 70 percent.

In 1942 the cutting off of supplies from Java and China by the Japanese and the urgent need to economize shipping led to a fall of about 25 percent in total world exports of tea. In that year the United Kingdom, which before the war imported more than the rest of the world combined, received 80 percent of her prewar supplies, and the United States only 60 percent. Rationing of tea had been introduced in Britain in July 1940 and in 1942 civilian consumption was cut to about two-thirds of the prewar level. The British Ministry of Food had contracted to buy the exportable surplus of India, Ceylon, and East Africa; and nearly all the available exports of tea were thus controlled by the Ministry and later were allocated by the London Tea Committee of the Combined Food Board (CFB).

In January 1942 MESC included in its first six-month import program a figure of 4,800 tons of tea for Egypt and the Mediterranean area, two-thirds from India and one-third from East Africa. The British Ministry of Food said that it would have great difficulty in meeting these requirements and urged the importance of reducing tea consumption and obtaining more coffee as a substitute. It agreed to release 1,400 tons from East Africa for Sudan, and in addition arrangements were made for the supply of 1,750 tons from India for

Persia and Iraq; but the Ministry could give no undertaking for the rest of the area.

When the second six-month program was submitted in June 1942, MESC pointed out that arrivals in the Red Sea area had in recent months been reduced to about 30 percent of normal imports and it pressed for larger supplies. This time MESC's urgent representations induced the authorities in London to agree to a total allocation for the half year of 24.5 million pounds (11,000 tons) for the whole Middle East. Two-thirds of this was to come from East Africa and one-third from India. It was also agreed that, while no coffee could be shipped from distant sources, the United Kingdom Commercial Corporation (UKCC) could buy up to 20,000 tons from East Africa, Ethiopia, and Yemen.

During 1942 recorded imports of tea reached the surprisingly high level of 22,600 tons, part of this being due to the use of uncontrolled tonnage for larger shipments from India than the program provided. The government of India objected to UKCC buying for Persia and Iraq on the ground that this would interfere with normal trade channels, and private exports were in fact permitted in excess of the six-month program of 3,000 tons for these countries. Even so, the high figure of 9,110 tons for recorded imports into Persia in 1942 is difficult to explain and probably includes some delayed entry of 1941 imports.

By the beginning of 1943 the shipping situation had worsened to such an extent that it was decided in London that Middle East supplies would have to be reduced to 50 percent of prewar imports. When it became known that uncontrolled imports in dhows were arriving in the Persian Gulf on a substantial scale, the governments of Persia and Iraq were warned that so long as this continued it would be necessary to reduce their regular quota.

At a later date, when it was proposed in London that Persia's quota should be increased in order to discourage smuggling, MESC had to protest and insist that, since Egypt and Sudan were short of supplies, there must be no discrimination in favor of the Persian Gulf area. The original January–June 1943 program for imports in controlled tonnage was only 1,700 tons for the Red Sea and Mediterranean area, and 2,000 tons for the Persian Gulf countries. But this program, which was prompted by instructions to place Middle East requirements on a "siege basis" during the final campaign in North Africa, was revised upward after the worst period of shipping diversion was over in March 1943.

For the second six months of 1943 the Red Sea area import program was raised to 3,600 tons, with an additional 3,200 tons for Libya, and the quantity to be shipped in controlled tonnage for the Persian Gulf area was set at 2,600 tons. At the same time, Persia's tea quota was increased to cover additional imports by dhow from India. The International Institute of Agriculture (IIA) recorded imports indicate that the 1943 programs, except in the case of Iraq, were in fact unfulfilled. Egypt, Sudan, Palestine, Cyprus, and Transjordan received less than half their prewar imports. If Persian customs entries for 1943 are to be trusted, only 1,640 tons were imported, compared with 9,110 tons in 1942 and 6,770 before the war. One of the reasons for the drop in Persia's imports was the delay which took place in organizing control of imports and distribution of tea following the prohibition of private imports and the decision to introduce rationing. Conversely, Iraq, which obtained her programed quota of 1,000 tons through controlled channels, had recorded imports of 2,835 tons in 1943, which exceeds the prewar average.

In 1943 the method of procurement of tea from India and Ceylon posed difficult problems. Both countries had agreed in principle to the allocation of world supplies by the London Tea Committee of CFB. Private exports were prohibited except under license, and tea controllers had been appointed to supervise bulk sales to the British Ministry of Food. The governments of Persia and Iraq were urged by MESC and their official advisers to tighten up internal control of prices and distribution, and to achieve this it was necessary to appoint either a single buyer or a pool of importers. For political reasons the government of India was unwilling to recognize UKCC as the single buyer for Middle East governments and was reluctant to break the normal trade connections of Indian exporters with their customers in the Persian Gulf area.

Lack of co-ordination between control of exports in India and control of imports in Persia and Iraq put a premium on smuggling and illicit trade. During the first three months of 1943 the government of India, in accordance with the policy laid down in London, had granted no export licenses for tea to Persia and Iraq. But in spite of this, substantial quantities in excess of the agreed quotas had been shipped in Arab dhows from small harbors on the northwest coast of India, where effective supervision by customs authorities was extremely difficult to enforce. There seemed little prospect of stopping this trade so long as there was an acute unsatisfied demand in Persia and Iraq, an exportable surplus in India, and uncontrolled shipping available for transport.

In Iraq an arrangement was eventually made in March 1943 that a private British firm, the African and Eastern Company, should act as sole importing agent for the Iraq government. For the first six months of 1943 Iraq's import quota of 500 tons was obtained by this firm from Ceylon. For the second half year the British Ministry of Food was able to arrange with the tea controller in India for the formation of a pool of tea exporters normally engaged in the trade with Iraq to handle orders received from the African and Eastern Company for the purchase, blending, and preparation for shipment of teas suitable for the Iraq market. The firm's agents in Calcutta checked the qualities and deliveries, were responsible for payments to the tea controller, and arranged shipment.

In Persia it took longer to regularize the position and work out satisfactory arrangements for government control of purchase and distribution. In March 1943 prohibition of private imports and centralization of supply were proposed by the American food adviser, Sheridan, as a means of enforcing price control and rationing of tea, which was introduced on April 1, 1943. Stocks of tea in the hands of private dealers were requisitioned by the government and, when tea rationing started, stocks in government hands amounted to 2,700 tons. The indigenous crop, which is picked in the fall, was expected to amount to 1,700 tons; but since the tea-growing areas were in northern Persia under Russian occupation it was uncertain whether this quantity would become available. As early as April, a tea buyer was appointed to go to India to act on behalf of the Persian government; but, as in the case of Iraq, some time elapsed before mutually satisfactory arrangements for purchase and shipment could be made. It was not till July that the Persian buyer arrived in Calcutta and had his first meeting with the tea controller to discuss arrangements for dealing with a pool of exporters to the Persian Gulf.

If the Persian tea-rationing scheme was to work, it was necessary to distribute 500 tons a month, sufficient to provide a nominal ration of 50 grams per head monthly for 10 million adults. A three-month reserve stock was needed to ensure distribution to outlying districts and to provide against irregularities of transport, especially during the winter months. MESC therefore estimated Persia's import requirements at 1,500 tons to the end of 1943. In October the official Persian buyer was authorized to purchase 2,000 tons for shipment over the next four months.

One of the incidental results of centralization of imports was to create a problem of "frustrated" exports—that is, stocks of tea bought in the normal course of trade for export from India and Ceylon, for which export or import licenses could no longer be obtained. About 28,000 cases (1,400 tons) of tea, which had been bought by Persian and Indian traders and licensed for export by rail across the land frontier in Baluchistan, were held up at Nokkundi, first by a breakdown on the railroad and later by prohibition of private imports. In May 1943, when these stocks had been lying in store or in the open air since July 1942, the Persian authorities asked the government of India to extend the validity of the export licenses and offered to purchase any quantity which was still in acceptable condition. This request was granted on the understanding that the tea would form part of Persia's quota, which had now been raised by the London Tea Committee of CFB to 90 percent of normal. But transport by rail from India to Persia continued to present great difficulties; and judging from the Persian customs returns, which show recorded imports of only 1,640 tons in 1943, it may be inferred that little if any of the Nokkundi tea arrived before the end of the year. The records do not show whether any of it was imported in 1944.

Similar difficulties arose in the supply of tea to Arabia. In October 1943 the Saudi Arabian government complained that importers were unable to obtain their normal supplies from India and MESC had to release small quantities from UKCC stocks purchased from Ceylon. Later the tea controller in Calcutta arranged for Messrs. Gellatley Hankey at Jedda to collect orders and payments from importers for supplying tea to western Saudi Arabia, and authorized the pool of Indian exporters to the Persian Gulf area to look after supplies allocated to eastern Saudi Arabia. Aden was supplied through UKCC out of MESC's Red Sea pool, for which supplies were drawn from Ceylon.

## CITATIONS

*1* Hugh Scott, *In the High Yemen* (London, 1942).

*2* Internatl. Tea Com., *Bulletin of Statistics* (London), June 1953.

*3* IIA, *International Yearbook of Agricultural Statistics, 1941–42 to 1945–46* (Rome, 1947).

*4* V. D. Wickizer, *Coffee, Tea and Cocoa: An Economic and Political Analysis* (Food Res. Inst., Studies on Food, Agr., and World War II, Stanford, 1951).

# Part VI

# SCIENTIFIC AID FOR FOOD PRODUCTION

CHAPTER 31

# THE FIGHT AGAINST LOCUSTS

One of the activities of the Middle East Supply Center (MESC) that had an important bearing on wartime food supplies was the antilocust campaign of 1943–45. From time immemorial periodical plagues of locusts have been a menace to the Middle East. If a major outbreak had occurred during the war, it could have resulted in a disastrous reduction of cereal and other crops, leading to diversion of ships for importing grain at the expense of munitions. This might have jeopardized, or at least delayed, the victory over Rommel in North Africa. The supply of munitions to Russia through Persia might have been slowed down or temporarily stopped, if locusts had helped the enemy by destroying crops as they did in Syria in World War I (*1*, p. 203; and ch. 4, above).

The mastermind behind the fight against locusts, which has been waged with growing resources and knowledge for three decades, has been Dr. B. P. Uvarov. It was through his initiative and under his direction that the Anti-Locust Research Centre was established in London in 1926. Before the outbreak of war a wealth of information had been gathered about the habits and movements of locusts, and enough data had been collected about breeding areas and meteorological conditions favoring infestation to make it highly probable that a peak period in the locust cycle would occur during the years 1943–45. Steps were taken to establish or to strengthen antilocust control measures in India, East Africa, and Sudan; and an interdepartmental committee was set up in London to co-ordinate and promote co-operation between governments and military and air authorities. Early in 1942 it was decided to create a Middle East Antilocust Unit to organize and carry through a concerted campaign as part of the Food and Agriculture Division of MESC. Among the more important breeding grounds, known to be a menace to neighboring countries, were Sudan, where control was already being undertaken; Persia, where a body known as the Teheran International Locust Council was set up in 1942 and the services of O. B. Lean (later to become chief locust officer of the Middle East Anti-Locust Unit) had been secured to establish control; and Saudi Arabia, where little was done until the winter of 1942/43. Maxwell Darling was assigned by the Sudan government to act as chief locust officer and carry out a preliminary reconnaissance. At the same time, arrangements were made for a party from India under D. Vesey Fitzgerald to work in Oman and eastern Saudi Arabia, and for missions from Egypt and Palestine to visit Hejaz and northern Arabia, including the Great Nafud. In spite of limited resources of material, personnel, and transport, and the many political and other difficulties that arose in opening up work in so vast and little known an area, valuable information was collected which formed the basis of the 1943/44 campaign.

In July 1943 an important conference on locust control was held by MESC in Cairo under the presidency of Lord Moyne, at which Uvarov met officers of the Middle East Anti-Locust Unit and a team of experts from India, Egypt, Sudan, Syria, Lebanon, Palestine, and the liberated territories of Eritrea, Cyrenaica, and Tripolitania. Another similar conference was held in January 1945 at which other countries, including the USSR, Turkey, and Saudi Arabia, were also represented. It was unfortunate that Ethiopia could not be represented at either conference (*2*).

The successful outcome of the campaign, which in size, scope, and extent of international co-operation was unparalleled before or since, was mainly due to a combination of three factors: first, a team of British and American technical experts and MESC administrators, who entered upon this novel and arduous work with something like missionary zeal; second, wholehearted co-operation from the military and air authorities in providing personnel, transport, and wireless facilities; and third, financial assistance provided by the British Treasury at the instance of the Inter-Departmental Committee on Locust Control in London. None of these would have been forthcoming in such full measure if the fight against locusts had not been recognized, thanks to Uvarov's pioneering research, as an urgently needed and practicable method of saving shipping and safeguarding the food supply of the Middle East. In Sudan, Egypt, Ethiopia, Eritrea, and Libya, as well as farther afield in India, East Africa, Turkey, and the USSR, governments and local administrations intensified their normal control measures and contributed and received technical information of the greatest value. Fortnightly reports about the appearance of swarms and the discovery of breeding areas were centralized in Uvarov's Anti-Locust Research Centre in London. MESC's main contribution lay in the work carried out, with the aid of the army and the Royal Air Force (RAF), by technical missions sent to Saudi Arabia and to Persia. The Arabian peninsula had long been regarded as the stronghold, hitherto undisturbed, of the desert locust and the strategic center for a co-ordinated campaign. Swarms arrive there from both India and Africa and multiply during the winter months. To meet the threat of infestation spreading to neighboring countries, the plan was to seek out and exterminate the locusts in their breeding grounds in Arabia.

Locusts are most easily attacked in the "hopper" stage, before they develop wings and become a flying swarm. On the ground they are readily attracted by poisoned bait, and experience had shown that the best bait was wheat bran with a 1–2 percent admixture of sodium arsenite. It was decided to send two expeditions, one to operate from bases on the west coast at Jedda and Yenbo, and the other from bases on the east coast from Bahrein to Sharjah. With the help of British army transport and equipment, a special Egyptian unit was organized to work in Hejaz in the neighborhood of the holy cities of Mecca and Medina under the leadership of Mohammed Hussein, entomologist in the Egyptian Ministry of Agriculture.

King ibn-Saud took a personal interest in the work of the missions and overrode the scruples of some of his advisers who were lukewarm if not opposed to the extermination of locusts. It must be remembered that locusts are a prized article of diet among the nomad tribes, and the government was rightly concerned about the risk of human beings and animals being poisoned. There were also some difficulties at first in obtaining permission for almost a thousand uniformed British troops to enter Saudi Arabia. But with good will on both sides most of these were solved. In particular the wearing of an Arab headdress—a *kefia* and an *algal*—as part of the uniform added a touch of glamour to the expedition and (at the same time) allayed the misgivings of the Saudi Arabian authorities.

General Headquarters was prevailed upon to provide two Palestinian transport companies and two platoons of a tank-transport company equipped with ten-ton trucks, with a total strength of 24 officers, 800 other ranks, and 329 vehicles. MESC was responsible for providing the civilian specialists as well as bait and other technical equipment. For the actual killing of locusts, Saudi Arabian labor was recruited to work under the supervision of Sudanese foremen.

In December 1943 the first mission, under Captain Hodden of MESC, proceeded inland from Yenbo about 300 miles into the interior around Hail, where extensive breeding was taking place. From the first moment of its arrival this mission was engaged up to the limit of its resources. By the beginning of May 1944 the area was reported clear.

The second mission, under Lean, traveled from Cairo to Baghdad and set up its base at Dharan, opposite the Bahrein Islands. Contrary to expectations, no serious infestation was found in the coastal areas along the Persian Gulf, and at the end of March the mission moved about 400 miles inland to the Shaqra area where heavy infestation had occurred and where contact with the first mission was possible. The Egyptian expedition reached the Hejaz at the beginning of February and had its hands full in coping with heavy infestation.

In Persia the help of the RAF was enlisted in carrying out the dusting of locust swarms in flight and of hoppers on the ground with poisonous dust—dinitro-orthocreosol. A Soviet air unit also operated from a base at Jiwani, making use of methods of dusting from the air already practiced in the USSR. Actually, the expected swarms from India and Oman were almost negligible and the Persian campaign worked mainly with poisoned bait on hoppers. In March it was found possible to transfer half the RAF unit for a similar operation in Kenya.

Early in March a threatened infestation of Upper Egypt was met with the assistance of a British transport unit. In Tripolitania there were severe attacks and arrangements were made to supply 700 tons of bait. Effective control measures were taken in Sudan and Eritrea; but in Ethiopia, partly because of the wild and inaccessible nature of the country and partly for fear of objections from the local population, it was not thought practicable to send a large-scale expedition into the region round Lake Tana, where locusts were believed to breed extensively.

The campaign in Arabia was successful in spite of the trying conditions of work. There was no abnormal sickness amongst the personnel, but the wear and tear on transport was terrific. Much of this might have been avoided if trucks had been equipped with low-pressure tires in addition to the hard tires used in the North African desert. The ten-ton trucks supplied by the United States under Lend-Lease proved of immense value, and only one of them in six months of continuous running had to be written off.

Periodical plagues of locusts still constitute a threat to the food supplies of the Middle East. What was done during the war, particularly in Saudi Arabia, has set an example for later campaigns conducted by entomologists working together in the Middle East. But the resources mobilized during the war exceeded anything attempted before or since, with the result that no severe outbreak occurred involving serious loss of food during what were expected to be the peak years of the locust cycle. Prevention of crop failure, famine, and famine prices by fighting the locusts in their breeding grounds may have saved the diversion of hundreds of thousand tons of Allied shipping which would have been needed to bring relief.

## CITATIONS

*1* George Antonius, *The Arab Awakening* (London, 1938).

*2* Unpublished MESC, The 1943/44 Anti-Locust Campaign (Agr. Rpt. No. 10), May 1944.

## CHAPTER 32

# IRRIGATION AND DRY FARMING

The war years stimulated interest in the scientific problems of Middle East agriculture. Since the war this has been followed up and intensified in the Point Four program, in technical-aid projects of the Food and Agriculture Organization of the United Nations (FAO), in the work of the scientific adviser to the British Middle East Office, and in surveys such as that undertaken by Overseas Consultants, Inc., in Persia. Experience shows that, whatever reservations the Middle East may have about Western influences in the political and economic fields, there is a keen desire among the educated minority to learn and profit from the teachings of Western science and technology.

One of the most important and successful projects sponsored by the Middle East Supply Center (MESC) was the Conference on Middle East Agricultural Development which met in Cairo in February 1944 (*1*). It was attended by representatives of 10 Middle East governments and technical papers were read by more than 30 agricultural experts. The main topics discussed were problems connected with dry farming and irrigation, including land reclamation and soil conservation. The Conference also devoted sessions to methods of improving agricultural techniques through research and extension work, and to some of the complex problems of land settlement and land tenure. Among the resolutions passed was a recommendation that a Middle East Council of Agriculture should be set up, composed of representatives of governments, to provide a forum for the discussion of common agricultural problems through periodic meetings and through the publication of a journal on Middle East agriculture. The Conference invited the Council, when formed, to consider the establishment of a central institute of agricultural development to serve the Middle East as a whole. The resolutions of the Conference and the draft constitution of a Middle East council of agriculture are printed in Appendix Notes III and IV.

The Conference met at a time when the Allies were entering on the final stage of the war. Roosevelt and Churchill had met at Cairo before and after the Teheran conference in December 1943, where the big three had concerted their policies for the opening of the second front. Rommel had been driven out of Africa; Sicily and southern Italy had been occupied; Mussolini had fallen; Badoglio's government had become a cobelligerent; and on January 22, 1944 a surprise landing had been carried out on the Anzio beachhead south of Rome. There was an atmosphere of expectancy and optimism among the assembled experts. At the Hot Springs conference the previous year FAO had been born and had set itself the goal of achieving "freedom from want." In his opening address the chairman of the Conference on Middle East Agricultural Development, E. E. Bailey, Deputy Director-General of MESC, emphasized that the Conference had met to deal with technical and scientific matters which transcended national frontiers and pointed to the encouraging growth of co-operation during the war (*1*, p. x): "Here in the Middle East some of us met in Cairo six months ago to tackle the locust problem, and as a result of our joint efforts a single co-ordinated campaign against the locust is at this moment being waged throughout the Middle East." He hoped that the work of the Conference would be another contribution in the same spirit to the practical welfare of the peoples of the Middle East. The assembled experts recognized that they were faced with a challenge not merely to show how technical problems of production could be solved but how modern techniques could be used to open up a better way of life for the fellahin.

## IRRIGATION AND WATER SUPPLIES

*Egypt.*—Discussion of irrigation opened with an account of the control of the waters of the Nile, which the Egyptian Minister of Agriculture, Mustapha Nosrat Bey, claimed to be the most complete and comprehensive control of a great river to be found anywhere in the world. A paper was read by Ahmed Khairy Bey, giving the story of the building and raising of dams and barrages during the last 50 years and of recent developments in the extension of covered drainage.

The original Delta barrage, constructed in the nineteenth century to provide a summer supply of water for cotton in the Delta, came into full use in 1901 and was reconstructed in 1940. The great Aswan Dam, which was built in 1901 and heightened in 1912 and again in 1933, has a storage capacity of 5,000 million cubic meters. This, together with the Gebel Aulia Dam in Sudan, with a storage capacity of 2,000 million cubic meters, stores floodwaters, which are at their maximum during August and September, and releases them during the spring and early summer months when the natural flow of the river is at its minimum. For controlling the flow of water a daily record of gauge readings is kept in the upper reaches of the Nile, and a program for emptying the reservoirs is drawn up. If the supply available exceeds the probable requirements for cotton and maize cultivation, the area planted under rice can be increased. Central control of irrigation by the government thus gives it an important influence in planning the area to be grown under cotton, cereals, and rice.

With the adoption of perennial irrigation the problem of adequate drainage had come to the fore. Under the traditional system of annual flooding no artificial drainage was required, since the ebb of the river itself provided natural drainage. For thousands of years, under basin irrigation no deterioration of the soil had taken place, since the subsoil-water level was kept naturally low during the growing period of the crops. But with the introduction of the perennial system, accumulations of salt occurred in the subsoil and caused damage to crops. In some badly drained spots barren patches appeared with incrustations of salt on the surface. It soon became evident that an elaborate network of main drains and pumping stations would have to be undertaken by the government. The over-all cost of this work before the war amounted to about 10 Egyptian pounds per acre; but the capital cost has been more than compensated by the marked increase in crop yields.

Many of the chief drainage channels are about 50 meters wide and 4 deep, run for 80–100 kilometers, and with their numerous ancillary drains may occupy between 5 and 10 percent of the cultivable area. Moreover, in the most densely populated districts peasant holdings are so small that their owners could not afford to construct private drains to connect to the main drains. The government was now therefore gradually extending the system of covered-pipe drainage which, though its original cost is two to three times that of open drains, costs less for annual maintenance and does not interfere with private irrigation channels or reduce the size of holdings. The first large-scale covered-drainage scheme, servicing 20,000 acres, was completed during the war in the Menoufia district about 40 miles north of Cairo, where a highly fertile soil had progressively deteriorated owing to excessive fragmentation of holdings and lack of proper drainage.

*Iraq.*—The account of irrigation in Iraq given by the assistant director of irrigation, Abdul Amir al Uzri, was very different. Compared with the Nile, the Tigris and Euphrates are virtually uncontrolled and in many respects more difficult to control. The Euphrates rises in the mountains of Turkey between Lake Van and the Black

Sea and passes through the northeast corner of Syria before entering Iraq. Out of its total length of 260 kilometers only 40 percent lies within Iraq. The Tigris and its tributaries have their origin in Turkey and Persia. To establish complete control of the floodwaters of these rivers by a system of dams and storage reservoirs and thus secure maximum utilization of their total water reserves would require the co-operation of four countries.

The total yearly volume of water in the Euphrates River that passes Hit in north central Iraq averages 1,600 million cubic meters, which considerably exceeds a normal year's flow of the Nile through Egypt. But the flow varies widely from year to year and there is marked seasonal variation, the average of the four months March–June being three times that of the low period from July to February. The lowest period comes in September and October at the end of the summer. Summer crops thus begin with an abundant supply of water and end with a low supply in September and October, while winter crops planted in November start with a low supply and have an abundant supply in April and May when they mature. The period of low supply in the Euphrates is thus the limiting factor for both winter and summer crops.

From these and other data it can be concluded that with proper control of irrigation, by flow and by lift, without reservoirs and storage schemes, present supplies would be sufficient for the cultivation of 130,000 hectares of summer crops and 624,000 hectares of winter crops[1] (*1*). The new flood-relief scheme at Habbaniya Lake, with a storage capacity of some 2,000 million cubic meters, would make it possible to increase the area under winter crops by about 200,000 hectares and the area under summer crops by about 60,000 hectares. When the new storage schemes at Wadi Tharthar and elsewhere are completed, the total area under crops with present water supplies could be increased still further.

But side by side with increased irrigation an extensive development of drainage would have to be undertaken. Under present conditions natural drainage is insufficient and in large areas the land under irrigation becomes saline and infertile through lack of drainage. Only about half the cultivated area is irrigated and half is left fallow. Iraq is exceptional in having an extensive rather than intensive system of cultivation on her irrigated land. If and when the Tigris and Euphrates should be controlled like the Nile, a consider-

[1] Sousa (*2*) gives larger figures for area under crops in the irrigation zone: winter crops, 1,179 million hectares; and summer crops, 400,000 hectares.

able increase in population would be required. But at the same time it would become imperative to reform the present system of land tenure and to give the cultivator greater security and more inducement to improve his methods of cultivation.

*Syria and Lebanon.*—Recent progress in irrigation in the Levant States was described by Major G. Howard-Jones, MESC agricultural representative in Beirut. He explained that no definite projects had yet been made in Syria for controlling the upper Euphrates by building a barrage for large-scale gravity irrigation; but the river plain was being increasingly irrigated by privately owned pumps for the purpose of growing cereals. In the more densely settled areas of Syria and Lebanon many small schemes had been carried out both before and during the war. The two mountain ranges, Lebanon and Anti-Lebanon, receive abundant falls of rain and snow during the winter months from November to March and give rise to numerous springs, 900–1,500 meters above sea level. These springs provide a constant flow of water for irrigation of the coastal strip on the west and of the central valley through which flow the Orontes to the north and the Litani to the south. Irrigation was practiced in Roman times, and an ancient Roman barrage near Homs had been rebuilt and heightened by the French before the war. A network of main and secondary canals was constructed to supply water in the summer to 20,000 acres. On the western slopes of Mount Lebanon where it is too steep or the limestone rock is too porous to build a large reservoir, a simple weir and take-off is built to lead the water into a feeder canal which continues along the side of the river gorge, sometimes cut into the rock and sometimes built out on reinforced-concrete supports. On reaching the coastal plain these canals can be used to irrigate thousands of acres of fertile soil. Little or no artificial drainage is required, the concrete lining of the canals reduces the cost of upkeep, and there is little silting up or weed growth. The risk of malaria is also diminished.

*Cyprus.*—Experience in Cyprus was described by C. Raeburn, who showed what could be done not by large irrigation schemes but by numerous small schemes. The Troodos Mountains, the area of greatest rainfall, reach a height of 2,000 meters and water that collects on their slopes runs with fairly steep gradients not more than 20 miles to the sea. The problem was to conserve the floodwaters of winter and spring for use in summer. Large reservoirs on the hillsides would be impracticable because of the steep gradients and the porous nature of the rocks. Before the war the main emphasis was on the installation of small pumping plants to tap the subsurface water. But early in the war it was realized that pumping equipment would be difficult to obtain, and that the only alternative way of getting more water for increased food production was by building small weirs and tanks with local stone and lime and some cement imported from Egypt. These schemes were financed partly by the British government from funds granted under the Colonial Development and Welfare Act and partly by contributions in cash or in kind from the villages. In the three years 1941–43 schemes had been completed covering about 30,000 acres and another 20,000 acres were planned for 1944. Practically all the 640-odd villages in Cyprus had been persuaded to improve their supply of water, and the benefits of the government grants were thus spread over the whole island. The effect of these minor irrigation schemes in increasing food production was claimed by Raeburn to be immediate and important.

The chief problem awaiting solution was how to retain in underground caverns and aquifers more of winter water for use in summer. It seemed likely that as much as half the water of perennial springs was running to waste in midwinter. If it could be stored in creviced rocks and caverns and drained off under control, summer irrigation could be much increased. In one district the underground storage capacity was estimated to be some 200 million gallons. But to exploit these possibilities elaborate hydrological and geological surveys were needed, involving experiments which naturally encountered some resistance from owners of existing springs and wells. As one delegate to the Conference observed, the ultimate goal of the irrigation department in Cyprus seemed to be to trap all the water that fell on the island and prevent any of it flowing out to sea in the normal way.

*Palestine.*—Three papers submitted to the Conference dealt with the problems of irrigation in Palestine. D. Stedman-Davies, controller of agricultural production in Palestine, described the various methods of using water from wells and springs. B. A. Lowe, in a paper on dry farming in the Beersheba district of Palestine, explained the practical difficulties of irrigation in that area. And R. F. Jardine, water commissioner for Palestine, gave a general survey covering both the hydrological and legal aspects of controlling the limited water resources of the country. In view of the political and economic implications of this problem and the exaggerated claims that have sometimes been advanced, the Conference took a special interest in what these experts had to say.

Jardine presented (*1*, p. 188) what may be called a water-supplies balance sheet for Palestine. The average annual rainfall provided between 7,000 and 8,000 million cubic meters. "If this quantity fell gently and evenly throughout the year there might be no need for irrigation." But actually rainfall is concentrated in the winter months from November to April and varies regionally from less than 100 millimeters in the Negeb and the Jordan Valley up to 500 in the coastal plain and over 600 in the northern hills. Moreover the khamsin winds in May and October, when the temperature rises to 116° F., cause severe loss of moisture through evaporation. Without irrigation only one crop can be grown a year, even in the favored regions, either during the rainy season or in summer after a winter fallow and repeated plowings. The problem is thus to control the distribution of irregular supplies of rain water so as to use it for growing crops.

Here there are favorable and unfavorable factors to be balanced. Compared with California, Palestine is favored by having a relatively low runoff. In the Santa Clara Valley of California it was estimated that at one time as much as three-quarters of the rainfall was carried out to sea and only a quarter percolated into the soil to replenish the underground waters. In Palestine measurements had been made which suggested that the runoff was less than 10 percent and after allowing for loss by evaporation more than half percolated underground. But this gain was balanced by the difficulty of tapping the water in the porous limestone strata of the highlands.

In the central plain the water is retained in sandstone and gravel resting on thick beds of impervious strata of unknown depth. The mountain water percolates to a considerable depth and much of it appears to descend below the impermeable clays on which the coastal underground water rests. The coastal-plain water is extensively used for irrigation by pumping and there are signs of a dangerous lowering of the water table. Much of the underground water from the mountains is lost or cannot be traced. Between Beersheba and Hebron, where much of the rainfall percolates, bores have been drilled, in one case to a depth of 317 meters, but no water has been found. In conclusion, Jardine emphasized the need for systematic hydrological research (*1*, p. 189):

Throughout the whole area where development is thought at all possible scientific investigation must be carried on, to determine, basin by basin, the catchment of the underground water horizons, the geology and occurrence of underground water, how it moves, where it goes, its quality, and where and how it may be recovered. This will involve an extensive programme of drilling experiments, and of tests, inside the laboratory and outside, to determine the permeability of water-bearing strata, and to obtain information of the movement of water through those strata.

Apart from a passing reference by Jardine to the scheme for controlling the headwaters of the Jordan both for irrigation purposes and for generating electricity, the Conference did not discuss the ambitious plans for a "Jordan Valley Authority," similar to the Tennessee Valley Authority, put forward by W. C. Lowdermilk and others. Nathan, Gass, and Creamer (*3*) have claimed that it might be possible to increase the area irrigated from 125,000 acres to 750,000 acres by using not only the Jordan but also water from the Litani in Lebanon and from the Yarmuk, which rises in Syria and flows through what is now the independent Hashemite Kingdom of Jordan. This would involve the agreement of four governments, which even at the time of the Conference hardly seemed politically possible. Worthington, in summing up the discussion (*1*, p. 190), emphasized the danger of interterritorial competition over water and cautiously suggested that some time during the next 50 or 100 years "some reorganization of the regional control of water may be necessary on a cooperative basis in the area we are now considering."

## DRY-LAND FARMING

Dry-land farming has been practiced in the Middle East from time immemorial and, except where irrigation is possible, it is still the prevailing method of cultivation. But only in recent years have its problems been studied by scientists, mostly in the United States. It was therefore with special interest that the Conference heard Harold E. Myers, who had come from Kansas to work as agronomist with MESC, B. J. Hartley, director of agriculture in Aden Protectorate, and B. A. Keen, Britain's leading soil scientist, contribute the results of their research and experience.

Myers, who defined dry-land farming as the practice of crop production under conditions of deficient rainfall, estimated that about 25 percent of the land surface of the world had a rainfall and temperature such that dry-land farming practices could be used. The most effective methods of conserving moisture were timely and clean tillage, summer fallow, conservation of crop residues, contour plowing, and spreading the runoff from occasional rains by means of dikes and terraces. But equally important with conservation of water in the soil was the efficient utilization of this water for crop growth.

This involved several factors including (1) choice of suitable drought-resisting varieties, (2) time of seeding, (3) rate of seeding, and (4) elimination or reduction of weed growth.

As to the first two the answer could only be found by local investigations. Myers concluded (*1*, p. 27) that the chief shortcomings in Middle East dry-farming practice were, first, use of excessive quantities of seed, resulting in waste and lowering of yields per acre; and, second, failure to check weed growth. "Clean fallow prepared on time and kept free of weeds is absolutely essential to proper utilization of dry land resources in the Middle East."

Commenting on Myers' paper, Keen agreed that the creation of a dry-mulch surface by cultivation does little or nothing to prevent loss of moisture by evaporation. Its main purpose was simply to destroy weeds and prevent them using up moisture and soil nutrients. On the relative advantages of deep and shallow plowing, he was not wholly in agreement with the view that deep plowing to a depth of a foot or more was always wasteful and uneconomical. In certain areas of Palestine experiments had shown that very deep plowing, to a depth of two or three feet, was well worth while, probably because it improved the drainage of the soil and prevented it becoming waterlogged. But he agreed that in relatively rainless areas no appreciable crop increase was obtained by deep plowing and he welcomed the prospect of properly controlled experiments in the Beersheba district to compare the traditional Arab method of scratching the surface of the soil with a nail plow with the normal Western method of plowing with a tractor-drawn moldboard.

That even the most primitive methods of cultivation, if they have stood the test of thousands of years, may be well suited to special areas, was brought out both by Lowe's paper on dry farming near Beersheba and by Hartley's picture of dry farming in the western highlands of the Aden Protectorate, where conditions are similar to those found in Yemen and in Asir in Saudi Arabia. In these parts of southern Arabia a simple set of farm instruments had been evolved well suited for growing millet, sorghum, wheat, and barley in an area where the rainfall is uncertain and averages only about 300 millimeters (*1*, pp. 37, 39):

The plough is a light wooden pole-draught implement shod with a flattened iron—nowadays mild-steel—share of about 1½ feet in length and of 14 lbs. weight. This plough does not invert the soil but lifts and stirs it. For sowing, a drill attachment comprising a funnel and tube down which the seed is fed by the sower is rigged to the plough, and this efficient arrangement allows seed to be run in behind the plough at the depths demanded by varying conditions of moisture in the soil.

For making field embankments and leveling the soil the farmer uses "an oblong set of boards some 2½ feet long by 1½ feet deep attached at the corners by four chains which are led to the yoke." For shifting the soil the farmer stands on the upper edge of the board which is kept in a slanting position, and as his oxen move forward the soil is scooped out and hauled in front of the board. This Arab version of the bulldozer is remarkably effective for conserving moisture and trapping the runoff from adjoining uncultivated areas.

The discussion of irrigation, dry farming, and soil conservation has been summarized at some length, both because these topics must figure in the forefront of any survey of Middle East agriculture and because it is in these fields that the impact of Western, mainly American, ideas is most evident and is likely to prove most far-reaching. On the more difficult question of how modern techniques can be used to improve the position of the fellah, the Conference was less explicit; but there were useful contributions on agricultural education, on extension services, and on the plans of the Egyptian government for setting up rural-welfare centers and agricultural centers. There was also a forceful appeal from two Egyptian health specialists that in making plans for irrigation the risk of spreading malaria and bilharziasis, as had happened in Egypt, should not be overlooked. Some of these points will be taken up in the following chapter.

## CITATIONS

*1* MESC, *The Proceedings of the Conference on Middle East Agricultural Development, Cairo, February 7th–10th, 1944* (Agr. Rpt. No. 6, Cairo, 1944).

*2* Ahmed Sousa, *Iraq Irrigation Handbook, Part I: The Euphrates* (Baghdad, Dir. Gen. Irrigation, 1944); cited by Doreen Warriner, *Land and Poverty in the Middle East* (Royal Inst. Internatl. Affairs, London, 1948).

*3* R. R. Nathan, D. Gass, and D. Creamer, *Palestine, Problem and Promise* (New York, 1947).

## CHAPTER 33

# BETTER USE OF RESOURCES

Few if any countries in the world can claim to make the best use of their resources. But in the Middle East it is only too evident that poverty and ill-health are largely due to failure to make the best use of land and water and failure to apply scientific knowledge. Organization of agricultural research is inadequate. There is need for a great expansion of experimental work in the field and in the laboratory, and for scientifically trained staff both to conduct research and to advise the producers. In the less densely populated areas millions of hectares are waiting to be developed by irrigation and by better methods of cultivation; and everywhere there is scope for improvement by such well-tried methods as use of better seeds, introduction of new crops, mechanization and better implements, scientific use of fertilizers, control of grazing, and eradication of pests and diseases of plants and animals.

Few countries again can claim to have achieved such a balance between growth of population and development of resources that per capita real income clearly rises. Technical advances in production need to go hand in hand with advances in public health, education, child welfare, and improvement in the status of women. All these are beginning to take root in the Middle East, but the general picture is still one of poverty, illiteracy, and a primitive pattern of living among the masses with only a small fraction of the population reaching a Western standard of living. The result of applying modern techniques has too often been a rapid increase of wealth accompanied by a correspondingly rapid increase of population. Both the national income and the population of Egypt have approximately doubled in two generations. The soil produces twice as much but has twice as many to support. As Keen says (*1*, p. 109): "The peasant is imprisoned within the walls of his own agricultural system: year by year his numbers grow and the walls remain." Economic progress in agriculture has mainly centered round production for the world markets of cotton (in Egypt) and of citrus fruits (in Palestine). There are few industries to provide outlets for the growing population and peasant agriculture is still largely for family subsistence rather than for urban markets. Irrigation schemes and land reclamation have increased the area of fertile land; the worst forms of disease and pestilence have been controlled; and veterinary science has been applied to the prevention of livestock disease. But these achievements have been largely neutralized by increase of the human and animal population, which has aggravated the worst features of absentee landlordism and fragmentation of holdings.

The Conference on Middle East Agricultural Development was attended by two British scientists, Keen and Worthington, whose reports to the Middle East Supply Center (MESC) on Middle East agricultural development and science (*1*; *2*) were published after the war. A companion volume on rural education and welfare was written by Allen of the Near East Foundation (*3*), who also took part in the Conference. Another book, written by Warriner (*4*), a member of MESC's staff, deals with land tenure and the economic position of the peasantry. Some of their most important conclusions and recommendations will be summarized in this chapter.

### LAND REFORM

Among his specific proposals Keen puts first the need for reform of the present semifeudal system of land tenure. No system of agriculture can be progressive and responsive to the application of scientific methods unless it is based on an economic farming unit. In the Middle East, the peasant holding often consists of a scattered collection of small plots, which may vary from time to time as redistribution takes place. Registration of title and consolidation of holdings is the first step in reform and is overdue in many parts of the Middle East; but this by itself is not enough. The creation of small holdings, whether freehold or rented, provides no remedy unless the holdings are of a minimum size and cannot be subdivided; but everywhere in the Middle East the laws of inheritance and family division of property need to be modified if the technical conditions of agriculture are not to be frustrated by pressure of population. When the density of population reaches a certain point, as in some provinces of India, production tends to fall not only per man but per acre of land. The soil is exhausted by being called upon to feed too many people and animals.

The cure proposed by Keen for the chronic disease of uneconomic farm units is that the governments should acquire large areas of land from the owners, either by purchase or on long lease. The areas would then be farmed as a large estate either by a public corporation acting as landlord, as in the Gezira Cotton Scheme in Sudan, or by a co-operative society consisting of the former peasant owners or tenants as members. The object would be to give the cultivator both security of tenure and some inducement to adopt improved practices and raise the value of his share in the joint enterprise. It would abolish the evils of absentee landlordism and excessive subdivision of the land. Keen suggests that a public corporation should be set up which would take over areas for initial development and training of personnel and then hand over responsibility to a co-operative society of tenant farmers. It would start in the less populous areas so as to simplify the progressive settlement of each area. Resettlement and transfer of population would be facilitated by movement of whole families and villages from areas where reform and reconditioning are most needed.

## EDUCATION

Side by side with land reform, rural education must be pressed forward. Emphasis is placed by Keen and Allen on the training of rural leaders. "Men—and women—drawn from the rural areas, not educated out of their rural outlook, but given a simple training and refresher courses in better agricultural methods, rural education, and welfare" (*1*, p. 12). Worthington refers (*2*, p. 189) to the possible impact of education on population trends. Elementary education, combined with child welfare, besides fostering a desire for a better life, may indirectly contribute to a fall in the birth rate and a reduction in infant mortality.

## SOIL SCIENCE

Keen was able to report that there was general agreement among Middle East experts as to the main lines of future research and development. Egypt and Sudan, Palestine and Cyprus, have shown outstanding achievements, but there is need for more fundamental research and controlled farming experiments. In many fields, but not in all, the solution of the problem is known and the main task is to persuade governments and cultivators to adopt the right techniques. More knowledge is needed about soil types and about the behavior and proper treatment of soils brought under irrigation. Agricultural departments should include a division of soil specialists staffed by qualified research workers and technologists, as is already the case in Egypt and Sudan. Closer association is needed between agricultural and irrigation authorities. Irrigation engineers are not, as a rule, familiar with modern soil science. There is need for a graduate school for hydrological engineers with facilities for postgraduate studies.

Methods of tillage and improvement of traditional implements need study. For dry farming, the primitive ox-drawn plow has certain advantages over deep plowing with tractors. Weed control in the early stages of crop growth is more important than deep plowing. Replacement of draft animals by tractors or small plow units is handicapped so long as present systems of land tenure persist.

### SOIL CONSERVATION

Soil conservation and study of soil-erosion problems have received too little attention in the past. The most important single factor has been denudation of the hilly regions in Palestine, Lebanon, and Persia by destruction of forests, which has been going on for centuries. This has been accentuated in recent years through increased demand for firewood and timber and through overgrazing by goats. Reforestation needs to be pressed forward and given more financial support. Remedies for soil erosion are well known and include contour plowing, terracing of hillsides, control of grazing, and restrictions on fuel and fodder collection. The building of highways, bridges, and culverts may sometimes cause preventable erosion. Keen proposes the setting up of an interdepartmental soil-conservation committee in each territory along the lines of those existing in Palestine, Cyprus, and Sudan. The proposed Middle East Council of Agriculture would have provided a useful forum for exchange of experience and technical advice.

### PLANT NUTRITION

Many problems connected with plant nutrition and the proper manuring of crops under tropical and semitropical conditions remain to be studied. Analogies drawn from experience in temperate climates may be erroneous under Middle East conditions. The investigations of plant physiologists have been mainly concentrated on valuable crops of cotton and citrus fruit produced for world markets. Under irrigation conditions the most important set of problems arises in connection with the influence of salts in the soil on plant nutrition and growth, and with the best manurial treatment and drainage systems required to counteract these conditions in nonirrigated areas where dry farming is practiced. There are important problems, such as the effect of organic manure on semitropical soils, the effect of legumes on succeding cereal crops, and the extent to which the growing of mixed crops in the same field may serve as a substitute for the more normal system of rotation.

### SEED SELECTION

Plant genetics and seed selection have been developed in connection with Egyptian cotton, but other crops, particularly cereals, pulses, oilseeds, and fodder crops, have received too little attention. As regards fruits, nuts, and vegetables, there is scope for further development of experimental stations and for the distribution at low prices of young trees, seedlings, and vegetable seeds.

Wartime experiments in seed production have on the whole been encouraging and there are areas in Palestine, Lebanon, and parts of Iraq which would be suitable if a seed trade is to be built up. Expert guidance is needed both in the technical and commercial fields.

The citrus industry in Palestine has probably reached its maximum extent with about 15 million trees on 75,000 acres, but it may be possible to extend the season of marketing by introducing early-ripening varieties of oranges.

### PESTS AND DISEASES

The study of pests and diseases has been little developed outside the special fields of cotton and citrus fruits. There is a wide variety of diseases and pests apart from periodical locust attacks which cause great damage to growing crops and to stored products. It would be impossible and wasteful for all Middle East countries to have fully equipped plant-pathology research stations, but a Middle East council of agriculture could do much to plan a co-ordinated attack on these problems for the Middle East as a whole.

### ANIMAL HUSBANDRY

Livestock improvement lags behind work on veterinary problems in the Middle East. Work on cattle has been mainly confined to the crossing of native stock with European breeds. There are a few examples of private efforts to grade up native cattle to obtain higher milk yields. Crossing with breeds from countries like India, where conditions resemble the Middle East, has not yet been attempted. For sheep and goats the main work has been the introduction of Merino and Angora stock. There was some development of a pig industry in Palestine during the war, but the market is naturally limited by Jewish and Moslem custom. Successful work in Palestine and Egypt has shown that native poultry can be improved by selective breeding. Egypt had a considerable egg-export trade before the war, and increased production and consumption of eggs would provide one of the quickest means of improving nutrition both in town and country. Methods of distributing improved livestock need to be developed. Cyprus has a system of supplying good-class sires for breeding purposes and in Palestine there was a scheme for the distribution of improved breeds of chicks.

### MIXED FARMING

Livestock improvement is linked with the problem of fodder crops and the study of existing pastoral conditions. There are possibilities of introducing new types of grasses and fodder crops suitable for both dry farming and irrigation farming. The place of fodder crops in different rotation systems deserves special attention. Agricultural development in many parts of the Middle East depends on the introduction of some form of mixed farming. At present, animal husbandry and crop husbandry are not well integrated and are almost competing rivals; but Jewish workers in Palestine have shown what can be done under the guidance of experts in animal nutrition and livestock improvement working alongside experts in fodder crops and plant nutrition.

### REGIONAL PLANNING

Planning and development are limited by political and financial handicaps and by lack of experienced administration. Worthington, who deals with scientific and technological problems outside the field of agriculture, emphasizes the need for planning and draws attention to an interesting experiment in Cyprus. Here, a land-utilization committee was set up in 1943 which included experts concerned with forestry, agriculture, land surveys, and water supplies. A plan was made to recondition three typical villages—one in the mountains, one in the foothills, and a third in the plains—by reforming the land-tenure system, abolishing strip farming, planning the use of the land, and intensifying health and education services. He also refers to an experiment in Sudan to develop all-round self-sufficiency in a native area 1,000 miles from the coast. In many Arab villages improvements depend on restoring a better balance between human population, animal numbers, forage, water, arable land, and supplies of fuel and timber. Examples of faulty experiments include the settlement of Armenians in Lebanon and of Assyrian refugees in Syria.

On the other hand, settlements of Jews in Palestine and of Italians in Tripolitania had been successful.

Large-scale planning should start with the home and the village as the unit, and then cover a whole country or river basin on lines similar to the Tennessee Valley Authority; but Worthington emphasizes that scientific and economic developments depend upon the growth of civic responsibility and a spirit of public service.

### RIVERS AND WATER

Water is required for domestic supply, livestock, irrigation, transport, and power. In general, irrigation should have precedence over power, since plenty of oil is available locally. Five of the seven chief rivers in the Middle East are shared by more than one country. International arrangements are therefore required. In the case of the Nile, co-operation is effective. The Tigris and Euphrates, with the Karun, concern four countries—Turkey, Syria, Iraq, and Persia. Flood-control and irrigation problems have been much less thoroughly studied here than in the valley of the Nile. There is need for better collection of hydrological data to form the basis of future programs.

The use of the Jordan was dominated by the hydroelectric scheme of the Palestine Electric Corporation and this conflicted with its full development for irrigation. Some progress was made during the war in the development of the Orontes Valley in Lebanon and Syria. Draining the swampy land of the Ghab would affect the river's flow in Turkey. An important question was whether it was advisable to drain such areas in a dry country, or whether it might not be better to impound the water in a lake where fisheries could be developed and the head of water used for power or for irrigation. Good progress was made in Cyprus during the war in securing the co-operation of peasant farmers in maintaining small-scale irrigation schemes.

Hydroelectric developments offer less scope in the Middle East than elsewhere. Schemes which would not conflict with the use of water for irrigation include the proposal to use the Qattara Depression in Egypt and to bring the Mediterranean into the Dead Sea by an underground tunnel through the Judean hills. During the war the British army's geologists and engineers developed many underground-water supplies. The traditional systems of tapping underground water include the *qanats* (underground watercourses) of Persia and the chains of wells in Cyprus. There are possibilities of developing subterranean reservoirs for storing water in the dry season. Sinking boreholes to provide water for domestic purposes and for stock grazing and small-scale irrigation could be further developed.

Roofed reservoirs were in use in the Nabatean Kingdom. Fencing and roofing of water holes, as already practiced in Sudan, would reduce pollution and losses from evaporation. The water supply in many small towns and villages is extremely bad. A pure supply piped to fountains in villages is essential both for health and for relieving the burden on the women, who have to fetch water in jars from the village pond. The experience of armies during the war should help in problems relating to the purification of water from rivers and other sources and also to questions of distillation of salt water and condensation of water from the air.

The settlement of water rights is an urgent problem that needs solution. In some countries the government has taken over all water from major sources and arranges distribution. Elsewhere special legislation is needed.

There is a center for training water engineers in the Fouad University at Cairo but, in general, hydrological engineering in the Middle East is backward. A central clearinghouse for information on water supply and hydrology would be useful.

As regards rainfall, Worthington concludes that, according to the weight of evidence, there appears to have been no great change in climatic conditions during the last 4,000 years. But during historical times there has undoubtedly been some deterioration through deforestation, soil erosion, and destruction of old irrigation works in the Euphrates Valley during the Mongol invasions.

### FORESTRY

The two main needs of the Middle East are water and shade. The latter is mainly provided by date palms and olive trees. High forest is limited to very few areas, namely, parts of Ethiopia and Sudan, the hillsides above the Caspian Sea in Persia, a corner of Iraq which runs up into the Kurdish mountains, and small mountainous areas in Syria, Lebanon, and Cyprus. Some forest reserves contain only shrubs and thickets which never grow to high trees. The greatest value of forests is to maintain water supplies and conserve soil. For centuries there has been progressive denudation of forests owing to cutting of timber and firewood and overgrazing by goats.

Afforestation in the Middle East is a laborious task. The first need is to restrict the grazing of goats; this has been accomplished in some forest areas of Cyprus. The goat is a valuable animal, both to nomads and to settled peasants, and the substitution of fencing and tethering for uncontrolled grazing is bound to take time.

Legislation to enforce the substitution of oil fuel for wood in lime burning and other industries is now operating in Cyprus and was proposed in Palestine. Under the Italians in Eritrea and Ethiopia, all cutting of trees was prohibited except under license, and for every tree felled, 10 had to be planted. This system was continued under the British Military Administration in Eritrea. Control of this kind is urgently needed in other Middle East countries. There is need for more systematic planning of land so that forest areas may be developed in such a way as to benefit agriculture. In southern Lebanon and parts of the Anti-Lebanon Mountains, there are areas now almost bare of trees which should be changed back into forest. Palestine is urgently in need of more forest cover. Natural regeneration, even in advanced areas, is extremely slow. In Transjordan, seeding of Mediterranean oak has been tried in place of growing young trees in nurseries. In Palestine, an area of some 2,000 acres on the western shore of Lake Tiberias was taken over by the soil-conservation board and then terraced and planted by the forest department. Tree planting was undertaken by the British Military Administration in Eritrea, and eucalyptus trees were planted along the railway joining Palestine and Egypt. The difficulty is to get the public to co-operate. In Beirut, a number of trees were planted in 1945 but within a few weeks the sticks to which the young trees were tied had been stolen for firewood and within a month or two, the trees themselves had all been taken.

Useful timber is produced by the forest departments in Cyprus and in Sudan, and some wood for plows, carts, furniture, and boatbuilding is obtained from the Mediterranean oak and other trees in Palestine and Syria.

Among forest products, gum arabic and tanning materials are obtained from Sudan; incense from Yemen; and *dom* nuts, used for buttons, from Sudan and Eritrea. Rubber was obtained in small quantity during the war from wild vines in the Ethiopian forests. In the Syrian Desert large quantities of the kali plant (glasswort) are obtained, which yields caustic soda, potassium chloride, and other salts when burned. The ash was in great demand during the war for soapmaking in Damascus. Derris powder is obtained from the roots of a climbing plant found in Ethiopia.

There is scope for development of village woodlands and plantations. In Persia, northern Iraq, and recently in Syria, poplar trees are grown in small irrigated areas and on canal banks. Trees may be usefully planted in swampy areas as an antimalarial measure. Olives in Palestine and Lebanon and carobs in Cyprus provide wood as well as fruit and nuts.

There are other trees which can be developed to provide fodder for animals. The Christ's-thorn, which is regarded as an inferior scrub in Palestine, is carefully tended in Yemen and Aden Protectorate and is pruned annually for fodder during the dry season.

There is urgent need for more trained personnel and for the establishment of training centers for junior forest officers in the Middle East. Worthington suggested that Cyprus might provide a suitable site.

### FISHERIES

Worthington points out that fish production in the Middle East is low in relation to the extent of seaboard and inland waters. It amounts to less than 1.5 kilos per head, compared with the world average of 7 kilos, and might at least be doubled. Fish provide high-class protein, and fish production could be developed with less effort than a corresponding increase in other forms of food production.

Sardine fisheries and trawling could be developed in the eastern Mediterranean, but the Red Sea is potentially more productive. During the war the Palestine government established an experimental fishing industry in the Gulf of Aqaba. Fish caught by Arab fishermen at the mouth of the Gulf of Aqaba were taken by a ship of 150 tons fitted with refrigerating plant to the village of Aqaba, where a quick-freezing and ice-making factory was set up. The fish were taken in refrigerated trucks to cold stores at Lydda and there sold to retailers in the towns. The installations and methods of distribution were expensive, and it was doubtful whether it would be economical when normal imports became possible. Farther down the Red Sea there has been little development owing to lack of local demand and the great distance from markets. In peacetime *Trochus* and other shellfish were exported from Port Sudan to China. There are possibilities of developing fisheries in the southern parts of the Red Sea along the coasts of Eritrea and Yemen. The fish consist mainly of shark, tunny, and sardines. In Aden Protectorate, fisheries are well developed and the coastal Arabs, and even their camels and cattle, eat large quantities of fish. An extreme shortage of fishing gear during the war reduced the supply of fish and contributed to the serious famine in the Hadhramaut.

The Persian Gulf might provide most productive fishing grounds, but little has yet been done to develop them. A fish-canning factory was established at Bandar Abbas in Persia on the northern shore at the mouth of the Gulf. The Persian government had a controlling interest and most of the production was exported during the war to other countries. The Anglo-Iranian Oil Company, recognizing the need for protein food among their staff of 4,000 and their labor corps of 100,000, organized a fishery scheme which produced 800 tons per annum for consumption at their refineries at Abadan. Both the oil company and the Iraq government were hoping to develop a trawler industry in the Persian Gulf.

In the Caspian Sea there was a flourishing fishing industry divided between the Persian and Soviet governments. Persia was mainly interested in the luxury trade in caviar. The Russians had done much to maintain the Caspian fisheries and every year increased the stock of fish, including sturgeon, by releasing many million fry.

The inland fisheries of the Middle East, although their areas are small compared with the sea, are of great importance. The inland waters of Egypt, with an area covering about one-fifth that of the agricultural land, produce about 25,000 tons of fish, which is far greater than the amount of sea fish landed. The bulk of the catch comes from the Delta Lake fisheries. Worthington urges that the nutritional value of the fish from these lakes should be carefully weighed before continuing the present policy of draining the lakes to make more arable land. In Sudan there were large undeveloped resources in the Nile, particularly the great reservoirs on the Blue Nile and White Nile. Insufficient attention had been given to the potential value of fresh-water fish as a source of protein food. Every acre of fresh water in Sudan and Egypt should produce from 10 to 40 kilos of fish per annum.

This was equally true of the Tigris and Euphrates, where between 5,000 and 10,000 tons per annum were produced, and this could be much increased. Before the war there was an export of fresh-water fish from Iraq across the desert to Tel Aviv in Palestine. The completion of the railway from Baghdad to Tel Aviv may enable this trade to be developed. Lake Tiberias in Palestine is still an important fishery and with the growth in population overfishing became serious. This was being remedied by limiting the number of fishermen and the size of mesh in nets. Production was about 400 tons per annum, or one-fifth of the total fish production of Palestine.

Other valuable fisheries were to be found in Lake Hula up the Jordan Valley, and in Lake Homs and the Ghab in Syria, which probably produce about 500 tons per annum. The effect on future food supply and nutrition of draining Lake Hula and the Ghab should be carefully considered. Any reduction of fisheries would accentuate the present lack of animal protein in Middle East diets.

Fish farming in the form of culture of carp in ponds had been developed in Palestine, where about 400 tons per annum were produced during the war. The carp is probably a more economical converter, and yields more high-class protein per unit area, than any domestic animal. Further research is needed and government control is required to deal with water rights and prevention of malaria. Fish farming is also being developed in Egypt, Syria, and Cyprus, and may have a future in Iraq, Persia, and Sudan.

In general, there is great need for international co-operation and assistance from outside. In his book, Worthington proposed the establishment of a bureau of fisheries, to serve as a clearinghouse of information and to publish a journal of abstracts of fishery literature. Since his book was published the Fisheries Division of the Food and Agriculture Organization of the United Nations has undertaken this task and has provided much valuable technical advice and assistance in the development of Middle East fisheries.

## NUTRITION

There is little detailed knowledge about nutrition in the Middle East, but it is probable that with a few local exceptions the whole area must be classed as one of the worst-nourished parts of the world, deriving more than 70 percent of its calories from cereals. Famine conditions and insufficiency of food mainly affect nomads and dry-land cultivators when reserves are exhausted. Malnutrition in the irrigated areas comes from unbalanced diets rather than lack of quantity.

Studies of food habits by spot surveys are needed, of the type of some recent studies in Palestine. Bedouin Arabs present an interesting problem and reports vary as to their nutrition, which is often far below the minimum. The safeguard in their diet is the supply of milk and milk products. In Egypt, the chief deficiency diseases are anemia, rickets, pellagra, and osteomalacia. Lack of calcium and shortage of protective foods is the main evil, particularly in cash-crop areas where cotton and sugar are grown. Following the Hot Springs conference, Egypt decided to establish a laboratory for nutritional research. This was the first in the Middle East. Iraq and Persia have problems similar to that of Egypt but less is known about them.

### HEALTH AND MEDICAL SERVICES

Health and medical services are extremely backward and conditions in hospitals are unsatisfactory; the rural areas are particularly ill served. Egypt requires two or three times as many doctors as there are today; to attain this, four times as many as now must be trained during the next 30 years. Medical students from the Middle East should be sent to Europe and America.

Before the war malaria was probably the cause of more ill-health and debility than any other disease. A serious epidemic broke out in 1943 in Upper Egypt, where malnutrition of workers on sugar estates was a contributing factor. Malaria control is closely associated with irrigation and requires co-operation between doctors, entomologists, engineers, and agriculturalists. In Egypt, bilharziasis affects something like three-quarters of the population and could be controlled either by destroying the snail vectors or by improved sanitary habits. Hookworm and tapeworm are also rife in Egypt. Typhus and other louse-borne diseases were controlled during the war by vaccination and destruction of lice by DDT. Eye diseases, typhoid, and dysentery are common throughout the Middle East and though curative treatment has been greatly improved, preventive measures, which involve tackling the fly problem, lag behind.

### STATISTICS AND SOCIAL STUDIES

Only in Egypt, Palestine, and Cyprus were population figures and vital statistics at all adequate. The statistical department of the Palestine government under the direction of George E. F. Wood, and later of P. J. Loftus, had acquired an outstanding reputation.

Both Worthington and Keen underline the need for improvement of Middle East economic and social statistics and refer to the proposal adopted at MESC's Statistical Conference in 1943 for establishing a permanent Middle East statistical office, which would concern itself both with the improvement of official statistics and with the training of qualified staff. The Statistical Conference drew special attention to the importance of demographic as well as of agricultural statistics in the Middle East.

Sociological studies are needed to reveal what is happening and to guide administration and planning for improvement. This is a field in which the Institute of Rural Life at the American University at Beirut has done pioneer work. In Sudan, the government has sponsored qualified scientists in sociological research work. Two of them, E. E. Evans-Pritchard and S. F. Nadel, were employed during the war by the British Military Administration, the first in Cyrenaica and the latter in Eritrea.

After this condensed account of the diagnosis and treatment of Middle East ills prescribed by the doctors of science, it is time to return to the economics of war and its aftermath. Measured by national indexes we shall find that there was little to show for all the efforts to expand production, except—and this is the important point—that there was no catastrophic fall in the total supply of food. Under conditions of war involving severe reduction of imports, that was no mean achievement on the part of Middle East producers and agriculturalists.

## CITATIONS

*1* B. A. Keen, *The Agricultural Development of the Middle East* (London, 1946).

*2* E. B. Worthington, *Middle East Science . . .* (London, 1946).

*3* H. B. Allen, *Rural Education and Welfare in the Middle East . . .* (London, 1946).

*4* Doreen Warriner, *Land and Poverty in the Middle East* (Royal Inst. Internatl. Affairs, London, 1948).

# PART VII

# RETROSPECT AND PROSPECT

## CHAPTER 34

# IMPACT OF THE WAR

This account of how the Middle East was fed during the war has branched out into a number of related fields—strategic, political, financial, and technological—and has involved a survey of data ranging over a score or more of countries. It is now time to bring the picture into focus and to offer some concluding observations on the impact of the war on Middle East agriculture.

### THE CHALLENGE

In the summer of 1940 it seemed hardly possible that the Middle East could be defended against the combined resources of Germany and Italy. After the fall of France and the entry of Italy into the war in June 1940, while Mussolini was planning the invasion of Egypt, Hitler was preparing to invade Britain. In Churchill's words (*1*, pp. 417–18):

> The eyes of the world were fixed upon the fate of the British Island, upon the gathering of the invading German armies, and upon the drama of the struggle for air mastery. . . . Nevertheless, the War Cabinet were determined to defend Egypt against all comers with whatever resources could be spared from the decisive struggle at home. . . . It is odd that, while at the time everyone concerned was quite calm and cheerful, writing about it afterwards makes one shiver.

The fateful question that faced the Prime Minister and the British Cabinet was how far the citadel of Britain could safely be "denuded" in order to defend the Middle East (*1*, p. 422). Had it not been for the decision to reinforce General Wavell's hard-pressed forces, there can be little doubt that Hitler and Mussolini would have realized their ambition of seizing Egypt and using it as a steppingstone for the conquest of the Middle East. From there it would have been a short step to domination of India and Africa, and to invasion of Russia from the south.

Once it had been decided to send reinforcements to the Middle East, no longer through the Mediterranean but right around the Cape, shipping shortage and losses from submarine attacks became the crucial factors determining the fate of the Middle East; and so they continued to be until the Mediterranean was reopened three years later. The greatest contribution that Middle East countries were able to make to their own defense was to cut down their civilian imports to the minimum, in order to release ships and port, road, and rail facilities for the transport of vast quantities of men and munitions.

To help governments regulate civilian imports and to ensure that Middle East countries would obtain their essential needs, the Middle East Supply Center (MESC) was created in April 1941. Within a short time the Germans had occupied Greece and Crete; Syria under Vichy control was placing air bases at their disposal; and German propaganda was stirring up Rashid Ali's revolt in Iraq. In June 1941 Russia was attacked and within a few months shipping had to be diverted in order to send munitions and supplies to her through Persia. During the three months April–June 1941, General Wavell was engaged in five simultaneous campaigns in Ethiopia, Libya, Greece, Syria, and Iraq. He had to retreat in Libya and met with disaster in Greece and Crete; but Egypt, Syria, Iraq, and the rest of the Middle East were saved from enemy occupation.

### MAINTENANCE OF FOOD SUPPLIES

For some months the threat of famine in the towns was added to the menace of enemy attack; for while the fate of the Middle East hung in the balance, the rains failed and hot winds scorched the ripening grain. In Turkey, Egypt, Syria, and Persia the grain crops of 1941 yielded 3 million tons less than the record harvests of 1939—a drop of 18 percent. Instead of having a surplus of over 100,000 tons of wheat for export to neighboring countries, as in 1940, these four countries received overseas wheat and flour imports of 250,000 tons in 1942. Total cereal imports into the Middle East and Turkey in that year required 643,000 tons of Allied tonnage—177,000 tons for the Allied forces and 466,000 for civilian consumption.

This unexpected and unwelcome drain on Allied shipping resources at so critical a time forcibly brought home to the authorities in London and Cairo the need for three main tasks for MESC: (1) expanding production to enable the Middle East to feed itself without imports; (2) centralizing imports and reserve stocks of cereals and other foods in the hands of the United Kingdom Commercial Corporation (UKCC) as the executive arm of MESC; and (3) organizing the collection of cereals at fixed prices to discourage hoarding and speculation.

After the experience of 1941/42, when emergency action had to be taken to stave off critical cereal shortages in Egypt and Syria, MESC got into its stride and established forward programing, centralized import of staple foods, and pooling of reserve stocks. The addition of Persia to MESC's sphere of responsibility in the second half of 1942 brought fresh problems. Bread riots in Teheran and breakdown of cereal collection, caused by dislocation of transport and rampant inflation, again necessitated diversion of Allied shipping. Programing of imports into Persia met with special difficulties owing to the weakness of internal controls and the lack of reliable statistics.

After many trials and setbacks cereal-collection schemes were successfully launched in Egypt, Syria, Persia, and Iraq—and on a more limited scale in Palestine, Transjordan, Cyprus, and Sudan—with the result that during the three years 1943–45 Middle East imports of wheat and flour from overseas averaged only 208,000 tons and were more than counterbalanced by exports of barley and rice from Iraq and Egypt. A major contribution to increased food production was made by Egypt, where a million acres were taken out of cotton in order to increase the area under cereals and to offset the drastic cut in fertilizer imports.

*Cereals.*—Before the war the eight countries for which figures are given in Appendix Table IV had an average grain production of just over 10 million tons. During the next seven years, 1939–45, there was only one year when the total fell below this prewar average—in 1941, 10 percent below. Weather conditions were more important than any other factor in causing good or bad crops.

Good crops in 1939 and 1940 resulted in a surplus for export which reached a record figure of 370,000 tons of grain in 1940. The poor harvests of 1941 led to net imports of 176,000 tons in 1941 and nearly 400,000 in 1942. In 1943, in spite of less-than-average wheat crops, barley and rice production was enough to produce a net surplus of 105,000 tons of grain for export; and in 1944 and 1945 wheat imports were all but counterbalanced by barley and rice exports. Detailed figures of production and trade, 1934–38 and 1939–45, are given in Appendix Tables IV and V and are summarized on the following page, in thousand metric tons.

From this tabulation, 1941 stands out as the only year when supplies, ignoring changes in stocks, fell below the prewar average. But in fact the position varied in different countries, and monthly

| Year | Production | Net trade | Apparent supply |
|---|---|---|---|
| Average 1934–38 | 10,362 | −271 | 10,091 |
| 1939 | 11,000 | −208 | 10,800 |
| 1940 | 10,400 | −370 | 10,000 |
| 1941 | 9,200 | +176 | 9,400 |
| 1942 | 10,600 | +397 | 11,000 |
| 1943 | 10,600 | −105 | 10,500 |
| 1944 | 11,000 | + 19 | 11,000 |
| 1945 | 11,900 | − 5 | 11,900 |
| Average 1940–45 | 10,600 | + 19 | 10,600 |

variations in stocks and arrivals were of more importance than the annual average. The figures of production are the amounts harvested each year and available during the succeeding twelve months, whereas the trade figures are for calendar years. Thus, imports in 1942 were mainly concentrated in the first six months of the year and owing to the better harvest of 1942, imports in the cereal year 1942/43 were quite moderate.

MESC sources give six-month shipments of cereals from overseas in 1942 and 1943, divided into civilian and army supplies. They were nearly all wheat and flour but included some rice from India. They are shown below, in thousand long tons:

| Period | Civilian | Armed forces | Total |
|---|---|---|---|
| Jan./June 1942 | 400.6 | 115.7 | 516.3 |
| July/Dec. 1942 | 65.1 | 61.5 | 126.6 |
| Total 1942 | 465.7 | 177.2 | 642.9 |
| Jan./June 1943 | 63.6 | 28.9 | 92.5 |
| July/Dec. 1943 | 105.4 | 141.3 | 246.7 |
| Total 1943 | 169.0 | 170.2 | 339.2 |

These figures are the quantities consigned to UKCC during the period, and include some provision for countries not included in Appendix Table V. They serve to bring out an important point: whereas the armed forces were permitted, and indeed encouraged, to buy wheat from Egypt in the first 18 months of the war, in the years 1942 and 1943, when shipping was scarcest, their cereal requirements (apart from some Egyptian rice) were obtained from overseas and not from Middle East production. Average cereal imports for the forces in these two years were sufficient to provide a daily ration of about half a kilo of flour for a ration strength approaching a million men (*2*, p. 218).

*Rice.*—The main problem with rice was to maintain exports from Egypt and thus help to meet the critical wartime shortage in Ceylon. After the Japanese conquest of Southeast Asia all rice-importing countries had to cut down their supplies. The United Kingdom, which imported 114,000 tons before the war, received less than half her normal quantity in 1942 and about a third in 1944. Palestine, Syria and Lebanon, Cyprus, and Sudan, which between them imported 40,000 tons in 1934–38, received only 10 percent of this quantity in 1942 and 30 percent in 1943 and 1944.

Egypt made an important contribution toward meeting the shortage by diverting acreage under cotton to expansion of rice. After a bumper crop in 1942, 50 percent higher than the prewar average, and good crops in the following years, she was able to export in 1943–45 at the rate of 100,000 tons a year, in addition to supplying the Indian troops in North Africa and elsewhere in the Middle East. Persia's production of rice, which was mainly concentrated in the Russian zone of occupation, fell during the war, and her exports in the critical years 1942 and 1943 were little more than half the prewar average. This reduction, combined with cessation of exports from India, caused an acute shortage in Saudi Arabia and the Persian Gulf Sheikdoms, which could only be met by inducing these countries to accept an unfamiliar diet of wheat flour. In 1944 Iraq came to their rescue by releasing part of her expanded production.

Egypt's exports of rice could have been larger if she had not chosen to retain part of her expanded output to meet increased home demand. Consumption per head increased by about 25 percent at a time when Palestine, Cyprus, Syria, and Lebanon were getting less than a third of their prewar supplies. But since rice and other bread grains were to some extent interchangeable, the Egyptian government could argue that increased consumption of rice reduced her own need for wheat imports and thus indirectly helped her neighbors.

*Sugar.*—Both as a source of calories and as a semiluxury which served as an incentive to producers to market their crops, sugar had a high priority. Though world supplies were not reduced to the same extent by Japanese conquests as in the case of rice—Java was the only important source cut off from the Allies—sugar made heavy demands on tonnage. In the United Kingdom consumption was reduced by rationing to about 65 percent of the peacetime level. Even in the United States and Canada sugar was rationed; imports in 1942 were restricted to 60 percent of prewar for the United States and 75 percent for Canada, solely to save shipping. Cuba's exports of sugar in 1942 were reduced to 70 percent of normal.

In the light of these reductions in North America and Britain, MESC was fortunate in getting as much sugar as it did for the Middle East. In 1942 net imports into the area were 63 percent of the 1934–38 average and in the worst year, 1943, 52 percent. Egypt was able to expand her production, and in spite of sugar rationing her consumption per head remained about the same as before the war. Palestine had two years, 1942 and 1944, when consumption per head fell to about 70 percent of prewar but for the remaining years it averaged only 10 percent below. In the two years 1942 and 1943, Cyprus, Syria and Lebanon, Persia, and Iraq, had the severest cut in consumption per head—to about half the prewar level.

*Fats and oils.*—The crucial factors in the vegetable-oil situation were, first, the reduction by 60 percent in Egyptian cottonseed output caused by cotton-acreage restriction in 1942; second, uncertainty and wide annual fluctuations of olive-oil production in Palestine, Cyprus, Syria, and Lebanon; and third, the extreme difficulty of obtaining reliable figures of total production of fats and oils, particularly of animal fats.

In the early war years Egypt was able to maintain and even to improve upon her prewar consumption by reducing her exports of cottonseed and cottonseed oil. Later supplies fluctuated close to the prewar level.

Palestine's worst year was in 1941, when the poor olive crop yielded only 26 percent of a normal supply. In this year consumption per head fell to about 70 percent of normal; but with good olive crops and higher imports in 1942 and 1943, supplies were sufficient to bring consumption above the prewar level. The year 1944 was again bad for olives, and larger imports were obtained to make up the deficit. Edible oils other than olive oil were rationed in Palestine.

Syria and Lebanon had two bad years—1941 and 1944—when olive-oil production fell far below normal; but exceptionally good crops in 1942 and 1943 provided a sufficient carryover to make them virtually independent of imports in 1943 and 1944. Average consumption per head was approximately the same or above the prewar level except in 1942 and 1944.

Persia and Iraq were self-supporting in fats and oils before the war, with a small net export. During the war they received small imports of technical oils for soapmaking. There are no reliable data to show how far consumption per head was affected by variations in home production of oilseeds, but it seems probable that the supply of animal fats was reduced.

That there was no critical shortage of fats and oils in the Middle East was in the main due, first, to the special efforts made to step up cottonseed imports from Sudan and, second, to MESC's strenuous advocacy of Middle East claims for supplies from India and East Africa at a time when Britain's total supply of fats (including butter) was about 25 percent below the prewar level.

When one looks back at what happened to food and agriculture in the Middle East during the war and compares it with what happened in occupied Europe, the conclusion reached is that there was less disturbance to customary patterns of food consumption than might have been expected, in spite of crises and of what seemed at times an imminent risk of breakdown. This was in large part due to the recognition that management of food and agriculture had a vital contribution to make to the defense of the Middle East. Planning of food imports, collection and distribution of crops, movement of supplies by land and sea from one part of the area to another, control of prices, and rationing of urban consumers were all part of a combined operation to save the Middle East from the fate that befell occupied Europe.

During the three years 1941–43, when military operations, inflation, dislocation of transport, and shipping shortage caused the greatest interference with food supplies, the average level of food consumption per head was inevitably lower than the prewar average. It is impossible to give any statistical measurement of the extent of the over-all reduction. Lack of consumer goods, particularly textiles, was felt by urban and rural populations alike; but the shortage of food hit the urban population more than the rural. Except for sugar, tea, and to a less extent fats and oils, the food supply of the settled population of the villages, which is mainly grown for local consumption, was probably not much below normal. It was the town dwellers who had to go short and were most exposed to the risk of breakdown in supply. Bread riots occurred in Teheran, Ahwaz, and Damascus; and there were two occasions when the bread supply was in jeopardy in Cairo and Alexandria. Famine conditions, due to crop failure and necessitating urgent measures of relief, were experienced mainly in Hadhramaut in Aden Protectorate and to a less extent in the extreme northeast of British Somaliland. Unrest in the towns and complaints about high prices of food were a source of continual anxiety to governments in Egypt, Palestine, Cyprus, Syria, Lebanon, Persia, and

Iraq; but regulation of imports, cereal collection, food subsidies, and rationing schemes of varying efficiency, supplemented but not wholly frustrated by smuggling and black-market activities, prevented the situation getting out of hand and setting off an explosion of civil strife.

### FOOD AND INFANT MORTALITY

It has been emphasized by the World Health Organization of the United Nations that one of the best indications of the state of public health in a country is the infant-mortality rate. There is also some evidence to suggest that changes in this rate, particularly over short periods, are related to improvement or worsening in the food supply. It is interesting therefore to look at records of infant mortality during the war years and to compare them with the average for years before and after the war. Unfortunately such records are only available for three countries in the Middle East. These are tabulated below, together with the rates for Italy, the Netherlands, and the United Kingdom. The figures show deaths of infants under one year of age per thousand live births (*3*, pp. 320–27):

| | | | Palestine | | | | |
|---|---|---|---|---|---|---|---|
| Period | Egypt | Cyprus | Jews | Moslems | Italy | Netherlands | United Kingdom |
| Average 1934–38 . . . | 163.9 | 128.9 | 65.4 | 153.3 | 103.1 | 39.2 | 60.1 |
| 1939. . . . . | 161.2 | 98.2 | 54.0 | 121.5 | 97.0 | 33.7 | 53.6 |
| 1940. . . . . | 161.8 | 88.9 | 59.1 | 147.1 | 102.7 | 39.1 | 61.0 |
| 1941. . . . . | 150.2 | 107.6 | 55.6 | 131.7 | 115.2 | 43.6 | 63.3 |
| 1942. . . . . | 168.4 | 184.7 | 58.0 | 140.3 | 112.4 | 39.5 | 52.9 |
| 1943. . . . . | 160.2 | 120.8 | 44.1 | 113.1 | 115.1 | 40.1 | 51.9 |
| 1944. . . . . | 152.3 | 81.8 | 36.1 | 102.9 | 103.2 | 46.3 | 47.6 |
| 1945. . . . . | 152.8 | 81.0 | 35.8 | 93.9 | 103.1 | 79.7 | 48.8 |
| Average 1940–43 . . . | 160.1 | 125.5 | 54.2 | 133.1 | 111.3 | 40.6 | 57.3 |
| Average 1946–49 . . . | 135.4 | 68.7 | 30.7[a] | . . . | 79.3 | 32.1 | 39.1 |

[a] Average for 1946–47.

The most significant point that emerges from these figures is that in the four worst years of the war, 1940–43, the infant-mortality rate averaged below the prewar rate in Egypt, Cyprus, and Palestine, as it did in the United Kingdom. In the Netherlands it was slightly higher and in Italy 8 percent above the prewar average. In Egypt and Cyprus there was only one year, 1942, when the rate rose above the prewar average. The worst years for Palestine were 1940 and 1942, but even so the rate remained below prewar. In Italy and the United Kingdom, the rate rose to its highest point (and was above prewar) in 1941. It was in the early part of this year that Britain's supply of food, other than flour and potatoes, was at its lowest point. This was when her dollar resources were nearly exhausted and before Lend-Lease had come into operation. The famine in the Netherlands in 1945 is tragically reflected in the rise of infant mortality in that year to more than twice its prewar rate.

These comparisons supply a significant commentary on wartime food management in the Middle East. The progressive reduction in infant mortality since before the war was of course primarily due to improved medical and social services; but the fact that there was only one year when the rate exceeded the prewar average is a tribute to the successful management of food and agriculture, both by the governments concerned and by the Anglo-American team in MESC, which co-operated with them to prevent any avoidable interruption in the flow of essential foods to the Middle East.

## CONTROL OF INFLATION

The key to anti-inflation, as Sir Theodore Gregory and Keith Murray said at the Middle East Financial Conference, lay in control of food prices. But it was equally true that collection and distribution of home-produced food depended on controlling inflation. The two were in fact interdependent and formed part of a combined policy. This was not sufficiently recognized in the early years of the war. Indeed, if all-round measures of control had been introduced at an earlier date and administered more efficiently—an important proviso—it is fairly certain that price inflation could have been prevented from going as far as it did. This is one of the main conclusions drawn by Prest in his critique of war organization in the Middle East (*2*, pp. 158, 218, 239).

And yet there is an alternative and not wholly inconsistent view: that it was too much to expect that price inflation could be kept within such moderate limits as it was in the United States or the United Kingdom, once the seeds of inflation had been sown, not by any action of the governments themselves but by factors outside their control, in particular the sharp reduction in imports and the vast growth of military expenditure.

It was of course overwhelmingly in the interest of the Allies, and particularly of Great Britain, that price inflation should be avoided.

But it was not so demonstrably in the interests of Middle East countries. Given a fixed rate of exchange, it was the degree of price inflation which largely determined the size of the postwar sterling balances. The price inflation that took place in India and the Middle East might in theory have been avoided, or at least reduced, if local currency had been bought not at fixed prewar parities but at rates of exchange determined from time to time by supply and demand. Excess of demand over supply would then have been reflected in a steady appreciation of the rate of exchange. The rise of prices in local currency would have been less; but the resulting level of the postwar sterling balances might have been much the same.

This is an unreal hypothesis, since there was of course no basis for a free market in exchange. But it has a bearing on the view commonly held during the war, and implied to some extent in Prest's analysis, that price levels in the Middle East ought somehow to have been kept at about the same level as in the United Kingdom and the United States. With imports of consumer goods cut to the bone and the Allies pumping in new money at such a rate, this could only have been done by imposing heavy direct and indirect taxation on a scale which the governments had neither the inclination to propose nor the power to enforce. The experience of Palestine, Cyprus, and Sudan illustrate the limits to which taxation could be pushed even under British administration; and Millspaugh's heroic efforts in Persia met with such resistance that they achieved only a partial success. Little, too, could be done in the Middle East to raise money by public loans or savings campaigns.

There remained the possibility of obtaining local currency by selling gold at market prices. This was done on a small scale and the results were satisfactory so far as they went. But Britain's gold reserves were too small to continue the experiment, and it would have required a much larger amount, which only the United States could have provided, to finance the war in India and the Middle East by the sale of gold coins and jewelry.

The general conclusion to which this analysis leads is that, after a bad start in 1941 and 1942, notably in Syria and Persia where military operations came on top of poor crops, the efforts made by governments and central banks to check inflation were not without effect and deserve more credit than they have received. There was always the risk that a moderate price inflation might develop into runaway inflation such as occurred in Greece and China during the war and as has happened more recently in Korea and French Indochina. Except in Persia there was no deficit financing and budgets were balanced—or nearly so. In Egypt a series of budget surpluses was achieved and government loans were issued locally for the first time. In Egypt, Cyprus, Palestine, and Sudan, subsidies were applied to keep down the cost of living and to stabilize wages, as in Britain; and this must have helped to slow down inflation. But perhaps the major contributions of Middle East governments to the fight against inflation were the measures to control the prices and distribution of essential foods. It is easy to point to the weaknesses and shortcomings of control. These were only to be expected. In the Middle East there were black markets, and controls were evaded or ignored, as in most countries where inflation occurred. But the significant question to ask is not so much why controls did not work better, but how they were made to work at all. Price control, cereal collection, and rationing in the Middle East recall Dr. Johnson's simile of a dog walking on its hind legs.

That inflation was kept in check, as much as it was, was in no small measure due to the fact that all over the Middle East, through careful planning of imports and organized collection of bread grains at fixed prices, the food supply of the towns was maintained.

## CITATIONS

*1* W. S. Churchill, *The Second World War: Their Finest Hour* (Houghton Mifflin Co., Boston, 1949).

*2* A. R. Prest, *War Economics of Primary Producing Countries* (Cambridge, 1948).

*3* United Nations, *Demographic Yearbook, 1952* (New York, 1952).

CHAPTER 35

# POSTWAR DEVELOPMENTS

It would be beyond the scope of this book to do more than touch on postwar developments, but a few observations may be offered as a postscript. Political and economic developments since the war have in some respects been in striking contrast to the hopes and fears entertained at the time when the Middle East Supply Center came to an end. In the political field hopes for the establishment of some form of Middle East federation, and particularly hopes of ending the antagonism of Jews and Arabs, were all too quickly dashed. But in the economic field recovery from the effects of the war proceeded more smoothly than was at one time feared. The expected postwar slump, involving mass unemployment and bankruptcies, did not occur. Even the necessity of adjusting Middle East prices to world prices has proved less painful than was anticipated at the time of the Middle East Financial Conference in 1944. The tendency of world prices to rise rather than fall after the war helped the Middle East to bring its prices into line with the outside world.

In 1944 the prospect of curing wartime inflation in the Middle East seemed likely to involve a choice between deflation and devaluation. There has been no severe deflation; and devaluation of local currencies in terms of dollars has been shared with the whole sterling area. Rapid expansion of Middle East oil production, loans from the International Bank for Reconstruction and Development, and continuance of a high level of prosperity in the United States have all helped to stimulate recovery in the Middle East. For five and a half years, from 1944 to the middle of 1950, when the Korean boom sent cotton prices soaring, the wholesale-price index and cost-of-living index in Egypt varied less than 5 percent up or down. A similar though less pronounced stability with more of a downward trend in prices prevailed during the period 1945–50 in other countries (see Appendix Table IX).

During the period of postwar recovery economic expansion has been aided by the favorable balance-of-payments position, in which an excess of imports of merchandise has been financed partly by drawing on sterling balances accumulated during the war, and partly from United States government credits and grants. Wartime price inflation has been worked out of the system and a reasonably healthy equilibrium has been established. The plethora of money and shortage of goods that prevailed during the war have become a distant memory.

## FOOD PRODUCTION AND POPULATION GROWTH

The comparative stability of Middle East prices, as the Food and Agriculture Organization of the United Nations (FAO) points out, has been partly due to expansion of agricultural production, which has helped to keep inflationary pressures in check (*1*, p. 7). By 1951, in the Middle East (not counting Turkey) both agricultural production and food production had risen 22 percent above prewar, and in 1952 (a year of good crops) the increase in food production reached 30 percent (*1*, p. 28).

Since the population in 1951 had also increased 22 percent above prewar, food production per head was no higher than before the war. In fact it may be said to have remained virtually unchanged for 15 years. From 1952 onward the FAO report held out hopes of food production expanding faster than the annual growth of population, which was expected to be 1.8 percent. But a warning was added that, according to estimates of the Population Division of the United Nations, the actual rate of increase for the period 1949–51 was 2.2 percent in countries for which adequate statistics were available; and, with an expected decline in death rates as a result of improved medical facilities, the net rate of population increase might be higher than the forecast (*1*, p. 29).

Given favorable weather conditions and continued technical progress, expansion of grain production was expected to be greatest in Persia and Syria and somewhat less in Iraq and Ethiopia. In Egypt, where cotton and rice have been more profitable crops than wheat and maize, production of these two latter crops during the five years 1946–50 has been lower than before the war and below the highest point reached during the war.

In the rest of the Middle East grain output per head in 1948–52 has been buoyant since the war. Syria (except in 1951), Iraq, and Ethiopia have had a higher production per head, and exports of wheat from Syria and of barley from Iraq have risen. Persia lagged behind in 1948–50, and it was not till 1951 that production per head recovered to about the prewar level. Only in Egypt has there been a decline in total grain production per head. In the five years 1948–52 it averaged 25 percent less than before the war, and the deficiency had to be made up by substantial imports.

The net result for the Middle East (not counting Turkey) is that grain production per head is little if at all above the prewar level. The FAO report recognizes that in some of the food-deficit areas (of which Egypt is now the most important), "the margin between population increase and the growth of production is too slim to permit any appreciable progress" (*1*, p. 130) toward the goal of an increase in food production at a rate 1–2 percent greater than the annual growth of population.

Increase of food production depends on economic and social progress over a wide front and not merely on technical aid to agriculture. Indeed, technical aid from outside can contribute little unless it is accompanied by simultaneous advances in education, political stability, and social reforms inside each country.

In the technical field the postwar period has been marked by some striking developments, many of them involving large-scale investment financed by loans from the International Bank for Reconstruction and Development. In Egypt, Sudan, Iraq, Persia, and Syria several plans are nearing completion for extending the area under irrigation. FAO estimates that while only 160,000 hectares, equivalent to little more than 1 percent of the present irrigated area, have been added in the last two or three years, projects still under construction will add 850,000 hectares, and a further 1.25 million hectares may eventually be covered by additional schemes for which financial provision has yet to be made. Assuming that 60 percent of the projects under construction are completed before 1955–56, an additional production of 1 million tons of grain (less than a third of that needed to reach the target increase of 3.4 million) might be harvested.

For the rest, progress depends on the rapid spread of improved farming techniques. There has been some progress in mechanization of large farms, particularly in Syria and Iraq. The most promising development in Egypt is the increased attention being given to selection of better seeds for wheat and rice and particularly the breeding and distribution of hybrid maize. But elsewhere the spread of well-tried methods—including greater use of fertilizers, systematic seed improvement, advances in animal husbandry and mixed farming, agricultural education, and development of research and extension services—have all been hampered by lack of resources and to some extent by lack of trained personnel.

If these handicaps in the technical field could be progressively removed or reduced, food production might possibly expand at a cumulative rate of 2 or even 3 percent per annum. But what meanwhile of population growth?

In the Middle East, as in other areas of high fertility, the main limiting factor in population growth is to be found in the premature death of infants and children. In Egypt it has been estimated that a quarter of those born die before they are two years old. One-fourth of those born are "dead at 1.8 years of age in Egypt, 2.0 years in India, 51.5 years in the United States (whites) and 58.4 years in New Zealand" (*2*, p. 117). But specific death rates from 5 to 40 are probably not excessive in the Middle East. Infant mortality is being reduced both by better medical services and by more food. If infant mortality were to fall as low as in the West, population in the Middle East with existing birth rates could easily grow by 2 percent, or 2.5 percent (as it did among the Arabs of prewar Palestine), or even 3 percent per annum. There is thus a strong presumption that, until birth rates fall, numbers will automatically grow as fast as food is increased; and vice versa, that unless food is made available to feed increased numbers (particularly of infants and children under five), population growth will slow down and wait for food increase to catch up. Unless and until the birth rate falls, there can be no real race between food and population; for the foregone conclusion, as it has been throughout the greater part of human history, is an inevitable dead heat.

As to the prospects of a fall in the birth rate, which is the core of the problem in Egypt and in some other Middle East countries, little can be said with confidence. Worthington (*3*, p. 189) says that "birth control must start largely with the woman and depends on her wish to limit the family. This wish is not likely to be expressed by the majority of women in Mohammedan countries for at least several generations." But he points out that emancipation of women, which must play an essential part in any slowing down of population growth, has at least made a start in the Middle East.

Economic and social progress, particularly in peasant countries, must necessarily be slow, judged by the span of a single generation and by the standard of what can take place in selected areas. But looked at in historical perspective, the Middle East, where agriculture originated and where the sickle, the plow, and possibly even the sowing of seed were first invented, is undergoing a revolution. And not only in the techniques of farming, but in the social and political outlook of the peoples. The application of scientific knowledge depends on the education of the producers; and a progressive agriculture, responsive to the teachings of science, involves changes in the system of land tenure, development of co-operative societies, regrouping of scattered holdings, and even changes in the laws governing inheritance and family division of property, if the establishment of economic farm units is not to be frustrated by pressure of population. Education of the fellahin will stimulate a growing demand for improved housing, sanitation, and medical services; and last, but not least in importance, women will seek to reach higher standards of living and demand an end to the tragic loss of child life and impaired vitality of mothers that necessarily accompany high birth rates and high infant mortality.

The chief legacy of World War II in the Middle East has been growing resentment against foreign intervention, and growing social unrest. It is too early to say whether the political and social ferment resulting from the war will lead to social reform and economic progress, or whether it will find a destructive outlet in violence and xenophobia. At present both tendencies exist, and much will depend on the character and vision of the leaders who are able to command popular support. History provides no guide as to which is likely to prevail.

## CITATIONS

*1* FAO, *Agriculture in the Near East. Development and Outlook. Part II. Current Development of and Prospects for Agriculture in the Near East . . .* (Rome, November 1953).

*2* C. V. Kiser, "The Demographic Position of Egypt," in Milbank Memorial Fund, *Demographic Studies of Selected Areas of Rapid Growth . . .* (New York, 1944).

*3*. E. B. Worthington, *Middle East Science . . .* (London, 1946).

# APPENDIX AND INDEX

# APPENDIX NOTES

## Note I

## RESOLUTIONS OF THE MIDDLE EAST FINANCIAL CONFERENCE, CAIRO, APRIL 24–29, 1944[1]

### PREAMBLE

The Middle East Financial Conference, which met in Cairo from April 24 to April 29, 1944, was attended by Ministers and technical experts representing eleven Middle East Governments and by representatives of the Government of India, of the British, American and French Treasuries, of the Occupied Enemy Territories Administration and of the Economic and Financial Department of the League of Nations. The following Resolutions are submitted for the consideration of the Governments concerned.

### I. GENERAL

1. The Conference records its satisfaction with the way in which Middle East currency and banking systems have stood up to the strain of war-time conditions. The most critical period was in the spring and summer of 1942 and during the last twelve months there has been steadily growing confidence in the stability of Middle East currencies.

2. There has never been any danger of uncontrolled inflation of the kind which occurred in certain central European countries after the last war and the Conference wishes to emphasize that monetary inflation (in the restricted sense of fiat money or fiduciary notes uncovered except by advances to the Government from the Bank of Issue) has not taken place in the Middle East.

3. All Middle East currencies are fully backed by real values in the form of gold or foreign exchange assets and there has been no significant flight of capital and no depreciation of exchange rates. These foreign exchange assets will be used for purchasing goods and capital equipment as the latter become progressively available. This will enable Middle East countries to expand their economies and raise the standard of living of their peoples.

4. The Conference notes with satisfaction the statement of the late Chancellor of the Exchequer in February 1943, that the British Treasury intends to pursue a policy aimed at maintaining the approximate level of prices now ruling in the United Kingdom after the war and thereby stabilizing the purchasing power of sterling. This statement is of special importance to Middle East countries linked with sterling and also has a direct bearing on the currency of Syria and the Lebanon, owing to the close connection now established between sterling and the franc following the Anglo-French Agreement of February 8, 1944.

The Conference also notes with satisfaction that the United States controls the prices of its exports and prevents them from getting out of line with the general level of domestic prices. It also notes with satisfaction that the

[1] Unpublished proceedings of the Middle East Financial Conference, Cairo, April 24–29, 1944.

price level in the United States has been stabilized, thus maintaining the purchasing power of the dollar, and that it is the express policy of the United States Government to maintain prices at approximately their present level.

5. The Conference recommends that all possible measures such as taxation, loans and control of prices (about which separate resolutions follow) and development of production should now be taken by Middle East Governments to bring the price levels in their respective countries into better equilibrium with one another and with external price levels.

6. The chief cause of the price inflation that has occurred in the Middle East has been the increase of various forms of purchasing power in circulation caused by military expenditure with no corresponding increase in the supply of goods, and the remedy is of course to reduce the flow of money and to increase the supply of goods. The Conference understands that Allied military expenditure in the Middle East has passed its peak and when hostilities in Europe are concluded will be substantially reduced. This will help to bring down prices and will release productive capacity and labor for increasing production of civilian consumption. Under war conditions the supply of goods available for civilian consumption has had to be reduced, and this makes it all the more necessary to neutralize excessive purchasing power by appropriate measures and thus prevent excessive increases in prices.

The Conference attaches the greatest importance to a large import of both consumer goods and capital goods as soon as conditions of shipping and supply permit.

7. The Conference has taken note of the work of the Standing Committee of the Middle East Statistical Conference and recommends Governments of the Middle East to give their support to the project for establishing a permanent Middle East Statistical Bureau.

8. The Conference is of the opinion that the range of statistical information available to Middle East Governments is insufficient and urges improvement in the organization and collection of economic statistics especially with regard to the following four matters:—

(a) Banking statistics require supplementation in the shape of the collection of figures relating to the aggregate of all debits to current accounts. This figure is required in order that changes in the velocity of circulation of bank deposits can be kept fully under review as an indicator of the volume of business activity.

(b) Bank balance sheet summaries in accordance with the standard form recommended by the League of Nations in 1934.

(c) Improved statistics relating to the balance of payments position of different countries. Information of this kind is necessary if Governments are to be in a position to follow intelligently the net effect of internal and external transactions on the equilibrium of their currencies.

(d) Statistics relating to the volume and composition of the national income and output of each country. It is impossible for Governments to pursue intelligent social and economic policies in the post-war period without much fuller information than they at present have at their disposal in this regard.

It is desirable that Governments should take into early account the necessity of producing statistics relating to the national income so far as possible on a uniform basis over the entire Middle Eastern area. The Conference recommends that each Government should consider the possibility of affording facilities for study of these questions in London and Washington to appropriate members of their Government staffs.

9. The Conference welcomes the confidential information placed before it with regard to the aggregate of past Allied military expenditure in the Middle East and considers it desirable that, subject to military exigencies, periodical information of this kind should be made available to the respective Governments in future.

10. The Conference welcomes the discussions now in progress among the United and Associated Nations having as their objective the establishment of permanent machinery for international monetary stabilization and co-operation. The Conference shares in the hope that it will become possible for foreign credit balances to be made readily transferable into goods from any source.

### II. TAXATION

11. The Conference recognizes that taxation is one of the most important means of reducing the superabundance of money and thus checking the rise of prices. It accordingly recommends that Middle East Governments should constantly keep under review the possibilities of absorbing more money by taxation, and consider the imposition of supplementary taxes.

12. In particular the Conference recommends (i) that a direct tax on excess profits due to the war should be introduced where it does not already exist; (ii) that direct taxation should be increased progressively at the higher levels of income and profits; (iii) that a compulsory savings element in the shape of post-war credits might be introduced into the tax system; and (iv) that indirect taxes and railway freights on non-essential commodities should be increased. The funds obtained by such increased taxation might assist the subsidizing of essential consumer goods.

13. One of the chief objects of increased taxation, in addition to absorbing excess spending power, is to enable Governments to build up reserves and strengthen their financial resources (a) for covering accumulated arrears of maintenance and renewals and (b) for post-war development schemes and investment in works of public utility which will increase the welfare, health and happiness of the peoples of the Middle East.

14. The Conference recommends that each Government should take energetic measures to modernize its tax machinery and to improve the system of assessment and collection. Evasion and delays in payment of taxes not only undermine confidence in the administration and impose an unfair burden on those taxpayers who meet their obligations, but neutralize the efforts to combat price inflation. It should be recognized that speeding up the collection of taxes may be just as effective as imposing new taxes in reducing surplus purchasing power.

15. The Conference recognizes that the administration of direct taxes has only recently been introduced in certain countries of the Middle East and that the lack of trained and experienced income tax officials adds much to the

difficulties of administration. It recommends that Governments should pay special attention to the training of income tax experts and that, in the field of taxation, arrangements should be made for pooling the experience of Middle East countries and for the provision of training facilities for technical staff.

16. The Conference notes with approval that certain Middle East Governments have not only had balanced budgets throughout the war but have succeeded in building up reserve funds for use after the war. It recommends that this policy should be adopted in other Middle East countries and that the practice of budgeting for a surplus at times when money is abundant and profits are high should be extended and developed as an important contribution to national stability and sound public finance.

### III. LOANS AND SAVINGS

17. The Conference congratulates those Governments in the Middle East which have for the first time raised internal loans during the war and have thus demonstrated the confidence which their public now have in the stability and credit of their financial systems. It understands that other Governments in the Middle East are considering the adoption of similar measures and suggests that these Governments may be encouraged and assisted by the example and experience of countries which have successfully raised internal loans.

18. The development of a capital market in Middle Eastern countries is bound to take time but the habit of saving and investment is being stimulated by the war and should prove of lasting benefit to the economy of Middle East countries. Its importance is emphasized by the fact that countries holding large sterling balances cannot expect to borrow further sterling in the U.K. after the war, and that they will need machinery which will enable the Governments to obtain control of such sterling resources as they may need by internal borrowing.

19. Governments are urged to consider carefully the particular type of public loans or savings which are likely to prove most attractive to their citizens, including municipal loans, premium bonds or lottery loans, post office savings and the sale of savings certificates. All these methods of saving and investment are useful but the particular choice must depend on the psychology and habits of different types of investors in each country.

20. The Conference welcomes the satisfactory progress of the War Savings Campaign conducted on varying lines in the different countries. In its view these gratifying results indicate conclusively that new ground has in fact been broken by the adoption of diverse methods of saving and that vigorous prosecution of savings campaigns in the Middle East holds out encouraging prospects.

21. The Conference wishes to emphasize the need for individual and collective saving. Saving has many social and moral advantages. It sets aside money for the satisfaction of future needs. It tends to reduce the uncertainties and anxieties of life. It encourages foresight and independence. In wartime it also helps to restrict ordinary spending to essentials so that maximum labor and shipping space can be released for war production. The Conference recommends that the various Governments should examine the possibility of promoting and extending the scope of their savings campaigns.

22. The Conference notes with special interest the schemes adopted or pro-

posed in various countries for compulsory collection of a special tax on incomes or war profits subject to repayment in whole or in part after the war. It recommends each Government to study the possibility of adopting an appropriate type of post-war tax repayment scheme as a means of absorbing surplus purchasing power, encouraging the habit of saving, and providing for resources to meet the problems of post-war adjustments.

### IV. PRICE POLICY AND PRICE CONTROL

23. The Conference considers:—

That the stage at which Allied military expenditure in the Middle East will fall, and the movement of goods will become freer, must now be regarded as sufficiently near to make it necessary to take account in present planning of this approaching development, and of the downward adjustment of the price level of Middle East products which will result.

The Conference accordingly recommends that the Governments represented should take every step in their power, in their various capacities as Governments of buying or selling countries, to bring about the downward adjustments of prices from now on in a steady and orderly manner, so as to spread out over a sufficient period of time the strain of readjusting the economies of Middle East countries from war conditions to peace conditions.

24. The Conference notes with the greatest satisfaction the various measures taken by Middle East Governments to establish and maintain war-time control of prices, and recommends that every effort should be made to extend such control and render it fully effective.

25. The Conference recognizes the vital importance of establishing close control of supplies and distribution in order to make any price control policy effective. Such policy should be designed:—

(a) to ensure the equitable distribution of essential goods at reasonable prices to all members of the community; and
(b) to bring about a reduction in the general level of prices.

It therefore urges that the Governments concerned should strengthen and, if necessary, extend their organization for controlling supplies and distribution.

In this connection the Conference draws attention to the Resolutions formulated by the Middle East Conference on Control of Distribution and Rationing held in Cairo in August 1943.

26. The Conference recommends that every effort should be made to reduce essential food prices to the lowest practicable level since this is a fundamental condition to the successful adoption of other anti-inflation measures. The Conference recommends that the Middle East grain collection scheme should be continued as a means of discouraging hoarding and ensuring supplies to towns, and other areas not producing sufficient for their own needs.

In this connection the Resolutions of the recent Damascus Cereals Conference should be taken into consideration by the countries which participated therein.

27. In order to obviate hardship and inequities of distribution as between the various sections of the community, the Conference considers that it will be necessary to continue war-time controls until such time as sufficient supplies of essential goods become available.

28. The Conference recommends that in the case of luxuries and of any articles the prices and distribution of which cannot be effectively controlled, the differential between the cost price (including reasonable profit) and the open market price should be appropriated by the Government for the public benefit.

### CONCLUSION

In conclusion the members of the Conference desire to express their appreciation of the initiative taken by the British Minister Resident in the Middle East in summoning this Conference and tender their thanks to the Royal Egyptian Government for the facilities and hospitality which have been extended to them during their visit to Cairo. The meetings have been both harmonious and fruitful and have afforded an opportunity for a most useful exchange of views and information between the experts attending the Conference.

## NOTE II

## RESOLUTIONS OF THE MIDDLE EAST CONFERENCE ON CONTROL OF DISTRIBUTION AND RATIONING, CAIRO, AUGUST 21–22, 1943[1]

1. This Conference of Official Delegates from the Middle East which met on August 21 and 22 in Cairo under the auspices of the Middle East Supply Center to discuss rationing and control of distribution desires to place on record the following resolutions which have been formulated as a result of interchange of views and experience between technical officers engaged in the administration of rationing. The resolutions are not binding on their respective Governments, and no Government is committed to accept the views expressed or the policies advocated, but the Conference considers Governments may find it useful, in framing their policies, to have before them this statement on methods of rationing and control of distribution in time of war.
2. Rationing in its most general sense includes all forms of allocation and distribution of goods at fixed prices as opposed to competitive buying and uncontrolled distribution at market prices. Rationing by cards and coupons may be called "consumer rationing".
3. Control of prices, by removing the free play of market forces and keeping prices at a level at which demand exceeds supply, needs as a general rule to be accompanied by some form of allocation or rationing if it is to prove just, efficacious and practicable. Price control without allocation or rationing cannot by itself achieve fair distribution.
4. At the same time we recognize that other measures to check speculation and profiteering and to stabilize and co-ordinate the general level of all prices, profits, wages and costs, in so far as they command general support, are necessary to counter inflation and restrict the demand for consumer goods.

[1] Unpublished proceedings of the Middle East Conference on Control of Distribution and Rationing, Cairo, August 21–23, 1943.

Among these increased taxation especially of excess profits, stimulation of savings and State borrowing play the most important role.
5. The possibility of effective rationing depends on the extent to which the rationing authority is able to gain control of the supply of goods, including stocks in the hands of distributors.
6. We recognize the special difficulties in obtaining control of home produced foods. The Conference has noted with particular satisfaction the progress made by many of the Governments in the collection of surplus bread grains from rural areas for the feeding of urban populations. We consider that it is not possible under present conditions to rely on the free marketing and movement of grain to ensure the bread supplies of all consumers.
7. In view of the importance of cereals in the national diets of the Middle East we consider that control of the supply of bread grains is one of the most important measures necessary to secure fair distribution of food. Such control will be facilitated to the extent that the Government or its appointed agents becomes the sole purchaser of bread grains, since the continued existence of a free market for grain tends to black market dealings, high prices, hoarding and speculation.
8. Supplies of imported goods are in general consigned either to the Government or to licensed importers. Strict control of the distribution of these supplies should be established where it does not already exist.
9. We consider that control of the supplies of essential processed or manufactured goods should also be undertaken where this has not already been done. Control of supplies of raw materials and transport offer opportunities of achieving effective control of the final products.
10. In the control of imports and wholesale distribution close co-operation between the controlling authorities and established traders is essential. Established traders should be licensed and, wherever possible, organized into special groups or associations. Either the Government may import the goods and employ traders as agents, or private importers may own the goods but distribute them according to the instructions of the Controlling Authority.
11. If Consumer Rationing is to work successfully, an accurate census or registration of the population is absolutely necessary. Improvement in agricultural and industrial statistics of production, together with complete returns of stocks, are needed.
12. Consumer Rationing may be either national or local. Card or coupon rationing is recommended for towns and urban areas. Villages and tribes may receive bulk allocations of essential goods. In both cases, however, it is essential to check the numbers of recipients to prevent fraud and duplication.
13. The Conference specially emphasizes the need for providing a fair share of consumer goods at reasonable prices to the rural producers in order to ensure the maximum supplies of food for the towns.
14. Government subsidies are among the recognized means of keeping the price of essential foods within the reach of the poorest consumers, and thus enable them to pay for their rations without giving rise to inflationary demands for increases in wages.
15. In the Middle East rationing cards or coupons are for the most part issued to families or householders rather than to individuals. This has advantages so long as there are not frequent changes in the composition of the household. Individual cards or ration books are preferable where possible.

16. The tying or linking of consumers to retailers simplifies distribution, but has the disadvantages of limiting competition between retailers. Where tying is adopted, we consider that consumers should be allowed to choose their retailers and change them periodically if desired.
17. Where satisfactory co-operation of retailers cannot be secured, Governmental or Municipal shops and co-operative stores are recommended as a means of ensuring fair distribution at fair prices.
18. Specific or straight rationing is appropriate for a commodity in universal demand which lends itself to being divided up either in equal quantities or in differential rations for defined categories of consumers.
19. Points rationing provides elasticity and freedom of consumers' choice and is considered appropriate where there are marked differences in consumption habits within an area or, as in the case of clothing, the variety of articles precludes straight rationing. In extreme cases of shortage of clothing, however, it may be necessary to adopt a system of special permits.
20. Some form of restriction of meals in restaurants is a necessary complement to household rationing. Whether or not meal tickets or coupons are surrendered for meals obtained in restaurants, supplies to restaurants should be allocated on the basis of the number of meals served.
21. Whatever rationing system is adopted, it should be simple and easily understood. Full explanations should be given by means of Press and the Radio and official announcements in Mosques, Churches, Schools, etc.
22. The elimination of the "black market" depends upon effective Government control of supplies, and the licensing of established traders to the exclusion of speculators and unauthorized dealers, the co-operation of the public and the infliction of heavy penalties on offenders.
23. The exchange of information and views which has taken place at this Conference has been of great value to the Delegates from the various territories and to the Middle East Supply Centre, since many of the methods of control and rationing adopted in some countries might with advantage be introduced elsewhere. The Conference recommends that information on methods of control and rationing, both in the Middle East and in other countries, should be circulated periodically by the Middle East Supply Centre to be competent authorities in each territory. To this end, Governments are requested to keep the Middle East Supply Centre informed of any additions to and changes in their methods of controlling supplies, prices, and distribution.

## Note III

## RESOLUTIONS OF THE CONFERENCE ON MIDDLE EAST AGRICULTURAL DEVELOPMENT, CAIRO, FEBRUARY 7–10, 1944[1]

1. The Conference has welcomed the opportunity for this exchange of views and of technical experience and wishes to express its gratitude to the Middle East Supply Centre for convening the Conference.

[1] Middle East Supply Centre, *Proceedings of the Conference on Middle East Agricultural Development, Cairo, February 7th–10th, 1944* (Agr. Rpt. No. 6, Cairo, 1944), pp. 207–08.

2. The Conference desires to emphasize the necessity for Middle Eastern countries represented at this Conference, severally and jointly, to conserve and develop their agricultural resources and to adopt an active policy towards this end.

3. The Conference is of the opinion that, in view of the many agricultural problems which are common throughout the area, a Middle East Council of Agriculture should be set up to consider the regional technical problems associated with agricultural development.

4. The Conference suggests that such a council might be composed of representatives of the constituent Governments, to provide a forum for the discussion of common agricultural problems through periodic meetings and through the publication of a journal on Middle East agriculture, and to disseminate agricultural knowledge through exhibitions.

5. Pending approval of the formation of this council by the Governments concerned, a Standing Committee of the Conference should be appointed to continue the work of the Conference and to formulate a constitution for the Council for the consideration of the Governments concerned. The Standing Committee should be empowered to appoint sub-committees to consider specific problems.

6. The offer of the Middle East Supply Centre to act as the Secretariat to the Standing Committee until the permanent Secretariat of the Council is established should be gratefully accepted.

7. The Conference considers that irrigation and other schemes for agricultural development initiated during the war should be carried on in the subsequent years and that those elements of permanent value achieved under the exigencies of war should not be allowed to lapse.

8. The Conference wishes to bring to the attention of Middle Eastern countries the growing dangers to their natural resources from soil erosion, accentuated by uncontrolled grazing and the destruction of protective vegetation. The Conference urges therefore that comprehensive measures of soil conservation and management should be pursued and accelerated.

9. The Conference attaches great importance to the improvement through research and education of agricultural techniques and rural standards of living; increased facilities for the training of personnel are essential.

10. The Conference requests the Council, when formed, to examine the possibilities of establishing a central Institute of Agricultural Development to supplement the work now being carried on in individual countries and to serve the Middle East as a whole by enabling fullest use to be made of such trained personnel and facilities as are now available.

11. In order to ensure the practical application of new knowledge and techniques the Conference stresses the need for the extension of suitable methods of technical education and instruction to the farming community.

12. The Conference records its conviction that agricultural progress is inseparably linked with the continued advancement of the agricultural population in all factors concerned in their welfare, particularly in nutrition, health and education.

13. The Conference wishes the Middle East Supply Centre to bring to the notice of supplying countries the importance of accelerating the arrival of

agricultural machinery, fertilizers and other agricultural requirements, in order to achieve an immediate increase in food production.

14. Finally the Conference expresses its confident belief that agricultural development in the Middle East must rest upon the constant exchange of agricultural knowledge, both within the area and with other parts of the world, and upon a growing sense of public responsibility to the land and the people who cultivate it.

## Note IV

## PROPOSED AGREEMENT FOR THE CONSTITUTION OF THE MIDDLE EAST COUNCIL OF AGRICULTURE

The Governments whose duly authorised representatives have subscribed hereto,

> desiring to promote the agricultural development and rural welfare of the Middle East,
>
> and having regard to the Resolutions of the Conference on Agricultural Development held in Cairo in February 1944,

have agreed as follows:—

### ARTICLE I

### ESTABLISHMENT OF THE COUNCIL

There is hereby established the Middle East Council of Agriculture (hereinafter referred to as "the Council").

### ARTICLE II

### SCOPE OF THE COUNCIL

The scope of the Council shall cover the agricultural development and rural welfare of the Middle East. As used in this context, agricultural development includes the science and practice of agriculture, animal husbandry, forestry and fisheries, together with their closely associated sciences and closely associated industries; and rural welfare includes problems relevant to the well-being of those primarily deriving their livelihood from the rural occupations and rural industries defined above.

### ARTICLE III

### OBJECT AND PURPOSES OF THE COUNCIL

The objects and purposes of the Council shall be as follows:

(i) To collect, collate and disseminate data and information regarding the progress and results of agricultural development and rural welfare investigations in the countries of the Middle East, and to obtain from any other sources similar information regarding problems of general and specific interest to the agricultural development of the Middle East.

(ii) To assist in promoting and maintaining the regular interchange of technical information between the member Governments represented and with the Middle East and other countries, particularly with a view to developing to the greatest extent direct contacts between both individuals and institutions concerned with similar problems and engaged upon similar lines of research, investigation or educational work.

(iii) To keep in constant review the agricultural development and rural welfare work being conducted throughout the Middle East and to indicate to the member Governments concerned ways by which existing knowledge or programmes of work might be supplemented.

(iv) To review methods of agricultural education and extension work now in progress in the various territories and to recommend action which might be taken to supplement existing facilities for agricultural education and extension work and for training of agricultural personnel.

(v) To formulate and recommend measures for individual or joint action by any or all of the member Governments, for the co-ordination of agricultural development projects and policies.

(vi) The form of activities of the Council within the territory of a member Government and the responsibility to be assumed by a member Government for carrying out measures recommended by the Council, shall be determined after consultation with and with the consent of the member Government. The Council may participate in the administration or execution of such co-ordination measures as may be authorised by the member Governments concerned.

ARTICLE IV

MEMBERSHIP

The members of the Middle East Council of Agriculture shall be the Governments signatory hereto and such other Governments as may, upon application for membership, be admitted thereto by a two-third majority vote of all the members of the Council.

ARTICLE V

THE COUNCIL

SECTION 1—Each member Government shall have one vote on the Council and shall name not more than two representatives. Each member Government may appoint such alternates to its representatives as may be necessary. The Council shall, for each of its sessions, select one of its members to preside at the session. The Council shall determine its own rule of procedure.

SECTION 2—The Council shall be convened not less than twice a year by its Secretary-General and shall meet, as may be convenient, in the territory of any of the member Governments.

SECTION 3—The Council may establish such committees (standing or ad hoc) as it shall consider desirable. The members of such committees shall be appointed by the Council. For technical committees the members may be members of the Council or others nominated by the Council for their special competence in their respective fields of work; and, where and when necessary, the consent of the Government concerned shall be obtained.

SECTION 4—All reports and recommendations of committees of the Council shall be submitted by the Secretary-General for consideration by the Council. Where such reports specifically affect the interests of a member Government, they shall be communicated in advance to the Council member representing the Government concerned so that the latter may have an opportunity of expressing his views. Such reports may be published with the consent of the Council.

SECTION 5—The travel and other expenses of members of the Council shall be borne by the Government which they represent.

### ARTICLE VI

### THE SECRETARIAT

SECTION 1—A Secretary-General shall be appointed to undertake the secretarial work of the Council and to maintain an office to facilitate the exchange of information and other activities of the Council.

SECTION 2—The Secretary-General shall make periodic reports to the Council covering the progress of the Council's activities.

SECTION 3—With the approval of the Council, the Secretary-General may appoint such subordinate staff as may be necessary to assist him in carrying out his duties.

### ARTICLE VII

### FINANCE AND RESOURCES

SECTION 1—In so far as its appropriate constitutional bodies shall authorise, each member Government will contribute to the support of the Council and its activities in order to accomplish the purposes set out in this Agreement. The amount and character of such contributions will be recommended by the Council. All such contributions received by the Council shall be accounted for.

SECTION 2—The Secretary-General shall submit to the Council an annual budget covering the necessary expenses of the Council and, from time to time, such supplementary budgets as may be urgently required for specific purposes. Upon the acceptance of budgets by the Council, the amounts, in proportions to be determined by the Council, shall be communicated to the member Governments for approval and acceptance.

### ARTICLE VIII

### LEGAL STATUS

The Council shall have power to acquire, hold and convey property, to accept gifts and endowments, to enter into contracts and undertake obligations, to designate or create agencies and to review the activities of the agencies so created, to manage undertakings and, in general, to perform any legal act appropriate to its objects and purposes.

#### ARTICLE IX

#### AMENDMENT

The provisions of this Agreement may be amended by a two-third majority vote of all the members of the Council.

Provided that amendments involving new obligations for member Governments shall only take effect when accepted by the member Government or Governments concerned.

#### ARTICLE X

#### ENTRY INTO FORCE

This Agreement shall enter into force with respect to each signatory when the Agreement is signed by that signatory, unless otherwise specified by such signatory.

#### ARTICLE XI

#### WITHDRAWAL

Any member Government may give notice of withdrawal from the Council at any time after the expiration of six months from the entry into force of the Agreement for that Government. Such notice shall take effect twelve months after the date of its communication to the Secretary-General. Upon withdrawal, the member Government concerned shall be deemed to have no claim in any form against the Council.

# APPENDIX TABLES

## Abbreviations and Symbols

| | |
|---|---|
| FAO | Food and Agriculture Organization of the United Nations |
| IIA | International Institute of Agriculture |
| MESC | Middle East Supply Center |
| UN | United Nations |
| ... | Data not available |
| — | None, negligible quantity, or entry not applicable |
| 1934/35 | Year beginning in 1934 and ending in 1935 |
| 1934–38 | Total, or average, for the five calendar years ending 1938 |

Totals and other calculations made from unrounded figures may not check exactly with the individual items shown. Rough conversions of weights and measures in the text are often rounded.

## Measures and Weights

### LENGTH

1 kilometer (km.) equals 1,000 meters, or .621 mile
1 meter (m.) equals 1,000 millimeters, or 3.2808 feet
1 millimeter (mm.) equals .03937 inch
1 mile (mi.) equals 5,280 feet, or 1.60934 kilometers
1 foot (ft.) equals 12 inches, or .3048 meter
1 inch (in.) equals 25.400 millimeters

### AREA

1 square kilometer (km.$^2$) equals 100 hectares, or .386 square mile
1 hectare (ha.) equals 2.471 acres
1 square mile (sq.mi.) equals 640 acres, or 259 hectares
1 acre (a.) equals .4047 hectare
1 dunum:[a]
  in Palestine equals .100 hectare, or .2471 acre
  in Cyprus equals .13378 hectare, or .3306 acre
  in Iraq equals .250 hectare, or .61775 acre
1 feddan (in Egypt) equals .42 hectare, or 1.038 acres

### WEIGHT

1 metric ton (m.t.) equals 1,000 kilograms or 1,000 kilos (kg.), or 2,204.6 pounds
1 long ton (l.t.) equals 2,240 pounds
1 short ton (s.t.) equals 2,000 pounds
1 pound (lb.) equals .454 kilogram

### EGYPTIAN CEREAL MEASURE

1 ardeb of wheat weighs approximately 150 kilograms
1 ardeb of maize weighs approximately 140 kilograms

[a] Sometimes called mishara in Iraq.

TABLE I.—AREA AND POPULATION OF MIDDLE EAST COUNTRIES, LATEST CENSUS AND 1949*

(*Thousand persons, except as indicated*)

| Country | Area (*1,000 km.*$^2$) | Latest census: Date | Latest census: Population | 1949 midyear population |
|---|---|---|---|---|
| Aden Colony | ...[a] | Oct. 8, 1946 | 81 | 82 |
| Aden Protectorate | 316 | ... | ... | 650 |
| Cyprus | 9 | Nov. 10, 1946 | 450 | 476[b] |
| Egypt | 1,000 | Mar. 26, 1947 | 18,967[c] | 19,888[d] |
| Eritrea | 124 | ... | ... | 1,086 |
| Ethiopia | 1,060 | ... | ... | 15,000[e] |
| Iraq | 435 | Oct. 19, 1947 | 4,800 | 4,800[f] |
| Lebanon | 10 | ... | ... | 1,238 |
| Libya: | | | | |
| Cyrenaica[g] | 855 | ... | ... | 327 |
| Tripolitania[g] | 353 | Apr. 21, 1936 | 666 | 797 |
| Palestine | 27 | Nov. 18, 1931 | 1,036 | 1,874[h] |
| Persia | 1,630 | ... | ... | 18,388 |
| Saudi Arabia[i] | 1,546[j] | ... | ... | 6,000[i] |
| Sheikdoms: | | | | |
| Bahrein | ...[a] | Mar. 3, 1950 | 110 | 110 |
| Kuwait | 21 | ... | ... | 170 |
| Muscat and Oman | 212 | ... | ... | 550 |
| Qatar | 22[j] | ... | ... | 20[g] |
| Trucial Oman | 15 | ... | ... | 80[g] |
| Yemen | 195 | ... | ... | 4,500 |
| Somaliland: | | | | |
| British | 176 | ... | ... | 500 |
| French | 22 | ... | ... | 56[g] |
| Italian | 514 | Apr. 21, 1931 | 1,022 | 972[g] |
| Sudan | 2,506 | ... | ... | 8,182 |
| Syria | 181 | ... | ... | 3,135[k] |
| Transjordan | 90[g] | ... | ... | 400[g] |
| Total | 11,319 | ... | ... | 89,281 |

* Except as otherwise indicated, data from UN, *Demographic Yearbook, 1952* (New York, 1952), pp. 89–97, 127. As will be seen, no census has ever been taken in most of these countries; the censuses shown for Aden Colony, Iraq, and Italian Somaliland were the first taken. Hence 1949 estimates are largely conjectural.

[a] Less than 1,000 km.$^2$: Aden Colony, 207; Bahrein, 598.

[b] Excluding persons in special military and internment camps, numbering 12,422 at the 1946 census.

[c] Excluding 55,073 nomads; including alien armed forces.

[d] Excluding alien armed forces and enemy prisoners of war.

[e] Other estimates range from 5 to 16 million.

[f] Midyear 1947.

[g] Data from UN, *Demographic Yearbook, 1949–50* (New York, 1950), pp. 71, 74, 77, 78.

[h] Midyear 1946.

[i] Data from UN, *Review of Economic Conditions in the Middle East, Supplement to World Economic Report 1949–50* (New York, March 1951), p. 43. Other estimates range from 3 to 6 million.

[j] Unofficial.

[k] Excluding nomads whose number was estimated at 288,400 in 1945.

TABLE II.—LAND USE IN SPECIFIED COUNTRIES*
(*Thousand hectares*)

| Country and year | Irrigated | Cultivated[a] | Cultivable[b] | Pasture[c] | Forest and woodlands |
|---|---|---|---|---|---|
| Aden Protectorate, 1947. | 110[d] | 110[d] | ... | ... | — |
| Cyprus, 1947 | 15 | 199 | ... | 405 | 169 |
| Egypt, 1948 | 2,445 | 2,445 | 3,495 | — | — |
| Eritrea, 1948 | 20[e] | 222 | 416 | 9,130 | 1,416 |
| Ethiopia, 1951 | 10[e] | 11,000 | 19,000 | 50,000 | 3,000 |
| Iraq, 1949 | 1,300 | 1,900[f] | 6,600 | 4,000 | ... |
| Lebanon, 1950 | 53 | 225 | 340 | ... | 75 |
| Libya: | | | | | |
| Cyrenaica, 1947 | ... | 41 | ... | — | 155 |
| Tripolitania, 1947 | ... | 2,260 | 2,986 | 6,542 | 19 |
| Palestine, 1944 | 50 | 800 | 870 | ... | 89 |
| Persia, 1947 | 2,200 | 16,600[g] | 50,000 | 10,000 | 19,000 |
| Saudi Arabia, 1947 | ... | 20 | ... | 55,000 | ... |
| Somaliland: | | | | | |
| British, 1949 | ... | 200 | 460 | 16,840[h] | 300 |
| French, 1950 | ... | 2[d] | 4 | 1,800 | 62 |
| Italian, 1951 | 301 | 7,977 | 15,119 | 25,658 | 7,142 |
| Sudan, 1947 | 250 | 717 | 1,317 | 24,038 | 94,111 |
| Syria, 1947 | 297 | 2,314[g] | 5,680 | 3,825 | 356 |
| Transjordan, 1946 | 26 | 480 | ... | 600 | 35 |

* Data from UN, *Review of Economic Conditions in the Middle East, Supplement to World Economic Report 1949–50* (New York, March 1951), p. 45; from FAO, *Yearbook of Food and Agricultural Statistics, 1949* (Washington, D.C., 1950), p. 16, for Eritrea and Libya; and from *ibid., 1952* (Rome, 1953), pp. 5–9, for Ethiopia, Saudi Arabia, and Somaliland, and irrigated area for Eritrea.

[a] Including fallow, except as otherwise noted.

[b] Cultivated plus unused but potentially productive.

[c] Called by FAO "permanent meadows and pastures"; here indicating pastures and semidesert steppe.

[d] Major crops only.

[e] Data for 1949.

[f] Excluding fallow.

[g] Including 11.9 million hectares of fallow for Persia and .7 million for Syria.

[h] Including wasteland.

Table III.—Population of Principal Cities and Towns in the Middle East*
(*Thousand persons*)

| Country and city | Population |
|---|---|
| Aden (1946): | |
| Aden | 57 |
| Bahrein (1950): | |
| Manama | 40 |
| Cyprus (1946): | |
| Nicosia | 34 |
| Egypt (1947): | |
| Cairo | 2,091 |
| Alexandria | 919 |
| Port Said | 178 |
| Tanta | 140 |
| Mahalla el Kubra | 116 |
| Suez | 107 |
| El Mansura | 102 |
| *Total* | *3,653* |
| Eritrea (1948): | |
| Asmara | 131 |
| Ethiopia (1951): | |
| Addis Ababa | 400 |
| Diredawa | 30 |
| Harrar | 25 |
| *Total* | *455* |
| Iraq (1947): | |
| Baghdad | 400 |
| Mosul | 203 |
| Basra (1937) | 180 |
| Karbala | 123 |
| Najaf | 107 |
| *Total* | *1,013* |
| Kuwait: | |
| Al Kuwait | 70 |
| Lebanon (1943): | |
| Beirut | 234 |
| Libya (1947): | |
| Tripoli | 136 |
| Bengazi | 96 |
| *Total* | *232* |
| Malta (1948): | |
| Valetta | 19 |
| Palestine (1951): | |
| Tel Aviv–Jaffa | 346 |
| Haifa | 147 |
| Jerusalem | 138 |
| *Total* | *631* |
| Persia (1950): | |
| Teheran | 619 |
| Tabriz | 279 |
| Isfahan | 196 |
| Meshed | 192 |
| Hamadan | 124 |
| Shiraz | 116 |
| Resht | 112 |
| Kermanshah | 108 |
| Abadan | 40 |
| *Total* | *1,786* |
| Saudi Arabia: | |
| Mecca | 80 |
| Riyadh | 60 |
| Jedda | 30 |
| *Total* | *170* |
| Somaliland (British): | |
| Berbera | 15–30 |
| Somaliland (French): | |
| Djibouti | 15 |
| Somaliland (Italian): | |
| Mogadishu (1948) | 74 |
| Sudan (1947): | |
| Omdurman | 123 |
| Khartoum | 68 |
| El Obeid (1948) | 66 |
| Port Sudan (1948) | 47 |
| *Total* | *304* |
| Syria (1943): | |
| Aleppo | 320 |
| Damascus | 286 |
| Homs | 100 |
| *Total* | *706* |
| Transjordan: | |
| Amman | 35 |
| Yemen: | |
| Sana | 25 |
| *Total listed cities* | *9,699* |

* Data from UN, *Demographic Yearbook, 1952* (New York, 1952); Royal Inst. Internatl. Affairs, *The Middle East . . .* (London, 1950); and *Webster's Geographical Dictionary* (Springfield, Mass., 1949).

TABLE IV.—PRODUCTION OF GRAINS IN SELECTED COUNTRIES, PREWAR, 1939–45, AND AVERAGE 1946–50*
*(Thousand metric tons)*

| Period | Egypt | Sudan | Palestine | Syria and Lebanon | Cyprus | Persia | Iraq |
|---|---|---|---|---|---|---|---|
| | | | | WHEAT | | | |
| Average 1934–38..... | 1,184 | 7 | 87 | 494 | 59 | 1,869 | 478 |
| 1939.......... | 1,334 | 8 | 89 | ... | 68 | 1,700[a] | 450 |
| 1940.......... | 1,361 | 7 | 136 | 602 | 48 | 1,500 | 478 |
| 1941.......... | 1,124 | 6 | 90 | 473 | 25 | 1,200 | 515 |
| 1942.......... | 1,262 | 7 | 104 | 507 | 77 | 1,400[a] | 532 |
| 1943.......... | 1,292 | 9 | 66 | 624 | 54 | 1,650 | 480 |
| 1944.......... | 946 | 20 | 88 | 532 | 30 | 2,080 | 332 |
| 1945.......... | 1,182 | 11 | 109 | 442 | 56 | 2,100 | 558 |
| Average 1946–50..... | 1,094 | 16 | ... | 749 | 52 | 1,959 | 490 |
| | | | | BARLEY | | | |
| Average 1934–38..... | 225 | 2 | 67 | 319 | 44 | 793 | 575 |
| 1939.......... | 238 | 1 | 86 | ... | 49 | 700[a] | 950 |
| 1940.......... | 241 | 1 | 102 | 339 | 36 | ... | 1,000 |
| 1941.......... | 210 | 1 | 69 | 275 | 22 | ... | 825 |
| 1942.......... | 277 | 1 | 114 | 249 | 62 | 600[a] | 859 |
| 1943.......... | 314 | 2 | 62 | 330 | 36 | 700[a] | 899 |
| 1944.......... | 227 | 1 | 68 | 284 | 18 | 1,260 | 743 |
| 1945.......... | 262 | 1 | 115 | 274 | 42 | 1,250 | 790 |
| Average 1946–50..... | 149 | — | ... | 320 | 46 | 788 | 723 |
| | | | | MAIZE | | | |
| Average 1934–38..... | 1,616 | 12 | 8[b] | 24 | — | ... | ... |
| 1939.......... | 1,524 | 11 | 6 | ... | — | ... | ... |
| 1940.......... | 1,530 | 7 | 9 | 45 | — | ... | 15 |
| 1941.......... | 1,282 | 5 | 8 | 40 | — | ... | 10 |
| 1942.......... | 1,452 | 5 | 3 | 43 | — | ... | 13 |
| 1943.......... | 1,377 | 5 | 4 | 22 | — | ... | 11 |
| 1944.......... | 1,559 | 4 | 3 | 28 | — | ... | 11 |
| 1945.......... | 1,697 | 10 | 5 | 32 | — | ... | 12 |
| Average 1946–50..... | 1,358 | 15[b] | ... | ... | — | 6[b] | 18 |

TABLE IV.—PRODUCTION OF GRAINS IN SELECTED COUNTRIES, PREWAR, 1939–45, AND AVERAGE 1946–50*—(*Continued*)

(*Thousand metric tons*)

| Period | Egypt | Sudan | Palestine | Syria and Lebanon | Cyprus | Persia | Iraq |
|---|---|---|---|---|---|---|---|
| | | | | MILLET, SORGHUM | | | |
| Average 1934–38..... | 426 | 713[a] | 49 | 71 | — | ... | ... |
| 1939.......... | 535 | ... | 43 | ... | — | ... | ... |
| 1940.......... | 454 | ... | 58 | 58 | — | ... | 17 |
| 1941.......... | 469 | ... | 65 | 47 | — | ... | 11 |
| 1942.......... | 964 | 478[a] | 58 | 89 | — | ... | 12 |
| 1943.......... | 773 | 544[a] | 31 | 44 | — | ... | 33 |
| 1944.......... | 764 | ... | 25 | 61 | — | ... | 9 |
| 1945.......... | 734 | ... | 37 | 80 | — | ... | 10 |
| Average 1946–50..... | 531 | 735[c] | ... | ... | — | 18[b] | 13 |
| | | | | RICE (PADDY) | | | |
| Average 1934–38..... | 609 | — | — | 3 | — | 423 | 205 |
| 1939.......... | 898 | — | — | 3 | — | ... | 280 |
| 1940.......... | 667 | — | — | 2 | — | ... | 215 |
| 1941.......... | 572 | — | — | 1 | — | 320 | 196 |
| 1942.......... | 940 | — | — | 3 | — | 320 | 182 |
| 1943.......... | 685 | — | — | 6 | — | ... | 241 |
| 1944.......... | 815 | — | — | 6 | — | 385 | 270 |
| 1945.......... | 866 | — | — | 16 | — | 423 | 329 |
| Average 1946–50..... | 1,187 | — | — | 22[b] | — | 430 | 277 |

* Data from FAO, *Yearbook of Food and Agricultural Statistics—1947* (Washington, 1947) and later issues for the years 1949–52; and IIA, *International Yearbook of Agricultural Statistics, 1941–42 to 1945–46*, Vol. I (Rome, 1947), except as follows: Egypt, Ministère des finances, Département de la statistique générale, *Annuaire statistique de poche, 1948* (n.d.), pp. 130–31, for millet and rice in Egypt; Jewish Agency for Palestine, Econ. Res. Inst., *Statistical Handbook of Middle Eastern Countries . . .* (Jerusalem, 1945), for millet in Palestine through 1944, for all grains in Syria and Lebanon, 1940–41, and average for corn in Syria and Lebanon; *International Reference Service* (U.S. Dept. Comm.), August 1947, No. 31, for millet in Palestine, 1945; [Gt. Brit.], Commonwealth Econ. Com., *Grain Crops . . .* (1950), for Sudan, 1939–45; Iraq, Min. Econ., Principal Bur. Stat., *Statistical Abstract, 1948* (1950) and *ibid., 1949* (1951), for Iraq, 1940–46 (see text, chapter 19, for comment).

[a] Approximations from records of MESC.

[b] Four-year average; Palestine maize includes a small amount of durra.

[c] Four-year average from FAO, *Current Development of and Prospects for Agriculture in the Near East. Second Near East Meeting on Food and Agricultural Programs and Outlook, Bloudane, Syria—28 August 1951* (July 12, 1951).

TABLE V.—NET TRADE IN GRAINS, SUGAR, AND VEGETABLE OILS IN SELECTED COUNTRIES, PREWAR, 1939–45, AND AVERAGE 1946–50*

(*Thousand metric tons*)

| Period | Total | Egypt[a] | Sudan | Palestine | Syria and Lebanon | Cyprus | Persia[b] | Iraq |
|---|---|---|---|---|---|---|---|---|
| | | | | WHEAT[c] | | | | |
| Average 1934–38.... | + 51.1 | + 7.2 | + 25.1 | + 70.3 | + 2.1 | + 22.8 | − 22.5 | − 53.5 |
| 1939......... | + 92.9 | + 6.5 | + 33.3 | +110.9 | − 32.1 | + 21.1 | − .0 | − 46.8 |
| 1940......... | − .5 | − 41.3 | + 16.8 | + 53.0 | − 8.6 | + 27.5 | − 15.0 | − 32.9 |
| 1941......... | +277.8 | − 19.6 | + 31.2 | + 95.7 | + 35.5 | + 48.3 | + 63.0 | + 23.7 |
| 1942......... | +417.6 | + 57.6 | + 24.3 | +147.5 | + 87.1 | + 42.6 | + 32.5 | + 26.0[d] |
| 1943......... | +152.7 | − 7.0 | − 2.3 | +122.8 | + 7.8 | + 1.9 | + 30.1 | − .6 |
| 1944......... | +160.2 | − 23.5 | .0 | +141.5 | − 15.2 | + 45.2 | + 11.8 | .0 |
| 1945......... | +311.8 | +153.0 | + 1.7 | +116.7 | − 4.6 | + 42.8 | + 2.2 | − .0 |
| Average 1946–50.... | ... | +316.2 | + 17.6 | ... | − 4.9 | + 44.0 | + 74.7 | + .9[e] |
| | | | | BARLEY | | | | |
| Average 1934–38.... | −240.5 | − 7.0 | − .1 | + 14.4 | − 26.1 | − 4.6 | − 12.6 | −204.5 |
| 1939......... | −238.3 | + .3 | + .0 | + 7.5 | − 28.8 | − 1.0 | − 8.2 | −208.1 |
| 1940......... | −192.8 | − 2.8 | + .0 | + 5.0 | − 6.5 | − 1.3 | − 4.3 | −182.9 |
| 1941......... | − 52.4 | − .3 | .0 | + .4 | + 2.2 | + .3 | + .0 | − 55.0 |
| 1942......... | − 40.9 | − 1.6 | − .0 | + 9.7 | + 6.7 | − 2.7 | + 1.1 | − 54.1 |
| 1943......... | −151.7 | − .4 | .0 | + 18.7 | − 4.7 | + 1.2 | + 2.3 | −168.8 |
| 1944......... | − 62.5 | − 1.3 | .0 | + 84.0 | − 2.4 | + 26.7 | + 2.5 | −172.0 |
| 1945......... | −160.6 | − .0 | + .0 | + 54.7 | + 8.7 | + 18.5 | + .3 | −242.8 |
| Average 1946–50.... | ... | − 11.1 | + .1 | ... | − 25.8 | − .5 | − 11.2 | −263.7 |
| | | | | MAIZE | | | | |
| Average 1934–38.... | + 2.8 | + 2.4 | − 3.5 | + 4.6[f] | − 0.2 | + .0 | .0 | − .5 |
| 1939......... | ... | + 1.3 | − 1.4 | + 6.0 | − 3.3 | + .0 | ... | − .1 |
| 1940......... | − 1.7 | − .2 | − .9 | + 1.3 | − 1.9 | + .0 | − .0 | − .0 |
| 1941......... | − 1.1 | + .6 | − 1.9 | + .2 | − .0 | + .0 | .0 | − .0 |
| 1942......... | + 33.8 | + 19.4 | − .9 | + 8.6 | + 6.6 | + .1 | + .0 | .0 |
| 1943......... | + 1.4 | − .0 | − .2 | + .0 | .0 | .0 | + 1.6 | .0 |
| 1944......... | − 1.3 | − .5 | − 2.2 | + 1.3 | .0 | + .0 | + .1 | .0 |
| 1945......... | − .6 | .0 | − .2 | + .0 | .0 | .0 | − .2 | − .2 |
| Average 1946–50.... | ... | +147.9 | − 8.9 | ... | + .8 | ... | + .3 | − .5 |
| | | | | MILLET, SORGHUM | | | | |
| Average 1934–38.... | ... | + 30.6 | − 63.5 | ... | ... | ... | .0 | − 27.6 |
| 1939......... | ... | + 4.5 | − 18.1 | ... | ... | ... | − .1 | ... |
| 1940......... | ... | + 12.3 | − 19.2 | ... | ... | ... | − .2 | ... |
| 1941......... | ... | + 7.1 | − 11.8 | ... | ... | ... | − .2 | ... |
| 1942......... | ... | + 3.2 | − 3.9 | ... | ... | .0 | ... | ... |
| 1943......... | ... | .0 | .0 | ... | ... | .0 | ... | − 12.3 |
| 1944......... | ... | + 1.6 | − 5.3 | ... | ... | .0 | ... | − 6.2 |
| 1945......... | ... | + .7 | − .7 | ... | ... | + .4 | ... | − 5.2 |
| Average 1946–50.... | ... | − 9.1 | + 5.0 | ... | − 11.0 | ... | − .6 | − 11.1 |

TABLE V.—NET TRADE IN GRAINS, SUGAR, AND VEGETABLE OILS IN SELECTED COUNTRIES, PREWAR, 1939–45, AND AVERAGE 1946–50*—(*Continued*)

(*Thousand metric tons*)

| Period | Total | Egypt[a] | Sudan | Palestine | Syria and Lebanon | Cyprus | Persia[b] | Iraq |
|---|---|---|---|---|---|---|---|---|
| | | | | RICE, MILLED | | | | |
| Average 1934–38.... | − 85.1 | − 94.6 | + 3.2 | + 16.4 | + 18.8 | + 1.7 | − 29.2 | − 1.4 |
| 1939......... | − 63.8 | −112.1 | + 3.6 | + 21.6 | + 20.2 | + 2.4 | + 1.0 | − .6 |
| 1940......... | −174.4 | −168.1 | + 1.5 | + 16.0 | + 9.2 | + 1.9 | − 33.0 | − 1.9 |
| 1941......... | − 48.6 | − 62.4 | + 4.0 | + 19.9 | + 17.9 | + 2.5 | − 24.6 | − 5.9 |
| 1942......... | − 13.2 | − 2.3 | + .4 | + 2.7 | + .8 | + .0 | − 14.5 | − .3 |
| 1943......... | −107.6 | −103.2 | + 1.5 | + 4.2 | + 7.4 | + .5 | − 17.7 | − .3 |
| 1944......... | − 77.6 | − 65.3 | + 1.9 | + 6.8 | + 1.8 | + 1.2 | − 20.4 | − 3.6 |
| 1945......... | −156.0 | −136.0 | + 2.5 | + 7.8 | + 9.9 | + 1.4 | − 40.5 | − 1.1 |
| Average 1946–50.... | ... | −248.6 | + 4.0 | ... | + 10.1 | + 1.8 | − 19.6 | − .9 |
| | | | | SUGAR | | | | |
| Average 1934–38.... | +170.2 | − 22.3 | + 27.0 | + 24.6 | + 31.9 | + 3.4 | + 68.4 | + 37.2 |
| 1939......... | +236.4 | + 1.3 | + 37.9 | + 27.7 | + 26.8 | + 3.4 | + 94.1 | + 45.2 |
| 1940......... | +175.1 | − 30.6 | + 28.9 | + 31.9 | + 14.2 | + 3.3 | + 86.4 | + 41.0 |
| 1941......... | +138.3 | − 38.6 | + 31.3 | + 20.3 | + 18.4 | + 2.7 | + 64.7 | + 39.5 |
| 1942......... | +108.0 | − 17.9 | + 24.4 | + 18.1 | + 24.1 | + 1.0 | + 43.3 | + 15.0 |
| 1943......... | + 88.1 | − 4.4 | + 18.2 | + 23.5 | + 10.3 | + 2.0 | + 26.0 | + 12.5 |
| 1944......... | +151.4 | − 5.9 | + 35.8 | + 17.2 | + 27.8 | + 2.6 | + 45.5 | + 29.4 |
| 1945......... | +141.4 | − 3.0 | + 20.1 | + 21.8 | + 18.9 | + 3.2 | + 48.4 | + 32.3 |
| Average 1946–50.... | ... | + 34.1 | + 39.8 | ... | + 30.9 | + 4.1 | +112.2 | + 57.8 |
| | | | | OILS, OILSEEDS (AS OIL)[g] | | | | |
| Average 1934–38.... | − 53.9 | − 39.6 | − 22.0 | + 9.1 | − .8 | − .2 | − .3 | − .1 |
| 1939......... | − 55.0 | − 32.9 | − 24.0 | + 10.4 | − 5.0 | − .3 | − 2.4 | − .7 |
| 1940......... | − 21.2 | − 15.2 | − 17.2 | + 11.5 | + 2.9 | + .1 | − 3.3 | + .1 |
| 1941......... | − 6.1 | − 7.7 | − 6.1 | + 8.8 | + 1.1 | .0 | − 2.4 | + .2 |
| 1942......... | + 7.8 | − 2.2 | − 9.6 | + 13.7 | + 5.1 | .0 | − .1 | + 1.0 |
| 1943......... | + 9.2 | + 20.7 | − 24.5 | + 11.8 | + .9 | − .2 | + .2 | + .3 |
| 1944......... | + 21.7 | + 24.2 | − 22.3 | + 19.4 | + .1 | + .0 | + .1 | + .2 |
| 1945......... | + 17.8 | + 20.3 | − 19.8 | + 15.1 | + 1.6 | + .0 | + .2 | + .3 |
| Average 1946–50.... | ... | + 9.6 | − 15.6 | ... | + 1.8 | + 2.4 | − 1.8 | ... |

* Data from FAO, *Yearbook of Food and Agricultural Statistics, 1948* (Washington, D.C., 1949) and later issues for the years 1950–53; and IIA, *International Yearbook of Agricultural Statistics, 1941–42 to 1945–46*, Vol. II (Rome, 1947), except at follows: Gt. Brit., For. Off., *Report by the Governor General on the Administration, Finances and Condition of the Sudan in 1945* (1948) and *ibid., in 1939–41* (1950), for Egypt's trade in rice, cottonseed, and peanuts with Sudan; Gt. Brit., Bd. Trade, *Statistical Abstract for the British Commonwealth, . . . 1936 to 1945* (Trade and Comm. Sec.) (No. 69, 1947), for Sudan's gross exports of millet, 1939–45, and for Cyprus' barley trade; selections from Cyprus, *The Cyprus Blue Book*, successive issues, and *Statistics of Imports, Exports and Shipping . . .* , successive issues, for Cyprus' trade in millet; Iran, Customs Admin., *Statistique annuelle du commerce extérieur de l'Iran*, successive issues, for Persia's trade, 1939–45.

[a] Trade with foreign countries and Sudan for wheat and flour, sugar, oilseeds, and rice, and for maize through 1939; trade with foreign countries only for maize, 1940–45, and for barley; trade with Sudan only for millet and sorghum.

[b] Year beginning March 21.

[c] Including wheat flour in grain equivalent at 70 percent extraction rate.

[d] Author's approximation. [e] Four-year average. [f] Includes durra.

[g] Trade in oilseeds converted to oil equivalent with factors from FAO, *Yearbook of Food and Agricultural Statistics, 1950*, Pt. 2 (Washington, D.C., 1951), p. 185, and *ibid., 1951*, Pt. 2 (Rome, 1952), p. 193; peanuts, shelled .43; peanuts, unshelled, .30; copra, .63; cottonseed, .155; sesame seed, .45; sunflower seed, .25; and linseed, .33.

TABLE VI.—EGYPT: AREA, YIELD, PRODUCTION, TRADE, AND APPARENT USE OF SELECTED CROPS, PREWAR, 1939–45, AND AVERAGE 1946–50*

*(Thousand hectares, quintals per hectare, thousand metric tons)*

| Period | Export crops | | | | | Import crops | | | | |
|---|---|---|---|---|---|---|---|---|---|---|
| | Area | Yield | Production | Net exports[a] | Apparent use[b] | Area | Yield | Production | Net imports[c] | Apparent use[b] |
| | | | BARLEY | | | | | WHEAT | | |
| Average 1934–38.... | 113 | 19.8 | 224.6 | 7.0 | 217.6 | 588 | 20.1 | 1,183.9 | 7.2 | 1,191.1 |
| 1939......... | 110 | 21.6 | 238.2 | ( .3) | 235.4 | 608 | 21.9 | 1,333.8 | 6.5 | 1,292.5 |
| 1940......... | 112 | 21.4 | 241.1 | 2.8 | 240.8 | 632 | 21.5 | 1,360.6 | (41.3) | 1,341.0 |
| 1941......... | 107 | 19.6 | 210.5 | .3 | 208.9 | 631 | 17.8 | 1,123.8 | (19.6) | 1,181.4 |
| 1942......... | 135 | 20.5 | 276.7 | 1.6 | 276.3 | 662 | 19.1 | 1,261.7 | 57.6 | 1,254.7 |
| 1943......... | 176 | 17.9 | 314.4 | .4 | 313.1 | 806 | 16.0 | 1,291.6 | (7.0) | 1,268.1 |
| 1944......... | 139 | 16.3 | 226.8 | 1.3 | 226.8 | 694 | 13.6 | 946.0 | (23.5) | 1,099.0 |
| 1945......... | 151 | 17.4 | 261.6 | .0 | 224.0 | 692 | 17.1 | 1,182.1 | 153.0 | 1,290.8 |
| Average 1946–50.... | 83 | 18.0 | 149.0 | 11.1 | 137.9 | 632 | 17.3 | 1,094.0 | 316.2 | 1,410.2 |
| | | | RICE[d] | | | | | MAIZE[e] | | |
| Average 1934–38.... | 174 | 34.9 | 609.0 | 94.6 | 301.2 | 649 | 24.9 | 1,615.6 | 2.4 | 1,618.0 |
| 1939......... | 230 | 39.1 | 898.0 | 112.1 | 415.6 | 650 | 23.4 | 1,524.4 | 1.3 | 1,524.2 |
| 1940......... | 214 | 31.2 | 667.0 | 168.1 | 371.2 | 647 | 23.6 | 1,529.5 | ( .2) | 1,530.1 |
| 1941......... | 188 | 30.4 | 472.4 | 62.4 | 369.8 | 642 | 20.0 | 1,282.1 | .6 | 1,301.5 |
| 1942......... | 283 | 33.2 | 939.8 | 2.3 | 517.7 | 833 | 17.4 | 1,451.6 | 19.4 | 1,451.6 |
| 1943......... | 270 | 25.4 | 685.2 | 103.2 | 380.1 | 819 | 16.8 | 1,377.0 | .0 | 1,376.5 |
| 1944......... | 260 | 31.3 | 814.6 | 65.3 | 393.5 | 794 | 19.6 | 1,558.9 | ( .5) | 1,558.9 |
| 1945......... | 265 | 32.7 | 866.4 | 136.0 | 359.9 | 789 | 21.5 | 1,697.4 | .0 | 1,695.7 |
| Average 1946–50.... | 302 | 39.3 | 1,187.0 | 248.6 | 523.0 | 657 | 20.7 | 1,358.0 | 147.9 | 1,505.9 |

TABLE VI.—EGYPT: AREA, YIELD, PRODUCTION, TRADE, AND APPARENT USE OF SELECTED CROPS, PREWAR, 1939–45, AND AVERAGE 1946–50*—(*Continued*)

(*Thousand hectares, quintals per hectare, thousand metric tons*)

| Period | Export crops: Area | Yield | Pro-duction | Net exports[a] | Apparent use[b] | Import crops: Area | Yield | Pro-duction | Net imports[c] | Apparent use[b] |
|---|---|---|---|---|---|---|---|---|---|---|
| | | | SUGAR (TEL QUEL) | | | | | MILLET[f] | | |
| Average 1934–38.... | ... | ... | 145.8 | 22.3 | 123.5 | 141 | 30.3 | 426.0 | 30.6 | 456.6 |
| 1939......... | ... | ... | 159.8 | ( 1.3) | 129.2 | 173 | 30.9 | 534.6 | 4.5 | 546.9 |
| 1940......... | ... | ... | 175.0 | 30.6 | 136.4 | 157 | 28.9 | 453.8 | 12.3 | 460.9 |
| 1941......... | ... | ... | 158.9 | 38.6 | 141.0 | 180 | 26.0 | 469.3 | 7.1 | 472.5 |
| 1942......... | ... | ... | 189.9 | 17.9 | 185.5 | 346 | 27.9 | 964.0 | 3.2 | 964.0 |
| 1943......... | ... | ... | 167.1 | 4.4 | 161.2 | 306 | 25.2 | 773.4 | .0 | 775.0 |
| 1944......... | ... | ... | 172.5 | 5.9 | 169.5 | 306 | 25.0 | 763.6 | 1.6 | 764.3 |
| 1945......... | ... | ... | 179.9 | 3.0 | 180.4 | 287 | 25.5 | 733.8 | .7 | 699.1 |
| Average 1946–50.... | ... | ... | 196.0 | (34.1) | 230.1 | 211 | 25.2 | 531.0 | ( 9.1) | 521.9 |
| | | | COTTONSEED[g] | | | | | OTHER OILSEEDS[h] | | |
| Average 1934–38.... | 746 | 10.3 | 771.2 | 64.4 | 55.1 | 20 | ... | 7.8 | 24.8 | 32.6 |
| 1939......... | 683 | 10.4 | 709.4 | 54.6 | 74.1 | 21 | ... | 8.4 | 21.7 | 29.1 |
| 1940......... | 708 | 10.5 | 746.1 | 35.9 | 95.2 | 22 | ... | 8.4 | 20.7 | 21.2 |
| 1941......... | 690 | 9.8 | 678.5 | 20.4 | 69.3 | 32 | ... | 11.6 | 12.8 | 18.1 |
| 1942......... | 297 | 11.5 | 342.0 | 8.7 | 70.2 | 38 | ... | 10.9 | 6.5 | 14.4 |
| 1943......... | 299 | 9.9 | 296.2 | (17.2) | 67.2 | 35 | ... | 11.3 | 3.5 | 14.2 |
| 1944......... | 358 | 10.8 | 385.9 | (21.3) | 79.1 | 41 | ... | 14.8 | 2.9 | 15.8 |
| 1945......... | 413 | 10.8 | 430.8 | (19.3) | 71.9 | 29 | ... | 11.4 | 1.0 | 14.7 |
| Average 1946–50.... | 636 | 9.8 | 624.0 | ( 2.2) | 98.9 | 31 | ... | 11.6 | 7.4 | 19.0 |

* Data from FAO, *Yearbook of Food and Agricultural Statistics—1947* (Washington, 1947) and later issues through 1953; IIA, *International Yearbook of Agricultural Statistics, 1941–42 to 1945–46*, Vols. I and II (Rome, 1947); Egypt, Ministère des finances, Département de la statistique générale, *Annuaire statistique de poche, 1948* (n.d.); and Gt. Brit., For. Off., *Report by the Governor General on the Administration, Finances and Condition of the Sudan in 1945* (1948) and *ibid., in 1939–41* (1950).

[a] Data in parentheses, net imports.

[b] Production minus net exports or plus net imports. For individual years the crop harvested in the calendar year indicated plus or minus the trade of the following year. (Averages simply as indicated.)

[c] Data in parentheses, net exports.

[d] Production and yield, rough basis; trade and use, milled basis at 65 percent.

[e] Trade with foreign countries 1940–45, including trade with Sudan through 1939.

[f] Millet trade only with Sudan.

[g] Production as seed, trade in oil plus oil equivalent of seed; apparent use, trade plus oil equivalent of production. (Seed considered to yield 15.5 percent oil.)

[h] Area and oil equivalent of production and trade of peanuts, linseed and sesame seed combined with trade in above oils plus coconut, palm, and olive oils, and copra in oil equivalent. (For oil-equivalent factors, see Appendix Table V, note *g*.)

TABLE VII.—SUEZ CANAL SHIPPING, 1938–50*

| Year | Number of ships passing through | Net transit tonnage (*millions*) | Passengers (*thousands*) | Revenue from tolls[a] (*million francs*) |
|---|---|---|---|---|
| 1938 | 6,171 | 34.4 | 480 | 1,626 |
| 1939 | 5,277 | 29.6 | 411 | 1,389 |
| 1940 | 2,589 | 13.5 | 168 | 621 |
| 1941 | 1,804 | 8.3 | 14 | 498 |
| 1942 | 1,646 | 7.0 | 1 | 457 |
| 1943 | 2,262 | 11.3 | 173 | 710 |
| 1944 | 3,320 | 18.1 | 419 | 1,215 |
| 1945 | 4,206 | 25.1 | 984 | 1,882 |
| 1946 | 5,057 | 32.7 | 932 | 5,689 |
| 1947 | 5,972 | 36.6 | 587 | 6,191 |
| 1948 | 8,686 | 55.1 | 455 | 16,394 |
| 1949 | 10,420 | 68.8 | 611 | 24,896 |
| 1950[b] | 11,751 | 81.8 | 664 | 26,980 |

* Data from the annual report of the Suez Canal Co., June 1950, and National Bank of Egypt, *Economic Bulletin* (Cairo), various issues.

[a] Tolls were raised by 40 percent on Jan. 1, 1941 and have not been changed since that date.

[b] From *Le Monde* (Paris), June 18, 1951.

TABLE VIII.—TONNAGE OF SHIPS IN EXTERNAL TRADE ENTERING HARBORS OF CERTAIN COUNTRIES, 1939, 1943, 1945, AND 1946*

(*Million net registered tons*)

| Year | Egypt[a] | Iraq[b] | Lebanon[c] | Palestine[d] | Persia[d] | Total |
|---|---|---|---|---|---|---|
| 1939 | 30.1 | .7 | 2.6 | 4.4 | 7.1 | 44.9 |
| 1943 | 12.6 | .4 | .6 | 2.2 | 3.4 | 19.2 |
| 1945 | 18.3 | .4 | .3 | 3.3 | 7.5 | 29.8 |
| 1946 | 37.0 | .5 | 1.0 | 4.5 | 8.6 | 51.6 |

* Data from UN Statistical Office; mainly *Statistical Yearbook, 1948* (Lake Success, N.Y., 1949), pp. 277, 279.

[a] Including ships passing through Suez Canal; including entrances into all Egyptian ports, even when more than one port is entered during one voyage.

[b] Port of Basra only.

[c] Port of Beirut only; including ships in ballast and coastwise shipping.

[d] Including ships in ballast; for Persia, figures refer to year beginning March 21.

[a] Currency *issued*, plus demand and time deposits.

[b] August 1939.

[c] January 1943.

[d] January 1948.

[e] Notes in circulation at the end of the year plus "Demand deposits in the Bank Melli and Other banks, less such deposits held by the Government and banks" in March of the following year.

[f] Currency *issued* plus demand deposits including government deposits.

[g] January 1940.

[h] Year 1939.

TABLE IX.—INDEXES OF MONEY SUPPLY AND COST OF LIVING IN SELECTED COUNTRIES, 1939–50*

*(December 1939 = 100)*

| End of year | Egypt | | Sudan | | Palestine | | Cyprus | |
|---|---|---|---|---|---|---|---|---|
| | Money supply | Cost of living | Money supply[a] | Cost of living | Money supply | Cost of living | Money supply | Cost of living |
| 1939 | 100 | 100 | 100 | 100 | 100 | 100 | 100 | 100[b] |
| 1940 | 137 | 113 | 105 | 110 | 110 | 118 | 109 | ... |
| 1941 | 183 | 144 | 169 | 130 | 153 | 149 | 165 | 192 |
| 1942 | 254 | 199 | 203 | 151 | 248 | 192 | 257 | 246[c] |
| 1943 | 337 | 238 | 241 | 177 | 400 | 210 | 386 | 235 |
| 1944 | 452 | 270 | 231 | 160 | 496 | 218 | 468 | 229 |
| 1945 | 565 | 269 | ... | 170 | 594 | 235 | ... | 231 |
| 1946 | 530 | 268 | ... | 183 | 610 | 244 | 626 | 249 |
| 1947 | 505 | 259 | ... | 229 | ... | ... | 577 | 330[d] |
| 1948 | 556 | 261 | ... | 289 | ... | ... | 545 | 317 |
| 1949 | 551 | 260 | ... | 307 | ... | ... | 531 | 303 |
| 1950 | 573 | 283 | ... | 265 | ... | ... | 508 | ... |

| End of year | Syria and Lebanon | | Persia | | Iraq | |
|---|---|---|---|---|---|---|
| | Money supply | Cost of living | Money supply[e] | Cost of living | Money supply[f] | Cost of living |
| 1939 | 100 | 100[g] | 100 | 100 | 100 | 100[h] |
| 1940 | 161 | 147 | 122 | 113 | 115 | ... |
| 1941 | 183 | 211 | 192 | 184 | 239 | ... |
| 1942 | 382 | 332 | 282 | 375 | 399 | ... |
| 1943 | 600 | 455 | 410 | 745 | 679 | ... |
| 1944 | 733 | 540 | 468 | 644 | 793 | ... |
| 1945 | 851 | 546 | 501 | 611 | 771 | 611 |
| 1946 | 784 | 467 | 530 | 575 | 752 | 548 |
| 1947 | 775 | 429 | 540 | 590 | 672 | 715 |
| 1948 | 859 | 415 | 548 | 656 | 662 | 593 |
| 1949 | 818 | 366 | 524 | 624 | 693 | 506 |
| 1950 | 964 | 384 | 581 | 538 | ... | 507 |

* Indexes of money supply, author's computation from currency in circulation plus demand deposits (except as otherwise noted) as reported in UN, *Statistical Yearbook, 1953* (New York, 1953), for Egypt; in A. R. Prest, *War Economics of Primary Producing Countries* (Cambridge, 1948), for Sudan, 1939–44; in Cyprus, *The Cyprus Blue Book, 1939,* and Treas., *Cyprus: Financial Report,* various issues, for Cyprus 1940–50; in *General Monthly Bulletin of Current Statistics* (Palestine, Dept. Stat.), various issues, for Palestine; in *International Financial Statistics* (Internatl. Monetary Fund, Washington, D.C.), various issues, for Syria and Lebanon, 1939–44, Lebanon, 1945–50, Iraq, and bank deposits for Persia; in Syria, Ministry Natl. Econ., Dept. Stat., *Statistical Abstract of Syria, 1950* (n.d.) and *ibid., 1951 and 1952* (n.d.), for Syria, 1945–50; in *Bank Melli Iran Bulletin* (Teheran), various issues, for notes in circulation in Persia. Data for 1939 in million units of domestic currency are as follows:

| Country | Unit | Currency in circulation | Deposit money | Total money |
|---|---|---|---|---|
| Egypt | pound (£E) | 31 | 32 | 63 |
| Sudan | pound (£E) | 2.7 | 1.2 | 3.9 |
| Palestine | pound (£P) | 8.5 | 12.8 | 21.3 |
| Cyprus | pound (£C) | .85 | 1.9 | 2.75 |
| Syria, Lebanon | pound ( £S, £L, £LS) | 51 | 32 | 83 |
| Persia | rials (rls.) | 1,010 | 1,320 | 2,330 |
| Iraq | dinars (ID) | 5.9 | 1.2 | 7.1 |

Indexes of cost of living, shifted to December 1939 base (except as otherwise noted), from Egypt, Ministre de l'economie nationale, Département de la statistique, *Annuaire statistique,* various issues, for Egypt, 1939–47; from Internatl. Labour Off., *Year Book of Labour Statistics* (Geneva), various issues, for Egypt, 1948–50, Sudan, 1945–50, Cyprus, 1945–49, Syria, Lebanon (Beirut), 1948–50, Iraq (Baghdad), 1950; from Prest, *op. cit.,* for Sudan and Cyprus, 1939–44; from Jewish Agency for Palestine, Dept. Stat., *Statistical Handbook of Jewish Palestine, 1947* (Jerusalem, 1947), p. 318, for Palestine (data for 1941–44 differ slightly from those shown in chapter 20 of text); from Syria and Lebanon, Conseil supérieur des intérêts communs, Services d'études économiques et statistiques, *Recueil de statistiques de la Syrie et du Leban* (Beirut), various issues, for Syria and Lebanon (Beirut), 1939–47; from *Bank Melli Iran Bulletin,* various issues, for Persia; from Iraq, Min. Econ., Principal Bur. Stat., *Statistical Abstract,* various issues, for Iraq, 1945–49.

See chapter 20 of text for further details, 1939–44.

# INDEX

# INDEX

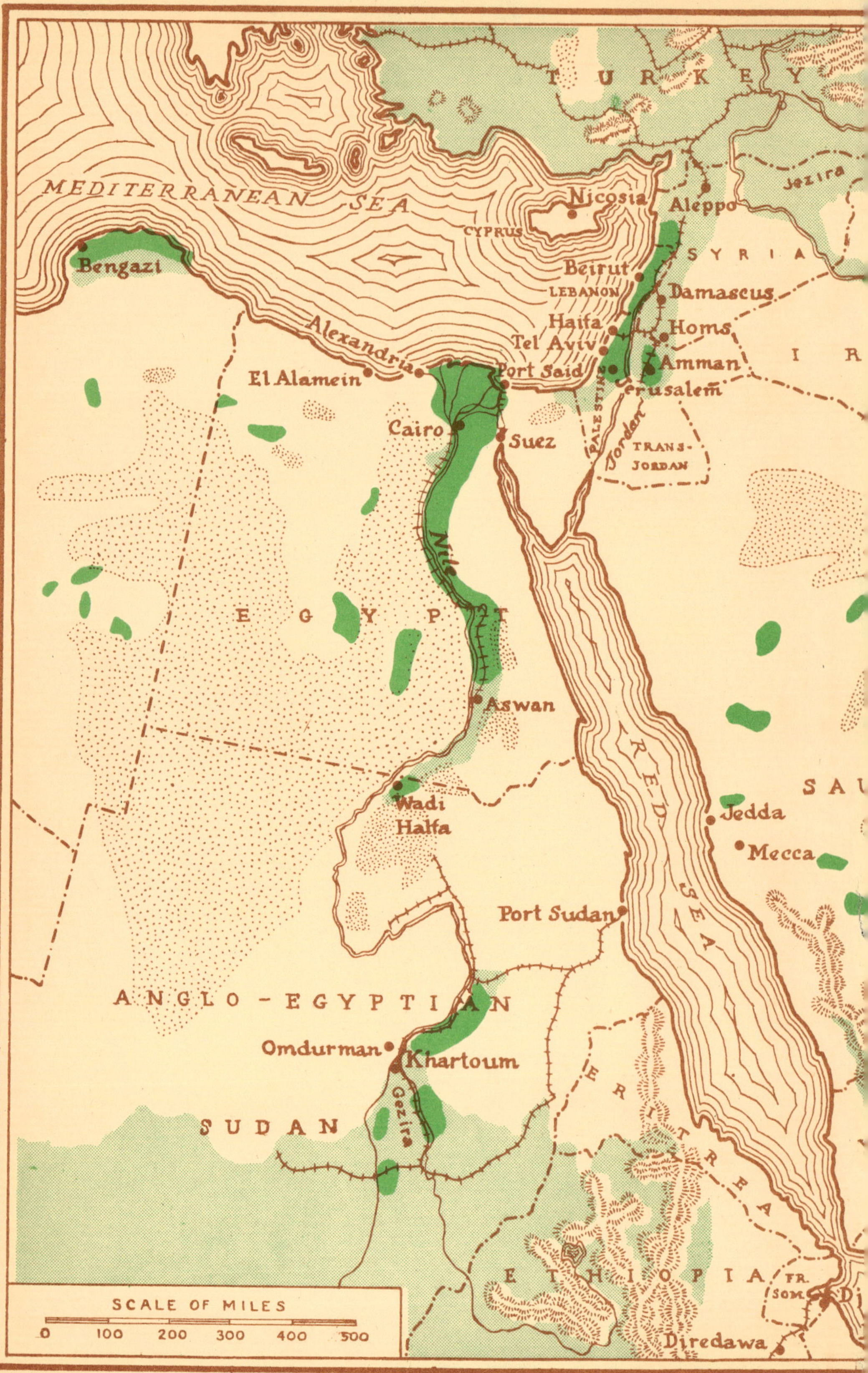

TURKEY
MEDITERRANEAN SEA
Nicosia
CYPRUS
Aleppo
Jezira
SYRIA
Bengazi
Beirut
LEBANON
Damascus
Haifa
Homs
Tel Aviv
Alexandria
Port Said
Amman
El Alamein
Jerusalem
PALESTINE
Cairo
Suez
Jordan
TRANS-JORDAN
Nile
EGYPT
Aswan
RED SEA
Wadi Halfa
Jedda
Mecca
SAU
Port Sudan
ANGLO-EGYPTIAN
Omdurman
Khartoum
Gezira
SUDAN
ERITREA
ETHIOPIA
FR. SOM.
Diredawa
SCALE OF MILES
0 100 200 300 400 500